Sarah Ditum is a columnist for the *Sunday Times* whose byline has also appeared in publications such as the *New Statesman*, *Guardian* and *Elle*. Her TV and radio appearances include Newsnight and Today.

T0349625

'Ditum's hotly anticipated book brilliantly captures the prevailing millennial mood of anti-nostalgia ... a damn good thesis'

Observer

'Ditum's prose is never overwrought, and she treats pop culture with a rare seriousness. She is right to do so. The women who came of age in the noughties are entering middle age, with all the agency that brings ... *Toxic*, Ditum's reframing of an era, suggests that the uproar over Brand may have been just the beginning of a reckoning'

Financial Times

'Ditum gets the tone right: critically engaged, well-researched, colourful without seeming exploitative ... a serious book of reportage ... For readers interested in real celebrity journalism, get off the internet and into a bookshop and ask for *Toxic*'

Irish Times

'A page-turning exploration of a time when new technology and old misogyny collided and the concept of privacy collapsed'

Daily Express

'Illuminating'

New Statesman

'Bracing'

The Bookseller

'Extremely compelling'

The Critic

Sarah Ditum

TOXIC

Women, Fame and
the Noughties

FLEET
2024

FLEET

First published in Great Britain in 2023 by Fleet
This paperback edition published in 2024 by Fleet

1 3 5 7 9 10 8 6 4 2

A CIP catalogue record for this book
is available from the British Library.

ISBN 978-0-349-72714-1

Typeset in Warnock by M Rules
Printed and bound in Great Britain by
Clays Ltd, Elcograf S.p.A.

Papers used by Fleet are from well-managed forests
and other responsible sources.

Fleet
An imprint of
Little, Brown Book Group
Carmelite House
50 Victoria Embankment
London EC4Y 0DZ

An Hachette UK Company
www.hachette.co.uk

www.hachette.co.uk

*To Jay and Maddy, the greatest content
created in the noughties*

I don't think we've even seen the tip of the iceberg. I think the potential of what the internet is going to do to society, both good and bad, is unimaginable. I think we're actually on the cusp of something exhilarating and terrifying . . . It's an alien life form.

David Bowie (1999)

I didn't feel bad because they were rich and famous and knew what they were signing up for.

Perez Hilton (2011)

Contents

Timeline

May 1966	Janet born
Feb 1969	Jen born
Dec 1969	Chyna born
Jan 1979	Aaliyah born
Oct 1980	Kim born
Feb 1981	Paris born
Dec 1981	Britney born
Sep 1983	Amy born
Jul 1986	Lindsay born
Sep 1998	'... Baby One More Time' released
Aug 2001	Aaliyah dies
Sep 2001	9/11
Nov 2001	Chyna leaves WWE
Dec 2002	*Gawker* launched
Aug 2003	MySpace launched
Dec 2003	*The Simple Life* first broadcast
Jan 2004	*The Apprentice* first broadcast

Feb 2004	Nipplegate
Feb 2004	Facebook launched
Apr 2004	*Mean Girls* released
May 2004	Last episode of *Friends* broadcast
Jun 2004	*1 Night in Paris* released
Sep 2004	Perez Hilton launched (as PageSixSixSix)
Dec 2004	*1 Night in China* released
Jan 2005	Brad and Jen announce separation
Feb 2005	YouTube launched
Nov 2005	TMZ launched
Mar 2006	Twitter launched
Oct 2006	*Back to Black* released
Feb 2007	Britney shaves her head
May 2007	Lindsay arrested for the first time
Mar 2007	*Kim Kardashian, Superstar* released
Jun 2007	Paris goes to jail
Oct 2007	*Keeping Up With the Kardashians* first broadcast
Jun 2008	R. Kelly cleared of child pornography charges
Sep 2008	Lehman Brothers declared bankrupt
Oct 2008	Britney placed under permanent conservatorship
Oct 2010	Instagram launched
Jul 2011	Amy dies
Oct 2012	*Gawker* publishes Hulk Hogan sex tape
Mar 2013	'Blurred Lines' released

Introduction

'A reasonable expectation of privacy'

This is a book about nine women so famous, you know them by their first names alone. Britney. Paris. Lindsay. Aaliyah. Janet. Amy. Kim. Chyna. Jen. It's about what celebrity did to them, how they changed celebrity, and why the early part of this century was such a monstrous time to be famous and female. It's about how the concept of privacy came undone and why that was a catastrophe for women. In the strange, febrile years of the noughties, the women in this book lived outsize lives in the popular imagination. Their bodies, their image, their personal dramas were all dissected in minutest detail across tabloid magazines and gossip blogs. Those of us who came of age around the millennium lived through Britney's descent from virginal schoolgirl to public disgrace, through Paris's sex tape, through Lindsay's partying. We lived through Aaliyah's death (and the peculiar coyness around her relationship with the man who publicly groomed her), through Janet's humiliation in Nipplegate, through Amy's destruction by the addictions she romanticised in her music. We lived through Kim's triumphant assault on fame, through Chyna's decline from athletic trailblazer to train wreck, through the tabloid creation of 'Sad Jen' and the incessant speculation over whether she'd have children.

When I say we 'lived through' these things, I don't mean merely that they happened while we were alive. Nor do I mean they were somehow ordeals that we, the public, had to suffer. (Whatever suffering there was, it belonged to the women this book is about.) What I mean is that the stories of these women, as told by the tabloid press and celebrity blogs, became vehicles through which we made sense of our own existence. For the public, tearing these women to pieces was both a social activity and a form of divination. In the entrails of their reputations, we hunted for clues about what a woman ought to be, and this has always been one of the functions of celebrity women.

Writing in the seventies, film critic Molly Haskell described the female screen stars of Hollywood's golden age as 'two-way mirrors linking the immediate past with the immediate future'.[1] The cast of this book – four singers, two actresses, two reality stars and a pro wrestler – were the two-way mirrors of the Millennial era. Fame has always been psychologically devastating to many of those it touches, and the media has often been cruel to women. But thanks to a peculiar mixture of new technology and old misogyny, the women I write about experienced a kind of hypertrophied celebrity that had never existed before. All the wrenching forces of the digital revolution were focused through them. Unsurprisingly, some of them shattered.

This book begins, though, with the story of an anonymous sixteen-year-old in a branch of Target in Tulsa, Oklahoma. In 2006, the girl stopped to look at some greetings cards, and a man stopped to look at her. His name was Riccardo Ferrante, and he was thirty-three. CCTV footage caught him crouching down beside her and using a digital camera to take pictures up her skirt while she browsed obliviously; a security guard saw the incident and notified the police. It was an open-and-shut case of voyeurism. Ferrante had seen a TV item about upskirting and been inspired to try it himself: he told police that 'he was a leg man and that he had intended to take pictures of her legs'.[2] It was also a sign of a growing problem, according to Corporal Mark Mears of the Tulsa Police: 'With digital cameras and phone cameras, it's very easy to get video. There's been, you can ask our cyber crimes guys, many of these that end up on the internet.'[3] At least in this case, the alleged perpetrator had been brought before the court. Then, in 2007, Judge Tom Gillert ordered that the charges against Ferrante be dismissed on the grounds that 'the person photographed was not in a place where she had a reasonable expectation of privacy', and in 2008, an appeals court concurred.[4] By being in a public space, the girl was understood to have made the most intimate parts of her body available to anyone who cared to look.[5]

Formally, this ruling was gender neutral: men as well as women could have no reasonable expectation of privacy in the Target stationery aisle. Practically, privacy had a different import depending on your sex: men were in no danger of being upskirted. 'The legal concept of privacy,' noted feminist legal scholar Catharine A. MacKinnon in 1989, 'can and has shielded the place of battery, marital rape, and women's exploited domestic labor.' The right to privacy functioned as 'a right of men "to be let alone" to oppress women one at a time'.[6] The Oklahoma legislature tightened its 'Peeping Tom' statute following the case,[7] but the same problem arose elsewhere. In 2014, a Boston man who upskirted women on the subway was exonerated on the same grounds.[8]

The violation Ferrante committed would not have been possible before the introduction of small, light point-and-shoot digital cameras in the early noughties. In fact, at the same time that Ferrante was being arrested for upskirting, professional photographers were taking exactly the same kind of picture, with no risk of police attention. The difference was that the paparazzi were doing it to famous women. The website Fleshbot, which covered pornography and was part of the *Gawker* stable of blogs, routinely published upskirt pictures of celebrities and maintained a conveniently cynical attitude towards its subjects. 'We always had a suspicion that when Britney, Lindsay, Paris, et al., "accidentally" flash their lady business to the paparazzi that it's a lot more calculated than their publicists would want you to believe. After all, there's no easier way to get your attention than to show some hoohah to your adoring public,' declared a 2007 post.[9] There were even sites, like the charmingly named Hollywood Tuna, dedicated to cataloguing compromising shots of famous women.

Readers saw the posts and assumed – with a nudge from the copy – that the women in question were sloppy exhibitionists. What they couldn't see was the way such pictures were obtained. In 2009, *Harry Potter* actress Emma Watson described how her eighteenth birthday celebrations in London had been mobbed by photographers. 'I realised that overnight I'd become fair game,' she told the *Daily Mail*. 'I had a party in town and the pavements were just knee-deep with photographers trying to get a shot of me looking drunk, which wasn't going to happen . . . The sickest part was when one photographer lay down on the floor to get a shot up my skirt. The night it was legal for them to do it, they did it. I woke up the next day and felt completely violated by it all.'[10] If an unknown sixteen-year-old in Target could have no 'reasonable expectation of privacy', such a right certainly didn't apply to a famous eighteen-year-old out celebrating.

Nor did the 'reasonable expectation of privacy' extend to pictures which had been taken privately and then somehow made their way into public view. In September 2007, nudes purportedly of *High School Musical* star Vanessa Hudgens (then eighteen) appeared on Fleshbot and the website

IDontLikeYouInThatWay.[11] Fleshbot concluded that the iden-
tification was probably 'wishful thinking', and the full-frontal
bedroom shots were likely to be of some other teen with 'cute
but bland features'. It published them nonetheless. Actually,
the shots were legit, as Hudgens's representative confirmed
to TMZ: 'This was a photo which was taken privately. It is a
personal matter and it is unfortunate that this has become
public.'[12] (Presumably, the pictures had been either hacked
from a cloud server or leaked by the original recipient, whoever that was.) This did not lead to any introspection about
the ethics of posting such pictures. Nor did the fact that
Hudgens was probably under eighteen when the pictures were
taken: Fleshbot noted that the nudes didn't feature Hudgens's
navel piercing but not the significance of her having got that
piercing when she was only sixteen.[13] Then again, it had been
happy to hit Publish when it believed the pictures were of an
unknown girl, of unknown age, with no indication of how they
had been acquired. Even in your own bedroom, there was no
reasonable expectation of privacy.

This was a time when feminism could not have been more
needed. And yet, perversely, it was a time when women's liberation had been declared prematurely redundant. Things that
the second wave of feminism had worked hard to make socially
unacceptable – pornography, sexualisation, painful beauty
standards – now made a resurgence. Only, this time, rather
than being imposed on women by men, women appeared
to be embracing them voluntarily. 'This new raunch culture
didn't mark the death of feminism ... it was evidence that the
feminist project had already been achieved,' wrote Ariel Levy
in her 2005 book, *Female Chauvinist Pigs: Women and the Rise
of Raunch Culture*. 'We'd earned the right to look at *Playboy*;
we were empowered enough to get Brazilian waxes. Women
had come so far, I learned, we no longer needed to worry about
objectification and misogyny. Instead, it was time for us to join

the frat party of pop culture, where men had been enjoying themselves all along.'[14] Levy was sceptical about this, but many were not. And besides, the more the public sphere adopted the pornified standards of the internet, the greater the exclusion faced by anyone who declined to participate.

If the noughties had a spirit of the age, it was probably embodied by Riccardo Ferrante, Tulsa's legally authorised upskirter. Which is why I think of the period covered by this book as the 'Upskirt Decade'. It begins in 1998, with the release of Britney's debut ' . . . Baby One More Time' and ends with the feminist backlash to Robin Thicke's single 'Blurred Lines' in 2013. History does not always fit within neat parameters. In *The White Album*, Joan Didion identifies the key years of the sixties as 1966 to 1971. The long nineteenth century runs from the French Revolution to the outbreak of the First World War. My focus here is on a kind of 'long noughties': fifteen years in which the world became so altered, it is hard now to recapture what it meant to live through them. Many of the incidents in this book seem improbably outrageous now the internet has become a settled part of life, subject to laws and norms. But in the time I describe, the digital world was a kind of Wild West. It was argued – and, more importantly, it was *felt* – that copyright, privacy, indecency and libel were all concepts that could have no force online.

I was sixteen at the start of 1998. In 2013, I turned thirty-two. The years I've covered in this book marked my passage from childhood to adulthood, but they also marked the passage of the internet from novelty to utility. At the start of this period, 30 per cent of the US population had access to the internet. (As late as 2005, gossip blogger Perez Hilton was spending most of his days in a coffee shop because he didn't have a connection at his home.)[15] By 2013, 71 per cent of the US population was online. In the United Kingdom, the rise was starker still: from 14 per cent to 90 per cent.[16] The increase in time spent online is even more instructive. In 2005, UK users spent an average of ten hours a week on the internet; a decade later, that figure had doubled, and the way people were accessing the internet had changed, too, with the widespread adoption of smartphones and the rise of social media.[17]

This change brought convenience and innovation, and much that is to be celebrated. It is not the argument of this book that the internet is bad. But any mass technological shift brings social change with it, and the digital revolution of the early twenty-first century affected men and women unequally because it exploded the distinction of 'private' and 'public' that had been more or less stable since the Industrial Revolution. As the Tulsa example showed, both public life and privacy were concepts that applied differently depending on whether you had a male or female body. At the same time, women were entering into public life in greater numbers than ever before and making decisions about their private lives that were of considerable public import – specifically, deferring having children or declining motherhood altogether. Fame is the phenomenon of private individuals en masse developing one-sided personal relationships towards public figures, which makes it the place where public and private collide. And so famous women were where all the stresses of the noughties were brought to bear. A common complaint about the noughties' celebrity culture was that it was the manifestation of a degraded, trivial society (a complaint often made, perversely, by the celebrity culture's most avid participants), and perhaps it was, but it was also a reaction to the era's most momentous happening.

The internet was a public place – the often-used metaphor of the town square made that clear – experienced in the privacy between user and screen. It allowed the private self to merge into the professional world of the workplace, where computer workers could check personal email and browse the web while they were on the clock. And it allowed the public life of the workplace to seep into areas previously reserved for the private self. In 2007 in the *New York Times*, one writer issued a frazzled wail in response to the power wielded over him by his BlackBerry (yet to be displaced by the iPhone as the default smartphone): 'Keeping out of touch is not a serious option, unless all systems were to crash everywhere. Nowadays, there is almost nowhere left to hide.'[18] As the range of messaging platforms expanded and the expectation of constant availability grew, it was a problem that would only become more acute. On message boards and social media, users often behaved as though they were in a private space, communicating among friends, only to realise belatedly that they were actually on public platforms, broadcasting to the world. The term *context collapse* described the strains this created.[19] In 2009, businesswoman Penelope Trunk caused a minor global incident when she live-tweeted her miscarriage during a board meeting. 'Twitter is not a public forum,' she wrote in an article for the *Guardian* about her experience.[20] But, clearly, it was. It just didn't always feel like one while you were using it.

The expression 'nowhere left to hide' described, too, the panopticon effect of mass digital camera ownership. Paparazzi were more pervasive, and more agile, than ever before: it would be considerably harder to get down in the gutter with a bulky analogue camera, while the move from physical rolls of film to digital memory cards freed up photographers to take more pictures, which could then be processed near-instantly. The concept of relative privacy in a public place died everywhere as it had died in Tulsa – another kind of context collapse, as places once moderately 'private' for celebrities (the insides of cars, the outsides of clubs) became unambiguously public. The proliferation of photography created new opportunities for the gossip magazines. Tabloids such as *Us Weekly*, *Star* and (in the United Kingdom) *Heat* had access to more shots than ever before, out of which they could conjure more celebrity speculation than ever before. Even if there was no news about a popular star in a certain week, a creative editor could always spin a story around a fleeting moment digitally captured. After all, the magazines needed to give their readers something: competition from the internet was eating into print sales, and a tantalising front page could make all the difference at the newsstand.[21]

But because magazines fundamentally relied on access to their subjects, there were still some things too explosively true or too scurrilously false for them to say. This was where the bloggers came in. 'I don't give a fuck about publicists,' boasted Perez Hilton in his book *Red Carpet Suicide*. 'I don't need access to their clients, and I don't have to keep them happy. I will rarely kill an item, because all gossip items were created equal! They are an inalienable right.'[22] For the blogs, celebrities were to be treated with an odd mixture of obsession and disgust. 'Updated daily, we will give you the real scoop. A brutally honest perspective on the stench we call celebrities,' promised Hollywood Tuna.[23] If the blogs were forced to take themselves seriously – which rarely happened, given that the signature tone of the noughties was an aggressive glibness – they would present themselves as a redistributive force, taking from the coddled elite of stardom and giving to the public. Or they would appeal to digital fatalism, as though their actions were not actions at all but, rather, an ineluctable consequence of the internet.

One of the 'fun' features of *Gawker* was '*Gawker* Stalker', a map providing instant updates on the locations of celebrities based on reader tips. (The internet, though libertarian in its underlying philosophy, often turned out to be totalitarian in effect.) When Jimmy Kimmel took *Gawker* editor Emily Gould to task about this on CNN in 2007, she responded with a post that cast offended celebs as entitled whiners demanding special treatment: 'It must be hard to be a celebrity and have people say mean things about you! The thing is, though, that everyone who's at all in the public eye, "celebrity" or no, is now subject to being insulted by anyone at any time, thanks to an innovation that makes it possible for anyone with a computer and a wireless connection to track people down and say mean things about them via email (that stands for "electronic mail"!) message or blog (sorry, "Web Log"!) post.'[24] Gould presented her website's work here as the morally neutral outcome of impersonal technological forces. Anyone who complained about the privacy implications was only demonstrating their own redundancy. (Gould left *Gawker* less than a year later, having 'realized the whole enterprise was bad for me and probably the world'.)[25]

It was fortunate for *Gawker* that Gould was a woman and Kimmel was a man. It helped to conceal an unsavoury truth about the way fame fell differently on the sexes. Maybe the perfect example of the noughties' attitude to the famous was the so-called Bling Ring – five middle-class LA teens, a boy and four girls (plus one older man), who stole more than $3 million of jewellery and designer goods from various celebrities between 2008 and 2009. (A *Vanity Fair* article about them was adapted into the 2013 movie *The Bling Ring*, directed by Sofia Coppola and starring Emma Watson.) Their victims included Paris and Lindsay, as well as Megan Fox and Rachel Bilson, among others. The thieves used the gossip blogs to work out when their targets would be out of town – exactly the kind of intrusion that Kimmel had warned would result from reporting celebrity locations in real time. Paris was their first victim because, the thieves reasoned, she would be 'dumb'. Part of their motivation was certainly financial, but that doesn't explain why they deliberately took small amounts of goods with the intention of going back again and again, or why their victims were almost exclusively young women who all shared a particular celebrity profile. (While they did burgle two men, both male victims were living with women who were the primary targets.) It doesn't explain why the thieves wore rather than fenced the designer clothes they took.

LAPD officer Brett Goodkin, the lead investigator, told journalist Nancy Jo Sales that he was struck by the 'stalkerish' quality of the offences: 'It may be a stretch, but is wanting to wear somebody's clothes that different from wanting to wrap yourself up in their skin, like that guy in *The Silence of the Lambs*?'[26] Burglary is usually imagined as a simple property crime. Actually, a great many burglaries are sexually motivated: for the perpetrator, breaching the house is a metaphor for breaching the victim's body.[27] The Bling Ring was not acting out of righteous disgust at fame, but more likely out of a desire to possess and violate the famous – a living reenactment of the 'Cry Me a River' music video in which Justin Timberlake takes his revenge on a cheating girlfriend who looks like Britney – and that desire was reinforced and abetted by the media they consumed. At the time of the arrests, one of the girls involved was being filmed for her own reality show (and she later ended up sharing a jail block with Lindsay Lohan).[28] Rather than being tactfully shelved, the series – called *Pretty Wild* – was broadcast on E!, home of *Keeping Up with the Kardashians*, in 2010.[29] (Meanwhile, *Gawker*, though it labelled the Bling Ring burglars 'terrifying' and 'insane', continued to post *Gawker Stalker* items until 2013.)[30]

The division of public and private has always been fraught for women in a way it hasn't been for men. The fact that women were identified with the domestic sphere made it questionable whether they had any right to public life at all. When public toilets were established in Victorian London, men's facilities were easily and widely accepted, but there was entrenched hostility towards providing the same for women: the reasoning, roughly, was that a decent woman should never be far from her house, so why would she need a public toilet?[31] By anthropologist Mary Douglas's definition, dirt is 'matter out of place', and to a society that believed a woman's place was in the home, a woman on the streets was dirt. Jack the Ripper's victims were classed as prostitutes not because there was evidence that they all sold sex, but simply because they had been in a public space when they were murdered.[32] In 1910, when the suffragettes marched on Parliament on what became known as Black Friday – a public assertion of women's right to a part in public life – the police put them down not merely with violence but with sexual assault, grabbing the protesters' breasts.[33] Women belonged to the private realm, and when they left it, they became public women, implicitly accessible to anyone, or any man – a logic that reached across centuries and continents and, eventually, modems to create the inescapable snare of the Upskirt Decade. Britney, Paris, Lindsay, Aaliyah, Janet, Amy, Kim, Chyna and Jen had all sought recognition; therefore, they had forfeited all boundaries. For women, attention was the vampire you invited in once and could never expel.

It's a truism that the internet never forgets, but it does decay. While it may be impossible to destroy any specific piece of information, the fabric of the internet itself is constantly eroding. Servers close. Websites disappear. URLs change, and the links are never updated, leaving a trail of clicks that end on 404 Error messages. More subtly, there's the problem of the internet's perpetual present: when a site is redesigned, old pages are served with the same look as the new ones, making it impossible to put the past into its proper context. Thanks to the internet, the noughties were more thickly documented than any era before; also thanks to the internet, that documentation turned out to be astonishingly fragile. One of the things I wanted to do with this book (and could only attempt thanks to the Wayback Machine, a website that preserves

archived versions of web pages) was to recover what was lost –
not just to establish a chronology of the Upskirt Decade, but
also to re-create the sensation of life in that hectic time. And
the hardest aspect of the past to reconstruct is our ignorance.

This book could have been written only after the reckoning of MeToo. Movie producer Harvey Weinstein's overdue
encounter with justice, thanks to the women who spoke out
about his abuses and the reporters who put that testimony on
the record in 2017, led to two crucial things.[34] First, it encouraged other women to talk about their own experiences in the
period I write about. Second, it created a public appetite to
hear those stories, and to reassess the past in their light. The
unspoken facts of female lives have long been a kind of dark
matter, apparent only in their effects. That some women's
entertainment careers would mysteriously founder, while
others slid into self-destruction – this appeared to be a natural
law, inexplicable but inarguable. Now we can understand that
the wasted talent and tabloid flameouts were, in many cases,
only the visible consequences of a mass system of sexual harassment, assault and discrimination. Actress Rose McGowan
has attested to being one of Weinstein's victims. But prior to
MeToo, she tended to be presented in the media as something
of a difficult woman, sabotaged by her own abrasiveness as
much as by Hollywood sexism.[35] Speaking to the journalist
Ronan Farrow about her assault after Weinstein's conviction
for rape in 2020, McGowan said, 'It altered my life in such a
monstrous way. Because also, at this point, I was already well
known ... and now all of a sudden you get raped and blacklisted. So then what do you do? What job do you go get? You're
trapped. You're stuck.'[36] Only with knowledge of the crimes
committed by Weinstein in private can the public life of the
women he abused be comprehended.

Still, I hope I have avoided the historian's sin of applying the
values of the present to the past. We could not know what was

coming: alongside the slow shock of the internet, the period I've covered saw the shattering abruptions of 9/11 and the 2008 financial crisis. In these latter two cases, events provided a drastic demonstration that a common understanding of the world was inadequate and would have to be retired. Where the catastrophe was immediate and visible, so, too, was the adjustment. In the case of the internet, a more subtle realignment took place. Many people were likely unaware of their attitudes changing, even as concepts around the public sphere and celebrity shifted radically in one direction and then another. Beliefs must be appropriate to the circumstances, and as the circumstances changed, other beliefs were quietly established.

Britney, Paris, Lindsay, Aaliyah, Janet, Amy, Kim, Chyna and Jen were all both subject to that process and sometimes participants in it. They appear in each other's stories. They sometimes did things you might disapprove of, as well as being the recipients of monstrous wrongs. 'Half victims, half accomplices, like everyone else,' in Simone de Beauvoir's formulation. How else could they be human? If this book succeeds in anything, I hope it is in leaving the conviction that these women – fetishised and objectified as they have been – are, after all, only humans who were forced to make imperfect choices within horrifyingly imperfect conditions. But, ultimately, I do not know these women as people. I only know them as celebrities. I only know their personas. I only know them as two-way mirrors linking the immediate past to the immediate future. We look into them to see who we were and who we might yet become.

1

Britney: Fame

'I'm Mrs. "Extra! Extra! This Just In"'

It ends in 2008 with a young woman strapped to a gurney, hemmed in by photographers, the legend 'CRAZYTOWN EXPRESS' stamped underneath her image.[1] But it starts ten years earlier, with a video: a chunky loafer kicking impatiently against the leg of a school desk; a pencil tapping on a notepad; an institutional-looking clock ticking with agonising slowness towards three, and a girl watching it. She's pretty in a soft-faced way, blonde hair pulled into pigtails and held in place with fluffy pink ties. Then the bell tears apart the quiet and the boredom, and, at the same time, pulsing piano chords break into the soundtrack. Led by the girl, the class spills out into the corridor – this is a classic American high school, the kind of place you know even if you don't know it, part of the universal grammar of being a teenager laid down by Hollywood – and starts dancing. The song was released in the United States in 1998 and was already a hit there, but when I first see it in the United Kingdom, it's February 1999. I'm seventeen, the girl in the video is sixteen, and I can't look away, can't break my attention from the melodrama of it all. 'Oh baby, baby,' the girl sings, in a way that falls somewhere between abject and accusing, 'how was I supposed to know?'

Her white shirt is tied above her waist to reveal her midriff and unbuttoned to below her cleavage, showing her black bra. In the gap between her thigh-high socks and skirt hem, there's a flash of skin, a mix of innocence and availability that is pure Humbert Humbert fantasy. I'd read *Lolita* the summer before, sprawled on the back lawn with the sun on my bare legs. The cover of my edition was a painting by Balthus called *Girl and Cat*, the subject reclining on a wooden bench with one sloppily socked leg hitched up, staring down the painter while the painter stares back at the white of her exposed knickers. The girl in the video has the same expression as the girl in the Balthus painting, her mouth gently set and unsmiling, dark eyes wide and frank.

Sometimes the camera cuts to the girl on her own, leaning against the wall, looking up in supplication: she begs for a sign, dragging the word *sign* out into a five-syllable cascade of agony, before she makes her demand – 'And hit me baby one more time!' I watch the ' ... Baby One More Time' video to the end and am immediately and forever a Britney Spears fan.

'Baby' is a great song, but more than that, it's an extraordinary *arrival*: every component of the Britney persona is established by the end of it. Her vocal is a perfectly controlled performance of losing control, half unstoppable purpose ('Hit me!'), and half frantic self-abnegation ('When I'm not with you, I lose my mind!'). Half child tendering her bruised naïveté and half woman: the drive of 'Baby' is unquestionably adult, and that's almost entirely a product of Britney's delivery. The song, with its escalating intensity and never-quite-resolved tension, feels like unrequited longing rendered into music, but the lyrics are tame. Aside from the masochistic double entendre of the chorus, there's not a single line you could describe as definitively sexual, and even the chorus was an accident, claimed songwriter Max Martin. He told the press that, being Swedish and not a native English speaker, he'd taken 'hit' to be US slang for 'call', in the sense of 'hit me up', and written the song in all unknowingness. 'Baby' was turned down by the R&B girl group TLC, who objected to the violent implications: 'No disrespect to Britney. It's good for her,' Tionne 'T-Boz' Watkins of the band told MTV in 2013. 'But was I going to say "hit me baby one more time"? Hell no!' Tellingly, by the time the song became Britney's, the words 'hit me' in the title had been replaced by a teasing set of ellipses: someone besides T-Boz seemed to have spotted the issue.*[2]

Britney took the provocation and turned it into the whole text of the song. She later told *Rolling Stone* journalist Rob Sheffield that she'd spent the evening before the 'Baby' recording session listening to Soft Cell's 1981 version of 'Tainted Love', another anthem of longing that ends up luxuriating in its own submission: singer Marc Almond starts by begging a lover to stay away, but come the outro, he's pleading to be touched. The aim, Britney explained to Sheffield, was always to sound 'sexy'.[3]

Everything about Britney's image asserted her innocence, and everything about that innocence's ostentatious performance encouraged at least one part of the audience to imagine

---

* The song TLC eventually chose as the lead single from their second album is practically the anti-'Baby': 'Creep' is a slinky ballad in which the narrator doesn't beg her neglectful boyfriend for attention, but cheats on him to make the relationship bearable.

her despoiling. There was a collective thrill over her having been a presenter on the Disney Channel's *Mickey Mouse Club* – what could be more perfect a symbol of all-American girlhood than that? Her publicity even made explicit reference to her intact hymen. She wore a 'purity ring', then popular among Christian teenagers in the United States, which signalled her formal commitment to remain a virgin until marriage – and this, it was expected, would be to her sweetheart and fellow teen pop sensation, Justin Timberlake, of the boy band 'NSync.

But the value of a virginity consists, ultimately, in its taking: a 'mystery businessman' allegedly approached Britney's record company to offer £7.5 million (the equivalent of £13 million today) for hers, and somehow the bid was leaked to the public, along with a quote from Britney calling this indecent proposal 'disgusting'. There was something deeply cynical about the way this information came to be reported. 'Britney Spears swirls her virginity about like a tasselled nipple,' wrote journalist Polly Vernon in the *Guardian*, before adding that 'the truly vile part of Britney's uniquely confused and confusing sexuality is that men find it so utterly intoxicating.'[4] But this, I knew from my Nabokov, was the essence of the 'nymphet' – the adolescent girls Humbert Humbert devotes himself to in *Lolita*, who, the character explains, exist on the fault line between 'the beastly and the beautiful', utterly naïve of their own depraving influence.[5]

Britney's image played so explicitly with the Lolita trope, it seemed impossible she wasn't doing it knowingly. In a 1999 shoot for *Rolling Stone*, photographer David LaChapelle captured her in her teenage bedroom, dolls ranked behind her, dressed in white knickers and a white push-up bra, lips parted and eyes wide. She had to be doing this on purpose. Didn't she? Part of the genius of Britney's presentation was that she addressed multiple markets simultaneously through the same imagery. To the tween girl sector (the audience she fostered through mall tours early in her career), she was the idealised version of what they might become post-puberty. To adult men, she was the perfect instance of pliant femininity. And to those who, like me, had crossed the boundary of female adolescence, she offered a model for the scrutinised life that seemed an inevitable aspect of being female. 'A woman must continually watch herself. She is almost continually accompanied by her own image of herself,' wrote John Berger in the 1972 book *Ways of Seeing*. 'She has to survey everything she is and everything she does because how she appears to others, and ultimately how she appears to men, is of crucial importance to what is usually thought of as the success of her life. Her own sense of being in herself is supplanted by a sense of being appreciated as herself by another.'[6]

Britney, with her unimpeachable command of the grammar of the male gaze, appeared to have mastered the business of being an object. She was, whether instinctively or calculatedly, an expert in being looked at. In her 2005 book *Female Chauvinist Pigs*, feminist writer Ariel Levy identified Britney as the exemplar of a culture that valued 'the appearance of sexiness, not the existence of sexual pleasure' in women. Britney, wrote Levy, was a 'shiny, waxy [blonde] who used to tell us over and over again that sex was something [she] sang about, not something [she] actually engaged in'.[7] This was not a positive thing. But at the same age as Britney, I wanted to believe that the devouring threat of male desire could be neutered, captured, turned back on itself through the power of girlish self-awareness. I Blu-Tacked a poster of the LaChapelle portrait up on my own bedroom wall, making Britney a kind of patron saint of sexual knowingness. When her debut album came out (also called ... *Baby One More Time*), the US cover showed her kneeling and looking up at the camera, head cocked ingratiatingly, legs slightly parted so you could almost (not quite) see up her denim mini, a discreet blur of shadow rather than the deer-tail white flash in the Balthus painting. I didn't know it yet, but the Upskirt Decade had begun. And at some point, the girl's perfectly controlled appearance of losing control would be replaced by genuine, terrifying helplessness.

Britney would be famous in a way that no pop star before her had ever been. This is not because she would be more successful than her predecessors, although she was extremely successful. It's because she was calibrated for a kind of celebrity that was about to cease to exist. The fame she was working towards with the release of 'Baby' was mediated through TV, radio, newspapers and magazines, and calculated in CD sales. It would bear almost no relation at all to the fame she had to negotiate over the next ten years because, shortly after Britney's arrival, the internet happened. She was simultaneously the next big thing and the last star of a dying age. Nineteen ninety-nine was the most successful year on record for the US music market, with a total value of $14.6 billion.[8] And within that historic high, Britney's debut album was one of the standouts.[9] But in June of the same year, peer-to-peer file-sharing service Napster was launched, allowing anyone with an internet connection to download anything they wanted, provided someone else on the network had made it available.[10] Suddenly, record labels were competing not just against each other, but against their own products being offered for free.

The industry went into immediate decline, and over the next ten years, its value almost halved: by 2009, US music sales totaled a mere $7.8 billion.[11] *Baby* sold fourteen million copies in America; Britney's 2007 album, *Blackout*, sold just one million, and while that partly reflected a dip in her popularity – the album ranked eighty-fifth out of the year's releases – the biggest-selling album of the same year sold only four million units in total. The traditional economics of pop music had flipped. With CD sales on the slide, concert tickets would have to compensate. In the eighties and nineties, Madonna had averaged one major tour for every two albums.[12] Britney toured every album and squeezed in an extra set of performances between her first and second albums. Between 1999 and 2004, she played 357 dates, 122 of them in 2000, not including her other promotional duties.[13] Every tour required planning, choreography and rehearsals. Every concert meant hours of travel and sleeping in another strange city. And in between this, she also had to record the albums that justified the live performances. It was a punishing work rate for anyone, never mind someone as staggeringly young as Britney was. But it was the only way for a pop star to be profitable.

In other words, Britney became successful at a time when even continued success could look a lot like failing. All the same, she was undeniably a phenomenon and rapidly became established as a peer of music's biggest names. In 2001, she was invited to duet with Michael Jackson at a concert to celebrate thirty years of his solo career: they delivered an awkwardly flirtatious rendition of 'The Way You Make Me Feel'. Two years after that, she performed with Madonna on a medley of 'Like a Virgin' and 'Hollywood' at the 2003 MTV Video Music Awards (alongside Britney's fellow young, hot singer and Disney alumnus Christina Aguilera, and rapper Missy Elliott). These events fixed Britney in the pop royalty line of succession, but there was benefit in both directions: she was so big by then that claiming her as an heir was a way for these acts to assert their continuing power. The VMA performance in particular has the feel of a reigning Mafiosa anointing a successor. At the climax, Madonna (who arrived onstage costumed as a kind of dominatrix bridegroom in black, with top hat and over-the-knee boots) bestowed a kiss on the lips to Britney, who was wearing a white lace bustier that gave her the virgin/slut look of a girl on her wedding night. It was a huge moment: although Madonna repeated the trick with Aguilera on her other side, the cameras had already cut to the audience's dazed reaction – lingering particularly on Timberlake, who was now Britney's ex.

This was a coup for Britney, who had looked in grave danger of losing control of her image over the previous few years. Obviously being a virginal schoolgirl wasn't a tenable persona in the long term: at some point, the public would have to be reconciled to the fact that Britney Spears was growing up. Doing that, however, had proved difficult, and in 2003, *Rolling Stone* noted 'it's undeniable that, as the former Mouseketeer has inched past the age of consent, she's had a much bumpier career ride'.[14] The *Oops! . . . I Did It Again* album, released in 2000, had teased a more provocative Britney, one who declared herself 'not that innocent' after all, although she still stopped short of claiming any sexual experience. *Britney*, in 2001, went further: the lead single, 'I'm a Slave 4 U', was an orgy of panting eroticism, with production team the Neptunes bringing her an edgier, R&B-influenced sound. Even so, nymphette elements remained, as the ballad 'I'm Not a Girl, Not Yet a Woman' made explicit. (This was also the key soundtrack moment in her 2002 movie *Crossroads*, a sweet coming-of-age story about three female friends that happens to include extensive scenes of Britney bouncing on a bed in her underwear and a plot that hinges heavily on whether and to whom her character will lose her virginity. The movie was perfect, the *Washington Post*'s reviewer declared, for an audience 'composed chiefly of 10-year-old girls and 50-year-old men'.)[15]

The last song on *Britney*, 'What It's Like to Be Me', warns a boyfriend that she won't give him 'everything' until she's sure his love is true; Timberlake co-wrote it and provided backing vocals. In a publicity Q&A, Britney explained that the song was 'talking about being in a relationship where the guy thinks he knows the girl inside and out and he tries to take advantage of her'.[16] In other words, Timberlake was constructing himself in the part of the player denied, grafting his reputation to Britney's profile – at the cost of positioning himself as the guy who can't get it. It was, at that stage of their respective careers, an acceptable bargain. Her first tour had actually been as an opening act for 'NSync – like Britney, 'NSync worked with Max Martin and were signed to Jive, so it made synergistic sense for the label to cross-promote the two. But their roles quickly reversed. When both acts made their VMA debut in 1999, the classroom-themed staging turned the boy band into an audience for her strutting and teasing; when she cooed, 'I'd like to introduce you to some friends of mine,' it was obvious which act held seniority. Britney and Justin were a pop power couple, but there was a hierarchy: the queen of teen, and her prince consort.

This was all well enough for building 'NSync's profile, but when Timberlake was looking to establish his solo career in 2002, something would have to change. If virginity was looking implausible on Britney, for Timberlake, it was downright humiliating. To be famous as a man who didn't get any was acceptable for a squeaky-clean boy band member maybe, but intolerable for a hot male singer whose debut solo album was pitched as the crossover between pop and R&B. When he and Britney split up, and rumors of her infidelity broke in the press, an opportunity presented itself. Timberlake could purchase his rebirth with a virgin sacrifice – or, rather, by sacrificing the myth of Britney's virginity (the myth he had in fact helped to construct on 'What It's Like to Be Me'). After years of gentlemanly discretion, he now couldn't stop running his mouth all over the media. In a radio appearance on Hot 97 FM, the DJ asked, 'Did you fuck Britney Spears, yes or no?'

'Oh man … Okay, yeah, I did it,' replied Justin, as the studio erupted in cheers.[17]

A cover line on an issue of *Details* magazine from 2002 summed up the break between old Justin and new Justin. 'Can we ever forgive Justin Timberlake for all that sissy music?' it asked, then answered itself: 'Hey ... at least he got into Britney's pants.' (Another feature was trailed on the cover with the line 'Forget Feminism: Why Your Wife Should Take Your Name', which says a lot about the political moment.)[18]

The centrepiece of the Timberlake reinvention came with his second solo single, 'Cry Me a River', released in November 2002. The song is addressed to an unfaithful ex – widely assumed at the time, and later confirmed by producer Timbaland, to be Britney Spears. But if the song was pointed, the video was a shiv. In it, Timberlake watches his ex leave her house, breaks in, and shimmies about inside it, dressed throughout like Tony Curtis in *The Boston Strangler*; at the end, the ex comes home, and Timberlake watches her taking a shower. It's a stalker's revenge fantasy, and the most sinister part of all is that the woman cast as the ex is a precise looka-like for Britney: if the pout and long blonde hair don't give it away, the fact that she wears Britney's then-signature baker boy cap throughout should be enough. It's a fantasy of inva-sion as punishment: if a woman was assumed to have failed at fidelity, she was assumed to have forfeited her boundaries alto-gether. Trespassing on her home was no trespass at all if she had shown herself willing to let other men through the door. If you can't keep your legs together, you don't get to complain about someone jimmying your lock. Or about a paparazzo aiming a lens between your thighs.

Director Francis Lawrence had previously pitched the 'Cry Me a River' concept to other artists (without, obviously, the Britney angle), but always came up against concerns about damaging the artist's image. Timberlake, though, was at a point in his career when damaging his image was the best thing for him. Although Britney was never mentioned in the discussions between Lawrence and Timberlake, the director took it as read that they both knew what this was. The label apparently did as well. Timberlake was still signed to Jive as a solo artist, and so still labelmates with Britney. In a 2017 interview, Lawrence explained, 'I think that there was momentary pressure from the "other party" that didn't last long. I think [Britney] had been shown the video before it was released. [The label] went through a moment where it was like, "What are we gonna do? Are we hurting a relationship with somebody else here?" But then it all went away.'[19] Britney told *Rolling Stone* that she had in fact been consulted and given her consent, but without a full understanding of what the video would be: 'I hadn't seen it. Then it came out, and I said, "I should've freakin' said no to this shit!" ... I think it looks like such a desperate attempt, personally. But that was a great way to sell the record. He's smart.'[20]

The video was a watershed for the reputations of both Britney and Timberlake. It marked him as a wounded bad boy, casting off his 'NSync stigma with no detrimental effect on his heartthrob status.* Britney, though, was turned into the villain – a faithless woman who could be rightfully shamed in regular rotation on MTV. The tabloid magazine *Us Weekly* plastered its cover with the question 'Britney and Justin: Did She Betray Him?'[21] In a TV interview, host Diane Sawyer pressed Britney relentlessly on the issue of how many people she'd slept with – and while Timberlake was celebrated for saying he'd had sex, there was no such applause for Britney. In her case, intercourse was treated as a grave and sombre matter for which she owed the nation an apology. Eventually, and to Sawyer's apparent satisfaction, Britney crumpled into sobs.[22] There was no sympathy here but, instead, the thrill of seeing

---

* Astonishingly, there was a crasser way to do this than the one Timberlake chose. His bandmate J. C. Chasez launched his solo career in 2004 with the album *Schizophrenic*, which features such triumphs of taste as the songs 'Some Girls Dance with Women' (an ode to lipstick lesbianism in the club) and 'All Day Long I Dream About Sex' (self-explanatory). On the cover, Chasez smoulders in a straitjacket. There was no second album.

celebrities break the fourth wall and turn gossip columns into art. You could enjoy 'Cry Me a River' as a song, but when you'd followed the backstory, there was an extra shiver of knowing-ness in watching the personal and the persona collide. The scandalous VMA kiss with Madonna put Britney, briefly, back in charge.

But it would be a mistake to think that Timberlake was operating from a position of uncomplicated power in the entertainment industry. Being male protected him from the sexism Britney suffered, but not from all forms of exploita-tion. 'NSync's first manager had been the entrepreneur Lou Pearlman, who had also managed the Backstreet Boys. Pearlman had started out in aviation, and he presented his musical concerns as simply another avenue for moneymak-ing. In Pearlman's own mythology, he had realised there were profits to be made from pop when bands started hiring private jets from him, and decided to get his own piece of the action.[23] After establishing Backstreet, he reasoned that their success made a competitor group inevitable, and he might as well profit from that, too – and so, 'NSync was born. Pearlman put his charges through a kind of boot camp, effectively estab-lishing the factory system that would dominate noughties pop. He even originated one of the first reality talent contests on TV, MTV's *Making the Band*. Alongside his small fleet of boy bands – including LFO, C-Note, Take 5 and O-Town – Pearlman had one girl band, called Innosense, which had briefly included Britney before she opted to pursue a solo career. His preference, though, was always for young men. 'Some may disagree with me,' he wrote in his 2003 autobiog-raphy, 'but my feeling is that young male performers are more coachable than young females.'[24]

By the time Pearlman wrote this, though, he was no longer managing either Backstreet or 'NSync. After years of relent-less work sustained only by Pearlman's promises of wealth to come and his father figure authority (he encouraged the band members to call him 'Big Poppa'), both Backstreet and 'NSync had realised Pearlman was ripping them off, and sued him. Among many pieces of sharp practice, he had written himself into the bands' contracts as both manager and 'sixth member', entitling him to a double share of the profits. Timberlake later described Pearlman's exploitation as like 'being financially raped by a Svengali'. The allusion to sexual violence echoed another allegation that emerged against Pearlman: that he had sexually abused his teenage charges. 'Some guys joked about it; I remember [one singer] asking me, "Have you let Lou blow you yet?"' said one-time Pearlman employee Steve Mooney, speaking to *Vanity Fair* in 2007. Another Pearlman protégé suspected that the manager had never actually expected his bands to become successful: 'I just think he wanted cute guys around him; this was all an excuse.'[25] But if Pearlman's interest was exclusively in young men, why had he been involved with the girl band Innosense? The unpleasant possibility raised by some observers was that they were simply bait for the boys. Pearlman had tanning beds in his home, which he invited the girls to use. He also reportedly had secret cameras installed in the room, and showed the resulting Peeping Tom footage to his boys.[26]

Pearlman did make money from his bands, even after the lawsuits, but not enough to save him. It transpired that his other businesses had been equally shady, and in 2008 he was convicted of running a Ponzi scheme that had syphoned millions of dollars from investors. He died in prison in 2016, aged sixty-two.[27] But despite his criminality, there was no doubting his influence. 'Pearlman did change pop culture. In some respects, we live in the world Lou Pearlman created – manufactured pop stars, boy bands, reality-TV singing contests. We just don't like to admit it,' wrote John Seabrook in an obituary for the *New Yorker*.[28] And this was the world that had made Timberlake.

Timberlake has never alleged that Pearlman behaved inappropriately with him; nor has he commented on the allegations of impropriety made by others. (Pearlman was never convicted of any sexual offences, and maintained his innocence up until his death.) Nonetheless, by the time 'NSync signed to Jive, the entire band had experienced the pop industry at its most predatory. In 2000, they celebrated their emancipation from Pearlman by naming their new album *No Strings Attached*. The truth is, however, that regardless of sex, very few performers in the factory system of the noughties were able to act with artistic impunity. 'Cry Me a River' could only happen because Jive wanted it to. Timberlake was the up-and-coming thing, while Britney was an act with diminishing returns and a worn-out gimmick. Betraying her was just business.

If Britney couldn't rely on her record company, perhaps she could rely on her family. After all, she had always been a family business: she was followed into show business by her sister, Jamie Lynn, and in Britney's early career, her mother, Lynne, was an omnipresent figure, playing the chaperone role and acting as the guarantor of her daughter's purity. Mother and daughter even produced two books together: the non-fiction *Britney Spears' Heart to Heart* in 2000, telling the 'inspiring story of how one little girl from a small town in the USA turned into a musical phenomenon',[29] and a novel called *A Mother's Gift* in 2001, about a girl from a small town in the United States with a 'dream of pursuing a singing career'.[30] These books were both brand extension and brand reinforcement. In the first place, they existed to draw more money from Britney's fans. (The ever-expropriative Pearlman noted in his book that, though young girls had limited disposable income, they would gladly spend it all on their idols: 'Once you've won their loyalty . . . they'll buy just about anything and everything that their favorite performers endorse.'[31]) In the second, they existed to prove that Britney really was a good girl who loved her 'mama', and therefore a safe role model for the tween market. The books had a subtler, tertiary role as well: to defend Lynne Spears to the public. Having divorced Britney's father, Jamie, over claims of his drinking and adultery, she presented herself as the paradigm of the fiercely supportive single mother, helping her daughter achieve her ambitions. Of Britney's risqué outfits, Lynne Spears wrote, 'I don't see any harm in it, and I don't believe it makes me a bad mother.' On the subject of drugs, sex and alcohol, she wrote, 'I know I have prepared her, I have told her how I feel, and I trust that she will make smart decisions.'[32] Still, there were hints, even in the controlled environment of the books, that everything was not quite right in the world of Britney. 'I am so not the party animal that it's kind of embarrassing,' protested Britney in a section of *Heart to Heart* called 'The Party Scene'. 'It makes it all the more crazy when the tabloids report that I was here or there, dating someone I never met.' There were further opaque denials from Lynne: 'What I can't understand is why they do it, why people make up nasty stories that aren't true and criticise her ... She's just a kid.[33]

But the tabloid stories didn't stop, and as Britney entered her twenties, it no longer made sense to call her a 'kid'. Her 2003 album, *In the Zone*, was pitched as 'a more adult affair' – and necessarily so, given the reports of her partying. *Star* splashed on an allegation of her sniffing coke in a nightclub bathroom – something Britney initially denied through a representative, but responded to more ambivalently in a follow-up interview with the magazine, when she said, 'Let's just say you reach a point in your life when you are curious.'[34] She even confessed to *W* magazine that she had indeed had sex with Timberlake.[35] But Britney's embrace of womanhood seemed, perversely, even more childlike than her Lolita era had been. There was something deeply fragile and naïve about her, and nothing showed this more than the song 'Everytime', her response to 'Cry Me a River'. A plaintive, pretty ballad, it contrasts sharply with the rest of *In the Zone*'s relentless performance of horniness and is delivered without Britney's usual battery of tics and growls: a simple address to an injured ex and a plea for forgiveness. Other songwriters had offered Britney tracks that would have fought fire with fire. (The Cathy Dennis song 'Sweet Dreams My LA Ex', eventually recorded by Rachel Stevens, was rumoured to be one of them. Its weary demand that the ex in question 'find somebody else to talk about' certainly fits the outline of the Britney-Justin drama.) Instead, she chose one of the most vulnerable songs she ever recorded. Unusually for Britney, she also co-wrote it.[36]

The video, though, is downright harrowing and frames the song less as a love story than as a response to the trauma of fame. This wasn't the first time Britney had addressed that subject in her work – the syrupy ballad 'Lucky', from her second album, *Oops!*, narrates the life of a starlet who cries every night despite her fame and riches, and to drive the point home, Britney plays both herself and 'Lucky' in the campy video. But the video for 'Everytime' seems to draw more directly on Britney's own experiences. It opens with Britney and a boyfriend exiting a limo and tussling with paparazzi as they enter a hotel. The boyfriend shoves a photographer back, then the couple start fighting, hurling objects at each other in their hotel suite. The video then shifts to a supernatural register. Britney sinks into a bath with blood blooming from a cut, then reappears, dressed in white, standing in a white corridor. We're now in a hospital. Britney, unnoticed by anyone else there, watches a woman give birth; back in the hotel room, her boyfriend rescues her from the bath, and she's taken away on a stretcher, with photographers pressing around the ambulance. At the end, we cut back to the bath – from which Britney emerges, smiling and cleansed, but the image feels like a tacked-on gesture to decency after what's gone before.

The video's director, David LaChapelle (the photographer behind the *Rolling Stone* bedroom portrait), said later that the concept had been Britney's: 'The only direction Britney gave me for the video was that she wanted to die, that she wanted to die in the video.'[37] But Britney has said that she didn't always feel like the one in control when working with LaChapelle. Recalling that earlier bedroom shoot during a 2003 interview with *GQ*, she said, 'He came in and did the photos and totally tricked me. They were really cool but I didn't really know what the hell I was doing. And, to be totally honest with you, at the time I was sixteen, so I really didn't. I was back in my bedroom, and I had my little sweater on and he was like, "Undo your sweater a little bit more." The whole thing was about me being into dolls and in my mind I was like, "Here are my dolls!"'[38] (Britney slightly misremembered here: she was seventeen at the time of the shoot.) LaChapelle's own account is that his shoots were always 'collaborative' and 'wholesome'.[39] Still, he had had his own misgivings about the 1999 photo session. 'I could tell even back then something wasn't right,' he declared in a 2019 Instagram comment.[40] And yet, if that's true, he was nonetheless able to master his discomfort and go on taking pictures of a teenage girl in her bra and pants for a national magazine.

If the 'Everytime' video was a cry for help from Britney, it didn't matter, because no one seemed to be listening. The 2003 VMA performance, rather than heralding a return to Britney's self-possessed prime, turned out to be the last high before a precipitous slide; she wouldn't be seen at the awards again until 2007. The constant stream of paparazzi shots showing her going in and out of nightclubs, sometimes in the company of fellow hot messes like Paris, generally in some state of intoxication, were one thing. More concerning was the incident in

January 2004, when she married her high school friend Jason Allen Alexander in a Vegas quickie; fifty-five hours later, the union was dissolved. The terms of the annulment included the troubling statement that Britney 'lacked understanding of her actions, to the extent that she was incapable of agreeing to the marriage'.[41] Months later, she was married again, this time to dancer Kevin Federline. This union was chronicled in a 2005 reality series called *Britney and Kevin: Chaotic*, based on camcorder footage filmed by Britney herself. It ran for five episodes and ensured that any vestige of glamour clinging to Britney was thoroughly extinguished. Highlights include her pointing the camera at her own knees and declaring delightedly, 'They look like my boobs, but they're my knees!' One of Britney's bodyguards voices a widely held scepticism when he says of Federline, 'this guy's just looking for a free ride'.[42]

The most perplexing question is why Britney would allow herself to be seen in this way – or why those around did not advise her against it. The answer may be strictly financial. Britney's 2004 Onyx Hotel tour had been cut short by a knee injury (perhaps unsurprisingly, given how relentless her schedule had been since 1999), and insurers had refused to pay out on the grounds that she had failed to disclose a pre-existing condition.[43] Selling behind-the-scenes footage to a TV network was a quick way to get money back into the Britney operation. But it may also have been simple naïveté. Reality TV was a relatively new medium and had been positive for many of its subjects: *The Osbournes*, which began in 2002, had transformed Ozzy Osbourne from a heavy metal has-been into the endearingly shambolic patriarch of an affectionate if disorderly family and launched his wife, Sharon, on a career as talent show judge and chat show host. For Britney, who had already made public her anger with 'tabloid lies' about her life, this may have felt like a chance to set the record straight.[44]

But reality could destroy an image as well as enhance it:

the same summer that *Chaotic* arrived on-screen, Bravo aired *Being Bobby Brown*, which followed the eponymous soul star and his wife, the regally beautiful and talented Whitney Houston. It was a disaster, cementing Brown in the public consciousness as a wife beater and Houston as his drug-addled victim. (Brown contests his representation as a domestic abuser, saying he only hit Houston once.[45]) Britney's foray into reality was not quite so damaging, but only because the gap between her image and the self she revealed through her own camcorder was not quite so vast. People already believed her to be white trash. *Chaotic* only confirmed this. In further bad news for Britney's reputation, celebrity blogging was just beginning to explode around this time. TMZ launched in 2005, and so did What Would Tyler Durden Do?, which took the nihilistic protagonist of *Fight Club* as a role model and epitomised the new savagery towards celebrities with its tagline: 'Because fuck them, that's why.' Perez Hilton had started his first blog in late 2004, but 2005 saw his antagonistic approach to the stars he covered gain mainstream recognition. He made a trademark of calling female stars 'sluts' and doodling ejaculating penises on their pictures, and Britney gave him an especially rich seam of material. One Hilton post about her was headlined 'Filthy Whore'.[46] Another, titled 'Attention All Britney Fans', demanded to know 'How can you still support this mess????'[47]

Between 2005 and 2007, Britney released no new studio albums and performed just nine times. She existed not as a pop star but as a tabloid presence, and the harder she crashed, the more traffic she generated and newsstand sales she racked up. Her marriage to Federline unravelled within two months of the birth of their second child in 2006. There was an abortive stint in rehab. She lost weight, gained weight, and was accused of being a 'bad mother' when she was photographed driving with her son on her lap. (She defended herself, saying that she had been trying to drive away from the photographers.) She lost custody of her children. There was also the concerning presence of a man called Sam Lutfi, who was acting as Britney's manager, and whom Britney's mother accused of drugging and controlling the singer (Lutfi denied this, saying through his lawyer that he had 'merely responded to cries for help'; Britney was granted a series of restraining orders against him).[48] And in February 2007, perhaps most shockingly, she walked into a hair salon in a Los Angeles, took up a set of clippers, and shaved her head. A few days later, she was photographed, shorn-headed and wide-eyed, taking an umbrella to a paparazzo's car outside a petrol station.

Britney had been the avatar of femininity in the new millennium, and her flowing blonde hair was integral to that. Remembering her daughter's birth in *Heart to Heart*, Lynne had written: 'An adorable baby girl to dress up like a little doll! A daughter to have tea parties with! I'd braid her hair! Luckily for me, Brit loved being a girl.'[49] Now, apparently, she didn't love it so much – or at least, did not love what being a girl meant. The hairdresser who spoke to Britney in the salon recalled her saying, 'My mom is going to freak.' Britney also spoke to a tattoo artist, who asked why she'd shaved her head. 'I don't want anyone touching my hair. I'm sick of people touching my hair,' was Britney's reply. Lutfi offered a more prosaic explanation years later – that by destroying her hair, Britney was destroying evidence that could be used in compulsory drug testing during her custody battle with Federline.[50] But the iconography of the act was profound. Consciously or not, this was a rebellion against the girlish compliance and availability that Britney had been groomed to perform.[51]

Even when Britney seemed to be rejecting her persona, though, she continued to be relentlessly documented: the bodyguards who were supposedly tasked with shielding her from the paparazzi chatted happily with photographers while all this happened, according to the hairdresser.[52] Some on the press side have claimed that the intimacy between Britney's camp and the paparazzi was long-standing, with 'her people' passing on information about her whereabouts.[53] Perez Hilton even alleged that Britney herself was sending in the tips: 'She used to call the agency X17 and invite them into her home to party!' he wrote in his book *Red Carpet Suicide*.[54] Britney has never confirmed this, but it is true that celebrities have an awkward symbiosis with the paparazzi, and many will develop relationships with the photographers who follow them day after day – Britney even dated one of hers for a time. At different stages in a celebrity's life, it's possible for them to welcome, rely on and resent those who pursue them for content. And why conduct the head-shaving in public at all? If Lutfi's theory was right, it would surely have made more sense for Britney to do this in her own home. Perhaps, having been on display ever since she was a child, she needed to be seen in order to feel her revolt meant anything. Or, perhaps, this was simply the way she had accepted her life should be.

The head-shaving was the moment she began to be described not merely as low-class or slutty, but as mad. Even more than losing custody of her children, Bald Britney seemed to symbolise her fall. Her sexiness was her most valuable asset, and she couldn't be trusted with it. In September 2007 – her hair long and blonde again, thanks to extensions – she made her return to the VMAs. What was billed as a glorious comeback turned out to be agonising shambles. Britney fluffed her choreography and looked vacant, and even her body was declared substandard. (There were reports that she had called herself a 'fat pig' while watching the rehearsal footage.) *X Factor* judge Simon Cowell considered the performance potentially career-ending. 'She wasn't ready for that show in every possible way,' he told the *Sun*. 'The song wasn't right, the image wasn't right and she just wasn't rehearsed.'[55]

Somehow, while all this was happening, she was also recording what would widely come to be considered her best album. From its substance abuse-baiting title on, *Blackout* tackled Britney's tabloid image directly. Released in November 2007, its standout track is the electropop assault 'Piece of Me'. The song's title, in classic Britney style, is ambivalent, both a challenge and a surrender: she's simultaneously calling the listener out and acknowledging the way she's been broken down for public consumption. Subject and object at the same time, forever conscious of the way she is surveyed: 'I'm Mrs. "Extra! Extra! This Just In" / I'm Mrs. "She's Too Big, Now She's Too Thin",' she sings. In the video, we see Britney rewriting her own press and taking revenge on her tormentors, with the help of a squadron of Britney lookalikes. (In what might be a callback to Timberlake's 'Cry Me a River' video, the Brit Army wear baker boy caps.)

But, in the song, something different happens, and the end result is less suggestive of someone taking back control than of someone entirely lost in her own image: her vocals are heavily pitch-shifted, so that she seems to disintegrate entirely in the middle eight. The human Britney has been consumed by the performance. And though Britney is singing the words, the words are not her own: critic Sady (now Jude) Doyle characterised *Blackout*'s lyrics as Britney's statement on her media treatment, but she's credited as a writer on only two of the album's songs, and 'Piece of Me' is not one of them.[56] (In interviews, Britney had expressed caution about autobiographical songwriting, which she dismissed as 'self-serving'.[57] 'Everytime' was an exception in her catalogue.) So, which version of Britney was real? The self-possessed woman in the video or the ghost in the machine of the song?

In January 2008, less than three months after *Blackout*'s show of defiance, the answer came. After an incident at her home, paramedics were called, and Britney was removed to a psychiatric ward. The image of her strapped to a gurney, surrounded by photographers, was a horrifyingly precise real-life rerun of the 'Everytime' video. Her father, acting with the support of her mother (despite their divorce), petitioned for Britney to be placed under a conservatorship, and for the next thirteen years, everything about Britney – her career, her finances, who she saw, where she went, even what she did with her body – would be controlled by him. According to lawyers acting for Britney, Jamie Spears would receive over $6 million through the conservatorship.[58] Another major beneficiary was the media, which had a shocking new twist for the ultimate celebrity narrative. The TMZ report ended with the cheerful injunction 'Keep refreshing for updates!'

There are a lot of ways to read *Lolita*, but this is my favourite: as a story of culpability. Over the course of the novel, Humbert is forced to recognise that Lolita was never the fantastical figure of innocent debauchery his libido cast her as, only a human girl, and a human girl who was injured by his predation and that of other men. She dies outside the scope of the story, in an obscure settlement called Gray Star, 'in the remotest northwest' (so remote, in fact, that it does not exist in the world beyond the novel). However fiercely she's desired, displacing her into a fetish means that the 'real' Lolita is always out of reach – something that Humbert realises much too late to deserve credit, never mind redemption. That's not the reading of *Lolita* that made its way into pop culture, which preferred the vision of the precociously sexual girl child. (In the song '10 Dollar', released in 2004, British rapper M.I.A. rhymes 'Lolita' with 'maneater' in a story about a child prostitute who propels herself to independence by extracting money from well-off men.) But it's the reading that matters most for understanding what happened to Britney. After her detention in 2008 and the establishment of the conservatorship, she effectively disappeared beneath her own image. Whatever the legal equivalent of Gray Star was, that's where Britney resided.

Not literally – she released albums (now a more profitable endeavour since the launch of Spotify in 2006 had created a legitimate substitute for illegal downloads), and she undertook tours and residencies. From the outside, Britney's conservatorship appeared to be a great success. In November 2008, *Us Magazine* announced that she was 'officially in comeback mode'.[59] The same month, MTV broadcast a fly-on-the-wall documentary called *Britney: For the Record*. It showed the public a Jamie Spears who was devoted to the welfare of his daughter and a composed, contrite Britney who was ready to acknowledge her past mistakes. 'I have definitely grown up. Big time,' she says. 'I had totally lost my way. I lost focus. I lost myself. I had that kind of nature in me that wanted to rebel out.'[60] Rebellion quenched, Britney could get back to her job of being a star. 'Letting her father Jamie run the show turned out to be the best thing for Britney,' announced Page Six in 2009. 'In addition to making her cheese grits, her dad took control of her finances and life. Jamie also purged all the negativity from her world and showed Britney the light.'[61] There were irregularities – she appeared vacant and inarticulate during a 2012 stint as a judge on the US version of *The X Factor*, and was not invited back – but overall, the narrative of Britney reborn held sway.[62]

But there was a problem with this, although many chose not to acknowledge it. If Britney really was better, what was the justification for her father's continued ownership of her life? And if Britney was still the fragile young woman everyone had watched coming apart in 2007, how could it be okay for her to be put on public display with each performance? There was no way to ask what Britney herself truly thought about this, because the terms of the conservatorship meant that everything she said to the media had to be filtered through her father. Even when she speaks directly to the camera in *For the Record*, she is speaking with the permission of Jamie Spears and with him as her primary audience. When someone holds the total power granted by a conservatorship, incurring their displeasure can hardly be advisable.

Throughout her career, in her music and her performances, Britney conjured ideas of submission and control with no apparent sense of irony. At the 2011 Billboard Music Awards, she duetted with Rihanna on a performance of 'S&M' wearing handcuffs. Onstage, she smiled radiantly, like someone delighting in her own subjection. 'Work Bitch', from her 2013 album, *Britney Jean*, became one of her signature songs: a celebration of the self-discipline through which she had attained the hot body, the martinis and the Maseratis that defined a successful lifestyle, according to the lyrics. The question of who, exactly, Britney was working for remained in the shadows – although, by 2020, a growing number of fans had started to express concern for her under the banner of #FreeBritney. And behind the scenes, Britney brought legal challenges to the conservatorship, beginning in 2014. In 2016, a court investigator reported that 'she feels the conservatorship has become an oppressive and controlling tool against her'. In 2020, her attorney told the judge that Britney was 'afraid of her father'.[63]

None of this, however, was enough to bring the conservatorship to an end. Britney's predicament was that, having been classified as mad, any objection she made to the constraints on her liberty could be dismissed as symptoms of her madness. It was only after the 2021 *New York Times* documentary *Framing Britney Spears* that popular opinion swung fully behind the idea that her situation was intolerable. That year, in a new hearing on the conservatorship, Britney delivered a devastating testimony of being, in her words, 'enslaved'. She said she had been 'forced' to tour by her management in 2018, and that her most private decisions had been dictated for her, including whether she could get married or try for a third child. (Her father, she claimed, had refused permission for her IUD to be removed; his attorney refuted this, telling the court, 'I'm not sure Miss Spears understands she can make medical decisions.')[64] She was compelled to take lithium, she said, which had made her feel 'drunk'. She had no privacy from the people in her father's employ: 'They watched me change every day – naked – morning, noon and night.' Perhaps the most painful detail was the disassociated way she spoke about her body, as though it were a separate entity. 'My precious body,' she said, 'who has worked for my dad for the past fucking thirteen years, trying to be so good and pretty. So perfect.'[65] (Jamie Spears, for his part, has maintained that the conservatorship was necessary to save Britney's life and denied the allegations against him of drinking and domestic violence.[66])

This, then, was what it meant to be the most objectified woman in the world. Under the performance of immaculate control that had been Britney's professional image throughout her adult life there lay an absolute schism between her body and her sense of personhood. As much as the public, Britney had turned into a spectator on her own physicality. The court granted Britney her freedom. At thirty-nine, the woman-child who had never lived an adult life – for whom holding a set of keys or buying a candle was a novelty – was able to begin again.[67] And yet, while she blamed her family for exploiting her, she was also angry about the way her situation had been covered in the media. For her, the sympathetic coverage of the *New York Times* (along with follow-up documentaries by the BBC and Netflix) was simply another way of turning her into content, just as the tabloids had done in the decades before. 'I feel like America has done a wonderful job of humiliating me ... and come on seriously is it honestly legal to do that many documentaries about someone without their blessing at all??!' she wrote in a 2022 Instagram post.[68]

Britney credited her emancipation not to journalism, but to her fans. Fame had come close to destroying her, and yet fame had given her love and support she had not experienced from those closest to her, including her own family. Britney was required to play the child while being held to an adult standard of responsibility for something as trivial as a teenage break-up. She felt betrayed by those who owed her a duty of care, believing her parents and her record label had placed profit over protection. Finally, she was forced into a legally mandated state of infantilisation that lasted almost into middle age. In the hypocrisy and cruelty of her treatment, the public life of women in the noughties was defined. Her debut had launched her into a kind of celebrity for which no one could have been prepared, one shaped by forces that few could have foreseen – least of all a sixteen-year-old. 'Oh baby, baby,' she sang in 1998, with the Upskirt Decade as yet an unimagined prospect, 'how was I supposed to know?'

2

Paris: Invasion

'I like attention'

In 2005, the gossip blogger Mario Lavandeira had a problem: What was he going to call himself? His website, PageSixSixSix, had become must-read material for anyone interested in celebrity and scandal, which was great news for his click rate and ad revenue, but it also meant he was attracting some inconvenient attention – including from the *New York Post*, home to the original Page Six gossip column.[1] The *Post* did not appreciate Lavandeira's demonic pun on its intellectual property, and Lavandeira didn't have the money to fight a lawsuit.[2] He was going to need a new brand. In fact, he decided to construct a whole new identity – a character he could play online as he participated in the great soap opera of trash talk and rumour.

For his new name, he wanted something funny. Something that represented the kind of celebrity he was writing about. And no one was more representative of celebrity in the noughties than Paris Hilton.

'These days,' Lavandeira wrote in 2009, 'fame is no longer limited to the actress on the red carpet, the rock star packing the arena, or the athlete tearing up the megadome. These untouchable, elusive, and private celebrities are being eclipsed by another kind of star.' The noughties were a self-consciously degraded time, and they needed a cast of self-consciously degraded characters to match: 'Now we have hiltons: people we confuse with celebrities. No one even knows how they became famous or, more accurately, how they became famous for being famous. You see, a hilton is someone who is skinny, notorious, mischievous, hot, loves to party, dates a lot, acts gorgeous, drives drunk, poses seductively for the camera, rarely works, dates some more, and doesn't eat . . . Hiltons lack any real talent, so they have to resort to using scandal and debauchery to catapult them to fame and celebrity status.'[3]

Mario Lavandeira rechristened himself Perez Hilton. And unlike the *New York Post*, this time the object of his wordplay didn't seem to take offence – not even at the obvious insult of making her the stand-in for a whole class of what Lavandeira called 'famous sluts'. Paris and Perez appeared on red carpets together; they partied together; in 2006, she accepted an award from him at the VH1 Big in '06 Awards. (The award, for 'Big Outlaw', was intended to honour celebrities who perpetrated the most entertaining bad behaviour.) In the video of her acceptance speech, she's smiling as she holds her trophy high. 'I never really thought of myself as an outlaw,' she says. 'I'm more of a girl who just likes to have fun and' – here her voice drops to a seductive purr – 'get in a little trouble sometimes.' The crowd whoops and cheers ecstatically for the unrepentant brat with the blonde hair and the angelic face. At this point, she's twenty-five, and the trouble she's been in so far includes being sentenced to thirty-six months' probation for reckless driving the previous September,[4] and – most notoriously of all – appearing in a sex tape. She looks radiant. 'This is so much fun. So, thank you to VH1 and all my fans!'[5]

When Paris first became famous back in the late nineties, it wasn't immediately obvious that she was going to revolution-ise celebrity. She seemed, instead, like a novel twist on an old model: the debutante. As the heirs to the Hilton Hotels for-tune, Paris and her younger sister, Nicky – at least initially, the two always seemed to appear as a double act – were following an American tradition with their assault on the society pages. 'New York has always had "It" girls, from Brenda Frazier and Cornelia Guest to Baby Jane Holzer and Edie Sedgwick,' noted the *New Yorker* in a short 1999 profile of Paris and Nicky. 'Now it has mini-"It" girls. At sixteen and eighteen, Nicky and Paris Hilton are the littlest socialites in town. Thin, blond, and wellborn – their great-grandfather was Conrad Hilton – they moved from LA with their parents three years ago, and are now out and about with the city's most entitled teens.' But, the article added, there was also something intriguingly new about these next-generation Hiltons, and something explicitly tied to burgeoning technology: 'Carrying twin candy-colored cell phones instead of tennis racquets, they're the Venus and Serena Williams of competitive socializing – made for the paparazzi and each other, too.'[6]

At the end of the twentieth century, mobile phones were still seen as more of a novelty than a necessity. (Even in 2003, when *The Simple Life* began, Paris's phone was portrayed as part of the 'life of luxury' she had to surrender along with her credit cards: with reluctance exaggerated for comic effect, she was filmed dropping it onto a silver platter held by a butler before she left the family mansion for a taste of 'real life' in

rural America.) In 1999, the only people permanently attached
to their handsets were either always-on professionals or those
with deep status anxiety, and Paris gave the appearance of
being both. She partied like she did it for a living, and though
there were other young women (including her sister) who
seemed similarly eager to court attention, Paris could always
beat out her rivals because she was always willing to be the
most shocking. By 2000, it was obvious that Paris was the
senior Hilton in terms of celebrity as well as age, as the *New
York Post* demonstrated in an article about 'hot young heiresses partying up a storm':

> They're young and sinfully gorgeous with multimillion-
> dollar trust funds, and their families are household names.
>
> But their penchant for nightcrawling – some of them in
> micro-minis, fishnet tops and four-inch stiletto heels – is
> upsetting their blueblooded elders who think they're pick-
> ing up a trashy reputation.
>
> Meet the daring heiresses of New York's social scene.
>
> The most outrageous is hotel-darling Paris Hilton, 19,
> a part-time model with a tendency to flash her thong. Hot
> on her Prada heels is sister Nicky, 16 – a high schooler who
> looks 25 – who's been seen at clubs drinking champagne
> and smoking cigarettes.[7]

Paris first, then Nicky: the double act was disintegrating.
But everybody came after Paris. She was the stereotype of the
celebutante: young, apparently dumb, gorgeous, and useless.
That supposed 'hot heiress' uniform – the micro-mini, fish-
net top and four-inch stilettos – was actually Paris's. She had
worn it in a portrait for that September's *Vanity Fair* taken by
David LaChapelle (the same photographer who, a year earlier,
had solidified Britney's Louisiana Lolita iconography with the
Rolling Stone bedroom shoot). In the image in question, Paris is

standing in her grandmother's opulently tasteful living room, flipping the bird at the camera, nipples on show and labia barely concealed by a scant band of magenta fabric. Above her head, in large letters, there's a quote from the accompanying interview with Nancy Jo Sales: 'People think I'm just this party girl. Well, I'm not like that.' Over the page, you could see her sprawled on a beach with one breast exposed, golden hair spilling across the sand and twenty-dollar bills scattered carelessly around her, soaking up seawater. And, again, the pull quote to make you hate her: 'Just tell 'em I'm a teenager … Tell 'em I'm a normal kid.' In the interview, this could be taken as either a self-aware joke or a bid for sympathy, but set against the picture, it was just invigoratingly obnoxious. Money and sex, sex and money, a provocation in the shape of an oblivious white girl.[8]

Could she really be as clueless as all that? Well, no. On the one hand, Paris genuinely wanted people to understand that there was more to her than going out and getting upskirted. In the *Vanity Fair* profile, she talked about a movie she'd made, some music she was working on, a fundraiser she had organised for breast cancer research. But she also said something that pointed to her singular insight into fame in the noughties – the reason that Paris would not only leave her socialite peers in the dirt in terms of profile, but also outrun whatever shame would subsequently be heaped on her. She knew, instinctively and profoundly, that the public didn't just want glamour from their celebrities. They wanted to see them brought low, too. While Sales was eating dinner with the family, the conversation turned to the rapper Puff Daddy (real name Sean Combs), recently in court on charges of gun violations, assault and bribery. (In 2001, Combs was found not guilty on all counts.[9]) 'Well, just because you're a celebrity doesn't mean you shouldn't get in trouble if you do something,' Paris said. Her family received this statement sceptically:

'Oh, yeah, celebrities think that all the time,' said Kathy, her mother. 'There are some people, I guess,' Paris continued, 'who feel they can get away with anything ...' Here, Nicky broke in contemptuously to say, 'This is just so ironic.'[10]

Just because you're a celebrity, it doesn't mean you shouldn't get in trouble if you do something. Nicky and Kathy seemed to think the joke was on Paris: the girl who never faced the consequences of her own actions. But as Paris continued her assault on fame, her success would come specifically from her understanding that people wanted to see her punished – for her privilege, for her beauty, for being Paris Hilton, for wanting to be seen. And though no one in the Hilton family knew it as they invited *Vanity Fair* into their home, Paris was only months away from doing the something for which she'd pay the highest price and draw the most attention. In May 2001, she (aged twenty) would have sex with her then boyfriend Rick Salomon (aged thirty-two). They would film themselves, using a murky night vision camera for some of it. And this would come to be the ruin, and the making, of Paris Hilton.

If Britney's crime had been to be white trash, Paris's was to be an unapologetic rich bitch. With her fake blue eyes and her fake blonde hair, she crafted herself into the perfect whipping girl, and in January 2003, it paid off when she landed her own reality show with Fox.

From its conception, *The Simple Life* was always intended to be punitive. Fellow LA scenester Nicole Richie, daughter of soul singer Lionel, was cast in the role of Paris's sidekick after Nicky passed on the gig,[11] and the two were transplanted to the Ozarks to live on a farm with the Leding family, where they were required to pitch in with 'regular' chores and take paying jobs. The point was not to see the two girls thrive as they took on the challenges of blue-collar life. It was to see them get dirty and fail. As Fox's then senior VP of casting, Sharon Klein, told the magazine *Television Week*, the fundamental concept was 'stilettos in cow shit'.[12] And the girls understood the game. In the opening of the first episode, broadcast in December 2003, an interviewer stops them on the red carpet and asks what their friends think about the show. 'They say we're not gonna make it, we are gonna love to see you guys suffer,' say Paris and Nicole together, laughing. By episode two, the show had delivered on the cow shit promise, after a stint on a dairy farm left them spattered with filth. They tried being petrol pump attendants, but got distracted flirting with the male customers. They went to the grocery store and couldn't keep to a shopping list, never mind a fifty-dollar budget. At their first dinner with the Ledings, the girls poked disconsolately at a meal made from chickens that, just a few hours earlier, had been scratching in the yard, and made oblivious small talk. 'Do you guys, like, hang out at Walmart?' Nicole asks, to the bafflement of the Ledings. Then Paris goes one better: 'What is Walmart? Is it like, where they sell wall stuff?'

It was a put-on, of course. 'I was in on the joke,' said Paris at a 2020 junket for the documentary *This Is Paris*. 'Sometimes it is annoying, people assuming I am the blonde airhead that I played on the show, but I like proving people wrong.'[13] In the noughties, however, the audience was happy just to have its preconceptions about Paris confirmed. Josh Wolk in *Entertainment Weekly* called it 'delightfully grounding'. But that pleasure at seeing Paris reduced to the mortal level shaded readily into darker fantasies of violence: 'You could swing a two-by-four at the back of her head, and the impact wouldn't cause her to change her expression one bit,' continued Wolk, 'although Cristal might start leaking out her ears.' Still, as Wolk acknowledged, if you wanted to see truly bad things happen to Paris Hilton, all you had to do was go online. 'Though Fox is trying not to overtly promote the show by mentioning Paris's sex video, I have to say that Paris's taped romp does add an extra layer of enjoyment to watching the show.'[14]

Because as much as *The Simple Life* represented a triumph for Paris, announcing her as a bona fide professional of the entertainment industry, it also appeared to precipitate her greatest humiliation. With legitimate success in the offing, someone decided it was the right time to try to ruin her.

The rumours had started soon after she signed the deal with Fox: *Did you know there's a Paris Hilton sex tape?* By the summer, the tape was being openly speculated about in the gossip pages, despite Paris's denials.[15] And just weeks before *The Simple Life* debuted, rumour became confirmed fact. On 12 November 2003, *New York Magazine*'s blog gleefully reported that the tape had been watched in the office. As one staffer was recorded saying, for pop culture hounds, this was 'like the newsroom of *Time* on election night!' Everyone stopped to crowd around a monitor and see Paris get screwed.[16] There was no acknowledgement here that it might be inappropriate to watch porn in the office, nor any curiosity regarding Paris's feelings about being exposed in this way. The spread was unstoppable. 'Thanks to videotape and Internet file-sharing, many Americans are now intimately familiar with the energetic love life of Paris Hilton,' said CNN's website two weeks later.[17]

From the beginning, there was very little sense that the tape was an erotic experience: 'They don't look like they're having much fun' was one verdict from the *New York Magazine* staff. At one point in the filming – the video was shot mostly in green-tinged night vision – Paris even breaks off the intercourse to answer her phone. 'It is so boring!' complained Amy Winehouse when the Paris tape came up during a 2006 appearance on panel show *Never Mind the Buzzcocks*. 'You know when you're on a ferry and you're like just being rocked, thinking, "I'll be there soon. I can see the Isle of Wight." She was just like that … It's not sexy.'[18] People weren't, for the most part, watching Paris have sex because they wanted to be turned on. They were watching because having seen the tape made you one of the information elite, set apart from the great mass of the uninformed. It demonstrated a kind of perverse moral superiority, too: to be unshocked by a celebrity sex tape showed you were above the petty puritanism of the mainstream. It was also (and this did have a libidinous charge for some viewers) an assertion of our power over Paris. All that money, all that status, and she still couldn't stop you from seeing her naked.

What kind of woman ended up in a sex tape? As far as the noughties were concerned, it could only happen if she either wanted it or deserved it. Either way, the fact of being exposed in this way marked her as undeserving of sympathy. The bible of sexual culture at the turn of the century was *Sex and the City*, the HBO comedy about four female friends in New York, which ran from 1998 to 2004. *SATC* introduced a horny world to Rabbit vibrators, straight anal sex and the aspirational ideal of a 'fuck-and-forget culture', where women did it just as unfeelingly as men had always somehow seemed able to. It also covered the etiquette of sex tapes, which had been thrust into the public consciousness with the appearance of the Pamela Anderson and Tommy Lee tape in 1996 – the first celebrity sex tape to be widely shared online, after it was stolen from the couple's home by a disgruntled electrician following a dispute over a bill.

In 'Models and Mortals', from *SATC*'s first season, Carrie (played by Sarah Jessica Parker) discovers that a male acquaintance who's obsessed with dating models is secretly taping himself having sex with them. Carrie's reaction to this is fascinating and (retrospectively) shocking: she doesn't care. Rather than remonstrate with him about the invasion of privacy, she lights up a cigarette and settles in to watch the show – although she does at least have the decency to warn her friend Samantha (Kim Cattrall) when Samantha later hooks up with the amateur film-maker. But, again, Samantha is more intrigued than outraged: 'What a pervert,' she purrs. The twist comes when Samantha is in bed with him and is insulted to discover that he isn't filming her after all. She insists that he hit Record, thereby proving that she's as hot as any model – and the two of them have a wonderful time.

The models didn't consent to be in the sex tapes, but as far as *Sex and the City* is concerned, they deserve it. Carrie and her friends – the 'mortals' of the episode title – complain about the unfairness of men only wanting to date models, while the models are presented as airheaded and callow: being taped having sex without their knowledge or consent is implied to be a fair penalty for the models' excessive beauty and numbing stupidity. Samantha wants to be on the tape, and so, by extension, she could not claim intrusion if it were later shared: whatever she gets, she would also deserve. This is, of course, a double bind. No matter what a woman's attitude is to being recorded or having the recording shared, the fact of being taped while performing a sexual act defines her as some-one with no right to set her own boundaries. Only a slut would be in this situation, and sluts don't get to say no.

This was an issue that Pamela Anderson had run into directly in 1996, when she and her then husband, Tommy Lee, had attempted to legally suppress the stolen tape of them having sex: when they pre-emptively sued *Penthouse* magazine in an effort to forestall the publication of stills from the video, *Penthouse*'s lawyers argued that the fact that Anderson had previously posed nude (for *Penthouse*'s rival *Playboy*) and that the couple had discussed their sex life in interviews meant they had forfeited any claim to privacy. This wasn't the clinch-ing argument for *Penthouse* – ultimately, the judge refused the injunction because it would have been unusual to issue a pre-emptive ban on publication – but nor was it dismissed out of hand by the court.[19] The fact that the tape had been dis-honestly obtained was irrelevant to the narrow legal issues at play and even less interesting to the wider public, which was largely inclined to assume the fame-thirsty couple had leaked the tape themselves. The term *revenge porn* – and the theft of the videotape was, categorically, an act of revenge – wouldn't be coined until 2007, over a decade too late to be of any use in explaining the injury done to Anderson and, to a lesser extent, her husband.[20]

But while they weren't responsible for releasing the tape, Anderson and Lee did inadvertently promote it. Before their legal action, the existence of the tape was only tenuously newsworthy, and reputable outlets had ignored it. The exist-ence of a lawsuit regarding the tape, however, was definitely a story, and blanket coverage ensued. Again, the concept that explained this wouldn't be invented for many years – not until 2005, on the blog TechDirt: 'How long is it going to take before lawyers realize that the simple act of trying to repress something they don't like online is likely to make it so that something that most people would never, ever see ... is now seen by many more people?' asked writer Mike Masnick. 'Let's call it the Streisand Effect.'[21]

Why Streisand? Because, in 2003, the singer and actress Barbra Streisand sued photographer Kenneth Adelman, who was documenting the erosion of the California coastline: she argued that by including an aerial shot of her Malibu home on his website, Adelman had violated the state's privacy law. Streisand lost the case and was ordered to pay costs, but even more crushingly, the lawsuit brought far more attention to the photograph than it would ever have gained otherwise. Before Streisand went to court, the image of her estate had been downloaded six times (twice by her own lawyers); in the month after she brought the action, the site received 420,000 visitors.[22] The story functioned as a parable of power on the internet. Streisand had belonged to the untouchable pantheon of true stars, but her wealth and status counted for little now that anyone with a modem could effectively act as a publisher. Privacy concerns around new technology, where they were acknowledged at all, were given short shrift.

In another post, about an Australian case where a man had been fined and had his phone destroyed after taking stealth pictures of women sunbathing topless, TechDirt grouched, 'If the woman were just lying topless on the beach, a public place, where any expectation of privacy doesn't exist, it's hard to see how this is a problem ... Because this woman decides to take her shirt off, it's suddenly a violation?'[23] There was no consideration at all here for the way in which technology had altered the relationship between public and private: nudity on a beach is very different to nudity surreptitiously photographed and then potentially uploaded to be viewed by others. Nor was there any reference to the feelings of the women, who would plausibly have experienced this as an intrusion regardless of its legality. The women had consented to be seen nude by other beachgoers, but not to be photographed nude.

The coastal photography project that had offended Streisand was a poor target for her lawyers. Adelman's environmental activism was obviously sympathetic, and it was entirely predictable that suing him would increase interest rather than protect Streisand's privacy – the example of the Anderson-Lee action against *Penthouse* already stood as a warning. Even if the legal case had been watertight, the strategy was terrible. But the backlash to Streisand contained an unmistakable note of glee which is hard to separate from the fact that she was a famous *woman* trying to defend a boundary. A blog post published on MSNBC was typical of the tone: 'Every time I start to believe that celebrities really are more talented, beautiful, and smarter than the rest of us,' wrote Mike Rogers, 'one of them comes along and does something downright stupid, making it clear that while they may have more talent and good looks than the average person, they're just as dumb as anyone else.'[24] The online magazine *CounterPunch* sniped, 'It is probably beside the point to suggest this diva get over herself.'[25] After all, the defining quality of the Streisand Effect was that no one had cared about looking at her house until she made it obvious she didn't want them to. The attraction was all in defying her 'no'.

So, in 2003, Paris's options for containing the sex tape were limited. The privacy angle had proved legally ineffectual for Anderson and Lee and was unlikely to be much more useful to her. And any legal action she did bring ran the risk, per Streisand, of further inflaming interest. At least initially, her strategy was simply to deny that any such a tape existed, as *New York Magazine*'s blog reported in August 2003 – in a post with one fascinating aside:

Hilton insists there's no video – at least that she knows of. '[Salomon is] a complete liar and scumbag,' she said last week in Ibiza, where she was vacationing with – of all people – *Girls Gone Wild* producer Joe Francis. '[Rick] is a very sick man. People love to talk shit because they're jealous. I don't care. Whatever.'[26]

Joe Francis, of all people. As Paris was undergoing a grotesque invasion of privacy, her holiday companion was the man who had done more than perhaps any other individual to eroticise and normalise this kind of intrusion. Paris was about to become the ultimate Girl Gone Wild.

Girls Gone Wild was the epitome of mainstream sexual entertainment in the noughties. The concept was brilliantly simple. Francis sent film crews to Mardi Gras, college campuses and spring break destinations – anywhere that attracted

young people looking for no-consequence fun – in search
of girls who could be coaxed into flashing their breasts for
the camera. It was also based on a deeply twentieth-century
business model. The footage was edited into DVDs, and the
DVDs were advertised via late-night infomercials. When
customers called the number to make an order, they weren't
just sold the latest *GGW* compilation; they were enrolled on
a subscription scheme, which meant they'd keep being sent
(and being charged for) *GGW* titles indefinitely, unless they
called the number to cancel, which was unlikely, given that
the company kept that number deliberately obscure.[27] It was
all very shady from a consumer perspective, but as *GGW*
production coordinator Ryan Simkin put it in his memoir of
working with Francis, 'that's why Joe has two jets and a fifteen-
bedroom resort in Mexico; that's why you have twenty DVDs
somewhere in your apartment, hidden from your girlfriend'.[28]

So, even at the peak of *Girls Gone Wild*'s success in the
early noughties, it was on borrowed time. Its revenue was tied
to inconvenience, and once online porn became prevalent, it
was more convenient (and cheaper) for its audience to use the
internet than to order a DVD in the first place. That, though,
was all in the background. The headline story of *GGW* was
that this was a cultural phenomenon riding the wave of post-
feminist liberation in the same way that Hugh Hefner had
surfed the sexual revolution with *Playboy*. Like *Playboy*, *GGW*
was delivering not just titillation but a lifestyle brand, some
aspiration to go with your erection. There were, of course,
some differences. In the fifties, the *Playboy* reader had been
conceived as a man of taste and culture, who was (at least in
theory) as interested in the short stories and reportage the
magazine published as he was in nude women. For the man
who bought into *GGW*, the dream was of a perennial party
life. But, crucially, both *Playboy* and *GGW* came with a veneer
of woman friendliness that redeemed them from pure sleaze.

Playboy called its Bunnies 'the most envied girls in America', with access to a 'glamorous and exciting world'.[29] *GGW* rested on a myth of celebrating women's sexual liberation. As one young woman told a *New York Times* journalist in 2004, shortly after lifting her top for a *GGW* camera, 'It's a very freeing feeling,' although she added that she was 'pretty drunk'.[30]

The problem for feminist critics of *GGW* was that the women were choosing to take part. They even signed legal documents before filming, to say they consented. They might have been tipsy, but they weren't being threatened or coerced. They weren't even doing it for the money: while Francis was raking in money from his franchise, the girls got no more than a branded T-shirt or trucker hat in exchange for stripping off. (For girls willing to go a bit further – particularly hot ones who could be induced to masturbate on camera or take part in some girl-on-girl action – the *GGW* crew was authorised to pay up to $150, and even this exceptional rate was strikingly low compared to the porn industry proper.)[31] Getting wild was, at least in the moment, a matter of pride. 'To most of the girls I've met,' wrote Ariel Levy in a 2004 report from a *GGW* shoot, 'bawdy and liberated are synonymous.'[32]

By the turn of the century, feminist opposition to pornography had become a relic, associated with censorship, puritanism and futility. Andrea Dworkin had been the pre-eminent thinker and activist of the anti-pornography movement: with the lawyer Catharine MacKinnon, she had drafted the Antipornography Civil Rights Ordinance in 1983, which addressed pornography as a threat to women's civil rights rather than using the legal framework of obscenity laws on which anti-pornography efforts had previously relied. Ingenious as this approach was, it was still incompatible with the US Constitution's protection of free speech, and attempts to turn it into law foundered during the nineties. To her ideological opponents, Dworkin had been a bogeyman, but when she died in 2005, obituaries cast her as a pitiable figure – too defeated even to be any kind of threat, a Queen Canute futilely opposing a tide of harmless smut. The website Salon memorialised her in distinctly patronising terms: 'The very opposite of self-reflective, she never reconsidered her position on porn, so she surely never wondered what all the time and energy feminists spent on the "Sex Wars" of the eighties might have accomplished if it had been redirected toward helping abused women gain the financial and emotional wherewithal to reclaim their lives.'[33] To Dworkin's ideological enemies, her crusade against pornography seemed so misguided that, in the end, the nicest thing they could say about her was that at least she'd failed in her life's work.

For women who grew up after the sex wars had apparently been settled, the question wasn't whether you were 'pro'- or 'anti'-pornography. Pornography existed whether you liked it or not, and to deplore it would mark you as shrewish and sexless. All that was left to decide was whether you preferred to silently tolerate it or would rather join in the fun with the boys. *GGW* and other 'real hot girl' ventures like the 'High Street Honeys' section in *FHM* magazine offered women the chance to become enthusiastic collaborators in their own commodification – although, inevitably, some women would change their minds about going wild on camera after the fact, when they belatedly realised that they would be seen not only by strangers, but also by classmates, friends and even family members. (Some would prove to have been legally incapable of consenting to appear in the first place: in 2008, Joe Francis pleaded no contest to charges of filming two underage girls in Florida in 2003. The fact that many of the women were visibly intoxicated should also have been a red flag as to the validity of their signed releases.)[34]

The official *GGW* policy was to help the regretful by iden-tifying and deleting their segments, but Simkin alleged that this wasn't always upheld in practice: 'If the girl was hot, and the footage was good, then Joe was known to say "Fuck her. Leave it in."'[35] For women, the appeal of *GGW* was the illusion of controlling their own sexualisation; but for men, the appeal was that they were getting to see something that would otherwise be hidden. What the *GGW* DVDs offered was a permanent record of something that would otherwise have been memory-holed under the rule of 'What happens on spring break, stays on spring break', and cameramen sought girl-next-door types because they knew the men in the audience were literally hoping they might see the girl next door.

'Basically, we wanted the kind of girl that seemed realistically attainable to whoever was watching the videos,' explained Simkin. 'A guy sitting in his dorm room watching a *GGW* DVD needs to be thinking that the girl in the video looks a heck of a lot like the girl who sits next to him in history class. That in turn should lead him to fantasize about the girl in history class showing him her tits and to believe that scenario is a real possibility. That is what Joe wanted, and that is what his consumers wanted.'[36] Self-described sex-positive feminist writer and *GGW* fan Greta Christina summarised the erotic promise of the tapes as 'humiliation': 'Not faked, not acted, not a fantasy. When the girls in Girls Gone Wild stepped over that line, it seemed like you'd be getting to watch, real-time, while they shamed themselves: like you'd be watching them let go of their dignity, place themselves in a position of public debasement, offer their bodies up for the crude enjoyment of a leering public eye.'[37]

GGW would go from cultural juggernaut to business basket case before the end of the noughties for several reasons, including Francis's legal troubles, a consumer crackdown on the dubious subscription model, and an increased unwillingness of men to pay for porn when so much was available online for free. It also became harder to find the kind of girls who were right for the brand – not because women were growing cagey about self-exposure but because, according to Simkin, they'd become too wild altogether. Paris's influence was part of this change, according to a *GGW* cameraman quoted in Simkin's book. 'I think Paris Hilton changed everything for these girls; I honestly think her sex tape had a huge impact ... It was like she gave these girls a "pass" or a reason to go wild.'[38] Women in America had lost their 'innocence', wrote Simkin. When the girls came pre-debased, the turn-on was gone.[39] But there was more to it than that. If the specific appeal of *GGW* was that you might see the tits of the girl in your history class, why would you bother phoning up to buy a DVD when there was a non-zero possibility that the tits you wanted to look at were already online somewhere? For men whose sexual taste bent towards seeing real girls doing things they might well regret, *GGW* had been a mere appetiser. By the mid-noughties, revenge porn had arrived as a genre in its own right.

One typical example was the site exgfpics.com, founded in 2005. Its self-explanatory tagline was 'Submitted Photos of Nude Ex Girlfriends & Former Wives', and it was utterly transparent about the subjects' lack of consent. The men sending the pictures were sometimes animated by resentment – they told stories of being cheated on, or complained that their ex had cost them too much money, or were just angry that they'd been dumped. Sometimes, they sent the pictures purely because they could: one set purported to show the sender's roommate's girlfriend sleeping naked. 'Imagine her surprise if her [*sic*] or someone she knows runs across these pics posted online,' gloated the site's creator in the caption.[40] And if your picture was published on this or one of the many similar sites offering a cocktail of voyeurism and vengeance, there was very little you could do.[41] Although many countries had 'malicious communications' laws to punish harassment, these were framed to criminalise direct contact between the perpetrator and the target, not the release of images to third-party sites. Copyright was held by the person who took the photo, not the person in it – meaning that if your boyfriend filmed you, the footage was his to dispose of. If the images in question were selfies, intellectual property would be on the woman's side at least, but bringing an action was slow and costly, and in any case, unlikely to stop the pictures from being circulated. As *The Economist* reported in 2014, there was little legal recourse for those who became the subjects of revenge porn:

> If images were stolen or obtained by subterfuge, a victim may have some redress. In February a jury in Texas awarded $500,000 to a woman whose ex-boyfriend posted a por-nographic video he recorded during a Skype call. But few victims bring such cases. Costs can reach $100,000 and legal proceedings will draw unwanted attention to the images. And most countries absolve websites that host user-generated material of legal responsibility for it. (Child pornography is usually an exception.) After 'basically begging' a site to remove images of herself, Bekah Wells, a Florida student, found her written appeal and photos fea-tured on its home-page.[42]

That is to say, a full decade after the Paris tape, the law still offered no protection to women whose private images had been publicly exposed – and the Streisand Effect ensured they would be punished for trying to defend their bounda-ries. What could you do in these circumstances? The only advice was not to take the pictures (or allow them to be taken) in the first place, which was out of victims' hands in many instances. As privacy blogger Kashmir Hill wrote at *Forbes* in 2009, 'If you're more Not-So Privately Progressive than me and you're cool with nude photos spreading on the Internet like [viral YouTube video] David after Dentist, then by all means, break out the camera in the bedroom. If not, it may be best to commit those nude images to memory rather than a memory stick.'⁴³ This was at least pragmatic (assuming you hadn't, for example, been creepshotted while sleeping), but there was no mention of the men who were responsible for the breach of trust. All moral agency was dumped onto the victim. What kind of woman ended up in a sex tape? By the end of the noughties, the answer was the same as at the beginning: one who either wanted it or deserved it.

To a lot of onlookers, it seemed obvious that Paris must have been the one behind the leak of her sex tape, particularly given its proximity to the launch of *The Simple Life*. In December 2003, the *Guardian* wrote that 'suspicions are growing that the entire episode might have been one giant and well-timed publicity stunt designed to further the career of America's newest celebrity obsession'.⁴⁴ Another Paris video truther was Perez Hilton: 'Paris got millions of dollars, a ratings boost for her show's debut, and the covers of magazines ... To this day, it's probably the best-marketed, best-selling, best-publicized sex tape in history.'⁴⁵ Actually, in February 2004, Paris sued Kahatani Ltd – an internet firm that had distributed the footage – for violation of privacy, illegal business practices and the infliction of emotional distress. According to a report from the news agency Reuters, Paris's filing stated that she had 'intended the videotape only for personal use and never intended or consented that it be shown to anyone else or distributed to the public'.⁴⁶

According to court documents, she had already successfully convinced another potential vendor of the tape to pull out. Pornography company Marvad had signed a $50,000 deal with a man named Don Thrasher, who claimed to be acting on Salomon's behalf and with Paris's blessing. In September 2003, Salomon sued Marvad and Thrasher for copyright infringement and invasion of privacy; Marvad countersued

Thrasher for damages, arguing (among other things) that he had falsely represented Salomon as the sole copyright holder when portions of the video had in fact been filmed by Paris: 'After learning from Paris Hilton that the rights Thrasher purported to grant were invalid, Marvad agreed with Ms. Hilton that it would not distribute or release the Video.'[47] The copyright strategy, while successful for Paris here, contradicted statements from her and her family claiming variously that there was no tape, or that if a tape existed, Paris must have been taken advantage of: in January 2004, Salomon brought a claim of slander against Paris and her parents, accusing them of 'orchestrating a malicious and outrageous campaign aimed at portraying Rick Salomon as a criminal'.[48] For the public at large, positioning Paris as an active participant in the video's production only served to make her seem even less innocent and, so, even less deserving of sympathy. 'She's already a socialite, hotel heiress, reality-show actress and gossip-page favorite. But soon Paris Hilton may have another job title on her resume: X-rated video director,' wrote *People*.[49]

But by mid-2004 all these various suits had been dismissed, and in July it was reported that Paris had reached a deal with distributor Red Light District Video, which was now working directly with Salomon: for a share of profits and a reported $400,000, Red Light District could go ahead with the commercial release of the tape, under the title *1 Night in Paris*.[50] (In an incongruous moment of compulsory respect, the video begins with a screen of the American flag and the words 'IN MEMORY OF 9/11/01 … WE WILL NEVER FORGET'. Although, one hopes that viewers were not actively remembering a terrorist atrocity when they started to masturbate.) Paris has repeatedly stated since that she received no money from the tape, and in the 2020 documentary *This Is Paris*, she says that she felt pressured into the filming by Salomon; the public release, she says, had been like being 'electronically raped'.

But at the time, the legal framework, as well as the mores of the noughties, had left little space for her to articulate her victimhood. Instead, she did what she had always done: she embraced shamelessness, as she described in her 2004 book, *Confessions of an Heiress*. Pitched as a kind of how-to guide for readers who wanted to live the heiress lifestyle, it included this advice for anyone dealing with difficult press coverage:

> If the media plays with you, well, play with them. I went on *Saturday Night Live* soon after my name was in the headlines every day for something I wasn't too proud of, and which had really upset my family. On 'Weekend Update' with Jimmy Fallon, the script had him asking me, 'Is it hard to get a room in the Paris Hilton? Is it roomy?' and he wanted to cut it. But I wouldn't let him. No way. That was the funniest line. And I got the upper hand with the media the moment he said it on national TV. That's when it all clicked and things started to change. People knew I could laugh at myself, and that one bad incident was not going to make me lock myself in my room.[51]

In other words, as soon as Paris realised that she could not deny the tape's existence or halt its distribution, she took the pragmatist's path and leaned into the narrative around it, assiduously folding it into her airhead celebutante persona. It even helped her to get – finally – a lead role in a movie. In the 2005 slasher film *House of Wax*, she plays a slutty blonde called Paige who is marked for a sticky end from the moment we see her enthusiastically making out with her boyfriend. When that end comes about two-thirds of the way through the movie, it's a blatant riff on the sex tape: the bad guy spears her through the forehead with an iron bar, then records her dying moments with a video camera. To drive home the fact that this was really about seeing bad things happen to Paris, the film was promoted with the slogan 'See Paris Die!' Paris posed next to signs announcing her own execution, doing that dazzling smile.[52] On the soundtrack, the score to Paige's death scene is titled 'Paris Gets It'.

An earlier part of the film even re-created the sex tape for cinematic audiences. It's after dark, and Paige and her boyfriend are in one car, while their friends are in another. When the car containing the other characters/murder fodder overtakes them, they can see Paige lying with her head in her boyfriend's lap: the friends whoop for the show, and one of them uses his video camera (the video camera that would later fall into the hands of the villain) to film them, using night vision. Briefly, we see Paris and the actor playing Paige's boyfriend, tinted greenish, engaged in something hard to see but definitely obscene-looking. Paris stares directly down the camera: the shot resembles, deliberately and undeniably, *1 Night in Paris*. The year after *House of Wax* was released, the singer Pink released a song called 'Stupid Girls', which – from an ostensibly feminist perspective – mocked 'porno paparazzi girl[s]' with blonde hair and tiny dogs. The video pastiched the sex tape, with Pink clowning it up in the Paris role. But since Paris had made the same joke at her own expense a year earlier, and in a Hollywood movie, someone else doing it had significantly less power to wound her. On Paris's own 2006 album, *Paris*, she played the stupid girl to perfection, with songs about going to clubs, stealing boyfriends and being hot. 'Everybody's looking at me,' she coos on 'Turn You On'. 'But that's all right, I like attention.'

All the same, you could push a joke too far. On 5 June 2007, Paris attended the MTV Movie Awards. Her legal issues – which she had jokingly referred to as 'a little trouble' a few months before at the VH1 Big in '06 Awards – had escalated. In January that year, she had pleaded guilty to a charge of reckless driving after failing a Breathalyzer test the previous September and been sentenced to three years' probation alongside alcohol education classes and a fine of $1,500 (eminently affordable for an heiress). But, a month later, she was pulled over again – and her punishment for driving with a suspended licence would be much harsher. On 4 May 2007, she was handed a sentence of forty-five days in jail. She was due to go directly from the ceremony to begin her sentence.[53] Paris, who had parlayed her troubles into coverage so deftly up to this point, must have been expecting her attendance to draw attention, but perhaps she imagined she would be treated as a collaborator in the joke. Instead, she was the butt of it.

Later on, stand-up comic Sarah Silverman, who was hosting the event, said that she regretted her joke at Paris's expense 'immediately',[54] but in the video of the performance, Silverman looks confident and commanding as she delivers it. 'Paris Hilton is going to jail,' says Silverman, and the audience cheers in response. The camera cuts to Hilton, smiling tightly and looking uncomfortable – an image broadcast not only to viewers at home, but also displayed on giant screens to everyone in the venue. Silverman presses in on the punchline: 'I heard that to make her feel, like, more comfortable in prison, the guards are gonna paint the bars to look like penises.' Cut back to Paris again, who looks notably displeased, gazing forward with her jaw clenched. 'I just worry that she's gonna break her teeth on those things.' Cut again, this time to the actor Jack Nicholson, sitting back in his chair and laughing as the rest of the audience loses it.[55] Perhaps he was enjoying a moment of 'there but for the grace of God' schadenfreude: despite his reputation for hellraising, he'd never ended up in serious legal trouble. Or, perhaps, like most of the world, he simply enjoyed seeing Paris suffer.

For public purposes, Paris could not be punished enough, and her misery was the finest entertainment she had ever delivered. The *New York Post* ran a report on her imprisonment with the gleeful headline 'Paris Bawls in Jail', alleging that she had received special treatment – including being exempted from the routine cavity search.[56] The same day, TMZ delightedly contradicted that coverage: 'The NY Post reported this morning that Paris was not required to undergo the customary "bend over and cough" search for contraband upon checking in to jail. Not true! TMZ has learned that Paris was forced to endure the "search." Humiliation at its finest!'[57]

There was no angle that Hilton could play here. If she was treated like any convict, the media gloried in her disgrace; if she retained any dignity, the media berated her for receiving 'celebrity justice'. When she was released from prison after four days to serve the rest of her sentence under house arrest, there was outrage at the supposed leniency. 'Thank God the authorities allowed this fragile flower to go home to her 100% Egyptian cotton sheets. Justice has been served, the media had a field day and I know Paris has learned an important lesson from this experience, which is "I really am better than everyone else and I do deserve special treatment,"' sneered a blogger at the *LA Times*.[58] After the uproar, the judge recalled her to prison, to much public satisfaction.[59] Actually, a more sober analysis by the same paper found that her original four days had been well within the average punishment for her crime. She ended up serving more time than 80 per cent of people with similar convictions.[60]

Not that this intrusion of reality made any difference. After the intense coverage of her imprisonment, there was room for one more surge of anti-Paris sentiment. The MSNBC news anchor Mika Brzezinski was globally celebrated when she refused to read an item about Hilton's release, tearing up her script on air and even trying to set fire to it. Her achievement, the *Guardian* reported, 'was to raise a defiant fist in the face of one of the most powerful forces in the modern world:

celebrity'.[61] (Rewatched today, Brzezinski's reaction looks more like a stunt, and one that her producers seemed happy to encourage.) Even *Us Weekly* – never formerly shy about Hilton content – got in on the act, plugging an issue with the promise that it was '100% Paris free', although media-savvy observers noted that may have been at least partly down to the fact they'd been scooped on the post-prison interview by rival magazine *People*.[62]

Even as the feminist argument caught up with the technological environment, Paris was left behind. In 2008, journalist Tracy Clark-Flory wrote an article for Salon about the new and alarming phenomenon of 'upskirting' and the failure of the justice system to address it: 'In non-legalese: Wear a skirt in public, and you might just get a camera in the crotch,' she wrote, with a justified sense of outrage. Even for Clark-Flory, though, Paris was an imperfect victim. 'Of course, not all subjects are entirely unwilling participants,' she wrote. 'Paris Hilton's and Britney Spears' pantyless crusade in front of paparazzi seemed intentional – if not sober or clearheaded. In some ways, it appeared to be an aggressive acknowledgment of their utter lack of privacy as famous females.'[63]

Paris had many advantages that the average woman in a *GGW* video did not. She was wealthy. She understood the media. She had access to legal resources beyond the means of most. But she was still a woman operating in a deeply sexist world. *GGW* appreciators of a liberal stripe, such as Greta Christina, liked to argue in terms of the female participants' 'agency', writing that 'when we treat the Girls Gone Wild with patronizing pity and contempt, when we stop respecting them and their sexual agency ... it's a small step from there to disrespecting every woman – and every man – who makes unpopular sexual choices'.[64] What was being advanced here was the doctrine often referred to as 'choice feminism', and it was an ideology to which Paris was frequently attached. 'Paris

Hilton: Feminist Icon to Be' was the semi-sarcastic headline on a 2003 *Gawker* post about the sex tape, which predicted that 'the sex tape will be made public on the internet, and Paris will become an ardent pro-sex crusader. She'll take her message to the streets of the world, celebrating young women's sexuality and freedom and the right to proudly wear little teeny outfits.'[65]

But 'choice', as the philosopher Michaela L. Ferguson wrote in her 2010 essay 'Choice Feminism and the Fear of Politics', is a weak substitute for power. By focusing on individual choices, Ferguson argued that choice feminism 'divorces choice from the broader institutional, political, historical, and social contexts in which choices take place. This means that choice feminism obscures how our choices are shaped for us.'[66] In a society that simultaneously judged sexually active women as 'sluts' while fetishising violation, Paris's decisions can be best understood not as expressions of liberation, but as stratagems for negotiating a hostile world. For all her privilege, she did not have the power to set her own terms as a famous woman.

There was some sympathy for Paris, but it came from a very unexpected quarter. In a 2007 column for *Slate*, writer Christopher Hitchens – a man who was rarely, if ever, in danger of being mistaken for a feminist – found himself disgusted by the circus around Paris, and he understood that the invasion into her life was fundamentally sexual. 'Not content with seeing her undressed and variously penetrated, it seems to be assumed that we need to watch her being punished and humiliated as well,' he wrote. 'The supposedly "broad-minded" culture turns out to be as prurient and salacious as the elders in *The Scarlet Letter*. Hilton is legally an adult but the treatment she is receiving stinks – indeed it reeks – of whatever horrible, buried, vicarious impulse underlies kiddie porn and child abuse.'[67] Hitchens was almost alone in his compassion for the fallen celebutante, though. 'Just because you're a celebrity doesn't mean you shouldn't get in trouble if you do something,' Paris had said back in 2001, and her role in public life ever since had been to stand for privileged nothingness, precisely so she could be berated for it. In the end, even the mass hunger to see her suffer was only one more thing for which Paris could be blamed.

'Sorry Paris Hilton, We Should Have Had Your Back,' announced a remorseful essay on *Elle* magazine's website in 2020.[68] In the previous thirteen years, Paris had certainly not locked herself in her room. While Nicky had settled into something more like the expected arc for a socialite, marrying a Rothschild in 2015, Paris had applied her gift for self-marketing to a dizzying range of products. Her fragrance line alone has racked up over $2.65 billion in sales.[69] She commands $1 million per show for DJ appearances.[70] Over the 2010s, Business Paris had gradually replaced Screw-Up Paris in the public imagination. She began to be recognised as the 'original influencer', the pioneer who had set the template for twenty-first-century fame. (Although the man who stole her name, Perez Hilton, thinks that title should actually belong to him. In a 2021 interview, he told me, 'Paris Hilton is not the original influencer. She was born an heiress, chose to become a socialite, then decided to work in television. I was the original influencer before that word influencer existed!')[71] In 2021 alone, she launched a Netflix series (*Cooking with Paris*), a reality show following her marriage to venture capitalist Carter Reum (*Paris in Love*), and a podcast (*This Is Paris*).

In 2020 – after the revelations of MeToo – Paris seemed to reason that the world was ready for yet another version of her: Survivor Paris. In the documentary *This Is Paris*, from that year, she not only talks openly about the trauma of the sex tape, but also alleges that she was physically and sexually abused at Provo Canyon School, the youth residential treatment centre to which her parents sent her at sixteen. (In a statement, Provo Canyon said: 'We do not condone or promote any form of abuse.'[72]) The slutty attention-seeker of the noughties was suddenly, obviously no such thing: Paris had been a damaged child acting out. It made sense that someone who felt let down by her family would look to sleazy older men like Salomon and Francis. It made sense that someone who said she had suffered and overcome institutional humiliation at Provo Canyon would intuitively grasp how to deal with the ritual shaming dished out to her by the media.

But this reinvention came with a reminder that, in the most important sense, Paris has always been Paris. At one point in the documentary, the director asks her why she didn't disclose her Provo Canyon experiences until now. 'I wanted to do something,' says Paris, 'but I was like, this is going to hurt my brand.' Implicitly, for her to reveal it at this point, she must have understood that it would now be *good for her brand*. If that suggests that Paris is capable of supreme cynicism, it should also be noted that her judgement was absolutely correct. In the noughties, victimhood won no consideration. The more she hurt, the greater the entertainment. In the fame system of 2020, though, trauma had become an asset: fans today want to see their idols talk about their pain and celebrate their bravery in overcoming terrible experiences. It is certainly an improvement on the noughties' theatre of cruelty, though it's impossible to evade the fact that female suffering continues to be the product. The same public that once revelled in Paris's humiliation now eats up her stories of anguish and survival. And Paris delivers the required content perfectly. She's always known, better than anyone, how to give the people what they want.

3

Lindsay: Apocalypse

'Yeah, motherfucker, I'm fine'

Britney, Paris, Lindsay. Three women who between them represented everything crass, tragic and trashy about women in the noughties – the Upskirt Decade's holy trinity, in the nickname that was given to an iconic photo of them together. It was a rare sighting, because they were not the close unit that their shared reputations suggested they might be. Paris had been out with Britney when Lindsay jumped into a car with them to take refuge from the paparazzi: Paris later remembered that it had been 'kind of awkward', because she was in some drama with Lindsay at the time. But the actual relationship between these three was less significant than the overlapping role they played in the popular imagination as avatars of feminine ruin, and to the public, there was always a sense that Lindsay was a cut above the other two in terms of squandered potential. Britney could sing and dance. Paris had savvy and charisma. But it was Lindsay Lohan who was always acknowledged to be the talented one, the one whose gifts were self-evident enough – at least at first – to repel the 'famous for being famous' sneer.

She was also the youngest of the three when fame came for her, just twelve when the 1998 remake of *The Parent Trap* was released. She'd been modelling since she was three and acting for years by this point, but the film was a significant challenge even with all that experience. She didn't just star in it: she also co-starred, playing twin sisters Hallie and Annie. She pulled it off magnificently. '*The Parent Trap* can't be imagined without its eleven-year-old [her age at the time of production] red-headed star,' said the *LA Times* review typical of the acclaim Lindsay received. 'Her bright spirit and impish smile make for an immensely likable young person we take to our hearts almost at once. Lohan's the soul of this film.'[1] It made her an instant star. 'I was thrown off by the whole fame thing,' she said in an interview in 2003. 'It came all at once.'[2]

Until 2004, she appeared exclusively in Disney movies. For Disney, Lindsay was both safe enough to be entrusted with valuable older properties and exciting enough to breathe new life into the studio's catalogue. Her characters sometimes broke the rules and often edged into brattiness, but she was so lovable that she could get away with being convincingly unlovable when the plot demanded. In TV movie *Life-Size* (2000), she's a girl who accidentally brings a doll (Tyra Banks) to life when she tries to revive her dead mother. In the 2003 do-over of *Freaky Friday*, Lindsay again had to act two personalities in one – the conceit is that her rebellious teen character swaps bodies with her tightly wound mother (Jamie Lee Curtis). The movie was a huge hit and confirmed Lindsay as a talent to watch. In *Confessions of a Teenage Drama Queen* (2004), she plays Lola (real name Mary, but 'I've known since I was five years old that my true name is Lola'), a New York girl who moves out to New Jersey with her mother after her parents' separation and decides to reinvent herself as the main character of her new school.

Confessions of a Teenage Drama Queen is no more than a mildly superior Disney TV movie elevated to cinematic status by Lindsay's burgeoning profile, but two things give it retrospective significance in the formation of her tabloid persona. Firstly, the plot involves Lola staging an intervention for a strung-out rock star, making Lindsay the agent of sobriety. It is not a role she could have been convincing in a few years later. And, secondly, there's an extended dream sequence in which Lola imagines herself as Marilyn Monroe. Lindsay has the blonde hair, the beauty spot and the deep-cut white dress with the full flippy skirt like the one Marilyn wears in *The Seven Year Itch*.

It was a cute, throwaway moment. It was also something like a calling card. Lindsay was seventeen now, old enough to be thinking about her transition to adult roles. Marilyn was an intimation of what could be: an actress who'd had the comedic chops and dramatic subtlety to transcend the limitations of her early career. It was also – though neither Lindsay nor anyone around her was aware of this at the time – the first in a string of occasions on which she would play with the iconography of Marilyn. Over time, the allusions held less sweetness and more irony. Over time, the same demons that had eaten Marilyn – the addictions, the self-loathing, the unreliability – seemed to have eaten Lindsay. Over time, people stopped expecting Lindsay to emulate Marilyn's career. Long before the end of the Upskirt Decade, watching Lindsay had become about waiting for one thing: it couldn't be long, surely, until she made like Marilyn in the ultimate way and self-destructed into the grave. There was something peculiarly morbid in noughties gossip culture. To understand that, you have to understand the place and time from which it emerged: Manhattan and the aftermath of 9/11.

Lindsay's Disney characters didn't have perfect families, but none of them had a family like Lindsay's. She was born and grew up in Long Island, New York – a very different kind of New York to the New York that existed in her films. In 1990, when she was five, her father Michael – then a Wall Street trader – was convicted of contempt of court and sentenced to four years in prison following an investigation into insider trading. (In interviews, he represented this as something almost honourable: his only crime, he said, was 'not talking'.)[3] In 1998, he was jailed again for violating his probation by visiting Lindsay on the set of *The Parent Trap*, and once more in 2000 for breaching an order of protection that his wife Dina had obtained to stop him from seeing their four children.[4] According to Michael, the source of the friction between him and Dina was Lindsay's growing success, and her other family members' efforts to alienate him so they could more securely attach themselves to the 'Lindsay gravy train'. In a 2005 interview, Michael railed against the implication that he was the bad parent when Dina's brother Paul Sullivan had been arrested over a scheme to defraud a 9/11 relief fund to the tune of $1.5 million.[5] (Sullivan pleaded guilty in 2006.)[6] But he also admitted to cocaine use and heavy drinking.[7] Dina's version was that she had acted to protect herself and her children from Michael's 'violent and unpredictable' behaviour. According to a 2005 letter to the press issued by Dina and Lindsay through their lawyer, 'he allegedly once threatened to kill his entire family'.[8] Michael professed confusion about this: 'It's just a shame, honestly, that my wife is putting my kids through this by not letting them be with their father,' he told an interviewer.[9]

The dysfunction between her mother and father forced Lindsay, by her own account, into the role of protector to her three siblings. 'I feel like a second parent in the sense that I helped raise my family,' she told *Allure* magazine in 2007. 'And I was put between my mother and father a lot. Well, I would put myself between them to try and keep the peace, and I felt good doing that.'[10] In 2005, Michael Lohan was back in prison after being convicted of assaulting his brother-in-law Matt Sullivan at a communion party for Lindsay's younger brother the previous year. That jail stint interrupted divorce negotiations between Michael and Dina, which ended up stretching out bitterly into 2007 – the couple was reported to be at odds over, among other things, whether Michael was entitled to $3 million a year from Lindsay's earnings.[11] Michael felt the whole nasty legal situation could have been avoided if only Dina had listened to him. 'At the beginning of the things, I suggested a reality show called *Living with the Lohans: Over or Starting Over?*' he told the *New York Observer*. 'When Dina served me the divorce papers, I said instead of going [to] trial, why don't we work this out in an amicable way – just show everyone we could end it the right way, and/or start over the right way. There would have been cameras on us the whole time. It would have guided us in the right way.'[12]

It was a spectacularly crass suggestion. But while it's unsurprising that Dina would pass on it, she was more than willing to put her family life on show elsewhere. In 2006, she told the *New York Times* that she was touting a reality show about mothers, to be called *CEO of Household*. 'We all have Band-Aids in our closet and Swiffers,' she said. 'We are the CEOs of our households. We go to the pediatrician or the doctor. We are the driver. We are the chauffeur.' In Dina's case, she was also the manager of her four children's careers. (The younger three were all signed to the Ford modelling agency, which also represented Lindsay.) But the former dancer wanted recognition in her own right: 'I have always been in the business, and I had children and put my career aside, and now it's my turn to put it back on the table,' Dina said in an interview at a launch party for her first magazine cover.[13]

CEO of Household would never happen – or rather, when something like *CEO of Household* did appear, it was called *Keeping Up with the Kardashians*, and it was built around the altogether more commanding figure of Kris Jenner. When the Lohan reality project finally materialised in 2008, it was a fly-on-the-wall-style show called *Living Lohan*, slipped into the E! channel's schedule as filler during *Keeping Up*'s off season and widely considered to be a *Kardashians* rip-off. (Lindsay kept her distance, appearing in only one episode and then as a disembodied voice on the phone.)[14] Dina's plan to make herself famous for being a stage mother had been a good one; it was just that she seemed to lack the skills to make her idea a success. There was an undeniable, and unappealing, feeling of desperation about her. Michael and Dina Lohan had an exceptional ability to become the story, and that story was irresistible to a public that thrilled to see Lindsay's appearance of button-nosed innocence degraded. In an era that could not get enough gossip, the Lohans seemed to exist purely to generate it.

As the public excavation of Lindsay's family issues began in 2004, Lindsay was also drawing attention in her own right for being what was euphemistically referred to as a 'party girl'. In the year she turned eighteen, reports of her being out on the town – sometimes in the company of her then friend Paris – were so routine that coverage adopted a weary, exhausted tone. 'Predictablt [*sic*], among the revelers were . . . Paris Hilton and Lindsay Lohan,' said a September 2004 post on *Gawker* about the *Entertainment Weekly* party. (The typo reflects the haste with which copy was thrown together and published.) The following was added in square brackets: 'Ed.note – Has someone invented a magical kind of vodka that caused these two to be cloned over and over again, allowing them to simultaneously attend every single event in Hollywood?'[15] Lindsay was leaving childhood behind. It wasn't just a question of how she had fun. It was also about the way she looked – something that *Saturday Night Live* played on when she guested on the show in May 2004. In one sketch, Lindsay appeared as Emma Watson playing Hermione in the *Harry Potter* films. The joke was that Hermione had got all grown up during the summer break, leaving the male characters incapable of doing anything but leer over her breasts, which were framed by a low V-neck sweater and a shirt unbuttoned to the cleavage. At the end of the sketch, Hermione left in frustration to take a bath; Ron asked Harry whether he still had the invisibility cloak, and the two rushed around the stage with excitement at the prospect of spying on their friend.[16]

The gag poked fun at adolescent male horniness, as well as the sleazy attention that focused on young women growing up in public like Lindsay and Emma Watson. But it also invited exactly the same kind of scrutiny it was parodying: at one point in the sketch, Lindsay held a giant magnifying glass in just the right position to display her chest to the audience. She was seventeen at the time, and it was in questionable taste to put her in school uniform with her bust on show. But in *SNL*'s slight defence, this sketch was hardly the first time Lindsay's body had been held up for public consumption. Speculation about her changing figure was so rampant that in an interview with the *Guardian* the same month, Lindsay was asked directly about rumours that she'd had breast implants. 'It's so retarded,' she said. 'I'm seventeen years old. My mother would never let me. I'd be deathly afraid, and it's unnecessary ...

but I'm glad people think I have a nice chest.'[17] Not even old enough to be legally considered an adult, Lindsay had to find a way to navigate the pornographic attention on her body. At least by making a joke of it, as with the *SNL* sketch, she could claim a modicum of authority over the way she was presented.

Being funny was one of Lindsay's greatest strengths, and so it made sense that her first non-Disney film would be a comedy. *Mean Girls*, which came out in 2004, was a perfect transitional vehicle for her. There was continuity with her previous work: Mark Waters, who had directed *Freaky Friday*, also directed here. And, as in *Freaky Friday* and *Confessions of a Teenage Drama Queen*, Lindsay plays a high school student. For the audience of girls who had aged up with her since *The Parent Trap* and were now high school students themselves, this was comfortable territory. But it was also a step outside the safety of the Disneyverse. The source material for *Mean Girls* was a non-fiction book called *Queen Bees and Wannabes* by Rosalind Wiseman, about the secret lives of teenage girls – lives of byzantine interpersonal politics enforced via emotional cruelty. Wiseman's book caught the attention of self-described former 'mean girl' Tina Fey, who was then a head writer on *SNL*.

Before Fey joined the show in 1999, *SNL* had a bad name for being a frat house, and a failing one. Under her watch, its ratings and critical reputation began to turn around as the show started to take on female-focused material from a female point of view.

Which is not to say that Fey's sensibility lay anywhere close to girl power fluff: there were jokes about waxing, trophy wives and sexual assault, plus liberal use of the words *slut*, *bitch* and *whore*. A *New Yorker* profile of Fey from 2003 (and the fact that she was the subject of a *New Yorker* profile at all demonstrates her cultural significance at this point) tells the story of a male *SNL* staff member asking Fey whether she was 'anti-woman'.

In reply, 'she told him that the show's business was to make fun of people, and if it didn't make fun of women the female performers would have no parts to play'.[18] Female characters deserved to be seen on-screen not because they were moral exemplars, but because they could be just as venal, stupid and degenerate – and, therefore, just as good a source of jokes – as the male ones. Fey's adaptation of *Queen Bees* into the *Mean Girls* script fit in with that philosophy perfectly. Lindsay's character is Cady, a girl who has been homeschooled in Africa by her anthropologist parents and is, therefore, utterly innocent of the 'girl code' when, at the age of sixteen, she returns to the United States and is enrolled at North Shore High School.

Cady makes two friends, gothy Janis and 'too gay to function' Damian. They encourage her to infiltrate the school's core clique of hot girls, known as the Plastics, and bring down the group's tyrannical leader, Regina George. Cady is all too successful in her mission: she goes full Plastic and not only displaces Regina but proves to be no better than her. In revenge, Regina distributes the Plastics' 'Burn Book', a private depository for cruel comments and vicious rumours about other girls, and pins the blame for it on Cady. This was an astute observation of high school machinations, but it wasn't just about high school. It was also about fame. When the Plastics make their first appearance, Damian describes them to Cady like this: 'If North Shore had *Us Weekly*, the Plastics would be on the cover every week.' And Regina George, as the biggest and meanest of North Shore's celebrities, was understood to be in need of the harshest correction: she gets her redemption, but only after she loses all her friends and gets hit by a bus. The Burn Book itself resembles nothing so much as the DIY culture of gossip blogging.

In the early noughties, gossip blogging was only just beginning to take shape: TMZ didn't exist yet, and nor did Perez Hilton. But *Gawker* did. Established by the New York-based

British journalist Nick Denton in 2002, *Gawker* would grow to become a whole family of sites: Fleshbot (founded in 2003) covered porn, Defamer (2004) did celeb gossip, Valleywag (2006) offered tech industry rumours, and Jezebel (2007) had a feminist angle. Denton and his employees 'didn't exactly invent the blog,' wrote Vanessa Grigoriadis in 2007, 'but the tone they used for *Gawker* became the most important stylistic influence on the emerging field of blogging and has turned into the de facto voice of blogs today'.[19] That voice could be summed up in one word: *mean*, although, in the argot of *Gawker, snarky* was more appropriate. The *Gawker* worldview was entirely unserious and wholly without mercy, which meant it could feel very serious indeed for those on the receiving end. Early blogging existed in a thrilling demi-monde – *Gawker*'s very name suggested being on the outside looking in, close enough to observe the world of traditional media, but detached enough to be unimpeded by the social codes (and, sometimes, the laws) that governed the industry.

Denton's sites held everything in contempt, including themselves, as the tagline on Defamer demonstrated: 'LA is the world's cultural capital. Defamer is the gossip rag it deserves.' This went in a sidebar, followed by a list of quotes about the site that could have been either condemnations or endorsements but that, either way, summed up the reasons to read it. 'Fearless . . . blithely malicious,' read one blurb. 'Total. Fucking. Bullshit,' said another. The very last blurb was from the site Radosh.net (last updated in 2010), and it read, 'Blah, blah – ooh, Lohanboobies!'[20] Brave truth-telling. Unmoderated rumour-mongering. A seventeen-year-old girl's tits. That, pretty much, covered the Defamer editorial mission. While *Mean Girls* had launched Lindsay towards adult stardom, her breasts enjoyed a parallel career creating clicks, wealth and employment for the Web 2.0 economy.

As for how Lindsay felt about this attention, the best insight probably came not from mollifying comments like 'I'm glad people think I have a nice chest', but from the lyrics to her debut single, 'Rumors', which was released in late 2004. It's a strikingly raw song, overproduced as it is. Where Britney sounds defiant when she addresses the media on 'Piece of Me' (2007), and Paris's tone is flirtatious in 'Turn You On' (2006), Lindsay is wounded and furious. 'I'm tired of rumors starting / I'm sick of being followed / I'm tired of people lyin', sayin' what they want about me,' she sang. (That her co-writers were Michael Jackson's nephews probably gave them a certain perspective here as well.) Of course, the song didn't convince the media to back off. Instead, there were leaks from the video's set about the status of her latest relationship.[21]

In 2005, Lindsay made her last Disney film, *Herbie: Fully Loaded*, the sixth (and final) film in the *Herbie* series about a Volkswagen Beetle with a mind of its own. It was a long way short of *Freaky Friday*'s heights, and the salivating media interest in Lindsay didn't help. The *Washington Post* headlined its review 'Old Engine in a New Body', wording that implied Lindsay's figure as much as the revamped intellectual property.[22] The *Chicago Tribune*'s review, by Robert K. Elder (who gave *Herbie: Fully Loaded* a damning one and a half stars from a possible four), noted the pressure that online coverage had put on the movie's reception: 'Director Angela Robinson has tersely denied Web-fueled rumors that Lohan received a digital bust-reduction to keep from offending family audiences. That rumor is dubious, but there is a valid point: *Herbie* is an odd role now for Lohan . . . She's matured, and no longer fits in the Disney mold.'[23]

Those rumours, of course, were heavily promoted via the *Gawker* sites. 'A reader reports that Lindsay Lohan's wildly overstuffed racing suit . . . might not be appropriate for a family flick,' panted one post on Defamer, illustrated with a disembodied close-up of Lindsay's cleavage.[24] Gossip also pointed to another problem on the set: Lindsay's partying was allegedly cutting into her professionalism, and there were claims that *Herbie*'s director had gone as far as starting to cast a Lindsay replacement.[25] Lindsay did her best to knock these rumours back. 'I relieve my stress by going out and having fun,' she told *W* magazine. 'Some people may go and take a yoga class, but people don't care about that. I'll be in LA, and if I drive to the gym, they take that picture but they never use it because that doesn't sell. Because people like the drama.'[26] It was a good line but difficult to square with the knowledge that she'd spent five days in hospital with what her publicist referred to as 'exhaustion', and what the gossip world casually assumed was either alcohol-related or cover for surgery to reduce the alleged earlier breast enlargement.[27]

Lindsay did look less voluptuous than she used to, and people were anxious to know why. One Defamer post about her figure ended with a gleeful cry of 'let the obsessive and creepy study of photographic evidence begin!'[28] If not surgery, then another possible explanation for her changing shape was an eating disorder, which again Lindsay shrugged off in the *W* interview. 'People lose weight when they grow up; they lose their baby fat,' she said. 'But, you know, I'm around girls, even in the movies, that are like, "I don't feel good, I just ate a lot, I'm going to go throw up." Like at the *Vanity Fair* shoot of all the young stars, no one ate. I was going straight to the pasta, and the other girls were eating salad. And I'm the one who people say that about.'

It was, again, a good line, but the accompanying photography – Lindsay shot from behind, kneeling and topless, glancing back at the camera, shoulder blades prominent on a slender frame and face startlingly childlike – did not seem to support it.[29] And all these purported issues – from the drinking to the rumoured eating disorder to the speculation about surgery to her parents' publicly disintegrating marriage – were seen as reflections on Lindsay's character rather than struggles she had to deal with. They seemed to show that she had never really belonged in the sweet, safe world of Disney because, underneath it all, she had always been trash. Here was an extremely young woman who had been on show for as much of her life as she could remember, who seemed to be treated as a meal ticket by her parents, and whose puberty had been picked over in the most public fashion. If she was rebelling, perhaps she had good reason to.

Growing up female is difficult even in unexceptional circumstances. For the child star, it can be a catastrophe. In her memoir, *I'm Glad My Mom Died*, former child actor Jennette McCurdy – who achieved fame at fifteen in the sitcom *iCarly*, having started acting when she was eight years old – recalls initially fearing that her breast buds were cancer. When her mother corrected her, she was not reassured: 'The only thing worse than a cancer diagnosis is a growing-up diagnosis.'[30] If being a child is your job, maturity is a loss and one that comes moreover with the perils of sexualisation. Working in children's entertainment offered little protection on that point. Intercourse might be non-existent on-screen, but offscreen was another matter. In 2021, Demi Lovato – another Disney performer, whose big breakthrough came in the 2008 film *Camp Rock* – said she had been raped by a fellow Disney star who 'never got in trouble for it. They never got taken out of the movie they were in.'[31] Both McCurdy and Lovato went on to struggle with bulimia and substance abuse.[32] It would be, if anything, more surprising for a child actor to come out undamaged.

And yet, for those raised to perform, it can seem impossible to imagine taking any other path. 'The transition from child stardom to a legitimate career as an adult in the entertainment industry is a notoriously tough one – even for young actors blessed with roles in credible films with credible directors,' wrote McCurdy. 'But for kids who start out on kids' TV, it's a career death sentence ... The second the child star tries to outgrow and break free from their image, they become bait for the media, highly publicized as rebellious, troubled, and tortured, when all they're trying to do is grow.'[33] Lindsay at eighteen could be read as a painfully conflicted person. She was following the outline of an acting career, but the self-sabotage of the 'exhaustion' suggested she was at least partly tired of being the good girl who did as she was told. She acted as sexy as anyone required, and yet, she seemed to be whittling her body away to fragile nothing. Still, she was trying to grow. After the misstep of *Herbie*, 2006 brought three Lindsay films that were far more strategically astute for a star developing an expanded range as a mature actress. Unfortunately, none of them was very good, and all of them were blighted by the Lindsay gossip machine.

Reese Witherspoon was ten years older than Lindsay and considerably further along in her reinvention from child actor to adult star. In 2005, she appeared in two films: Johnny Cash biopic *Walk the Line* (she played Cash's wife June, and won an Oscar for it), and a fantasy romance called *Just Like Heaven*. Pairing lower-budget, critically credible releases with more populist films had been Witherspoon's long-standing habit, and it had paid off. She'd established herself as a talented actress who could also pull multiplex crowds, and escaped the trap of pigeonholing. Lindsay's 2006 had a similar spread: two lower-budget prestige features, one popcorn-friendly rom-com.

Lindsay's most respectable movie of the year was the Robert Altman-directed *A Prairie Home Companion*. It was sentimental and uneven, and got mixed reviews – much of the praise had an indulgent tone, from critics who knew this was likely to be Altman's last film – but it placed Lindsay in an ensemble cast with supreme talents like Meryl Streep and Lily Tomlin, stamping a seal of approval on her acting. She also made *Bobby*, an Altmanesque take on the hours leading up to Robert F. Kennedy's assassination, directed by Emilio Estevez. Like *A Prairie Home Companion*, the film presented Lindsay alongside a raft of major names, including William H. Macy, Harry Belafonte and Sharon Stone. 'Lindsay's agents were rabid in attaching her to the movie. Rabid. They wanted to give her an extreme career makeover,' said Estevez.[34] The result, though, was lacklustre, and the film never received general release.

Finally, *Just My Luck* was closer to her old Disney films. She starred as a girl about NYC who lives a charmed life working as a publicist, until she crosses paths with a hot loser (played by Chris Pine) and the two exchange luck. The movie feels infantile rather than delightful – 'Like many another former child star, it's time for her to move on to more challenging roles,' said a disappointed Roger Ebert[35] – and it deservedly bombed, leaving the $7.5 million Lindsay was reportedly paid looking like a very bad bet. Lindsay's 'extreme career makeover' was not going to happen.

Lindsay in 2006 was stuck, and her films showed it: no longer young enough to be precocious, but unable to grow up convincingly on-screen, she was caught between mutually contradictory personas. But, taken as a whole, the films also demonstrated the predicament that American popular culture was in. All of them, in different ways, showed how the United States was floundering as it tried to come to terms with 9/11. It had now been five years since the city where *Just My Luck* was set had been the target of a terrorist attack of unprecedented – and, two decades on, unequalled – violence. On 11 September 2001, 2,753 people were killed when a group of Islamist terrorists hijacked two commercial airliners and flew them into the twin towers of the World Trade Center. One of the landmarks of the Manhattan skyline was razed in a single, incomprehensible day: many New Yorkers said that the first they knew of the horror was a rain of papers falling onto the city streets, from the offices that had been ripped open. For the West in general, Americans in particular and New Yorkers most of all, suddenly nothing and nowhere felt safe. The Manhattan air was a charnel house, grotesquely polluted with concrete dust, jet fuel and human remains. (The devastation was not limited to New York City. One hundred and eighty-four of those killed that day were in a plane that was crashed into the Pentagon, and forty of them were killed when a hijacked plane, presumably intended for the US Capitol Building, crashed in a field near Shanksville, Pennsylvania.)

In a still-fragile America, *A Prairie Home Companion* and *Bobby* could both be seen as a retreat by their film-makers into a comforting version of the past. (*Bobby* was Estevez's requiem for the politician he regarded as liberalism's last best hope: 'The killing of Bobby was the death of decency and the death of hope, the death of manners, the death of grace and formality. We unravelled culturally and spiritually after his death,' he told the *Guardian*.[36]) Meanwhile, in *Just My Luck*, it's as though nothing bad has ever or could ever happen in New York. Within the film, the city is a place of possibility and happenstance, in which Pine's character can gatecrash a party and be treated as a delightful addition rather than a security threat. This mass denial was far from unique to bad rom-coms. *Sex and the City* dealt with 9/11 by editing out the twin towers from its credits sequence and never mentioning their fall.[37] It was as though the attacks were simply too large and too disturbing to be acknowledged in entertainment for the most part. And yet, the people who made American entertainment had in many cases been deeply affected, especially because so much of the media was based in New York City. In the 2003 *New Yorker* profile of Tina Fey, the interviewer describes Fey beginning to cry as she talks about 9/11. 'In New York you get to have little moments of fear every day now,' she said. 'Right after September 11th, I thought, we got to get out of here. My dad talked to me about how important it was to go back to work. But it has not been easy.' Fey had, she said, been obsessively imagining hand-to-hand combat with a terrorist.[38]

In the raw months after 9/11, some had hoped that a traumatised nation would rediscover its better nature. In early January 2002, the *Wall Street Journal* published a column by critic Terry Teachout reflecting on the recent success of jazz singer Diana Krall. 'I'm no trend-sniffer, but as a critic who spends much of his time going to performances of all kinds, I've been thinking that it might have a little something to do with Sept. 11 ... unless I miss my guess, beauty is becoming fashionable again,' he wrote. America, Teachout believed, was ready to think once again in terms of good versus bad, artistically as well as morally.[39] In fact, a hardening of judgement did take place, but it was more about politics than aesthetics: in 2003, country-pop band the Dixie Chicks (renamed the Chicks in 2020) were blacklisted by radio stations after lead singer Natalie Maines criticised President George W. Bush onstage at a concert in London.[40] A more accurate guess than Teachout's about the trajectory of post-9/11 culture came from satirical newspaper *The Onion*. Less than a month after the attacks, it published an article headlined 'A Shattered Nation Longs to Care About Stupid Bullshit Again':

Shaken by the tragic events of Sept. 11, people across the nation have abandoned such inconsequential concerns as the Gary Condit scandal and Britney Spears' skimpy outfit at the 2001 MTV Video Music Awards. No longer are they talking about shark attacks or what's-his-name, that Little Leaguer who was too old to play. Instead, they're focusing on the truly important things in life: friends, family, and being good to one another.

'How long can it go on like this? ... Some are wondering if their priorities will ever be in the wrong place again.'[41]

And, in large part, the 'stupid bullshit' returned.* There was a political rationale for this, which was that any shift to seriousness would have amounted to capitulation. Islamism held that films, music and salaciousness were all marks of a degraded culture, meaning there was a kind of justified pride in cleaving to what the attackers most reviled. (And perhaps the 9/11 memorial card at the beginning of *1 Night in Paris* almost makes sense by this logic.) According to Amy Odell's biography of *Vogue* editor Anna Wintour, 'On September 12, 2001, Anna went to work ... She seemed to believe that if Vogue stopped, if fashion stopped, if the world stopped, the terrorists would have won.'[42] By acting as though nothing had happened, *Sex and the City* and *Just My Luck* were simply following Wintour's example. But this also injected a hefty sense of self-importance into a culture industry that had not been short of self-importance in the first place. After 9/11, American media was ripe for a dose of British piss-taking, and there happened to be a Brit in New York City perfectly placed to do it. The nihilistic cruelty of Nick Denton's *Gawker* blogs was the most compelling form of 'stupid bullshit' available to a media-savvy audience.

Someone like Teachout might have imagined that apocalyptic times would drive people towards beauty; a visionary like Denton saw that what an audience really wanted at the end of the world was savagery. *Gawker*, wrote Vanessa Grigoriadis (after she herself had been mocked by the blog for her *New York Times* wedding announcement), was 'about the anxiety and class rage of New York's creative underclass. *Gawker*'s social policing and snipe-trading sideshow has been impossible to

---

* For more on the influence of 9/11 on gossip culture, see Chapter 6: Amy.

resist as a kind of moral drama about who deserves success and who doesn't. It supplies a Manhattan version of social justice.'[43] But a Manhattan version of social justice is not the same as actual justice, and the gossip bloggers' choice of targets feels barely defensible in retrospect. For example: all the while that Lindsay's flameouts were being catalogued and dissected, Harvey Weinstein was pursuing his campaign of sexual assault and harassment within his company Miramax. Weinstein's predations were an open-ish secret in entertainment, to the extent that Tina Fey's sitcom *30 Rock* could make a joke about them in its 2012 season: the vain, promiscuous actress Jenna declares she's so undaunted by Hollywood power players that she 'turned down intercourse with Harvey Weinstein on no less than three occasions. Out of five.'[44]

Yet, for all the self-proclaimed fearlessness of the blogs, it took until 2017 for Weinstein's depravity to be placed on the journalistic record – and when it happened, it was done by the *New York Times* and the *New Yorker*, two pillars of traditional print publishing.[45] Apparently, Defamer's 'blithe malice' only reached so far up the entertainment hierarchy. Still, one of the quirks of Lindsay's story is that she defended Weinstein in 2017, posting a video to Instagram in which she said: 'I feel very bad for Harvey Weinstein right now ... I don't think it's right what's going on.'[46] Perhaps she felt more solidarity with someone she saw as a fellow victim of the media than she did with the women Weinstein had assaulted.

Reports of Lindsay's hard living had continued unabated through 2005, especially from the set of *Just My Luck*, which was filmed in the notoriously boozy city of New Orleans.[47] With camera phones now widely on hand, every night out was liable to be documented by the public, and it was no longer plausible to pin her troubles on 'exhaustion'. Instead, her 2006 publicity campaign started with a confessional interview and a front cover for *Vanity Fair*. In the article, she admitted to using drugs 'a little'; she admitted to bulimia as well. 'I was making myself sick,' she told the journalist. The article emphasised her talent and included testimonials from satisfied directors – Altman said she was 'excellent', although *Herbie* director Angela Robinson declined to be interviewed – but it didn't entirely suggest that Lindsay was turning over a new leaf. Her mother seemed oddly sanguine about Lindsay's health. 'She took it a little too far, maybe, and pulled back quickly and is fine,' Dina said of Lindsay's extreme skinniness. On the partying, Dina's response was a cry of exasperation: 'What did you do when you were a teenager?' Lindsay's last word on the matter was this: 'Yeah, motherfucker, I'm fine.'

And then there were the photos. These were taken by Mario Testino, and showed Lindsay on a beach with tousled blonde hair, wearing a chunky sweater that's almost (not quite) long enough to be a dress. In one, she was crouched down and smiling straight at the camera.[48] It looks unmistakably like one of Marilyn Monroe's last-ever shoots. The beach, the chunky knitwear, the hair, the dazzling expression, even the poses – all suggest a series of pictures taken by George Barris in 1962.[49] There was a compliment in the allusion, of course: it implied that Lindsay was Marilyn's equal as an actress, a sex symbol and an icon. But there was foreboding, too. However beautiful Marilyn had looked that day on the beach, those photos were a memento mori. They were taken when Marilyn had recently been fired from *Something's Got to Give* for her own lateness and absenteeism; a few weeks later, she would be dead from an overdose. Lindsay's story appeared to have been written in advance, and Marilyn was the archetype.

One of the misfortunes suffered by Lindsay's character in *Just My Luck* ends with her being arrested. On 26 May 2007 – just over a year after the film's release and not long after completing a stint in rehab – Lindsay was arrested for real, on suspicion of driving under the influence and possessing cocaine after crashing her car in Beverly Hills. There was another go at rehab in July, followed by another arrest. She pleaded guilty to driving under the influence and cocaine possession. Her sentence was one day in prison, ten days of community service and three years' probation. In November, she served just eighty-four minutes of her prison sentence, owing to jail overcrowding.[50] This incident was fatal to any remnant of her good-girl image, so it was fortunate that she wasn't playing good girls any more. Her first movie of 2007 was *Georgia Rule*, a female-focused drama in which she took the role of a tearaway Californian teen sent to her grandmother in Ohio (Jane Fonda) to be reformed. Reportedly, Lindsay's on-set behaviour was regrettably close to the character's. She was so frequently late or absent that the head of the production company sent her a letter accusing her of acting 'like a spoiled child' and warning that she would be held 'personally accountable' and pursued for 'full monetary damages' if she caused any more disruption. The letter was leaked.[51] (When asked about the allegations, Lindsay breezily replied, 'There were no problems. It's a great movie, everyone should see it.')[52]

Georgia Rule was a critical and commercial disappointment. Her next film, though, was a disaster. *I Know Who Killed Me* was Lindsay's first horror movie – a blend of Brian De Palma psychological excess and *Hostel*-influenced torture porn. It also marked the moment that Lindsay's persona overtook her performances. She played twin sisters, separated at birth, one of whom is adopted by a nice middle-class family while the other remains with their drug-addicted birth mother and grows up to be a two-bit stripper. But, really, she was playing a version of Lindsay Lohan, the girl who was cast as twins in *The Parent Trap* and had seemed so sweet but turned out so bad. In one scene, a psychiatrist uses MS Paint to write the word 'DELUSIONAL' in magenta across Lindsay's picture. This was a nonsensical thing for the character to do within the film. Its inclusion could only be explained as a fourth wall-breaking nod towards Lindsay's appearances on Perez Hilton's blog, where he adorned celebrity images with his hot-pink 'doodles'. Low-budget as it was, the film lost money, and it took eight awards at the Golden Raspberries, a show set up to honour the worst of Hollywood's output. Three went to Lindsay: she doubled up on Worst Actress for the dual role and took Worst Couple for her portrayal of the twins to boot.[53]

From now on, Lindsay's career would be on a notably smaller scale. She made one more film before the end of the decade – a very low-budget comedy called *Labor Pains* in 2009, which didn't even receive a theatrical release in the United States.[54] With her history of arrests, hospitalisations and showing up late to set, there were reports that it was difficult for her to get cast because it was difficult for her to get insured.[55] If you hired Lindsay for your film and she wasn't able to see it through for any reason, there were very few companies willing to bail you out. Towards the end of the noughties, there was also a feeling of fatigue with the whole gossip circus. A *New York Times* article in January 2008 on 'celebrity trainwrecks' placed Lindsay front and centre, alongside Britney and Paris. 'Is there any measurable way to prove what many of us feel in our gut, that 2007 was the year when the excesses of our most reliably outrageous personalities finally started to feel, well, excessive?' wondered the article, which included comments from Defamer editor Mark Lisanti. For Britney, Paris and Lindsay, said Lisanti, 2007 had been 'the culmination of their life's scandal work ... It was the snowball rolling down the hill, and it finally got to the bottom.' The part Lisanti and Defamer had played in pushing that snowball went unmentioned.[56]

Lindsay was now a byword for squalour and wasted talent. When the *Guardian* profiled Ellen (now Elliot) Page for the UK release of *Juno* in 2007, Lindsay was recruited as the exemplar of everything Page was not: 'If [Page] and her contemporary Lindsay Lohan were put on an attention-seeking sale, they would certainly be at polar ends.'[57] As the financial crisis slouched into view, *Gawker* was even briefly moved to announce the end of hedonism, in a post called 'Taradise Lost' (a pun on the name of actress Tara Reid, who was nearly Lindsay's equal in reputed trainwreckdom). Writer Richard Lawson made an explicit link between the post-9/11 sense of apocalypse and the impulse to party: 'The early aughts saw the rise of the Tara Reid and Lindsay Lohan mentality, one that celebrated and encouraged hard, rusty-jointed partying (and simulatneously [*sic*] loved to condemn it). Sure there was a war on and the world seemed to be ending, but when one thing ends another begins, and these folks wanted to hurl themselves, underpantsless crotches first, into the big new whatever ... Like the dirty bliss era of disco before it, is this new party era being killed by a recession? We think so!' Even Lindsay, the post suggested, had cleaned up her act: 'Lindsay Lohan is comfortably dating a deejay named Samantha Ronson (yes, dear readers, that's a woman! Maybe they'll get "married!" Keep reading Page Six to find out more!) and she's partying like a lot, lot less than she was before.'[58] It was a hopeful assessment. Her relationship with Ronson, which lasted until 2009, turned out to have its share of drama, aggravated by the casual homophobia it attracted. Ronson (sister of Amy Winehouse collaborator Mark) was 'attacked every day', recalled Lindsay later.[59] On his blog, Perez Hilton, despite being gay himself, habitually referred to Ronson as 'SaMANtha'.[60]

All the same, neither Lindsay nor Ronson retreated from publicity. In 2008, both of them appeared in the video for 'Everyone Nose (All the Girls Standing in Line for the Bathroom)', by N.E.R.D, the band formed by Pharrell Williams and Chad Hugo of the Neptunes. The lyrics were a celebration of coke-sniffing club girls. So much for *Gawker*'s assertion that the party era was over. 'From that Paris, Lindsay, Britney, Mary-Kate and Whitney / People say that they clean, motherfucker, don't bullshit me,' rapped Kanye West on the remix. The Lindsay of 'Rumors', the one who had angrily denounced the gossip about her life, was long gone. Now gossip was everything she was. She hadn't been able to resist it, and so, she embraced it – and the same media that had mocked her for covering up her bad habits as 'exhaustion' now scolded her for being open about them.

One of the most controversial things Lindsay did in 2008 was to sit for another Marilyn-themed set of portraits – this time for *New York Magazine*, a recreation of Marilyn's so-called 'Last Sitting' with photographer Bert Stern in 1962. The 'Last Sitting' had not in fact been Marilyn's last sitting (it took place a couple of weeks before the Barris pictures that had influenced Lindsay's 2006 shoot with Testino), but it holds a particular place in Marilyn lore nonetheless. *Vogue* published the photos the day after Marilyn died, which would make them poignant enough even if the pictures weren't hauntingly vulnerable. In them, Marilyn is mostly naked, often drinking champagne, and frequently sprawled across a bed with a sleepy-eyed look of intoxication. It's a scene that prefigured her death – in bed, from a sedative overdose – and Stern underlined the sense of fate in his recollection of the shoot: 'I wanted to photograph her one last time. She wasn't moving. I looked around the room. It was like a bomb had gone off, bottles of champagne all over, Marilyn's shoes in the corner, an overturned champagne bottle. I opened the door carefully. It was all over, she was asleep.'[61]

Still, the urge to photograph Marilyn one last time must have been strong, because, in 2008, Stern invited Lindsay to be his substitute Marilyn.[62] Ginia Bellafante, writing in the *New York Times*, called the photos 'macabre': 'The pictures ask viewers to engage in a kind of mock necrophilia. They are sexual, funereal images ... For the 10,000th time we are forced to ask:

Lindsay, what were you thinking?'[63] With the condemnation came attention: for three days after publication, the magazine's website was receiving twenty million daily pageviews, compared to its daily average of 1.2 million.[64] Bellafante was right about what had drawn all those clicks, though. The mix of Lindsay's naked body with the heady possibility that this body might soon expire was sublimely titillating. (That titillation was perhaps heightened by the fact that the previous year, the model Anna Nicole Smith – a former *Playboy* playmate who had lifted her image wholesale from Marilyn – had been found dead of an accidental overdose.)[65]

As for Lindsay, she was dismissive of any suggestion that she might be due to follow Marilyn to a tragic ending, simply saying, 'I sure as hell wouldn't let it happen to me.' But she did add her own insight into the original Marilyn pictures: 'Here is a woman who is giving herself to the public ... She's saying, "Look, you've taken a lot from me, so why don't I give it to you myself." She's taking control back.'[66] It was the signature error of the Upskirt Decade – to think that by surrendering the boundaries others were intent on breaching, you could regain your power. Marilyn had died regardless of how she looked in the pictures, and Lindsay herself did not seem very in control by this stage.

After multiple issues around the terms of her probation for the 2007 DUI, including being fitted with a SCRAM (Secure Continuous Remote Alcohol Monitor) ankle bracelet to monitor her alcohol use, she was sentenced to 90 days in prison in 2010. (She served two weeks.) A subsequent stay in rehab ended with her being accused of assaulting a staff member, though the charges were dropped. In 2011, she pleaded no contest to stealing a $2,500 necklace and received 120 days in prison.[67] In 2012, she finally completed her DUI probation, but police were called out to two altercations involving her, one of which was with her mother. (No charges were filed.)[68]

Professionally, Lindsay was reduced to riffing off her persona, with diminishing returns. The 2010 exploitation picture *Machete* gave her a bit part as a slutty teenager who gets drunk and makes a sex tape. (There never was a Lindsay porno, but it's the kind of thing girls like her were expected to do.) In the 2012 documentary *Love Marilyn*, she was one of a raft of actors reading Monroe's letters – and the only one to do it in Marilyn drag, with platinum hair and red lips. The same year, she had a substantial role as Elizabeth Taylor in the biopic *Liz & Dick*, but it was still casting that drew on her off-screen life as a casualty of fame to inform her on-screen portrayal of another one. It was also a made-for-TV Lifetime movie: some fall for the girl who'd been supposed to be the new Marilyn.

Then, in 2013, there were three movies – all bad, two execrable. *Scary Movie 5* and *InAPPropriate Comedy* were both abysmal low-rent comedies. In *Scary Movie 5*, her character makes a sex tape with Charlie Sheen (her male equal in tabloid scandal), shows off a SCRAM-type bracelet and crashes a car. The third film was better than either of these by a considerable distance, but it was also the one that probably caused her the most damage. When Paul Schrader, the screenwriter behind *Taxi Driver* and the director of *American Gigolo*, cast her in his LA sleaze-drama *The Canyons*, there were raised eyebrows. After Lindsay's behaviour on the set of *Georgia Rule*, her co-star James Deen was considered the safer bet – even though he was an actual porn performer, taking his first mainstream role here. (Two years after *The Canyons*, Deen would be accused of rape by several female porn performers; Deen denies the allegations, and there were no criminal charges.)[69] But this was a new kind of film-making: ultra-low budget, crowdfunded rather than backed by a traditional production company, and intended for the emerging video-on-demand market rather than cinemas. And the script, by novelist Bret Easton Ellis, had a cynical attitude towards celebrity that reflected the preceding decade's obsession with the dark heart of fame. In a 2011 essay for the Daily Beast, Ellis had declared the old 'Empire' of celebrity decorum to be dead: 'Do [audiences] really want manners? Civility? Empire courtesy? No. They want reality, no matter how crazy the celeb who brings it on has become.'[70]

For a post-Empire movie about a post-Empire world, Lindsay was perfect. But once again, the gossip was that she was tardy about her call times and disruptive when she did show up. As luminous as she could be on-screen – Schrader compared the film hopefully at one point to *The Misfits*, Marilyn's last film – Lindsay's flakiness cut into the shoot and forced compromises that were ultimately to the film's detriment. A set report in the *New York Times*, headlined 'Here Is What Happens When You Cast Lindsay Lohan in Your Movie', sealed her reputation for chaos. The Empire might have been over, but it was far from clear how to make a film without it. Near the end of the shoot that she had come so close to sabotaging, Lindsay spoke to the journalist. 'I needed time to figure out all the crap in my life that I'd created for myself, essentially, and I kind of realized, what am I doing? I like doing this. I like being here. This makes me happy,' she said. 'There was a line in the "Elizabeth" movie where she [i.e., Liz Taylor] says, "I'm so bored, I've never been taught what to do when I'm not working," and I'm kind of figuring that out now.'[71] It would be six years before she released another movie. For now, Hollywood was done with Lindsay.

Since 2004, part of the media's fascination with Lindsay had consisted in the imminent possibility of her death. Perhaps it would be in a car crash, perhaps it would be of an eating disorder. Ideally, it would be the full Marilyn: in bed, strung out, beautiful and broken. And yet, stubbornly, Lindsay stayed alive. Not only alive, but unrepentant. She's never seemed to ask to be loved in the way Britney has. She's never pivoted to sympathy like Paris. She's never seemed to take herself seriously, and this is infuriating (especially for those who cast her in the hope that she would prove to be a serious actress), but it's also strangely heartening in an industry where the more usual vice, as pilloried by *Gawker*, is pretentiousness. Lindsay seems to accept herself as what she is and asks no one else to take responsibility for it – even when she could arguably blame her parents, the entertainment industry's exploitation of child stars, or the hypocritical attention of the media. In 2022, she turned thirty-six, outliving Marilyn.

The last time she impersonated Marilyn, it was in the very bad sketch anthology *InAPPropriate Comedy*. In it, Lindsay re-creates the scene from *The Seven Year Itch* where Marilyn stands over the subway grille wearing the white dress with her skirt flipping up. It was a long, grimy way from the innocence of *Confessions of a Teenage Drama Queen*. In the sketch, the paparazzi gather round and get their pictures. Then Lindsay asks if she can take a shot, and the joke is that she does it with a gun, not a camera. The publicity material for the film pitched this as 'Lindsay Lohan living out her fantasy of taking an ultimate revenge on the salivating paparazzi who haunt her'.[72] As it appears in the movie, though, it's much bleaker. We see her from under the grille, from the perspective of a Peeping Tom (played by the film's director) – a full upskirt view with no consequences at all, and although it's not actually Lindsay's crotch, the scene is enough to make the revenge concept hollow. She could survive, but the message seemed to be that a woman like Lindsay could never decide how much she wanted to give.

4

Aaliyah: Possession

'There's a part of me that will always be just for me'

Some celebrity deaths hit hard because they have a desperate, fated quality: Whitney Houston's grotesque public decline, or Amy Winehouse narrating her own self-destruction in her lyrics. Aaliyah's wasn't like that. Her ending was neither anticipated nor ghoulishly willed. When she was killed in a plane crash on 25 August 2001, at the age of twenty-two, it hurt so much because it made no sense. Her peers and collaborators issued heartbroken statements. Vigils in her memory assembled across America – in New York City (her birthplace), in Detroit (her home town),[1] and in LA (the capital of the entertainment industry).[2] A thirteen-year-old named Delilah Coles, quoted in the *New York Times*, said very simply, 'It's terrible because she was so young and so talented.'[3] This was someone whose life and career had been defined by a meticulous command over the details. Since she first became famous at fourteen, every note she sang, every artist she worked with, every aspect of her image had been considered, deliberate, purposeful. Nothing had seemed careless, apart from her death: the small plane carrying her and seven members of her entourage home from a video shoot in the Bahamas had been overloaded by at least seven hundred pounds when it took off. The charter company had no licence to operate in the region, and the pilot, who had pleaded no contest to a charge of cocaine possession twelve days earlier, was not even certified to fly the plane. (At autopsy, metabolites of cocaine were found in the pilot's urine, and alcohol was found in his stomach contents.)[4] There were no survivors.[5] The negligence was incomprehensible.

So, too, was the timing. Aaliyah had been in entertainment for over a decade, but somehow everything still seemed to be ahead of her. She'd released three hit albums, starred in the kung fu/hip-hop crossover movie *Romeo Must Die* and had a thriving sideline as a model. But all this success felt like the preamble to true greatness. Everyone agreed that the twenty-first century was when Aaliyah was really going to happen. She was 'ready for superstardom', declared *Vibe* magazine in a cover profile from August 2001.[6] Her acting career was flourishing – she had just finished filming the lead in an adaptation of the Anne Rice novel *Queen of the Damned*, and was about to start shooting a role in the two *Matrix* sequels. And on the music side, the very fact that her latest album was self-titled seemed a statement of intent. *Aaliyah*, announced *Rolling Stone*'s review, 'shows that she has come into her own as a woman ... And the joy you hear in her voice, in the grooves, is rooted in independence.'[7] On 8 August, MTV had broadcast an episode of its *Diary* series, following Aaliyah through her various duties as a pop star: dance rehearsals, picking out looks with her stylist, meet-and-greets with her fans. 'I've just begun to show you what I'm capable of,' she tells the camera, gazing out from under the trademark wave of sleek black hair that fell across her face.[8] Aaliyah always seemed to be veiled from onlookers – by her hair, by baseball caps, by sunglasses, sometimes by an eyepatch. She both invited you in and held you at a distance.

The world would never get to see the rest. All that beauty, all that promise came to a violent halt a few hundred feet from the end of the runway of Marsh Harbour Airport. There was one more piece of horrific timing to the tragedy: seventeen days after the Bahamas crash came 9/11, and the small horror was subsumed by the greater one. Celebrity mourning can feel tenuous under the best circumstances, but for Aaliyah's fans, this left them with a grief curtailed.[9]

The story of Aaliyah in the Upskirt Decade is the story of how mass grief could preserve stardom even when the star herself was gone. But it's also the story of how a teenage girl was publicly groomed and privately abused in the nineties; how she and her family subsequently fought to exclude that fact from her public profile; how her rapist continued to prey on victims, even after his criminality was a matter of record, even after he had indicted himself in his own art; and how both the entertainment industry and the media that covered it winked at this man's depravity while profiting from his work. The story of Aaliyah in the Upskirt Decade is, tragically, inextricable from that of Robert Sylvester Kelly.

The important thing to understand is that the relationship between the two was never a secret. From the beginning, the facts of who R. Kelly was – and what he was to Aaliyah – were openly available. They were in the songs Kelly wrote and performed himself. They were in the songs he wrote and produced for her. They were laid out in legal documents and reported by journalists. It took a collective act of voluntary ignorance to dismiss all this as gossip and rumour, but it was a collective act of voluntary ignorance in which nearly everyone – from the perpetrator and victim, to the music industry and media, down to fans and the wider public – partook. This willed disbelief protected Kelly from criminal sanctions. It protected those around him from acknowledgement of their complicity. It did not protect Aaliyah, but it protected her reputation – which seemed an even more important duty after she was dead. In her 2021 book, *Baby Girl*, journalist and Aaliyah fan Kathy Iandoli writes that she had initially intended to leave Kelly out of it: 'As someone who loved Aaliyah dearly from afar, I felt I was disrespecting her legacy by spreading this part of her life on Front Street when her family never had. I also didn't want to dignify R. Kelly with any credit for her career, despite him being one of the main reasons we learned about Aaliyah in the first place.'[10] Still, Iandoli did write about him in the end. It's impossible for any honest account of Aaliyah's life and fame to avoid him. The first time the public at large heard her name, it was in his mouth; and the first time most people heard her voice, she was singing his words.

The two were introduced in 1991, when she was twelve and he was twenty-four, by their shared manager, Barry Hankerson. Hankerson was also Aaliyah's uncle, and her career had been a family business since her early childhood. Even her name suggests parental expectation: it means 'highest, most exalted one' in Arabic, and she had embraced celebrity as her destiny.[11] At ten, she had appeared on CBS's talent contest *Star Search* – the same show a young Britney would appear on three years later (and like Britney, she wouldn't win). At eleven, she'd performed in Vegas with Motown star Gladys Knight. (Knight had been married to Hankerson and had remained close to her ex's family despite an ugly divorce.)[12] Impressive as this all was, none of it had brought Aaliyah a record deal. Kelly was already signed to Jive, and by persuading him to take Aaliyah under his wing, Hankerson hoped to turn his aspiring child star niece into the real thing.

Perhaps the red flag should have been Kelly's first single, released in 1991. 'She's Got That Vibe' is a swaggering piece of new jack swing, mixing soulful seduction with R&B aggression. Although the lyrics consist of Kelly imploring a woman to let him take her home, in comparison to his later music, it's practically chaste: 'Cuddle me in your arms like I'm your teddy bear,' goes the rap. In the interlude, Kelly throws out the names of twenty different girls, all of whom he declares have 'got that vibe'. But one of them stands out, the only one honoured with adjectives: 'little cute Aaliyah's got it'.[13] There's a grim quality to hearing an adult man describe sex in the infantile imagery of soft toys when you know he's addressing an actual child within the song. Kelly's 1993 album, *12 Play*, ought perhaps to have raised more questions about his appropriateness as a mentor for Aaliyah: besides naming the collection after a pun on 'foreplay', the tracklist included 'Bump n' Grind', 'I Like the Crotch on You' and 'Sex Me Part I/Sex Me Part II'. And then there was 'It Seems Like You're Ready', with lyrics that suggest (though never outright address) taking a young woman's virginity. But *12 Play* was also a phenomenal success, making Kelly an undeniable asset to the Aaliyah project.

Kelly's working process with Aaliyah should definitely have struck people as troubling. 'Her and Robert spent a lot of time together going to arcades and bowling so that Robert could catch her vibe and write the songs that fit her,' recalled former Jive A&R representative Jeff Sledge in 2016. 'When we finally heard the album we were blown away ... It was basically like listening to an R. Kelly album, but with a little girl singing. Obviously the subject matter wasn't sexual, but the overall production and the sound of the record was like a Robert album as a little girl.'[14] Actually, it wasn't obvious at all that the songs Kelly wrote for Aaliyah were devoid of sexual content. The album – released by Hankerson's Blackground Records through a distribution deal with Jive in 1994 – was titled *Age Ain't Nothing but a Number*. It's a phrase that simultaneously invokes both Aaliyah's youth and her maturity, but it also carries well-worn implications of underage sex. In the title song, the line immediately following is 'Throwing down ain't nothing but a thing.' Did that mean what it sounded like? You could ask the same question of the lead single 'Back & Forth'. For Retha Powers, writing in the *New York Times*, it was plain that the song's refrain 'referred to the rhythm of the sex act ... It was easy to forget that the song was performed by a girl in the tenth grade.'[15]

But the point was precisely *not* to forget that this was being sung by a girl in tenth grade. 'Nothing charms grown-ups like seeing kids imitate them,' writes critic Margo Jefferson (in an appreciation of Michael Jackson's child star era). 'Children make our needs and habits entertaining; they follow our scenarios. Who do we want them to be? Wounded innocent? Flirt? Vixen? Naughty little chip off the old block? They know how to do it, but they can't know exactly why they're so alluring. They embody adult secrets, and that gives us the upper hand.'[16] Kelly wrote lines like 'Take control of me; fulfill my fantasies' for Aaliyah to sing back to him on the song 'I'm So into You'.[17] On 'No One Knows How to Love Me Quite Like You Do', she croons the title, and he replies, "Liyah, you're the only one for me.'[18] On the album cover, she's foregrounded, while he looks at her from the background, proprietorial. When they made promotional appearances together, they wore matching baggy clothes, and there was an evident understanding between them. And yet, while the intimation of broken boundaries gave Aaliyah an edge and helped her album shift a million copies, the acknowledgement of any actual breach of decency between her and Kelly would have been ruinous for them both.[19] She would have been damaged goods, and he would have been a criminal.

So, when Aaliyah was asked during a joint TV interview whether they were 'cousins' or 'girlfriend and boyfriend', she shut the query down firmly and politely: 'We're just very close. This is my best friend.' Kelly's response was considerably less deft: 'I better go get me a white jeep' – a jokey reference to the vehicle O.J. Simpson used when he attempted to flee arrest for the murders of his ex-wife Nicole Brown Simpson and her friend Ron Goldman.[20] What was Kelly invoking here? Simpson's assumed guilt or the idea that he, like Simpson, was a prominent black man being threatened with destruction through the law? As usual with Kelly, it seems like the answer was both at once: it's an apparent admission and an assertion of victimisation in the same gesture. And the story refused to go away. In fact, it got considerably worse when a marriage certificate from August 1994 with both their names on it – and a false date of birth for Aaliyah, making her eighteen rather than her true age of fifteen – was unearthed by *Vibe*.[21] 'It was a horrible scandal, a horrible situation for everybody involved, so we tried to keep the focus on the music and the videos,' Jeff Sledge remembered in 2016. 'It wasn't like now with social media. Twitter wasn't on fire with it. But once *Vibe* did that article, it definitely put a whole different energy around the project and about her and Robert.'[22]

A horrible situation for everyone involved, most of all Aaliyah – although the concern here was less for her as a victim of sexual exploitation than for the risk to her image. When MTV reported the marriage story, the item ended with a banter-y sign-off: 'Whether or not she's in legal trouble for passing off fake ID remains to be seen. We will keep you posted.'[23] The story was reported as juicy gossip, rather than a narrative of abuse; there was no suggestion that Kelly might face repercussions for raping a minor, only that Aaliyah could be identified as delinquent. Behind the scenes, Aaliyah's family had moved fast to end her connection with Kelly as discreetly as possible. The marriage was annulled, and in September 1994, Kelly, Aaliyah and her parents signed a legal document dissolving all professional and personal relationships between the Svengali and the prodigy. It also committed both parties to permanent public silence about each other – 'due,' in the words of the document, 'to the nature of the music industry and its ability to engender rumors and disseminate personal information, both true and untrue'.[24] Aaliyah's parents took over management duties from Hankerson (who retained Kelly as his client until an acrimonious split in 2000), and Blackground (which remained her label) cut ties with Jive. For the rest of her life, Aaliyah would dismissively refer to her entanglement with Kelly as 'that mess'.[25] Kelly's 2012 autobiography, *Soulacoaster*, more tantalisingly, began with a note stating that 'certain episodes could not be included for complicated reasons'.[26]

When Aaliyah's next album came out, in 1996, she had a new distributor (Atlantic) and new collaborators (Timbaland and Missy Elliott, whose twitchy beats meshed impeccably with Aaliyah's smooth vocals). She had a new look, too: out with the tomboy layers, in with sex shop leathers (in which she somehow still looked demure) for the 'One in a Million' video.[27] The album, of the same name, sold two million copies and put Kelly thoroughly in Aaliyah's past.[28] When, during an interview around *One in a Million*, she was pressed on the absence of her onetime 'best friend', Aaliyah used her answer to make it absolutely clear that she was the one calling the shots: 'That was a decision that I made. I thought it would be best for my career and me personally to move on and really take control of this album … Honestly, there were negative things that were said in the past, and that was one reason why I did feel it was best for me to move on. That was a rough period for me and my family – a very tumultuous time, but I'm a very strong person. I think it says a lot that I'm here today and I answer the questions.'[29] *Negative things were said.* What things were done, who by, and to whom was not even acknowledged.

After 1995, her music, too, gave no suggestion that she was a young woman with a traumatic history. *Age Ain't Nothing but a Number* had been about as personal as a record could be – both the implement by which a girl was groomed for sexual abuse and the document of its happening. The contrast between that and her subsequent recordings is total. On *One in a Million* and *Aaliyah*, she is rigorously, unyieldingly impersonal. Though her voice and style are distinctive, the words she sings could have been delivered by anyone. Her lyrics contain no allusions to her offstage life. Her strongest songs feel not like addresses to the public, but like murmurs to one individual man, who could be any individual man (which meant that any girl could imagine herself in Aaliyah's place and play the cool seductress). On 'Try Again', she encourages a prospective lover not to give up his efforts; on 'More than a Woman', she promises 'constant pleasure that no scale can measure', a dream of undemanding feminine compliance; 'Rock the Boat' is a sinuous list of instructions for getting her off. 'Many of her songs,' wrote *New York Times* pop critic Kelefa Sanneh, 'weren't really songs at all, but simple vocal riffs, repeated and refracted to echo the manipulated loops that create digital rhythm ... She sounds like the mirror image of David, the robot-boy in the film *AI*: a real person chasing an ideal of electronic perfection.'[30] Long before she died, Aaliyah seemed to have disappeared inside her music.

Ignoring the R. Kelly issue would not have been sustainable in the twenty-first century. In the nineties, a publicist could broker deals for access, declaring certain topics off-limits to the press in exchange for interviews. Social media and blog-ging would, as Jeff Sledge pointed out, end all that. Aaliyah died three years before Facebook was founded and four years before TMZ began: her image was preserved in a time when it was still possible for a star to control their own narrative and when even unambiguous evidence of Kelly's interest in young girls could be held at bay.

In December 2000, the *Chicago Sun-Times* had published an exhaustive account of Kelly's multiple sexual relationships with minors and the civil suits he had quietly settled with his victims – including Aaliyah. The article, by Jim DeRogatis and Abdon Pallasch, had been meticulously sourced from legal documents, witness testimony and the voices of some of Kelly's victims who were willing to go on the record. Although by the time the report was published, these women were well into their twenties, there was a desperately childish note to the way they spoke about Kelly. 'He treated us very well,' said one, who had first had sex with Kelly when she was sixteen and he was twenty-four. '[We got] anything we asked for, but we weren't going to ask for much – a pair of Air Jordans or $100 was a lot of money to us ... I still love R. Kelly's music; I don't hate him. He reminds me of a boyfriend who hurt you that you still love.'[31]

Shockingly, Kelly had first found this victim in his former high school's choir, which he had continued to attend as an adult at the invitation of music teacher Lena McLin. (McLin had been a mentor to Kelly, and *Soulacoaster* is dedicated jointly to her and his mother Joann.)[32] Just as his solo hangout time with Aaliyah had failed to raise eyebrows, there was an astonishingly lax attitude here about a grown man socialising with children. Twentieth-century understandings of sexual predation focused disproportionately on 'stranger danger', in which an aggressor unknown to the victim used force to get what he wanted. There was little understanding of the subtler processes by which adults exploited affection and trust to bring children and teenagers into compliance. The term *grooming* only began to be used in courtrooms during the noughties, replacing the oddly Victorian (and unhelpfully titillating) word *seduction*.[33] Besides, celebrities were by definition not strangers: they were people you felt you knew. Asked by the *Sun-Times* for comment on Kelly's apparently using her class as a pick-up site, McLin did not reflect on the possibility that this represented a failed duty of care on her part, but put the focus instead on the victims' morals: 'I don't know what he did outside of school. But in the school, there was no hanky-panky. If they were involved in that, the sad thing is, it takes two to tango.'[34]

For many, the default reaction towards a girl who had sex with an adult man was not compassion, but condemnation: having sex marked her as a slut, and so the very act that harmed her proved she was someone who could not be seriously harmed. This was an especially powerful force with the black girls Kelly picked as victims, who, according to racist stereotypes, could readily be characterised as oversexed and unrapable. Conversely, it was easy to sympathise with Kelly, whose success had made him a hero of Chicago's black community. When DeRogatis first received the tip-off about R. Kelly, via fax in November 2000, his initial instinct was to dismiss it as the work of 'one more reactionary jerk trying to disparage a black superstar'.[35] There is a complicated entanglement between sexual violence and racism in American history. Charges of sexual impropriety against black men have been used – most notoriously in the 1955 murder of fourteen-year-old Emmett Till – as the excuse for lynching. But there was also a tradition of downplaying and disregarding violence against women when it was presented in the context of resistance to racism. In her classic 1991 essay 'Mapping the Margins', legal scholar Kimberlé Crenshaw wrote, 'People of color often must weigh their interests in avoiding issues that might reinforce distorted public perceptions against the need to acknowledge and address intracommunity problems. Yet the cost of suppression is seldom recognized in part because the failure to discuss the issue shapes perceptions of how serious the problem is in the first place.' There was a racist stereotype of black men being sexually violent, and the imperative to counter this created a culture of silence around genuine acts of sexual violence by black men – which, in the majority of cases, would be committed against black women. A supposedly anti-racist impulse ultimately served to entrench the victimisation of black women specifically.[36]

An extreme version of the conflict between race and sex as axes of oppression even presented sexual assault as politically justified. Black Panther leader and convicted rapist Eldridge Cleaver, in his 1968 essay collection, *Soul on Ice*, wrote that having been politically awakened to the realities of racism, 'I arrived at the conclusion that, as a matter of principle, it was of paramount importance for me to have an antagonistic, ruthless attitude toward white women.' But demographics meant that the most accessible victims for a black man like Cleaver were, of course, black women: 'I became a rapist. To refine my technique and modus operandi, I started out by practicing on black girls in the ghetto – in the black ghetto where dark and vicious deeds appear not as aberrations or deviations from the norm, but as part of the sufficiency of the Evil of a day – and when I considered myself smooth enough, I crossed the tracks and sought out white prey. I did this consciously, deliberately, willfully, methodically ... Rape was an insurrectionary act.'[37]

Cleaver's history of sexual violence did not impede – and, to some minds, even enhanced – his status as a civil rights figurehead. This attitude endured up to the new millennium. In an introduction to *Soul on Ice*, included in a 1999 reissue, the writer Maxwell Geismar credited Cleaver with 'a secret kind of sexual mysticism ... which adds depth and tone to his social commentary'; and a 1998 obituary of Cleaver in the *New York Times* recalled that he 'was hailed as an authentic voice of black rage in a white-ruled world'.[38] The women harmed by this rage were a side issue – and the black women who were not even his primary intended victims but merely 'practice' were the most sidelined of all.

'Although racism and sexism readily intersect in the lives of real people, they seldom do in feminist and antiracist practice,' noted Crenshaw.[39] The demand for a simple, emotionally satisfying narrative rendered invisible the crosscurrents of victimhood and culpability within groups and even within individuals. This meant in practice that there were two culturally available strategies for rejecting women's testimony against black men: the belief that women lied to hurt black men and the belief that if black men did hurt women, that mattered less than the fact of racism. DeRogatis's original impulse about the story he broke turned out to be prescient of its reception. It was treated as either a private issue for the black community or a deliberate attempt to ruin a black hero. 'We expected the piece to have real impact the next day,' DeRogatis wrote in his 2019 book, *Soulless: The Case Against R. Kelly.* 'It didn't.' There was practically no pick-up from other news outlets, and public affection for Kelly seemed to rally rather than falter. After the *Sun-Times* story came out in 2000, Kelly's song 'I Wish' was reportedly the most-requested song on Chicago radio.[40]

Kelly's popularity, and the ease with which a black girl could be cast as a traitor to her race or simply a 'ho', further heightened the stakes for Aaliyah's image. She walked a careful line between playing with her sexuality and cultivating a certain impenetrable aloofness. She presented herself to the world as a sensual person. 'My mother always said that she feels like I always had sex appeal,' Aaliyah told *Vibe* in the 2001 interview. 'Even when I was very young, when I would take pictures, there was something sexual about me. I do feel sexy for sure. I embrace it, and I'm comfortable with it. I enjoy it.'[41] But did she ever actually have sex? It was hard to say, because she kept her private life strictly private.

For example, when she died, she'd been dating hip-hop impresario Damon Dash of Roc-A-Fella Records for some months, but they were never publicly linked while she was alive.[42] Compare this with the relationship between Dash's label co-founder Jay-Z and Beyoncé, which started around the same time and similarly matched a rap tough guy with an R&B princess, to the ultimate benefit of both their profiles. Another counterpoint is the alliance between Whitney Houston and Bobby Brown, which, at least initially, worked to toughen her image and domesticate his. Romance has an almost unmatched power in celebrity presentation, and Aaliyah could have benefited a great deal from announcing that she was with Dash: it would have marked her coming of age, emotionally and musically, and granted her by association some of the credibility, grit and glamour of Roc-A-Fella, the most prestigious brand in black music at the time. But to do so would have been to create a conflict with the profile she had cultivated, because her allure was all in what she didn't give away.

And she stood out for it. The *NME* review of *Aaliyah* had compared her to Neptunes protégée Kelis and to Destiny's Child, and found Aaliyah the superior in both cases. She was, wrote John Mulvey, 'abnormally mature': 'She doesn't hate him so much right now, and she isn't milking him to pay those bills, bills, bills either.'[43] (Kelis's debut had been the towering hymn to the betrayed woman's rage, 'Caught Out There', while Destiny's Child had had a hit with the slinkily pragmatic 'Bills, Bills, Bills'.) Such emotional outpourings and expressions of materialism were totally at odds with Aaliyah's rarefied presentation. Fundamentally, she was a nice girl from a nice family, one who worked hard and didn't neglect her studies – she graduated high school with a 4.0 average, despite the disruption caused by her music career. She just happened to also be an exceptionally beautiful global superstar.[44] This lent her a relatable quality that undercut the reserve of her music and bonded her to fans, especially black girls who'd grown up listening to her. She was, wrote Iandoli, the kind of celebrity with whom you could have an 'imaginary friendship'.[45]

After Aaliyah died, the teen mourners at the vigils for her universally emphasised her virtue. 'It was refreshing to have someone not talk about drugs and sex and violence and all that stuff . . . Her music was clean,' said Moricia Sylvester, aged fourteen, from New York.[46] And though Aaliyah did, obviously, sing about sex (and had dropped a reference to 'dope' on 'Rock the Boat'), the point was really that her version of sexuality was not the panting, frantic one that other young female stars were offering at the time. 'In this business, church girls become prostitutes because they want to be stars, but she would never let stardom interfere with who she was,' said Parrish Johnson, an executive vice-president at Blackground.[47] In all this, there was no space to mention – and her younger fans may truly not have known – the complicating fact that she had been briefly married to a man twelve years older than her. 'I think the girls should look up to her more than Britney Spears' was the cutting verdict of Shavonne Moore, aged eighteen, of Harlem. 'Britney Spears is always taking off her clothes. Please.'[48] Less than a month later – as if to prove Shavonne right – Britney released 'I'm a Slave 4 U', her most panting and frantic song so far, written and produced by the Neptunes. She promoted it with a VMA performance for which she wore nothing but a bikini and a snake.

For some, Aaliyah's death was more than the demise of one talented individual: it marked the moment music was inherited by teeny-bop phonies. Journalist Christopher John Farley turned around a superfast biography of Aaliyah, published the November after her death. He threw in eight references to Britney, whom he deemed less gifted, less interesting, more derivative and more manufactured than Aaliyah.[49] The unspoken concession of this comparison was just how much Britney – who had been signed to Jive after the termination of Aaliyah's contract – owed to the Lolita template of her teen queen predecessor. They were products of the same machine, and in both cases, the assertion of purity was heightened and eroticised by the display of sexuality. *Age Ain't Nothing but a Number* had shown that there was a market for nymphette pop, but the barely contained scandal about Kelly and Aaliyah had also shown how combustible it was as a concept. If you wished to turn adult male desire for adolescent girls into a marketable commodity, you had better not allow that adult male desire to become an embarrassment to your product. The lessons from Aaliyah's time at Jive could be seen in the styling of Britney on '... Baby One More Time'.

In obituaries, the Kelly issue could be either dodged entirely or hedged with Aaliyah's and Kelly's denials.[50] Kelefa Sanneh, in the *New York Times*, went the furthest of any critic at the time in acknowledging both the scandal and the way sexuality was bound into Aaliyah's image. 'She didn't sing like a little girl [on *Age Ain't Nothing*] – even then, she had a stronger voice and a more sophisticated approach than most pop singers – and she didn't act like one, either,' wrote Sanneh, who was also one of the strongest advocates in the media for Kelly's music. 'The child star was reported to be a child bride, secretly married to her mentor, the R&B crooner R Kelly. (Neither ever confirmed the marriage.)'[51] It was, at best, clumsy phrasing, implying that the (supposedly unconfirmed) sexual relationship was a mark of Aaliyah's maturity, both personal and artistic, rather than an act of predation by an adult man.

This was a kind of 'sophistication' that edged Aaliyah uncomfortably closer to 'prostitute' than 'church girl'. Was there no way for her to break out of that dichotomy? The depressing answer to that is probably 'no'. Two years after Aaliyah's death, Paris found herself stranded in the same no-woman's-land of sexual victimhood – subject to an injury that somehow damaged her reputation more than that of the man who had harmed her. And Paris was white and well-born, while the man who wanted their sex tape in public view had minimal social capital of his own. Aaliyah was black, her only assets were her own talent and image, and her violator was regarded as a hero and a genius. It is very hard to imagine what option was open to Aaliyah besides denial. It's also possible that Aaliyah, like some of Kelly's other victims, continued to regard him as a boyfriend rather than an abuser: this, after all, is the essence of grooming. It was also what the world wanted to be true. Sympathetic posthumous renderings of Aaliyah in popular culture pushed the 'true love' line for many years: as late as 2014, the Lifetime biopic *Aaliyah: The Princess of R&B* portrayed hers and Kelly's relationship as the equal match of 'two creatively connected souls' sundered by the cruel misfortune of timing.

But no matter how diligently Aaliyah closed down the subject of Kelly, her rigorous strategy of 'no comment' could never have survived the frenzied attention of fame in the noughties. Despite the underwhelming reaction to their original scoop, DeRogatis and Pallasch continued to pursue the R. Kelly story. In early 2002, they had a significant breakthrough. An anonymous source delivered a videotape to DeRogatis at his home: it showed R. Kelly with what appeared to be an underage girl, likely no older than her mid-teens. What DeRogatis saw on there, he said, was more graphic and more disturbing than any of the evidence about Kelly to have emerged so far. A story published by the *Sun-Times* on 8 February described the video's contents in the stark terms of journalistic objectivity:

'the underage girl refers to Kelly as "Daddy" while they have sex. The sex acts include intercourse, fellatio and urination.'[52] (Later, DeRogatis would summarise it for another journalist in more emotive terms: 'This girl has the disembodied look of a rape victim and he's urinating in her mouth. It's a sickening spectacle.')[53] The video became known, colloquially, as the 'pee tape'. The *Sun-Times* passed it on to the police (a surprisingly controversial decision with other journalists, some of whom believed that the paper had breached reporting ethics by handing evidence of child abuse to the authorities),[54] and in June 2002, Kelly was indicted on forty-nine counts, including possessing and making child pornography and soliciting an underage partner.[55]

Before now, Kelly had been protected by the media's indifference to his entanglements with young girls and by the fact that his most prominent victim was as invested as he was in downplaying the abuse. By 2002, though, the internet had changed the stakes. The 'pee tape' had been uploaded to the internet at some point, making it a particularly unwholesome part of the celebrity sex tape canon. On forums, posters pruriently analysed it: How old was the girl? Was the man really R. Kelly, or could it be a case of mistaken identity? Were the acts in the video inherently disgusting or part of the acceptable variety of human desire? (The uncensored internet had thrown open all manner of fetishes to public view.) Would they be able to listen to R. Kelly's music again?[56]

On that last point, the answer for most people seemed to be a solid 'yes': while his defence team exploited every possible stalling tactic to delay the trial, Kelly enjoyed some of his richest years, both creatively and commercially. There had always been a sentimental side to Kelly's music – in 1995, he had delivered the mawkish ballad 'You Are Not Alone' to Michael Jackson, which aided Jackson's rehabilitation after he was similarly accused of abusing children (in Jackson's case, mostly white boys). After 2002, Kelly emphatically embraced his gospel tendencies with songs like 'U Saved Me', presenting himself as a justified sinner in a way calculated to appeal to churchgoing black audiences. But while Jackson turned away from the lascivious side of his music after the sexual allegations against him, Kelly kept the filth coming alongside the godliness. 'Ignition (Remix)' was released in late 2002 and became one of his biggest hits yet. It compares a woman to a car, with Kelly as the driver who's going to take a ride: 'Girl, I'm feelin' what you're feelin' / No more hopin' and wishin' / I'm about to take my key and / Stick it in the ignition.' In a typical Kelly quirk, it was a remix of a song that hadn't even been officially released. The original had been on an album called *Loveland*, which, like the incriminating videotape, had been leaked onto the internet. Kelly responded by reworking the entire collection. The resulting album, called *Chocolate Factory*, was both fantastically dirty and a huge success.

It's not that people didn't notice Kelly's brazenness in this period. (On the remix of 'Step in the Name of Love', he even christened himself 'the Pied Piper of R&B', a self-identification with the fairytale childcatcher that the *Guardian* noted was 'dubious'.)[57] But, if anything, the shock element made him a more intriguing proposition. 'Mr Kelly, the legendarily freaky R&B star, long ago established himself as one of the greatest singer-songwriters of his generation,' wrote Sanneh in a 2006 live review. 'The sex scandal that threatened to derail his career in 2002 ended up doing the opposite: it made him more productive, more successful and, somehow – maybe because more people began paying attention to his excellent music – more respected than ever before.'[58] And the music really was good. Kelly became an in-demand collaborator. He made 'Outrageous' for Britney's *In the Zone* album (sample lyric: 'Outrageous! / My sex drive'), and he gave boy band B2K a No. 1 with 'Bump Bump Bump'. 'We definitely did weigh it,' said

Max Gousse of B2K's label, Epic, in 2004, when asked how he felt about the charges against Kelly, 'but it was undeniable – a hit record is a hit record.'[59]

Besides, it was impossible to be shocked by the allegations Kelly was facing, because he had made a profession of outraging public morals for so long, as the comedian Dave Chappelle pointed out in a 2004 routine from his Comedy Central vehicle *Chappelle's Show*. 'I mean, say what you want to say about his scandal, but the music is scandal-proof, you know what I'm saying?' he said in a stand-up section. 'And any real fan of R. Kelly wouldn't let that scandal stop them, because if you was paying attention to his music all these years, you might have seen it coming like I did.' The riff introduced a sketch in which Chappelle – dressed in sunglasses and a do-rag, with a neatly trimmed goatee – pastiched R. Kelly. 'Take me to your special place / Close your eyes, show me your face,' Chappelle sings in a passable falsetto. 'I'm gonna piss on it.' The audience responded with a thrilled mix of horror and hilarity, and Chappelle had landed on the essential truth of Kelly: his priapism was so transparent that you couldn't take it seriously as a fan without admitting your own complicity.

In 2008, when the trial finally took place – six years after the indictment – Kelly was found not guilty. His team argued that the video had been faked (a technological impossibility); that if it was real, then Kelly's partner in the video was not underage (it helped them that the young woman had refused to testify); that Kelly's accusers were motivated by money and resentment; and that girls in general were simply not credible. 'She is a thirteen-year-old-girl having raunchy, dirty, nasty sex ... with a superstar who's won Grammy Awards and she tells no one?' said Kelly's attorney incredulously. 'You couldn't keep a thirteen-year-old girl's mouth quiet about having Hannah Montana tickets!'[60] But girls keep secrets all the time. (And the plot of *Hannah Montana* is that a girl superstar leads a secret double life.) Whatever had happened between Aaliyah and Kelly, she had taken it to the grave.

Fortunately for Kelly, pop music soon supplied other topics of gossip. Rihanna – who signed to Roc-A-Fella in 2004 at age sixteen – was in many ways Aaliyah's inheritor: although nineties peers like Brandy and Monica bore an obvious resemblance to Aaliyah and her self-described 'street but sweet' style, it was Rihanna who pursued the experiments Aaliyah had started to their logical outcome. She had an Aaliyah-like knack for blending herself seamlessly into a production without losing her identity, and the more that pop music leaned on the intensely manufactured 'track-and-hook model' that Timbaland had helped to pioneer with Aaliyah, the more valuable that combination of pliability and recognisability became. Insistent, insinuating songs like 'Umbrella' – which could be heard as an innocent promise of care for a boyfriend, but which also ended with the singer imploring 'come into me' in a way that sounded guilelessly dirty – had made Rihanna the biggest thing in pop music by 2009. She was also half of an exquisite musical power couple with R&B singer Chris Brown. Both were scheduled to perform at the 2009 Grammys – a moment that should have sealed their joint status at the top of the entertainment business. It never happened, though, because, the night before, as they were driving home from a pre-awards party, the couple had argued. Brown had tried to throw Rihanna out of the car. When that failed, he had beaten and choked her until her eyes were blackened and her lip was split.

Learning the truth of what happened to Aaliyah during her lifetime had been a grinding process of tracking down documents, and whatever was uncovered was limited in its reach by the constraints of print and broadcast media: in the late nineties and early noughties, if you hadn't read the specific edition of *Vibe* or the *Sun-Times* or seen the relevant MTV news bulletins, you couldn't know for sure what the charges against Kelly consisted of. Within hours of Brown's attack on Rihanna, gossip site TMZ had published full details of the police report – followed, eleven days later, by photographs of Rihanna's battered face.[61] (In August 2009, Brown was sentenced to five years of probation and six months of community service for the assault.[62]) From a publicity perspective, this was a disaster for Rihanna. Her persona had leaned on girl-next-door sweetness and fashion-plate elegance. Now, she was in the far less aspirational position of being a victim – or, to Brown's fan base (which overlapped heavily with hers), a woman who must have done something to deserve the assault. There was no way to contain the story once it started replicating across blogs and social media. For Rihanna's career to survive, the only option was somehow to own this catastrophe. *Rated R*, her next album, was precision-engineered to eliminate any sense of Rihanna's vulnerability, explained John Seabrook in his book *The Song Machine*: 'From the Ellen von Unwerth cover photo of the unsmiling artist in mesh and black leather, palm cupped over one of her previously blackened eyes as though it still ached, to the lyrics . . . the whole album obliquely refers to the beating.'[63] But managing the tension between sex and violence in Rihanna's image didn't end there – not least because she would continue to be romantically linked with Brown for several years to come, even while he was on probation after pleading guilty to the original assault.[64] In the video for 'We Found Love', from 2011, we see Rihanna in a chaotic relationship with a handsome boy who has close-cropped hair like Brown's: at one point, she slams her hands on a car dashboard, and he lashes out at her. It follows, precisely, the account Rihanna gave to police of how Brown started his assault on her – the account that everyone had read thanks to TMZ. (In a report on the music video, the site accused Rihanna, with no apparent sense of irony, of 'exploiting' the beating.[65]) In 2012, shortly before the couple broke up for good, they even recorded a duet together, called 'Nobody's Business' (which, in another spectacular irony failure, chided the public for caring about a relationship that was being publicly performed in the song). Looked at plainly, this was disturbing stuff, but through it, Rihanna adapted her image to the reality of being a battered girlfriend and placed herself in control of her story.

Meanwhile, Brown's career was mostly unscathed, though he did lose an endorsement deal with Wrigley's chewing gum.[66] But he was spared imprisonment, and by the end of 2009, he was recording and performing as usual. His album of that year, *Graffiti*, alluded to what reviews euphemistically called his 'fall from grace'.[67] But while Rihanna had to pull off the difficult task of projecting empowerment while being a victim, all Brown had to do was show that he was sorry – often, it seemed, for himself, as on 'Lucky Me', where he bemoaned the travails of being famous.

His apologies found a receptive audience. After watching a somewhat contrite interview with Brown on *Good Morning America*, Diane Sawyer (the same anchor who had once reduced Britney to tears with questions about whether she had cheated on Justin) agreed with her co-host that 'it had finally sunk in' for Brown. His rehabilitation was confirmed, and his next album, *F.A.M.E.*, went double platinum, vindicating his label's decision to stand by him. Why would it have done anything else? Brown was signed to Jive, and if Jive's experience with Aaliyah and R. Kelly had instilled one lesson, it was that scandal (when properly handled) could always be turned into product, while the implosion of the Britney-Justin relationship had demonstrated that a male star could count on audience sympathy when a break-up turned hostile. Regardless of his predations, R. Kelly had made Jive an estimated $150 million during his career.[68] A hit, as the record industry liked to say, was a hit.

Kelly stayed with the label for as long as it existed, and when it was rolled into parent label RCA in 2011, his deal rolled over, too. By then, Kelly was forty-four. He wasn't the irresistible force he'd once been – 'Ignition (Remix)' had been the last of his songs to dominate the charts – but he had become something else instead: a true musical eccentric, restlessly pursuing his muse. In 2005, he'd released the first part of his 'urban operetta' *Trapped in the Closet*, a histrionic drama of entangled infidelities that would ultimately extend to thirty-three 'chapters' – narratively continuous videos in which the story is sung by Kelly while a cast acts it out.[69] The 'wildly convoluted plot', as summarised by one critic, 'involved an outbreak of mass cuckoldry, a shooting, the outing of a gay pastor and a dwarf stripper called Big Man'.[70] If it was intended as deflection, it worked. After Kelly had unveiled the second tranche of episodes, and with his child pornography trial under way in Chicago, the *Guardian* wrote, 'even if he is found guilty, R. Kelly has made at least 22 other videos that are weirder and more inexplicable than the one where he is said to urinate on a teenager'.[71] Meanwhile, Aaliyah's music wasn't even available, for the most part. Blackground Records, which owned the rights to the majority of Aaliyah's recordings, had become embroiled in legal issues during the late noughties; by the middle of the next decade, it had ceased to function as a business, and much of its catalogue – including *One in a Million* and *Aaliyah* – languished unlicensed to streaming services.[72] As physical formats fell into redundancy, Aaliyah seemed to be preserved in a separate realm entirely, as inaccessible and untouchable as ever.

The first definitive sign of Kelly's luck running out came in 2014. In 2013, he had recorded a song with Lady Gaga called 'Do What U Want'. The lyrics interweave disturbing sexual imagery with a bitter discourse about fame. 'Do what you want with my body,' sings Gaga, and then, shifting from addressing a lover to addressing the media: 'Write what you want / Say what you want about me ...' When Kelly joins the song, he is also denouncing his press coverage, although, for him, the refrain goes, 'Do what I want with *your* body.' Even if he saw himself as a victim of public opinion, he still played the aggressor in sex. The music video, directed by fashion photographer Terry Richardson, placed the song in a medical fetish setting, with Kelly as the doctor and Gaga as his patient. (This, like the Rihanna video before it, was a riff on real events in the star's life: Gaga had recently had hip surgery.) To underline the theme of calling out the media, a naked Gaga writhes about on a carpet of newspapers.

Richardson had once described his artistic mission as uncovering the 'internal porn star' in his subjects, and to that end, he had published pictures of himself having sex with models.[73] He was regularly described as 'controversial'. Like Kelly's hypersexual lyrics, the Richardson aesthetic dovetailed immaculately with an era where pornography was only a click away, no matter where you were, and lent even potentially staid collaborators an edge: in 2007, Richardson had shot Barack Obama (then campaigning to become the Democratic presidential nominee) for *Vibe*.[74] When the actual Hannah Montana, Miley Cyrus, relaunched as an adult artist, Richardson filmed her nude for the 'Wrecking Ball' video. But, as with Kelly, there had been persistent allegations that Richardson's sleaziness was more than a pose: for years before the Obama portrait, models and assistants had gone on the record to accuse him of degrading and assaulting them on set. The supposedly mutual sex he had documented himself having was, according to several women, coerced.[75] (Richardson has denied these allegations, and in a 2017 statement to BuzzFeed, claimed 'all of the subjects of his work participated consensually'.[76])

The combination of Kelly, Richardson and an ostensibly feminist artist like Gaga was too much for audiences to take. Gaga pulled the video, though not the song. Page Six quoted a source calling the clip 'literally an ad for rape'.[77] It would be another four years before Richardson was declared *persona non grata* by the fashion industry, and two more years after that before Kelly finally fell. In 2019, Gaga removed 'Do What U Want' from streaming, replacing it with a version in which Christina Aguilera took the Kelly part. She also issued a statement apologising for her 'poor judgment' in working with Kelly. 'What I am hearing about the allegations against R. Kelly is absolutely horrifying and indefensible,' she tweeted.[78] It seemed improbable that she could be just 'hearing about' those allegations in 2019. Could she really have missed all the *Sun-Times* reporting? The court cases? Nearly two decades of pee tape jokes? Kelly's own lyrics? There had always been enough information to condemn him. All that had ever been lacking was the will. (Beyoncé and Taylor Swift, who both worked with Richardson in 2013, may well have counted themselves fortunate to have missed the backlash.)

In 2017, DeRogatis reported another story about Kelly, this time for BuzzFeed, describing how the singer was maintaining an abusive 'cult' of women, many of whom he had groomed (a word now firmly in the popular lexicon) as underage girls.[79] This time, the reaction was very different from the silence DeRogatis had encountered in 2000. Two black women, Oronike Odeleye and Kenyette Barnes, organised the hashtag campaign MuteRKelly, which succeeded in pressuring several venues to cancel the singer's shows. 'My hope for the movement is that we can shut R. Kelly down,' said Odeleye in *Glamour* magazine. 'If I make him such a hot potato that no artist wants to work with him, that no record companies want to have him, then we've done our job.'[80]

Kelly was fifty by this time, and his biggest hits were behind him; there was less tolerance in general of men fooling around with girls, and he had lost his shine. He called the protests against him a 'lynching', but public feeling was no longer on his side.[81] There was now an appetite to see purported predators brought down. With MeToo in the air, 2017 saw Richardson blacklisted by multiple publications and fashion brands: the adjective most often attached to his name was no longer 'controversial', but 'disgraced'.[82] In 2019, the documentary *Leaving Neverland* put Michael Jackson's extensive abuse of boys beyond doubt. And the same year, Lifetime – the channel that had whitewashed the Aaliyah-Kelly relationship in *The Princess of R&B* – broadcast the documentary *Surviving R. Kelly*, which showed Kelly's victims speaking in their own words. It was, finally, incontrovertible public testimony of a lifetime of predation. Kelly's label abandoned him – although it could do so easily, knowing that his most profitable days were already gone.[83]

Police resumed investigations into Kelly, and in September 2021, he was found guilty of nine counts of racketeering and sex trafficking in relation to six women. Five of them testified; the sixth was Aaliyah.[84] Partly because the evidence was by now overwhelming, partly because of the changed public attitude towards grooming and sexual abuse, Kelly's old tactics of sowing confusion and slandering his victims were no longer so effective. The trial heard testimony that he had been seen having sex with Aaliyah when she was thirteen or fourteen.[85] Perhaps most horribly, Kelly's tour manager testified that he had conspired with Kelly to obtain the fake ID that enabled Kelly and Aaliyah to marry. There was no romance here. Kelly was moved not by love but by fear that she was pregnant. The marriage was intended to circumvent the risk of a statutory rape charge while obtaining an abortion.[86] The scene described was a bleak one: adult men deciding together how to deal with the problematic body of a child. Kelly was sentenced to thirty years in prison. In February 2023, a Chicago jury convicted him of a further six charges. The woman who had once denied being in the so-called 'pee tape' was among the victims who testified. She had been fourteen when Kelly filmed himself abusing her.[87]

Aaliyah's immaculate self-possession in her later career was, in part, the response of someone carefully managing the repercussions from a situation in her early life when she had held no power at all. In the end, it's difficult to be sure exactly how much control she truly clawed back. One of the revelations of Iandoli's 2021 book was that Aaliyah may not even have been awake when the plane crashed. A witness reported that Aaliyah had been anxious about the flight and was refusing to board the plane; eventually, a member of her entourage gave her a pill, which put her to sleep, and she was carried aboard unconscious – a human puppet after all.[88] Her death that day shielded her from the brutal scrutiny noughties fame would have inflicted: she never had to contend with public recognition that she had been the child bride of the man in the pee tape.

But it also denied her the restitution that MeToo might have delivered, when that movement belatedly provided a framework for describing her victimisation. For some, the decades it had taken for Kelly to receive some measure of justice were evidence of the institutional disregard for black girls and of the bias of MeToo towards white women's suffering; but they were also evidence of the might that celebrity afforded men, both black and white.

On 20 August 2021, almost exactly twenty years after she died, Aaliyah's Atlantic albums were finally released to Spotify. They sound, still, exquisitely futuristic and blissfully sensual – they sound like the work of an artist who had more to say. Her death cut off not just the possibility of more music, and of all the normal experiences she might have lived to have, but also of her ever speaking for herself about what was done to her when she was a girl.

The February after she died, *Queen of the Damned* was posthumously released. In it, the Vampire Lestat (played by Stuart Townsend) awakes from his tomb and decides to become a rock star. As one of the 'new gods' of entertainment, he realises he will be able to pursue his human victims openly. The more Lestat announces his own depravity, the more his fans indulge him. The film is a laughably poor mush of nu-metal clichés, and Aaliyah is hopelessly adrift in the B-movie camp; it is very far from the legacy she deserved.[89] But its story hits on one of the grotesque truths of the entertainment industry. As Kelly could have taught Lestat, there's no better way for a male performer to deflect from his predatory nature than by ostentatiously announcing to the world that he's a monster.

5

Janet: Indecency

'It was very embarrassing for me'

It had taken Janet Jackson three decades as an entertainment professional to be invited to perform at the *Super Bowl XXXVIII Halftime Show* in 2004, and it would take less than one second for her career to be derailed in one of the greatest disgraces of the Upskirt Decade. A Super Bowl performance was – and remains – one of the pinnacles of a music career. Audiences expect as much action from the break as they do from the game. So do broadcasters, who, by the noughties, had learned that a lacklustre halftime would see viewers drifting away and advertisers reconsidering the exceptional prices that a Super Bowl spot commanded. For artists, the Super Bowl doesn't offer great financial rewards: acts are paid union rate, and cover most of the staging costs themselves.[1] And it's high-pressure: a whole stadium-standard performance must be crammed into less than thirty minutes, including the time taken to assemble and dismantle the stage.[2] But for all the expense and all the risk, acts still want to do it, because the Super Bowl puts you into the living rooms of America and announces you as the biggest thing in music that year.

Viewing habits were changing in the early noughties. An increase in the number of channels and the emergence of digital recording devices like TiVo meant that television was becoming less of a mass experience and more reflective of individual taste. 'I think there's something going on in the world that's very profound,' Michael Powell, chair of the Federal Communications Commission, the agency that governs broadcasting in the United States, had said in 2003. 'We're moving to a world of incredible intimacy in mass media.' But he added that the Super Bowl remained a special case, a TV event the whole nation wanted to watch and to watch at the same time.[3] Ninety million viewers would see Janet perform live on 2 February 2004. That's ninety million people who would be exposed to her music – some for the first time – and who might become fans and ultimately buy her records or go to her concerts. In the end, it was ninety million who saw her bared breast in a fumbled costume reveal that transformed her from the personification of sexual empowerment into a global avatar of indecency and inadvertently changed the way we consume media for ever. This is Nipplegate.

If it hadn't been for the boob, Janet would probably be remembered as the best bit of an otherwise sketchy halftime. In an interview with MTV before the show, her choreographer had promised 'some shocking moments'.[4] (The halftime show was produced by MTV, which was owned by media conglomerate Viacom, which had recently been given permission by the FCC to purchase CBS, the channel that was broadcasting the Super Bowl in 2004.[5] Cross-promotion was one of the benefits of consolidation.) But as the performance approached its end, there was little sign of its delivering anything that would be memorable for the right reasons. It had started with a short film for MTV's 'Choose or Lose' voter registration campaign (2004 being an election year). Then Jessica Simpson – another Viacom asset, thanks to her reality show, *Newlyweds: Nick and Jessica*, on MTV – appeared, shouting, 'Houston! Choose to party!' A marching band played 'I Like the Way You Move' by OutKast, and then Janet did her first number, 'All for You', wearing a pirate-inspired costume designed by Alexander McQueen.[6] Her glossy black bustier had nods to fetishism, with a built-in choker and red lace trimming the cups, but the outfit was remarkably modest by the stripper chic standards of female singers in the noughties, thanks to three-quarter-length trousers and full sleeves. It was also modest by Janet's own standards, considering she had once appeared on the cover of *Rolling Stone* with only a pair of male hands covering her breasts.

After this, though, things got a bit more ragged. Two years earlier, the *Super Bowl Halftime Show* had consisted of a stripped-down, heartfelt performance by U2 in front of a screen showing the names of the victims of 9/11. That had ended with a costume reveal of a more dignified kind, as Bono opened his jacket to show the Stars and Stripes on the lining.[7] Now, in 2004, all that sombreness had been left well behind. Following Janet, P. Diddy (the name Sean Combs, previously known as Puff Daddy, was using at the time) and Nelly came onstage and delivered a breakneck mashup, involving crotch tweaking and dancers who whipped their skirts off on command. This was followed by Kid Rock thrusting his hips while roaring his own name and wearing Old Glory as a poncho. For more conservatively minded audience members, this was uncomfortable viewing – and it was, of course, about to get much worse. Janet returned to the stage for 'Rhythm Nation', a 1989 hit with a political edge suited to the Choose or Lose theme; and then Justin Timberlake emerged through the floor, and the two began a performance of his song 'Rock Your Body'.

A few months earlier, Timberlake had made headlines for his awkward reaction when his ex-girlfriend Britney kissed Madonna onstage at the MTV VMAs; now, with Janet, he was the young up-and-comer receiving the eroticised approval of an industry icon. Not just any icon, but an actual Jackson – which had particular resonance for Timberlake. In leaving the boy band 'NSync to forge a solo career, he was plainly hoping to emulate Janet's big brother Michael's passage from stand-out member of the Jackson 5 to King of Pop.[8] Timberlake's sexy falsetto and slick dancing were obvious points of contact with Michael Jackson, but maybe even more important was the way both artists combined influences from traditionally white and traditionally black genres. Michael Jackson started in Motown and headed towards pop; Timberlake began in the Max Martin pop factory and had since embraced elements of hip-hop and R&B.

Meanwhile, Janet was thirty-seven and had been in show business for thirty years, which made her the definition of established. She was the youngest of the nine Jackson children, all of whom had been cultivated for fame by their father, Joe, and she had undoubtedly had an easier time getting into entertainment than her siblings had. As boys growing up in Gary, Indiana, the Jackson 5 had played the segregated nightclubs of the sixties alongside 'bad comedians, cocktail organists, and strippers,' as Michael wrote in his autobiography, *Moonwalk*.[9] Janet got her start participating in her brothers' variety show to a mixed audience in Las Vegas,[10] and when she was ten, she was cast in the CBS sitcom *Good Times* – one of a raft of black-led prime-time programmes in the seventies that showed America a more inclusive version of itself.[11] For the older Jackson siblings, their first memories were of living crammed into a three-room house in Gary.[12] Janet's were of their 'English Tudor home' just outside Los Angeles.[13] She also got fewer paternal beatings than her brothers. 'We'd perform for him and he'd critique us,' recalled Michael. 'If you messed up, you got hit, sometimes with a belt, sometimes with a switch.'[14] (In later life, Michael said that simply seeing his father made him physically sick, to which Joe responded, with his typical fatherly tenderness, 'He regurgitates all the way to the bank.')[15] Janet received gentler treatment. 'I believe that by the time I was born my parents had grown tired of disciplining,' she remembered in her own autobiography, *True You*.[16]

Nonetheless, her father did hit her at least once, and she did fear him. His will was the rule in the Jackson family: when she was fourteen, he decided that, regardless of her own prefer-ence for acting, it would be more profitable for her to pursue a singing career.[17] (This reorientation may have been influ-enced by Michael's having fired their father as his manager around the same time, leaving Joe short of a musical prod-igy to hawk.)[18] Joe arranged a contract for Janet with A&M Records; the result was two lacklustre pop-soul albums that left almost no mark on the charts at all.[19] After that, Janet took charge. She cut professional ties with her father and moved to Minneapolis to work with Prince associates Jimmy Jam and Terry Lewis. The album they made together was called *Control*. This wasn't Janet's first gesture towards establishing her independence – in 1984, at eighteen, she had secretly mar-ried fellow singer James DeBarge; the marriage was annulled after a year when Janet, in her own account, became aware of the scale of DeBarge's drug problems[20] – but it was the first gesture to succeed. *Control* went to No. 1 when it was released in 1986. That transformed Janet from the underperforming baby of her family to one of the few artists who came close to matching Michael's stupendous sales and cultural currency. *Control*'s title was a statement of intent: this was a woman who ran her own show, both creatively and sexually. Sex was part of the way she showed she wasn't her daddy's little girl any more.

So was politics. In a *Rolling Stone* interview with her, journalist David Ritz compared Janet's socially charged 1989 album, *Janet Jackson's Rhythm Nation 1814*, to Marvin Gaye's civil rights classic *What's Going On*. Her lyrics addressed poverty, violence and prejudice; but her presence alone was a political statement in its own right. Music in the United States had historically been as segregated as the nation itself. In the forties, *Billboard* compiled separate charts for 'pop' (music made by white artists and marketed to white audiences) and 'race' (music made by black artists and marketed to black audiences) records. By the mid-twentieth century, the latter category had been updated from 'race' to 'R&B', but the distinction remained.[21] When MTV launched in 1981, black artists received negligible airplay. Janet and Michael were among the artists who broke that informal apartheid. Their impeccable grasp of visuals made them irresistible to the music channels, and so did the imperatives of the market: the United States had a growing black middle class, while white audiences that had come of age since the repeal of Jim Crow laws were now open to what previous generations might have seen as 'musical miscegenation'. Janet was a true crossover star. *Rhythm Nation 1814*, wrote Joseph Vogel in a twenty-fifth-anniversary appreciation, 'positioned a multifaceted, dynamic black woman as a leader, as someone whose ideas, experiences and emotions mattered'.[22] On the title track, Janet sings of wanting to 'break the color lines', and she did precisely that with her career.

Nonetheless, it was the sex part of Janet's image that had dominated in the years after *Rhythm Nation 1814*. In the same

Rolling Stone interview where he compared her to Marvin Gaye (for the issue with the iconic topless cover), David Ritz also lingered over her body, remarking on her 'snappy booty' and 'sensual mouth'.* Was the sex all a publicity ploy? he asked her. No, she replied, it was absolutely genuine: 'Sex has been an important part of me for several years. But it just hasn't blossomed publicly until now.'[23] Janet wanted the public to understand that her sexiness was never a put-on, never manufactured; it was all authentic self-expression. (Later, she would say that the sexualised version of herself had been at least partly constructed by her then husband, René Elizondo Jr, the man who provided the hands for the *Rolling Stone* cover and with whom things had ended so badly, she wrote in her autobiography, that she was legally prohibited from discussing him.)[24] By the time she made *All for You* in 2001, the 'blossoming' had reached full bloom. The song 'Would You Mind' included the lyrics 'Kiss you, suck you, taste you, ride you / Feel you deep inside me.' This was so provocative that some retailers felt compelled to add parental advisory stickers. (Eventually, her label, Virgin, issued a version with the offending track cut.)[25] The album was banned outright in Singapore, on the grounds that it was 'not acceptable to our society'.[26]† None of this outrage did anything to stop *All for You* from becoming Janet's fifth No. 1 album in a row.

But by the time she performed at the Super Bowl in 2004, *All for You* was three years in the past. There were questions about her relevance. Thirty-seven was considered perilously mature in an industry that worshipped youth to the point of having established a virginity cult around Britney. So, it was

---

* Janet can't have been very offended by this, as she would later co-write her autobiography with Ritz.
† The same year, I visited Singapore and bought a copy of *The Singles* by Bikini Kill, whose track 'New Radio' includes the line 'Let's wipe our cum on my parents' bed'. The censors had probably taken a day off.

important for Janet to show that she still had it, and playing Mrs. Robinson to the world's hottest young heartthrob seemed like a very effective way to do that.

Timberlake was dressed more conservatively than Janet when he arrived onstage, in slacks, T-shirt and jacket. It made him a slightly incongruous addition to her show – the plumber on a call to a fetish club. Aesthetic mismatch aside, they looked good together: two beautiful people flirting in the middle of the biggest party on earth. He pursued her, she strutted and teased, and as the song reached its climax, they stood together on a riser at the centre of the stage, in full view of the stadium, in full view of the world. 'Talk to me, boy,' she cooed at him, and he sang a promise back to her: 'Bet I'll have you naked by the end of this song.' Then he reached across her torso, grabbed the right cup of her bustier, and pulled. And this is the moment when something seemed to go wrong. In the dress rehearsal, Janet had worn a detachable skirt for Timberlake to snatch away, but no one had been happy with the result, and the reveal was taken out of the choreography. Following that, Janet's costume designer had spent the day of the performance making hurried alterations to the outfit, and just before showtime, Timberlake had been summoned to Janet's dressing room for a last-minute conference. No one has ever disclosed what was said at that meeting.[27]

What ought to have happened, according to Janet's spokesman after the event, was that the outer fabric of the bustier should have detached, leaving the red inner layer in place.[28] What actually happened was this: latex and lace came away together in Justin's hand, and Janet was left, breast out, in the full glare of the cameras – a 'wardrobe malfunction', in the language both her camp and Timberlake used in their initial apologies.[29] Only a sunburst-shaped nipple shield covered her – bathetically, Nipplegate did not even involve a visible nipple, and if anything, that made it worse, because it implied premeditation. But Janet's face suggested this was not quite how the performance had been planned. She looked down at her chest and appeared immediately stricken, while the show ploughed grimly on around her. At the back of the stage, oblivious to the world-changing flash that had just taken place, an array of pyrotechnics went off, while Janet clutched a hand – too late – across her breast. The timing was excruciatingly, appallingly perfect. In the background, a burst of 'Choose or Lose' branding appeared on jumbo screens to remind viewers they should also be voters, and then the sponsor's chirpy message came in: 'Thank you for watching the AOL Topspeed Halftime Show!'[30] It was the perfect punchline to the moment's horrible comedy. Of course, it had to be sponsored by an internet service provider, because the internet was the third reason – along with the media consolidation that had created this riot of brand synergy and the fact that it was an election year – that Nipplegate became the nightmare it did for Janet.

Two days after the Super Bowl, the BBC reported, 'Janet Jackson's breast has become the most searched-for image in net history.' A spokesman for the search engine Lycos said that Nipplegate had received sixty times as many searches as the Paris Hilton sex tape, eighty times as many as Britney Spears, and more even than the previous record for most searches in a twenty-four-hour period, which, according to the article, had been held by 9/11. People didn't just want to see Nipplegate once; they wanted to see it again and again and again. The flash, the fireworks, the thrill of outrage. Flash, fireworks, outrage. On and on and on. TiVo revealed that it was the most replayed moment in the service's existence, and it drove a flurry of sign-ups.[31] In a time when it was hardly difficult to find pictures of breasts to look at, there was something irresistible about this one breast in particular – and about the whole concept of the 'wardrobe malfunction', an expression that immediately entered the lexicon. It was a euphemism of delicious pomposity and built-in irony. A lot of people believed the costume had functioned exactly as intended. 'Gosh, what a happy coincidence ... that her costume just happened to have a breakaway bra cup,' snarked *Washington Post* TV columnist Lisa de Moraes.[32] It was hard to take Janet's claim to be a victim of pure accident seriously, not only because the moment appeared to have been planned in some degree (as Janet's eventual explanation about the costume confirmed), and not only because she was renowned for sexual provocation, but also because the teasing display of female flesh was in fashion in the noughties. Alexander McQueen, the designer of Janet's Super Bowl costume, had been pioneering the approach in his catwalk shows since the nineties: waistbands cut so low they showed hipbones and ass cracks, bodices slashed open to reveal almost everything bar the nipples, hemlines higher than the crotch.[33]

This was dazzling, provocative stuff, and it had crossed over into the style mainstream. It was also stuff that, when translated to bodies with more flesh than a size-zero model and situations with more movement than a catwalk, was perilously liable to go wrong. The cover of the October 2004 issue of *Hustler* was blazoned with the line 'Lil' Kim's Private Parts', advertising a spread of pictures of the rapper onstage, her mini-dress riding up and her vulva clearly visible thanks to the camera aiming directly up her skirt.[34] (The website ContactMusic referred to this, of course, as a 'wardrobe malfunction', although it might have been more accurate to call it a photographer violation.)[35] Like Paris's sex tape, such moments fell into the compelling overlap between 'she was asking for it' and 'she didn't want this'. The exposure was only possible because the woman had chosen to wear something exposing; it was only titillating because we, the viewers, got to see something that she hadn't chosen to expose. Not only was it acceptable to peer right up Lil' Kim, but peering right up her was a just punishment for her courting of indecency in the first place. In the case of Janet's breast, all this was heightened by the fact that she had spent her whole adult career seducing her audience while asserting strict boundaries around what she would show. There was an intoxicating joy in seeing those defences fall.

If Janet and Timberlake had been looking for attention, they'd certainly got it – and Timberlake's first comment to the media suggested that this had indeed been the intention. 'Hey, man,' he blithely said to *Access Hollywood* in a post-show interview. 'We love giving ya'll something to talk about.'[36] Janet, however, had left the stadium immediately after the performance, without speaking to anyone, and would not address what happened until the following Monday. This left a vacuum where speculation and shaming would flourish.[37] The release of her new single, 'Just a Little While', was brought forward immediately following the Super Bowl, heightening the impression that Nipplegate had been a publicity stunt, though her representative said the rescheduling was simply because the song had leaked to the internet.[38] However, there was one problem with the theory that Janet and Justin had done it for the coverage: none of the coverage was good.

CBS was 'deluged' with angry phone calls during the broadcast, according to a report in *USA Today*.[39] The reveal had happened 'completely without our knowledge', said a spokesperson for the network. 'We are angry and embarrassed.' The feeling spilled over onto CBS's own news website, which published an article headlined 'Janet's Bared Breast a PR Stunt?' The copy made it clear that the question mark was very much for show only. 'Gone are the days when a powerful performance is all that's needed to deliver a watercooler moment,' it fumed. 'Nowadays, a barely there outfit, same-sex smooching or foul language – and now, a flash of nudity – are what's required to get America talking.' The network was presented as the hapless victim of a tacky celebrity's relentless hunger for relevance.[40]

MTV also disavowed responsibility, calling the incident 'unrehearsed, unplanned, completely unintentional'. The NFL said it was 'extremely disappointed',[41] and that dismay was doubtless aggravated by AOL demanding the return of some of the $10 million it had paid to sponsor the halftime show. The original deal had been for AOL to rebroadcast the performance to its twenty-five million subscribers. The fact that so many people clearly wanted to see it would have made this a bargain for AOL, except that one of the service's key features was the inclusion of strict parental controls, which was hardly compatible with Janet's unleashed boob.[42] Everyone wanted to look at Janet, but no one could afford to be associated with her. And Nipplegate seemed likely to grow even more costly for those implicated, as the FCC launched an immediate investigation with the stated intent of imposing the maximum possible fine on CBS. (The eventual penalty was $550,000.[43]) 'I am outraged at what I saw during the halftime show of the Super Bowl,' said chairman Michael Powell in a statement. 'Like millions of Americans, my family and I gathered around the television for a celebration. Instead, that celebration was tainted by a classless, crass and deplorable stunt. Our nation's children, parents and citizens deserve better.'[44] Janet's breast was not, apparently, the kind of 'incredible intimacy in mass media' that Powell was excited by. Eventually, the FCC would receive more than 540,000 complaints about the incident, making it the most-complained-about moment in US television history.[45]

Nipplegate made Powell and Janet into antagonists (by his choosing rather than hers), so it's easy to overlook how much the two had in common. Like Janet, Powell represented the kinds of possibilities available to black Americans who grew up after the civil rights movement. He was born three years before her – although, being a man in politics rather than a woman in show business, he could still be described (with only moderate sarcasm) as a '38-year-old wunderkind' when he took the post of FCC chairman in 2001[46] – and, like Janet, he understood both the benefits and the burdens that came with a famous name. His father, Colin, had gone from being one of the United States' most respected military figures to a political career in the Republican Party, serving as the country's first black secretary of state under George W. Bush from 2001 to 2005.[47] This left his son, Michael, uncomfortably vulnerable to the charge of benefiting from nepotism, and there were rumours that family friend John McCain had lobbied for his original appointment to the FCC. Michael Powell shrugged off such efforts to diminish him, saying, 'Sure, go ahead and underestimate me. I don't have time for negative people.'[48]

By 2004, though, Powell had made it clear that he stood on his own merits. The FCC had responsibility for telecoms infrastructure as well as broadcasting, and the digital revolution in both sectors meant that Powell now occupied one of the most significant roles in American public life. 'The FCC is the EPA [Environmental Protection Agency] of the twenty-first century,' said media commentator Clay Shirky. 'Americans spend more of their lives in the media landscape than in the natural one, putting the FCC in charge of the environment most of us really inhabit.'[49] And Powell was intent on reinventing that environment. The policy of supporting consolidation in the media industry, with the theory that this would promote competition, had begun under Clinton: in 2000, the FCC had approved Viacom's acquisition of CBS for $30 billion, giving the resulting company control of a 35 per cent share of the broadcasting market.[50] As chair under the free-market-friendly oversight of a Republican government, Powell made deregulation his personal mission, and as a former lawyer, he was considered to have the skills to bring it off. He was also genuinely excited by new technology, enthusing in interviews about TiVo and the potential of the internet. Some observers suspected that Powell saw the FCC as a stepping stone to the same high office his father enjoyed – there was speculation that he might run for governor of Virginia;[51] or perhaps even hope to become attorney general, if Bush won a second term.[52] He was a powerful man, and now Janet had his full attention in the worst possible way.

She would carry Nipplegate alone. People made jokes about Timberlake's imperviousness – he was called the 'Teflon man' (because nothing seemed to stick),[53] and 'the Houdini of pop' (because he got out of everything)[54] – but there was never any serious prospect of his being held responsible. In press coverage, he became mysteriously invisible. 'What Janet Jackson did was bizarre, deliberately flopping out of her costume like that,' wrote Tony Kornheiser in the *Washington Post*, as though the breast were capable of voluntary movement entirely by itself.[55] All blame accrued to the woman who had been exposed rather than to the man who had exposed her. CBS's first response was to ask Janet, and only Janet, to make a statement claiming sole responsibility for the incident.

Which she did: 'The decision to have a costume reveal at the end of my halftime show performance was made after final rehearsals. MTV was completely unaware of it. It was not my intention that it go as far as it did. I apologize to anyone offended – including the audience, MTV, CBS, and the NFL.'[56] This unambiguous mea culpa still didn't go far enough: the next day, she, and not Timberlake, was asked to make a video reiterating her individual guilt.[57] Even that didn't satisfy. A few days after the Super Bowl, both she and Timberlake were scheduled to appear at the Grammys, also broadcast by CBS. He performed as planned and received an award, giving a tearful apology for the Super Bowl incident during his speech; she was disinvited.[58] (Perhaps even more gallingly, one of the other attendees was R. Kelly, who had been indicted on child pornography charges two years earlier and was still awaiting trial.) Janet had become so toxic that Disney World even removed a statue of Mickey Mouse dressed in her Rhythm Nation costume.[59] Apparently, just the suggestion of her clothes was enough to corrupt innocent eyes with the idea of what was underneath.

Even taking into account the ill-advised nature of attempting a high-stakes costume reveal at the Super Bowl, something about Nipplegate made it shocking out of all proportion with the scale of the incident itself. And though Justin was erased from the reaction, it's worth asking how significant he was to the furore or, more specifically, how significant it was that he was white and Janet was black. The far-right website VDARE certainly noticed: it called Nipplegate 'interracial and brazenly so'. 'Breaking down the sexual barriers between the races is a major weapon of cultural destruction,' the site fulminated, 'because it means the dissolution of the cultural boundaries that define breeding and the family and, ultimately, the transmission and survival of the culture itself.'[60]

This was extreme bigotry, but the taboo against interracial relationships persisted in the mainstream, too. Interracial marriage was legalised in the United States in 1967, and by 2003, it had the approval of 70 per cent of the public – meaning 30 per cent did not approve.[61] When *Romeo Must Die* was released in 2000, a kiss between Aaliyah and Jet Li was cut after test audiences reacted badly to a romance involving a black woman and an Asian man.[62] The same year as Nipplegate, Gwen Stefani's debut solo album featured a duet with André 3000 of OutKast called 'Long Way to Go', which samples Martin Luther King and presents attraction between a black man and a white woman as the next frontier in civil rights: 'When snow hits the asphalt / Cold looks and bad talk come,' the two sing together.

After Nipplegate, Janet especially but also Justin were more marked by their race. For both, crossover status was diminished – and for Janet, it was almost destroyed. Her work in the remainder of the Upskirt Decade was mostly targeted at black audiences, whose affection for her was resilient in the face of efforts to make her untouchable. She appeared in populist black auteur Tyler Perry's 2007 all-black ensemble film *Why Did I Get Married?* and in its 2010 sequel. There was a toll on Timberlake as well, albeit a less dramatic one. In 2005, VH1 broadcast a comedy series by the five-man multiracial collective Ego Trip, called *Race-O-Rama*. One episode, summarised by the *New York Times*, dealt with white people who had achieved 'honorary black' status: 'the singer Justin Timberlake, who a scant two years ago held honorary soul-brother status, has since had his ghetto pass revoked for abandoning Janet Jackson during their Super Bowl brouhaha'.[63] The colour lines Janet had once broken seemed to have been firmly reasserted in Nipplegate's wake.

When she appeared on *Letterman* nearly two months after the Super Bowl, Janet expressed her astonishment that 'this little breast' had caused such a commotion. But the problem was that her breast had been unleashed into a raging moral panic. At the time of the Super Bowl broadcast, there was increasing pressure on the FCC to impose penalties on indecent broadcasts – one of its first acts after Michael Powell became chairman had been to levy a $7,000 fine on a radio station for playing a censored version of an Eminem song[64] – but there was also uncertainty over how 'indecency' should be defined. During the 2003 Golden Globes broadcast on Fox, Bono had celebrated receiving an award with the words 'This is really, really fucking brilliant!' The show was not time-delayed, so there was no opportunity to cut away or bleep his profanity. There were complaints, but the FCC investigation determined that an adjectival use of the F-word did not attain the legal standard of 'patently offensive as measured by contemporary community standards for the broadcast medium'. It was a widely mocked verdict, but for linguist John T. McWhorter, writing at the end of 2003, this was merely the perverse but inevitable product of a United States in which the counterculture had won.

America's executive class in the noughties consisted not only of straights in suits, but also of people like Judy McGrath. McGrath was president of the MTV Networks Group within Viacom and had responsibility for MTV and VH1. Under her leadership, the channels had moved successfully into reality TV with shows like *The Osbournes* and *Newlyweds: Nick and Jessica*; she'd also overseen the evolution of the shock value aesthetic that underpinned the Super Bowl show. McGrath told interviewers that she was a Radiohead fan, and her office decor included a crucifix-topped font, which she used as a candy dish.[65] McGrath was a Baby Boomer: she had been a teenager in the sixties and seventies, when tuning in and dropping out were the highest imperatives, and her taste reflected that. By the noughties, people like her were the architects of the culture, and taboo-smashing was mainstream. 'Like it or not,' wrote McWhorter in the *Washington Post*, 'we'd better get used to it. We are today a society that elevates giving the finger to "the man" to a sign of enlightenment. So, there are bound to be more such rulings, and at the end of the day, we are best advised to fasten our seat belts and accept them.' US media was regulated by the Communications Act of 1934, which had established the FCC. McWhorter continued:

This law, penned by people born in Victorian America, decreed to be publicly inappropriate language that 'describes or depicts sexual or excretory activities or organs.' But this only leads to a question: If we are now so comfortable acknowledging, discussing and even displaying our most private 'parts' in public, then precisely what is the logical justification for refraining from using words that connote what we do with them?

After all, this is an America where the actress Tea Leoni purrs in TV Guide about having 'mated often' with an ex-lover, academics celebrate the profanity in rap music as visionary, sensitive adults are warmly fascinated by Eminem, R-rated movies are common coin among teenagers, unmarried celebrity couples casually announce the expectation of babies, young men show their underwear above their belts, and young women in 'low-rider' jeans display a netherly fissure celebrated in some places as 'the new cleavage.'[66]

Janet's flash, then, was arguably perfectly acceptable according to the 'community standards' of noughties media. Others, however, were not prepared to resign themselves so easily to such degradation. The Parents Television Council (PTC) had been set up in 1995 with the mission of 'leading the national effort to restore responsibility and decency to the entertainment industry'.[67] The organisation had a convoluted backstory, having originally been a project within the explicitly rightwing Media Research Center. The MRC had been founded to counter an alleged liberal bias in the media, which, it claimed, was undermining 'traditional American values'. In the Media Research Center's worldview, the entertainment industry was no more than a vast propaganda machine, seducing Americans into an unholy tolerance for abortion, homosexuality and sex outside marriage[68] – as well as spreading the 'media myth' of global warming.[69] (The MRC received funding from oil giant ExxonMobil.[70])

Even after the PTC was spun off as a separate entity, it was unclear how much independence it truly had – the two organisations shared premises, and the PTC's president was the Media Research Center's founder. But while the MRC was a traditional lobbying group and explicitly Republican-aligned, the PTC was non-partisan (formally, at least) and presented itself as a grassroots campaign. And while the internet was a relentless source of turpitude, it was also a critical tool for the PTC. Members didn't need to pay a fee, merely register via the website to receive outraged bulletins and calls to action. The PTC's weapons were constant vigilance and mass complaint campaigns. It employed 'entertainment analysts' to watch hundreds of hours of potentially indecent television and meticulously log each possible infraction.[71] This was necessary because of that 'incredible intimacy in mass media' of which Michael Powell had spoken. In an environment where viewers with digital recorders could conveniently watch only the programmes they wanted at the times they chose, and where much of the most concerning material was on subscriber-only cable, you couldn't rely on audiences to simply stumble across degenerate shows like *Sex and the City* or plastic surgery drama *Nip/Tuck*. They would have to be directed to the offence. This meant that the PTC was in practice a Streisand Effect generator: the more it objected to something's existence, the more attention it drew towards it.

But despite a wealth of potentially revolting material to choose from, the PTC had struggled to pick its targets effectively: a campaign against World Wrestling Entertainment for allegedly encouraging fatal violence between children ended with the PTC and Media Research Center paying WWE $3.5 million in damages and making a lengthy public apology.[72] (WWE got its revenge on-screen, too, parodying the PTC as a stable of villains under the name 'Right to Censor'.)[73] For the PTC, then, Nipplegate was a gift. Here was something legitimately gratuitous, apparently premeditated and broadcast live on network television to a vast audience that included millions of children. The same day as the Super Bowl (and a day before Janet broke her silence), the PTC released a floridly disgusted 'e-alert', calling Nipplegate 'obviously scripted' and rejecting all apologies from the broadcasters involved. 'To those who insist that a parent's sole remedy for such filth is to simply "turn the channel," we ask this: Does this mean that parents shouldn't allow their children to watch football games anymore?'[74]

The alert directed PTC supporters to help by 'forwarding this message to everyone in your address book' and linked to an automated complaint form. All an affronted party had to do was fill out their details and click the Sign-and-Submit button to dispatch a carefully phrased email to all five members of the FCC.[75] Prior to the noughties, expressing your displeasure had at least required the minimal commitment of writing a letter and walking to a postbox. Now, thanks to the internet, you could merge yourself with the mass voice of the moral majority with just a few taps of your keyboard. It's not clear from contemporary reports whether the FCC made any effort to disaggregate multiple complaints from the same sender, and even if it did, the fact that the e-alert urged the interested to canvass their friends was a sign that not all the outrage over the Super Bowl was an organic response from the audience. A technologically savvy chair like Powell might, perhaps, have appreciated this. Instead, he identified himself wholly with the PTC agenda. 'As a parent, I share the displeasure and fatigue of millions of Americans about the erosion of common decency standards on television,' he testified to the FCC. 'Indeed, the Commission has already begun wielding our sword in several important respects.'[76] This embrace of paternalism contradicted Powell's well-established deregulatory credentials. But the Super Bowl incident required a strong response from him because, although he didn't openly say as much, it was the realisation of some conservatives' worst fears about his media consolidation project.

There had been opposition to Powell's reforms from, as one might expect, the anti-corporate left and from musicians who worried that a lack of competition in radio would make it harder for smaller or more controversial acts to get airplay. The latter was not an idle concern, as the blacklisting of the Dixie Chicks in 2003 had shown.[77] But there had been resistance from Powell's own side of the aisle, too, from those who feared the effects on free speech as media ownership became concentrated within a tiny cluster of companies.[78] One of the Dixie Chicks' most principled defenders had been Republican senator John McCain – the same John McCain who had supported Powell at the start of his political career and who would now become one of the most powerful critics of Powell's reforms, which he saw as inadvertently enabling the suppression of minority views. 'It's a strong argument about what media concentration has the possibility of doing,' said McCain to Cumulus Media's chairman during a Senate hearing. 'If someone else offends you, and you decide to censor those people, my friend, the erosion of our 1st Amendment is in progress.'[79]

Others on the right, though, were animated less by high-minded anxiety for the Constitution and more by self-interested fear that their own viewpoints could be squeezed out of the public square. As the existence of the Media Research Center showed, there was a persistent belief on the right that liberals dominated the airwaves. That belief may or may not have been based in reality, and it may or may not have been advanced in good faith, but if cultural conservatives wanted an example of their monopoly nightmare in action, Viacom was it. Take MTV's Choose or Lose campaign. In theory, it was a non-partisan voter registration drive. In practice – and the inclusion of token Republican Kid Rock in the *Super Bowl Halftime Show* notwithstanding – the constituencies MTV reached were inevitably younger and more liberal. Democrats, in other words. 'MTV serves as the Democrats' main youth outreach program,' griped conservative commentator Jonah Goldberg.[80] Other Viacom output was even more explicit in its allegiance. On Comedy Central, Jon Stewart's *The Daily Show* delivered left-leaning topical humour, and the politics were at least as important as the jokes. 'It would be no over-statement to say that, in the pre-Obama years ... the leader of Democratic resistance was Jon Stewart, and he was holding rallies weeknights at 11 p.m. Eastern on Comedy Central,' wrote Devin Gordon in a 2022 retrospective on Stewart's career.[81] In its e-alert on the Super Bowl, the PTC had explic-itly mentioned the corporate ties between MTV, CBS and Viacom.[82] Powell had delivered immense power to Viacom, and with it, Viacom had beamed a naked breast straight into the eyes of America's children. 'Values' were pushed forward as an issue for the forthcoming presidential elections, and as a Republican politician – with, perhaps, ambitions for a cabinet position – Powell had a strong incentive to answer his critics on the right.[83] Adopting an uncompromising line on decency generally and Janet specifically may have been a way of doing just that.

Powell wasn't the only person with an interest in making a target of Janet. Les Moonves, the CEO of CBS, publicly expressed his determination to fight the fines imposed by the FCC and framed any decency crackdown as a violation of free speech.[84] But Nipplegate had been a vast and expensive embarrassment for both his network and for him personally, and Moonves had a reputation for being unforgiving to those he perceived to have wronged him. That included, according to a 2018 investigation by the *New Yorker*, multiple women who stated that they had rejected his overt sexual advances and found their careers at CBS stymied. (Moonves denied the allegations.)[85] It also apparently included Janet. According to reports, Moonves believed the wardrobe malfunction had been deliberate and that Janet had been insufficiently contrite, despite her two apologies, and directed MTV, VH1 and Viacom's radio stations (the largest group of stations in the United States) to blacklist her.[86] In the post-Nipplegate moral panic, competitor outlets followed suit. It was said to be Moonves who nixed Janet from the Grammys. There were claims that he was still intent on punishing her as late as 2011. When the publisher Simon and Schuster (owned by CBS) signed Janet's 2011 autobiography, *True You*, Moonves reportedly threatened to fire those responsible, railing, 'How the fuck did she slip through?'[87]

If the allegations against Moonves are true, the absurdity of the situation is difficult to comprehend. This is a man who, according to multiple women, forcibly kissed female employees and potential employees in the workplace, or put his hand up their skirt, or pinned them to the couch in his office – and who was simultaneously so distressed by a momentary, possibly inadvertent glimpse of Janet's breast that he attempted to choke her career. But as contradictory as these two positions appeared to be, they cohered around the principle that women's bodies should exist at the man's convenience; if those bodies offended by failing to comply with the man's demands, the man was entitled to apply whatever penalties were in his power to inflict.[88] Although her name was everywhere, Janet's music had been effectively suppressed, and the injury to her career was profound.

Even when she was able to appear in the media, the focus was all on the boob rather than the music. When she guested on *The Late Show with David Letterman*, ten minutes of a fifteen-minute interview were taken up with questions about what had really happened at the Super Bowl. Only after a blushing admission from Janet that 'it was supposed to kind of happen like that but ... I wasn't supposed to come out of it the way that I did' did Letterman ask about her new album, *Damita Jo*.[89] *Letterman* was broadcast by CBS, so there's a question here about why Moonves's alleged blacklisting didn't apply: perhaps it was supposed to be another stop on her apology tour, or perhaps Letterman himself was too powerful to be dictated to. He had a long history of flirtatious interviews with Janet that had made her a favourite guest on the show. His questioning, though, showed little sign of being tempered by their previous relationship, and it was painful to watch Janet – even at this late stage – continue to flounder over the subject. The damage of Nipplegate was compounded by her failure to own the incident with a brisk explanation and a shameless attitude. Whatever viewers remembered from the *Letterman* segment, it was more likely to inspire them to hit up a search engine than a record store.

Damita Jo was not a failure by the standards of most artists, given that it went to No. 2. But it was a failure by the standards Janet had set for herself. After five consecutive No. 1 albums, this was her first to miss the top of the charts since the bad old days of being ruled by her father, and given that she was under an $80 million contract with Virgin (a record-breaking deal when it was originally signed in 1996),[90] *Damita Jo* qualified as disastrous. Rather than reinvigorating Janet's sexualised image, the Super Bowl incident had fixed her in the public imagination as absurd and desperate: that fraction of a second of skin was broken down into static images for newspapers and blogs, replayed by disapproving news channels, looped at will on TiVo or the internet – and it defined her. The *New York Times* described her as 'aging' and criticised her for 'dusting off oldies' in her halftime show – unfair criticism because the Super Bowl has always been a venue to play the hits rather than a showcase for new material. (The year before, Sting had performed 'Message in a Bottle' as a duet with No Doubt, a song that was more than twenty years old.) But Janet's problem as a female artist was that she had been around long enough to have songs that could be regarded as oldies at all. Nearly two decades before the Super Bowl, she had made the transition from child star to adult that had recently caused Britney so much anguish. The move into middle age, however, would prove far more challenging for her.

Part of the blame for that must be put on *Damita Jo* itself. In 1998, Madonna had navigated the difficult passage into her forties as a pop star with the album *Ray of Light*, but it had taken a detour into movie musicals (*Evita*) followed by a musical reinvention (working with trip-hop producer William Orbit), a spiritual awakening (she publicly embraced the Jewish mystical tradition of Kabbalah) and an image do-over (having been barely dressed for much of the nineties, the video for *Ray of Light*'s lead single shows Madonna in a witchy full-length black gown; her signature look for the album campaign was double denim). But in 2004, Janet was delivering more of the same raunch she always had. With songs like 'Sexhibition', 'All Nite (Don't Stop)' and 'Moist', *Damita Jo* 'makes R. Kelly sound subtle', said the *Rolling Stone* review, perfectly if inadvertently articulating the double standard around women and sex.[91] The album wasn't totally without novelty – for one track, she brought in Kanye West, who was fresh enough then for the *Guardian* to describe him as 'new hip-hop wonderboy'[92] – but it consisted largely of more Jam and Lewis tracks, and it left the impression that their collaboration with Janet was finally exhausted. The biggest issue, though, was that the Super Bowl incident had done irreparable damage to Janet's image. It wasn't the indecency that was the problem – Janet could probably have worked with mere indecency – as much as the total failure of the Janet camp to establish an effective narrative around it. Her attackers called the incident a desperate calculation; Janet's account suggested it had been a chaotic error. Neither interpretation fitted with the confident sensuality Janet had projected since *Control*.

Nor did they fit with each other. The Janet of the record – the one singing 'relax, it's just sex' – and the Janet of the multiple abject apologies for showing some skin could not both exist in the same universe. 'One of the reasons it is difficult to believe in the "wardrobe malfunction" story is because, on the evidence of this album, Jackson is an extremely savvy operator,' wrote Alexis Petridis in the *Guardian* review (one of the most positive verdicts on the record).[93] Album Janet corroded Super Bowl Janet. But, noted Neil Strauss in his review for *Rolling Stone*, Super Bowl Janet also corroded Album Janet. 'As far as this CD is concerned, Janet Jackson's sin was not in exposing her breast during the Super Bowl. After all, the lady just wanted to show off a new piece of jewelry. The sin was in stripping down without titillating anyone. Overnight, she destroyed the highly sexualized persona she'd been cultivating for the last ten years and undermined *Damita Jo*, which is all about her sexuality.'[94] (Strauss would shortly become a sexual celebrity in his own way, by popularising the 'pick-up artist' subculture in his 2005 book *The Game*.) There was something besides the Super Bowl, though, that made sex into an unprecedented liability for Janet: her brother. Four months before the Super Bowl, Michael Jackson had been arrested on charges of child molestation. And while his fans remained steadfast in their support for him, the aura of something inappropriate about the Jacksons and sex persisted – and adhered to Janet. The BBC website review of *Damita Jo* opened by saying that, in light of Nipplegate, 'her troubled – that's putting it mildly – brother, Michael, looked positively wholesome in comparison'.[95] Posters on the fan website Janet Xone thought the same thing: 'She is just like her brother and has no respect for kids,' one fan wrote.[96]

Asked in the 2022 documentary *Janet* whether the allegations against Michael had affected her, Janet replied, 'Yeah ... guilty by association' (although she has never publicly accepted her brother's guilt).[97] Even without the Super Bowl incident, the Janet of 2004 – unacceptably old for a female pop star, tainted by her brother – would probably have struggled to convincingly sell sexiness, but Nipplegate fatally crystallised the problem with her persona in one endlessly replayable moment. After the Super Bowl, she was no longer the one in control. Instead, she was the perpetrator of a graceless stunt, the victim of a capricious media, an unwilling character in a morality play about the degradation of American values. After her 2006 album, *20 Y.O.*, proved as much of a commercial disappointment as *Damita Jo* had been, she parted ways with Virgin.[98] Her fall was complete.

Janet's body had been an asset to her career, but it had also been a problem to be solved, even before the Super Bowl. *Good Times* belonged to the seventies' halcyon period of liberalism in American TV,[99] but that did not necessarily make working on it a liberating experience for a girl of ten like Janet. 'Before production began,' she recalled in *True You*, 'I was told two things: I was fat and needed to slim down, and because I was beginning to develop, I needed to bind my breasts. In both cases the message was devastating – my body was wrong. The message was also clear – to be successful, I had to change the way I looked ... Each day of shooting, I went through the ordeal of having wide strips of gauze tied across my chest to hide the natural shape of my breasts. It was uncomfortable and humiliating.'[100] *True You* was published in 2011 and doesn't mention the Super Bowl: at this point, Nipplegate was a mortification that Janet wanted to leave in her past. Instead, the book frankly details a lifetime of body issues. Since she was a child, Janet had been told her figure was too obvious, too provocative, too *much*. A lifetime of being blamed for the way other people looked at her. Objectifying herself in her music and performances had been a means of reclaiming her body, and then the fever of prurience over Nipplegate had taken even that away from her.

Through the rest of the noughties, Janet belonged to that cadre of mostly female celebrities whose weight gain was a source of constant column inches. In 2006, TMZ wrote, 'Once upon a time, Janet was the good-looking Jackson. But after a nude sunbathing video made the internet rounds, people began to wonder if Justin Timberlake could even find that nipple ring now.'[101] Snicker, snicker. She had wanted attention, and now she would be scrutinised whether she liked it or not – and judged, too. *True You* is, as well as an autobiography, a diet book, in which Janet explained how she learned to 'eat better, exercise better, look better, feel better, be better'.[102] The little girl who got called fat found her apotheosis in embracing thinness. The book ended with a selection of weight-loss recipes from her personal chef.[103]

Nipplegate had left Janet irrevocably diminished. In the end, almost everyone who was in close contact to the scandal came off the worse for it to some extent. For Michael Powell, the consequences arrived almost immediately. His decency crusade proved to be a distraction from his beleaguered deregulation programme, and both faltered. By the summer of 2004, he was being criticised in the press for 'lacking basic political skills' – hardly a recommendation for higher office.[104] In December, Powell contributed an op-ed to the *New York Times* walking back his commitment to clearing up the airwaves. 'The high pitch at which many are discussing the enforcement of rules against indecency on television and radio is enough to pop an eardrum,' he wrote – which was true enough, even if the piece did fail to mention that, just a few months earlier, he himself had been the one 'wielding swords' in the name of morality.[105]

Les Moonves remained in his post at CBS until September 2018, when he left after sexual harassment allegations against him were made public.[106] (Per a settlement reached in 2021, he received nothing from a potential $120 million severance package.)[107] Despite all the forces arrayed against her, though, Janet persisted. Gradually, the hysteria over the Super Bowl incident receded into a baffling historical artefact. Who, after all, could have gotten so agitated about one little breast? Younger performers began to acknowledge Janet's influence. (Katy Perry performed a snippet of 'What Have You Done for Me Lately?' as a tribute to 'Miss Janet Jackson' during her 2018 tour.) In 2019, Janet was inducted into the Rock and Roll Hall of Fame.[108] It was a gesture not only of respect towards her, but also of hurried apology to the entire female sex for the endemic discrimination women had suffered in music.

In 2018, the past also caught up with Justin. With renewed attention on Janet and Britney came a reconsideration of his part in their lives, and the verdict was not kind to him. The 'Teflon man' to whom nothing seemed to stick became instead the repository for all the crimes of the culture. His 'golden boy status' had faded, wrote critic Maria Sherman in *Slate*: 'The new reckoning around him feels like a cultural exorcism, a chance to use the boy band vessel to purge ourselves of the evils he now represents to many.' Those evils included not only the misogyny some saw in the treatment of Britney and Janet, but also, allegedly, indirect racism. Justin's privilege as a white man was suddenly glaringly obvious to some onlookers, and an appearance at the 2018 Super Bowl underlined the disparity between his and Janet's treatment. (Tactlessly, he included 'Rock Your Body' on the setlist.) 'By 2018, cultural appropriation had permeated mainstream discourse,' wrote Sherman, and by that light, Justin's history of collaboration with R&B producers and his adoption of hip-hop influences could look like further evidence of racism rather than its opposite.[109] It was, in a curious way, a resurgence of the division between 'pop' and 'race' music that Janet had breached back in the eighties: it implied that there was a clear distinction between 'black' and 'white' music, and that a white boy should only ever play 'white' music.

Actually, Justin had long seemed conscious that he had benefited from racism and sexism in the distribution of punishment after Nipplegate. 'If you consider it 50-50, I probably got ten per cent of the blame,' he said in a 2006 interview with MTV. 'I think America is harsher on women ... and I think America is unfairly harsh on ethnic people.'[110] But, in 2018, the world wanted someone to answer for that harshness, and it was him. Now he got 90 per cent of the blame, and his once-invisible hand was all that anyone could focus on. The fact that it had been Janet's choreography and Janet's wardrobe was forgotten. Forgotten, too, was the fact that Timberlake – a former boy bander at the precarious beginning of his career in 2004, only a few years free from the predations of 'NSync manager Lou Pearlman and highly reliant on the goodwill of the media – was not particularly powerful in entertainment industry terms. The harm to Janet had overwhelmingly been directed by less famous, and less photogenic, men. Nonetheless, Justin's part was cast. 'Timberlake,' wrote Sherman, 'has become the perfect emblem of a bygone era that rewarded guys exactly like him – until it didn't.' Justin issued multiple apologies in an effort to appease an angry fandom, but the taint remained, just as it had for Janet in the noughties.[111]

The PTC could perhaps claim to have instilled a new spirit of caution in the media, even if the legislative changes Powell promised never came good. Broadcasters introduced a delay on live broadcasts like the Oscars, to insure against their ever being ambushed by celebrity indecency again.[112] For the next six years, the Super Bowl would swerve the possibility of a Nipplegate rerun by only inviting heritage acts to provide the halftime entertainment – Paul McCartney, the Rolling Stones, Prince, Tom Petty, Bruce Springsteen, the Who. It is not coincidental that all those performers were male. The best way to prevent a bared breast from appearing on the stage was apparently to make sure that nobody with breasts was anywhere near it: one upshot of Nipplegate was the collective punishment of female artists for the sin of having female bodies. When Black Eyed Peas brought pop back to halftime in 2011, they needed to soothe the organisers' qualms over the fact that one of their members was a woman. 'They were nervous about that,' said band member Will.i.am, and 'checked our wardrobe like we were going through freakin' security at the airport.'[113] The MTV brand seemed considerably less shaken, as illustrated by a stunt at the 2005 Australian VMAs in which Anna Nicole Smith bared her breasts on stage to reveal MTV stickers covering her nipples in what Fox News called 'a spoof of Janet Jackson's Super Bowl "wardrobe malfunction"'.[114] Ultimately, the PTC could claim only a temporary victory. Not only did it fail to expel vulgarity from the public sphere, but it also turned out to be wholly wrong about the relationship between party politics and the moral agenda. Crudity and liberalism did not inevitably move together. The next Republican president after Bush would emerge not from the sacred environs of the megachurches, but from the carnival chaos of the PTC's old enemy, the WWE.

There was one winner from Janet's disgrace, though. Nipplegate had seeded an idea. Programmer Jawed Karim had been one of the millions searching for a video of Janet's humiliation, and he had been struck by how difficult it was to find and watch. In 2004, putting films online required coding knowledge and daunting amounts of bandwidth: there was no large-scale portal for uploading user-generated videos to the internet, no centralised site to contain them. So, Karim suggested to Chad Hurley and Steve Chen, two fellow Silicon Valley entrepreneurs, that they make one. The result was YouTube, launched on 14 February 2005 – just over a year after *Super Bowl XXXVIII*.[115] The fervour to watch and rewatch a woman's exposure, to savour again and again the exact instant her image disintegrated, was powerful enough to drive a technological revolution. In 2009, the first music star to be made on YouTube emerged: a clean-cut fifteen-year-old called Justin Bieber. He was, noted the *New York Times*, 'a creature of this era: a talented boy discovered first by fans on YouTube, then cannily marketed to them through a fresh influx of studiedly raw videos on the Web site.'[116] Bieber represented stardom adapted to the online environment. He understood how to harness the 'incredible intimacy' with the audience, which was finally fully realised through social media, and translate that into a relationship with his fans that happened on his terms. Janet would never quite be able to benefit from the lessons she had helped a generation of performers to learn, or the technology she had helped to inspire. She stood, instead, as a permanent example of the limits of innocence for women who commodify their sexuality, a living sacrifice to the political machinations of more powerful men.

6

Amy: Reality

'Without girls like you, there'd be no fun'

When Amy Winehouse died in 2011, she was doing what millions of people had been doing for the previous five years: looking at Amy Winehouse. At the inquest into her death, her bodyguard testified that when he'd last seen her alive, she had been in her bed watching clips of herself on YouTube.[1] This, he said, was unusual: he'd never seen her doing it before. Otherwise, she'd seemed to be 'her usual self, nothing out of the ordinary' when he brought her an Indian takeaway that evening. When he checked on her the next day, there were empty vodka bottles on the floor. Amy had recently spent several weeks sober but had started drinking again because, she told her doctor, 'she was bored'. But her doctor had not thought her a suicide risk: 'She specifically said she did not want to die.'[2] There was vomit in the bathroom – either a result of intoxication or evidence of the bulimia that had pushed her weight dangerously low.[3] She had no pulse. She wasn't breathing.

By the time her body was removed from the house, the crowds had already gathered, just as they would have for any Amy performance, whether she was singing or under the influence and acting erratically in public. Photographers captured two black-suited men stretchering her out in a burgundy body bag.[4] The press coverage made much of her age: twenty-seven was not merely appallingly young; it was also the age at which Janis Joplin, Jimi Hendrix and Kurt Cobain had all died. This made Amy a member of the so-called 27 Club, a morbidly sentimentalised involuntary collective of too-fast-to-live artists.[*] In death as in life, all eyes were on her, and everything was being recorded to be fed back into the Amy mythology.

For a long time, that mythology kept me from enjoying Amy's music. She was a jazz singer with a voice of extraordinary depth and richness that seemed all the more remarkable for emerging from such a tiny body. Her lyrics valorised hard living and having one's heart broken by terrible men – the classic subjects, and the traditional habits, of jazz singers going back to the pattern of Billie Holiday in the mid-twentieth century. Amy's 2006 breakout song, 'Rehab', was a boast about refusing to seek help: she was a mess, yes, but a mess of her own making, and she chose to be this way. It felt like a defiant

---

[*] A study in the *British Medical Journal* concluded that the 27 Club had no statistical force, although it did make the gloomy observation that 'fame may increase the risk of death for musicians, probably due to their rock and roll lifestyle'. 'Is 27 really a dangerous age for famous musicians? A retrospective cohort study', *BMJ*, 20 December 2011.

assertion of agency, if you ignored the fact that agency is a hard quality to come by as an addict. Amy performed her part so exaggeratedly, and with such a large quantity of eyeliner and hair, that eventually it had the appearance of a drag act (and drag acts recognised this and returned the compliment, which resulted in multiple versions of 'Amy' appearing on *RuPaul's Drag Race* over the years).

But she meant every single word. There was no irony here – what she sang about, she did, and what she did was obviously destroying her. Whatever I loved about her – and there was plenty, from the towering evocation of sixties girl groups, to the lyrics that alternated between acid observation and tender self-exposure, to her vamped-up look, to, most obviously, the way she sang – it wasn't enough to overcome the queasiness I felt about the fact that listening to her records felt like bystanding at a suicide. Her music did not become macabre because it foretold her death; it was always macabre, because it was the script for someone who was killing herself in public. As reality TV took over pop music in the Upskirt Decade, Amy's confessional art and tabloid trials made her the focus of the ultimate reality show.

My favourite video of Amy on YouTube is a clip from the Sunday morning music show *Popworld*, broadcast in 2004. It's shortly before that year's BRIT Awards, and she's been nominated in two categories for her debut album, *Frank*. The pretence is that she's campaigning for the win as though for political office. She shares a quick joke about ham sandwiches with host Simon Amstell. (They're both Jewish, and Amstell often alluded to his background on-screen.)[5] Then Amstell and Amy set off around London in a tiny silver car, using a loudhailer to shout, 'Support Amy Winehouse!' out the windows at confused passers-by. Part of the gag is that the BRITs are not in fact decided by the public, so this canvassing is futile: a mockery of the sort of thing that reality hopefuls had to do, but not an artist like Amy, who depended on critical acclaim rather than the popular vote. 'This is fun!' she says, cackling madly in the back seat. She looks young – she was twenty-one at the time – and though the hair is big and the make-up pleasingly brassy, she isn't the tiny figure tottering under a beehive and painted with sweeping eyeliner that she would become. She's funny. She's charismatic. She's mischievous. She's enjoying herself, and it's enjoyable to spend time with her. She looks like an ordinary north London girl, and she looks like she's going to be a star.[6]

It would take a little while for her to become one, though. *Frank* was a success, but its success was of the minor, domestic kind. (Its highest UK chart position was thirteen, and the album didn't even get an American release.) Amy wanted more than that. At twelve, she had applied to the Sylvia Young Theatre School – one of the most established pipelines for developing talent – and her personal statement showed that, even then, her aims were uncompromisingly high. 'I have this dream to be very famous, to work on stage,' she wrote. 'It's a lifelong ambition. I want people to hear my voice and just forget their troubles for five minutes. I want to be remembered for being an actress, a singer for sell-out West-End and sell-out Broadway shows. For being ... just me.'[7]

She was accepted, and during her time at Sylvia Young, she got her first TV credit, appearing as an extra in a sketch on *The Fast Show*.[8] But Amy found it difficult to settle down in education and changed school several times. Her adolescence and teenage years saw the beginning of many of the self-destructive behaviours that would dominate her later life. In interviews as an adult, she said that she had started self-harming at the age of nine, the same year her parents, Mitch and Janis, separated.[9] At around twelve or thirteen, she discovered weed and alcohol.[10] As a teenager, Amy told her mother that she had invented a new 'diet': eating and then making herself sick; her mother remembered 'brushing the remark aside'.[11]

In 1999, after leaving school with five GCSEs, she was accepted at the BRIT School, the stage school that would also produce singer Adele and actor Tom Holland. Once again, Amy didn't fit in. She had chosen to specialise in musical theatre, and soon regretted it, as her mother remembered: 'In Amy's eyes, musical theatre was all about playing the game – about having a good voice, having a good performing arts background and getting up on stage and repeating the same show night after night. She saw no originality in it.' And originality – authenticity – was what Amy prized most of all. She left the BRIT School after a month. But she was still on the books at Sylvia Young's talent agency, and in 2000, when she was sixteen, the agency recommended her to the National Youth Jazz Orchestra. Within a month, she had her first performance. She also started playing pub gigs with Tyler James, a friend from Sylvia Young who already had a record deal with the management company Brilliant 19.[12]

In 2001, when she was seventeen, Brilliant 19 signed Amy, too. The deal meant she could give up her day job working for a celebrity news agency. The next year, she signed a publishing deal with EMI, and soon after came a recording contract with Island. Between them, these amounted to about half a million pounds. 'She was terrible with money and behaved like most people would do at that age, like she'd won the lottery,' James writes in his book, *My Amy: The Life We Shared*. She wasn't planning for her future: she was thinking about her present, and what she wanted in her present was to be independent. She rented a flat, moved out of her mother's basement and spent her money exactly like a teenager who had suddenly become rich would do: on Louboutins, dresses, guitars and takeaways.[13] And she also began working on the songs that would become *Frank*.[14]

Her youth is evident on *Frank*. Though the music shows the

eclectic influences that would later distinguish her, drawing especially on hip-hop, there's an unformed quality to it: the sound too often drifts into the bland realm of 'easy jazz', as the BBC website's review put it.[15] (*Frank* was not distributed in the United States, so all the contemporaneous reviews are from the UK.) The two things that made Amy stand out at this point were her voice and her lyrics, both of which suggested a maturity beyond her age. She was innocence and experience at the same time, and an important part of her appeal was that the experience was personal: 'She claims that she can only write about what she has already learned,' noted the *Guardian* approvingly.[16] Amy's words were never formulaic or clichéd. If she was singing about it, it was because she'd lived it or seen it.

One of the album's standout songs, 'Fuck Me Pumps', is a piece of sharp social observation pillorying the women who hung out in London bars providing fodder for the tabloid press: wannabe footballers' wives with sky-high heels, big handbags and boob jobs. The kind of women Amy would have covered during her brief career in showbiz gossip. 'Without girls like you, there'd be no fun / We'd go to the club and not see anyone,' she coos. 'October Song' is about the death of her pet canary, Ava.* 'Stronger than Me' is addressed to her ex-boyfriend and takes him apart in savage terms. 'Are you gay?' she complains, cheerfully jettisoning political correctness.[17] Then she compounds the offence in the chorus, where she calls him a 'ladyboy'.[18] The title of *Frank* was a statement of intent. In a world of robotic pop – the kind of processed, impersonal

---

* Sadly for Ava, although she got to be a muse, she was not a particularly well-cared-for pet, in Amy's mother's account: '[Amy] used to open the cage regularly and let Ava fly around the room, but, unfortunately, feeding her regularly didn't top Amy's list of priorities. "Mum, I don't think Ava's very well," she told me one day; and the next week I woke early to another phone-call: "Mum ... I think Ava's dead. Can you come over?" Ava was certainly dead: Amy had found her under the sofa as stiff as a board. That poor canary. She would have had no idea that when Amy set eyes on her she'd be popping her clogs within a matter of weeks.' Winehouse, *Loving Amy*, p. 102.

music Aaliyah had pioneered and for which Britney had become the avatar – Amy was defiantly flesh and blood.

But with her commitment to authenticity came insecurities about her status as an artist. Firstly, she was unhappy about the promotional campaign. 'I've given them [her label and management] a lot of control – I made the music because I know how to do that, but then for the promotional side I stepped back and thought "I've got to trust this lot, because I've never done this before." That was the wrongest thing I could have done,' she told one interviewer. 'All they know how to do is what's already been done and I don't want to do anything that's already been done. I don't ever want to do anything mediocre. I hear the music in the charts and I don't mean to be rude, but those people have no soul.'[19] By the February after *Frank*'s release, Amy was even badmouthing the album itself, claiming that some of the tracks and mixes had been forced on her by her record label. It was, she said, 'fucked' from production to release.[20]

And then there was the problem of her management. Brilliant 19 was funded by Simon Fuller, the man behind the international talent show franchise *Idol* (beginning with *Pop Idol* on ITV in 2001) and, before that, the Spice Girls. The UK press had nicknamed him 'Svengali Spice'.[21] Amy despised the reality shows. 'I wouldn't have gone on one of those shows in a million, billion years,' she told an interviewer, 'because I think that musicality is not something other people should judge you on. Music's a thing you have with yourself.' And as brutal as she could be in her lyrics, she found the harshness of the reality shows difficult to take: 'Even though the people who go on those shows are shit, it's really damaging to be told that you are.'[22]

Still, a cynical person who knew of the Fuller connection might have looked at Amy's 'authenticity' and 'originality' and seen nothing but clever branding. The jazz singer and the pop puppet seemed to come from opposite universes, but they could be merely two versions of the same product offered by the same canny marketer – two living Bratz dolls differently accessorised. The impression that Fuller was responsible for Amy's success was a drag on her reputation, as she conceded when she was asked about him in a 2004 interview: 'My A&R man is paranoid about it because he doesn't want people to think he [Fuller] did it.'[23] It was an impression that she was determined to avoid. The next – and final – phase of her career would be defined by the total rejection of Fuller and the manufactured pop he was identified with.

However Amy felt about her connection with Simon Fuller, by the mid-noughties she – and pretty much everyone who worked in music – was living in his world. The germ of what would become the *Idol* phenomenon had come to Fuller in 1997, after the Spice Girls sacked him as their manager. It was an experience that showed him the limitations inherent in his business model: as huge as he had helped the Spice Girls to become, there was in the end nothing to stop them from dispensing with him. He needed to think bigger. Next time, Fuller would not place himself at the mercy of the talent. He would own the concept, and the talent would be replaceable. In 1999, he began pitching a TV show called *Fame Search* to British TV networks. Presciently, he conceived it as an internet talent competition, with contestants applying online. Too presciently: the internet was still a fringe technology then, and the networks were sceptical about basing a mass-market TV show on it.[24]

But the appetite for something like *Fame Search* was out there. In 2000, with the concept now renamed *Your Idol*, Fuller approached television executive Nigel Lythgoe. Lythgoe was keen, but, unfortunately, he was already attached to another singing contest that would be broadcast in early 2001, called *Popstars*. This one was based on a format Lythgoe had seen in New Zealand and become fascinated by. And what fascinated him most was the window it offered into the audition process. 'Seeing the good, the bad and the ugly, then the honesty of the judges – that was what hooked me,' he explained in a 2021 interview. 'We didn't add any gloss. We showed the down 'n' dirty side of showbiz.'[25] Compared to the hyper-slick creature that reality television would become, the original UK *Popstars* was endearingly low-key. Not only did it lack the online element that Fuller had envisaged, but there also wasn't a public vote. There wasn't even a studio audience. The only opportunity to participate came at the end of the series, when the winning act had made and released a single that viewers could buy (the bottom having not yet fallen out of the physical music market).

Unglamorous as it was, *Popstars* set the tone for the *Idol* franchise to come. And the most important way it did that was through the judging. Early noughties viewers did not want to see contestants given gently constructive feedback. They wanted to see ambitions dashed, weaknesses exposed, harsh truths delivered – and on *Popstars*, Lythgoe was the one to do it. For journalist Richard Rushfield, who covered *Idol* for the *Los Angeles Times*, this acidity was a reaction to the cloying style that had dominated culture in the nineties: 'By speaking the truth in the setting of an entertainment audition, Lythgoe did not merely cut through the clutter of smarm that had, so the sentiment went, poisoned civic life; he was, in a sense, standing up to the mediocrity of entertainment that had been foisted down the public's throat in recent years.'[26] The press nicknamed Lythgoe 'Nasty Nigel', and he revelled in it. 'I loved it because it brought attention to the show,' he said, although he undoubtedly also enjoyed the attention that it brought him in his own right. Lythgoe became more famous than most of the people who auditioned for him, moving on to judge *American Idol* and *So You Think You Can Dance* in the United States.

For the objects of his cruelty, it was a less pleasant experience. After the audition process had winnowed the hopefuls down to a five-member group called Hear'Say, *Popstars* went on to follow them as they recorded their first single and were prepped for stardom. This meant working on their image as well as their music. In one episode, Lythgoe informs the band that they needed to slim down. 'Do you think I'm fat?' asks singer Kym Marsh. 'I think you've put weight on over Christmas, and I think you needed to lose weight before Christmas,' replies Lythgoe coldly. Marsh was reduced to tears on-screen.[27] This was Saturday night TV in the United Kingdom, and the kind of thing that Amy, a young girl with an eating disorder, might have watched for entertainment. Later, Marsh revealed that she, too, had suffered from bulimia when younger.[28]

In her autobiography, Marsh describes this incident as the moment she realised that she and her bandmates hadn't just been competing for a shot at stardom – they had also been the raw material for another kind of entertainment, one over which they had very little control. 'Suddenly it was horribly clear. I felt like me and the others were just puppets or characters in a soap opera. We were presented as caricatures of ourselves and we were being used to make viewers laugh or gasp with shock. And that was a horrible feeling.' Lythgoe had chosen the character of the villain, but Marsh got no choice about being put into the role of his victim: 'I, for one, was sick of having my strings pulled. Nigel seemed to have forgotten that I was actually a real person with real feelings.'[29]

Being in Hear'Say would not be Marsh's problem for very long. The band broke up on 1 October 2002 (Marsh had already left): from launch to implosion, they had lasted eighteen months.[30] For those pulling the strings, though, the band had been a huge success. In 2001, Lythgoe joined Fuller's company Brilliant 19 as head of TV development, and in October 2001, *Pop Idol* finally arrived on screens – complete with public vote and the crucial addition of Simon Cowell in the 'mean judge' seat. The essential elements of the format Fuller would take to America in 2002 were all in place. An audience of 22.8 million would watch Kelly Clarkson win season one of *American Idol*. In a time of divided attention and flagging ratings across the networks, watching a sneering British man devastate young singers' egos was what the nation wanted.[31]

It wasn't just TV that was becoming tougher. In 1997, Princess Diana was killed in a car crash while being pursued by photographers, causing the press to undergo a spasm of high-mindedness in which many swore off the use of paparazzi pictures. It didn't last long. In 2001, the editor of the *Mirror* was Piers Morgan. A few weeks after 9/11, he announced that his paper would be taking a new, more serious approach to the news in keeping with these new, more serious times. That did not mean, however, that the *Mirror* would cease to run celebrity coverage. (Morgan's background was in gossip reporting, and he understood the value of star power to his paper.) It meant, instead, that it would no longer offer copy and picture approval to its famous subjects – the practice of allowing celebrities or, at any rate, their representatives final say on what gets published. 'I just got fed up with PRs and agents calling the shots,' Morgan said. 'I just thought, the time has come – we've got to stand up to these people.'[32] The attacks of 11 September 2001, he explained, had 'empowered us to put celebrities back in their box', and the dignity of this statement was only slightly undermined by the fact that it came in response to a spat with Richard and Judy.[33]

Perhaps 9/11 did sharpen Morgan's appetite for taking on the famous, but he was being disingenuous here: he had constructed his most important weapon in his war against celebrities a year earlier. In 2000, the *Mirror* debuted a new gossip section called the 3AM Girls, so named because they were girls, there were three of them, and they were encouraged to stay up until the early hours partying with the stars on whom they were reporting. Morgan had envisaged them as a direct take on the 'ladette' archetype – fun-loving, hard-living young women who could match the men drink for drink and look hot doing it. The archetype, in fact, that Amy would also fit. 'I liked the idea of a little pack of ladettes marching around, mainly because I knew that all the male stars would be extremely susceptible to their charms,' Morgan said. 'A kind of intellectual Spice Girls. A parody of what showbiz is like now.'[34] Morgan cast himself in the Svengali role, assembling his girl band of gossips – a journalistic version of Simon Fuller.

Their sex alone made the 3AM Girls a very different proposition from the male journalists who then dominated celebrity coverage. But they were also different in attitude. 'Our brief was to leave celebrities very afraid,' wrote Jessica Callan, one of the original 3AM Girls, in her 2007 memoir of her time on the column. 'If someone behaved like a prima donna to us, we were given the green light to name and shame them in the column. Our favourite stories? Celebrities fighting and fucking.'[35] The approach was so successful, the 3AM Girls became famous in their own right: *Vanity Fair* ran a profile of them, written by Nancy Jo Sales, the era's leading chronicler of celebrity culture. For the 3AM Girls, drama was the most important thing. In the same way that Fuller's reality shows were edited to create protagonists, antagonists and narrative arcs, the 3AM Girls took the raw material of star encounters and gossip tit-bits and turned it into something like a soap opera. 'You need a cast of characters, long-standing feuds, it makes the column more interesting,' Callan said in a 2002 interview with the *Guardian*. 'Anyway, they like being in papers. They need us just as much as we need them.'[36]

Not every celebrity agreed with this assessment. The same year Callan gave that quote, the *Mirror* was the subject of a legal action claiming wrongful disclosure of private information brought by supermodel Naomi Campbell after the 3AM Girls published a photo of her leaving a Narcotics Anonymous meeting. Campbell said this was a violation of her privacy; Morgan disagreed. At the hearing, he argued that celebrities had already traded away their boundaries: 'If you are going to voluntarily enter Hannibal Lecter's cage, then eventually you are going to get nibbled round the back of the neck. If you are going to relentlessly use the media to promote a commercial image of yourself, if you are going to continue to talk about very intimate private parts of your life . . . you have less right to privacy than the man or woman in the street.'[37]

Paparazzi shots were, it turned out, far from the most intrusive technique used by the press in the noughties: this was also the golden age of phone hacking. Minimal security on voice mail meant that it was easy to access public figures' messages and write them up as stories. Another technique was 'blagging', in which a journalist would call, say, a doctor's office pretending to be a representative of a celebrity in order to access their records. It was an atmosphere that bred paranoia and isolation among the victims, who, not knowing how the press was getting these stories, feared that someone they trusted was selling their secrets.[38] By 2020, settlements with victims and legal expenses had cost the implicated tabloids hundreds of thousands of pounds.[39]

Campbell won her case against the *Mirror*, but at least as far as popular opinion was concerned, the moral victory seemed to be with Morgan.[40] The caustic style of celebrity coverage was overwhelmingly what the British public wanted. *Heat* magazine had launched in 1999 as a straightforward culture magazine, to general readerly indifference. In 2000, editor

Mark Frith relaunched it as an aggressive gossip tabloid, known for its 'circle of shame' – a red ring added to celebrity photos to highlight such indignities as cellulite, a make-up-free face, or body hair. This was a media culture where female bodies and behaviour could be held up for scrutiny without apology or alibi: it was the culture Amy was absorbing before she became famous and the culture that would absorb her when she was. Frith defended his magazine against accusations of intrusion by describing what it did as a 'fame tax'. It was, he said in a 2004 interview, all in the game of modern celebrity: 'This is part of being famous and, apart from a couple of major Hollywood stars, I don't think they recoil from that.'[41] Morgan concurred: 'The good celebrities, the ones I have respect for, can always laugh at themselves,' he said in 2002.[42]

Amy, by this standard, was one of the good ones. She took herself seriously as an artist, but not as a celebrity: on that point, she was happy to play along, as in her fake election campaign for *Popworld*. She was friendly to the paparazzi, and when they started camping outside her flat in the hope of a picture, she'd bring them cups of tea and stop for a chat.[43] Darren and Elliott Bloom, brothers who worked together as celebrity photographers, say they were approached by Amy's management to be her 'official' paparazzi, giving them privileged access.[44] (Many of the most famous images of Amy would be shot by their team – including, eventually, a picture of her in a body bag.) And in a time when audiences wanted to see what Lythgoe called the 'down 'n' dirty side of showbiz', Amy was willing to share that, too, spilling out her irritation with the pop machine in interviews. Her tongue-lashings were easily as fearsome as anything a talent show judge could offer. She was, in short, a perfect star for the Upskirt Decade. If celebrity was a game, Amy belonged to the elect who seemed to understand the rules. None of this would save her from being turned into a character in the columns and blog posts of the gossip world. First, though, she was going to follow the path set by Fuller and break America.

Back to Black is one of those miraculous records in which every element seems to have fallen perfectly into place. Like *Frank*, it wears its influences on its sleeve: the jazz is still there, and so is the hip-hop, as well as ska, soul and sixties girl groups. But, this time, Amy doesn't sound like she's paying homage to anything. She takes the pieces and turns them into something new, something of her own – something entirely and profoundly personal. She described her writing process to her friend Tyler James like this: 'You get a pen and slash it into your arm and bleed all over the pages.'[45] It's an image that suggests songwriting as self-revelation but also, disturbingly, as a version of the self-harm she had been resorting to since childhood.

The album came out in the United Kingdom in late 2006, when Amy was twenty-three. This time she got an American release, too, in early 2007. The critics largely adored the record and were fascinated by her. 'A wonderfully time-twisted batch of songs,' said the *New York Times*.[46] *Entertainment Weekly* called the album 'near-perfect', and declared it to be 'not just the arrival of a fully formed talent, but possibly the first major salvo of a new British Invasion'.[47] Even the reviewers who were less convinced, like Joshua Klein on Pitchfork, recognised that there was something compelling about Amy: 'Winehouse isn't a typical pop singer. If she winds up as popular in the US as she is at home in the UK, it'll be despite her reluctance to embrace the monotonous realities of promotional mechanics. Oh, she'll talk, but there's no guarantee what she'll say … She'll be scheduled to perform, but there's no guarantee what she'll do, or even if she'll make it through the show. And she'll sing about her problems, but she won't give a shit what you think of them.'[48] If Amy's reputation for no-shows was already established, something, clearly, was not right – but this seemed to generate intrigue rather than concern.

The album sold in phenomenal amounts: No. 1 in the United Kingdom, No. 2 in the United States. Amy hadn't won any BRIT Awards for *Frank*, despite her campaigning efforts, but *Back to Black* earned her Best British Female Artist. She did even better at the Grammys, where she was honored with five awards: Song of the Year, Record of the Year (both for 'Rehab'), Best New Artist, Best Female Pop Vocal Performance ('Rehab' again), and Best Pop Vocal Album. (Mark Ronson also won Producer of the Year, Non-Classical, for his production work, which included *Back to Black*.)[49] *Rolling Stone*, which had offered one of the cooler verdicts in its original review, put Amy on its June 2007 cover, accompanied by a profile that gave wide-eyed witness to her drinking, self-harm through cutting and 'exceptionally thin frame'. She had, unmistakably, made it, although she already sounded disillusioned. 'I don't want to be ungrateful. I know I'm talented, but I wasn't put here to sing,' she told *Rolling Stone*. 'I was put here to be a wife ... and look after my family. I love what I do, but it's not where it begins and ends.'[50]

Maybe the most miraculous thing about *Back to Black* is that it got made at all. By 2005, Amy had only a few songs sketched out for a putative follow-up to *Frank*, and her live performances had become infrequent. There were rumours that Island Records was considering dropping her, and her relations with Brilliant 19 had hit a low. This wasn't just because of tensions over the association with Fuller and *Idol*. In the downtime between albums, Amy had become a regular on the Camden pub scene in London, and her manager, Nick Shymansky, had grown concerned about her heavy drinking. He tried to convince her to go into rehab.[51] She refused, and Shymansky's failed intervention would go on to provide her with the lyrics to 'Rehab' – *Back to Black*'s first track and the lead single announcing her return after the post-*Frank* hiatus. (According to Tyler James, the line 'I'd rather be at home with Ray' is a nod to Raye Cosbert, her live booking agent who would become her manager after Shymansky declined to leave Brilliant 19.)[52] In Amy, creation and self-destruction went hand in hand.

In the nineties, Camden had been the hub of the Britpop scene, and in the noughties, another generation of guitar bands and bright young things flocked there – and the paparazzi flocked after them. Kate Moss was a regular; so was Pete Doherty of the Libertines (who became a friend of Amy's and whose own addiction issues were heavily documented).* It was where everybody who was somebody, and everybody who wanted to be somebody, went to hang out. 'It was a scene dominated by blokes in bands but also a type of character, which Amy fitted like a glove,' recalled Tyler James. 'She was a female solo jazz singer, but she was also a bit of a fella. Basically, it was all about being a full-on rock 'n' roll nutcase.'[53] Even if Amy wasn't making music, she could maintain her artistic credentials by getting wasted with those who were.

This was the period when Amy's tabloid persona became established and the girl next door began to be permanently effaced by something else. From early on, the sense of establishing a character had been a part of Amy's public image. When she had her first major TV appearance, in 2004 (on *The Jonathan Ross Show*), her mother recalled, 'She looked beautiful and she talked eloquently and assuredly, but her eyeliner was thicker than I'd ever seen it. And, as for her accent? It looked like Amy, but it didn't sound like Amy. It wasn't an accent she'd ever used at home. It was thick and

---

* One especially lurid, and dubious, tabloid story about Doherty claimed he had offered a kitten 'a specially-made mini crack pipe', after which the animal was allegedly removed from his care by the RSPCA. Rosie Swash, 'Kittens, just say no to cracknip', *Guardian*, 7 September 2007.

cockney.'[54] Amy would develop this character over time, acquiring elements magpie-style, the same way she accrued influences in her songs: something of the gangster's moll from London, something of the Latina street style she saw in Miami during the sessions for *Back to Black*, something of the music she loved.[55] Former Ronettes front woman Ronnie Spector recalled performing in London and seeing Amy in the audience: 'She looked just like me. She had the same hairstyle as me and everything. It scared me.'[56]

But in noughties tabloid culture, the visual language that made up Amy stood for Amy alone: a beehive hairdo and cat's-eye make-up, coupled with either the shortest and tightest of pin-up-style dresses or skinny jeans and vests on her increasingly tiny body. On her feet, either fuck-me pumps or ballet slippers. On her skin, a growing collection of sailor-style tattoos. By the time *Back to Black* came out, she was startlingly unlike the Amy of *Frank*, and she was an instantly recognisable icon. In a season two episode of *Keeping Up with the Kardashians*, Bruce (later Caitlyn) Jenner takes in a calendar picture of Kim with backcombed hair and heavily winged eyeliner and announces, 'Oh my God! Doesn't she look like Amy Winehouse there?'[57] The Amy look was unmistakable.

Remaking yourself as a character could be a way to manage the pressures of fame, as another British reality star and peer of Amy's would explain. Sarah Harding was a member of Girls Aloud, the group that won the second season of *Popstars*, in 2002. As badly as Harding wanted to be a singer, she was nervous about the spotlight. So, when the press gave her the nickname 'Hardcore Harding' in recognition of her party girl tendencies, she grabbed at the persona as an answer to the problem of her identity. 'For me, it was like, "Oh! That's who I am then. I've been looking for my role in the band, so this must be it,"' she writes in her autobiography (published shortly before she died of cancer at the age of thirty-nine).

'So, in that respect I suppose it became easy for me as well. Convenient. I mean, I liked a drink, I was a bit rebellious, I liked to go out partying, so it was a win/win. Until it wasn't.'[58] In 2011, Harding entered rehab to treat depression and alcohol addiction.[59]

The trouble with playing the party girl for the paparazzi was that you had to go full Method to carry off the role. However much that might have initially felt like a pose, the damage was ultimately real. This was the case for Amy, and her persona was creeping into her real life in other ways, too. According to Tyler James, she was fixated on playing a certain part in her most intimate relationships. 'She had a thing about always listening to your man, like someone from the 1950s,' he wrote. 'At that time, the biggest female pop stars in the world were singing about independence, making their own money – Destiny's Child's "Independent Woman," TLC singing "I don't need no scrubs." Amy hated all that. The only love songs she cared about were ones that said, "I will throw myself under a bus for you."'[60]

To become the surrendered woman of the kind of songs Amy wanted to write, she needed a man who could play the aggressor, and she found her muse during her Camden drinking sessions. Blake Fielder-Civil was one of the lesser figures on the scene, a hanger-on of the Libertines with a heroin addiction and a girlfriend. Other boyfriends, like the one who inspired 'Stronger', had not supplied the kind of high-drama masculinity Amy craved – the kind that involved those essential elements of a good story as defined by the 3AM Girls: 'fighting and fucking'. But Fielder-Civil could perform that role perfectly, and within weeks of meeting him, she had a tattoo of his name over her left breast.[61] *Back to Black*'s lyrics draw intimately on the couple's chaotic on-again, off-again, substance-infused relationship. 'The songs literally did write themselves,' Amy told *Rolling Stone*. 'All the songs are about the state of my relationship at the time with Blake ... I had never felt the way I feel about him about anyone in my life.'[62]

Out of her pain came great music. 'Tears Dry on Their Own' has a gorgeous defiance: the narrator still loves her man, as terrible as he's been for her, but she accepts that he is walking into the sunset. 'Back to Black' is bleaker: the title phrase means the narrator is returning to obliteration in drink, while her lover returns to his ex, 'that same old safe bet'. 'Wake Up Alone' is the sweetest and saddest song on the album: the narrator keeps herself distracted from her heartbreak in the day and holds off from drinking, but at night, she dreams of him. Her delivery is muted by grief; the lyrics are suggestive and lovely. 'Pour myself over him, moon spilling in / And I wake up alone.' (The narrator might be dry for now, but she still experiences love in the language of inebriation – she pours herself like a drink.)

Amy and Fielder-Civil were separated when she made the album, and had they stayed broken up, *Back to Black*'s intensity might be remembered as simply the hyperbole of a deep but brief heartbreak for her. She would have got what she needed from him – creatively as well as emotionally – and moved on. Instead, when 'Rehab' became a top-ten hit, Fielder-Civil reappeared in her life. In May 2007, the two got married.[63] From then on, their relationship was no longer the subject of songs but of relentless gossip coverage. Certainly, the lyrics to *Back to Black* suggest unfinished business between them romantically, but some of Amy's friends and family saw a more cynical reason for a junkie with no discernible income to attach himself to a woman with sudden success and wealth. He was now, wrote James, 'an addict whose drugs were all paid for' and paid for, moreover, by profits from an album that demonstrated in extreme detail why he was so very bad for Amy. Fielder – who later dropped the 'Civil' part of his surname after a breach with his stepfather – has said in interviews that he never intended to 'sponge off' Amy, but she was nonetheless one of his few sources of income both when she was alive and after her death: in 2014, he received payment for posed photos of himself at Amy's grave.[64] Had she had more experienced management at this point, perhaps they would have intervened to protect her, as Shymansky had tried to do in 2005; but then, one of the reasons Amy had broken with Shymansky was his propensity to get between her and her habits.

The temptation in looking back at Amy's life is to try to identify the point at which she could have been saved. If there was one, it had probably passed before *Back to Black*'s success. The window of semi-sobriety that made the album possible had closed up fast. In 2006, Amy made another TV appearance with Simon Amstell, who had now moved off *Popworld* and was hosting the BBC's music panel show *Never Mind the Buzzcocks*. She is still funny and unguarded – her impression of the Paris Hilton sex tape wins resounding laughter – but she is obviously drunk, and her expression is vacant much of the time. At one point, she spits on the floor, and Amstell seems genuinely shocked.

'Can we resuscitate the old Amy Winehouse?' he pleads. 'This is no longer a panel show, this is an intervention.'

'She's dead,' whispers Amy, stroking his face. 'She's dead.'

Still, she finds the composure to come to the defence of Jessica Garlick – a top-ten contestant from series one of *Pop Idol*, who appears in *Buzzcocks*'s 'identity parade' round. This was usually an opportunity to make cruel jokes at the expense of someone who was no longer really famous, and Amstell rolls out some unkind puns on Garlick's name.

'I don't know how much you're getting paid, but I'd ... smack him,' slurs Amy.

'They get paid, they know what's gonna happen,' riffs Amstell in return: the fame tax in action. 'God, you sound like a pimp,' jokes one of Amy's teammates. Amy broods over her mug (which presumably contained wine) as this plays out, her tower of hair sliding sideways. For this moment, she's a hold-out against the cruelty of noughties celeb culture, protecting a reality also-ran from media scorn. For this moment, she's visibly staggering under the weight of it all.

Amy would never make another album after *Back to Black*. Hers is a painfully scant legacy, especially for someone who saw herself as a peer of the great jazz vocalists. Frank Sinatra and Sarah Vaughan recorded albums well into the double digits. Even Billie Holiday, whose drug and alcohol issues made her a model for the 'chaotic chanteuse' role Amy occupied, produced more than ten albums before she died at forty-four. Yet, while the remainder of Amy's life was creatively bare, she would spend it being more famous than she had ever been – very famous for being just her, exactly as she'd hoped when she was twelve. And the thing she was most celebrated for was the thing that was destroying her. When *Idol* came to the United States, one of the things audiences had loved was the distinctly un-American rudeness offered by head judge Simon Cowell.[65] Amy brought a similar culture shock – only, in her case, what appealed was the unashamed commitment to hard living.

One of the first mentions of her in the US press was in a *New York Times* blog post from 2007, which described her as 'Britain's boldly anti-rehab star'. The post started by mention-ing Britney's troubles: Craig Ferguson, host of *The Late Late Show*, had recently performed a monologue in which he took the media to task for its prurient interest in the struggles of a 'vulnerable' young woman. 'But there's always the possibility that [Britney's] difficulties may yet lead to great music,' mused the post. 'Consider a British singer who wears her vices on her sleeve and is just about to hit the states: Amy Winehouse.'[66] For the media, the fact that Amy was turning her life into art provided an alibi for their own business of turning her life into content. The fact that the promotion for *Back to Black* had been punctuated by slurring performances and no-shows was treated as proof of her rock and roll credentials, rather than a cause for concern.

Some events, however, still managed to stir even the most prurient celeb watchers to shock. In August 2007, photos taken by Amy's 'official paparazzi', the Bloom brothers, showed her and Fielder-Civil with clear signs of having been in a fight. Her temple and knuckles were bruised, her knees and feet were bloodied, red stains blooming at the toes of her trademark pink ballet shoes; he had scratches on his face and neck. Perez Hilton – who considered Amy one of his celebrity friends – linked to the photos in a post titled 'Warning: This Is Too Real'. He used the first person plural – which he'd adopted at this time for some reason – and referred to Amy by his regular nickname for her, 'Wino'. 'We do believe in God and we pray that he is able to help save Amy from death, which she keeps inviting into her life,' he wrote. [67]

Still, the prayers – however sincere – did not stop Hilton from continuing to draw content from Amy. In response to his initial post, Amy sent him a series of texts begging him to 'set the record straight' and asserting that Fielder-Civil was 'the best man in the world' and that the couple 'would never ever harm each other'. Blake had, she wrote, 'saved my life'. Hilton dutifully published these as a follow-up, thereby both respecting his friend's wishes and conveniently pulling in even more traffic. [68] By this point, Amy had, in fact, almost entirely ceased to have a private life. She no longer needed to make music to tell her story of romanticised self-harm: the media would record her life for her.

In December 2007, the *News of the World* turned its front page over to a letter from Amy's mother, begging her then-estranged daughter to get help.* In her memoir, Janis Winehouse says that, though she agreed to publish the letter out of a desire to reach Amy, she didn't actually write it: it was concocted by the paper.[69] While Janis seemed naïve about the workings of celebrity, Amy's father was actively pursuing it on his own behalf. He signed a record deal to make his own jazz album, and made multiple TV appearances – he even signed up to make a documentary about parenting an addicted child, which was sold on the premise that it would include footage of his daughter, although that project was never completed.[70] 'He was so caught up in her success I felt like he didn't see his daughter for who she was anymore, and maybe not even himself,' writes Tyler James of Mitch Winehouse at this time. 'It was like he was a character in his own way, "Amy Winehouse's Dad."'[71] Mitch offers a more high-minded version of his involvement – 'I wanted the public to know about the heartaches and dilemmas that such people live with'[72] – but it seems at best a misguided decision. Even what should have been Amy's most private and nurturing relationships were absorbed into the great soap opera.

No one provided more drama here than Fielder-Civil. In 2008, he was imprisoned for perverting the course of justice and grievous bodily harm after he assaulted a landlord and then attempted to pay him off (with Amy's money, inevitably).[73] In another instance of how tabloidised Amy's life had become, the court heard that the plot had been uncovered by journalists from the *Mirror*.[74] In 2009, despite her frequent avowals that she could never let Fielder-Civil go, the couple divorced. Amy got breast implants around this time, which made her just a little more like the women she'd once disparaged in 'Fuck Me Pumps' and implies that at least one surgeon

---

* In 2011, the *News of the World*'s parent company elected to close the title down in response to the paper's implication in the phone-hacking scandal.

believed she was healthy and stable enough to be operated on.[75] In determining her suitability for the procedure, whoever performed it was apparently not paying attention to her performances, which were more shambolic than ever – profitably so, from the perspective of those whose income derived from chronicling her slide. One of the very last posts about Amy on Perez Hilton's blog before her death reported that she had shown up late and wasted to a private performance for the billionaire Roman Abramovich, and wearing no underwear: 'Grrrossss!!!!!!!!! Who needs to see cracked out snatch?' wrote Hilton, the days of prayers apparently fully behind him.[76]

The public disintegration of Amy was, for some, the limit of their patience with the rock-and-roll trope that equated damage with authenticity. When *Frank* was finally issued in the United States in 2007, after the triumph of *Back to Black*, one reviewer declared himself sick of the whole circus. On the website Pitchfork, Douglas Wolk wrote that 'the self-destructive tortured-artist routine' was 'bullshit': 'her look-how-messed-I-am public persona is now screwing up her art something fierce'. But he didn't blame Amy alone. He also held her audience, including himself, accountable for its complicity in the Billie Holiday kitsch. 'We can at least think very carefully about what our participation in that narrative means. And who are we to say we wish she'd stop going on about how she doesn't need any help and get some goddamn help already? Not vultures, that's who.'[77] When she died in 2011, the vultures had been waiting for nearly five years.

Amy's official cause of death was alcohol poisoning.[78] It is impossible to say that fame killed her – both her substance abuse and her eating disorder were established long before *Back to Black* made her an icon of self-destruction – but it is probably true that fame created the conditions in which she could only get worse and never better. Amy's public commitment to the role of 'Wino' meant her addiction became irrevocably entwined with who she was. In an era when Saturday primetime entertainment consisted of a reality judge calling an objectively slim woman 'fat', Amy's private war with her flesh become part of a mass war on the female figure. Her pathologies were inseparable from her celebrity self, and her celebrity self could live only at the expense of her mortal body.

Her demise left a gap in the market. The same year she died, another self-professed jazz singer emerged who would test the arguments about 'realness' and stardom almost to destruction. In 2011, Lana Del Rey self-released a woozy, beautiful ballad called 'Video Games'. In it, she adopts the persona of a neglected but irrevocably devoted girlfriend: 'It's you, it's you, it's all for you,' she swoons, while the boy in the song cracks open a beer and ignores her. The song became an instant alternative hit, widely boosted on music blogs, including Pitchfork, which took Del Rey at face value as an indie proposition and compared her to lo-fi chanteuse Cat Power. (It certainly didn't hurt the song's popularity that Del Rey looked very much like the fantasy girlfriend every alt-culture boy would have loved to be able to take for granted.)

Like Amy's, Del Rey's sound merged classic stylings with hip-hop influences. She even embraced the same girl band elements: 'Ultraviolence', from her third album of the same name, interpolates a fragment of the Crystals' 1962 single 'He Hit Me (It Felt Like a Kiss)', and as her use of that song suggests, Del Rey embraced a vision of sexuality that was even more flagrantly masochistic than Amy's. Her videos and cover art frequently showed a man pressing a hand to her throat, implying choking. Asked about this by an interviewer in 2014, Del Rey replied, 'I like a little hardcore love.'[79] This submissive streak was entangled with the kind of singer she was: 'I'm your jazz singer and you're my cult leader,' she murmurs at the end of 'Ultraviolence'.

But unlike Amy, Del Rey appeared to have arrived fully formed. There was no apprentice piece equivalent to *Frank* in her discography. 'Video Games' was the work of an admirably polished performer. Suspiciously polished, in fact. Soon after the song's release, footage of a New York performer called Lizzy Grant began to circulate. Grant sounded like Del Rey. She looked like Del Rey (albeit with the appearance of slightly thinner lips). She *was* Del Rey, and it transpired that she'd already recorded one album with a high-powered producer, although it was impossible to listen to it because it had been thoroughly scrubbed from the internet. Suspicion flourished into scepticism as it became known that Del Rey was no struggling outsider, but had been signed to a major label. Once-supportive websites turned critical, triumphantly announcing that Del Rey was not 'really' the helplessly surrendered girl she played in the song. Lana Del Rey was pronounced a fake. Fake name, fake lips (though she denied having fillers and said she was just pouty when she sang), fake image: fake, fake, fake. Commentators declared themselves disgusted at the deceit. When Pitchfork reviewed her debut album under the Del Rey name, *Born to Die*, in 2012, it was deemed 'the album equivalent of a faked orgasm – a collection of torch songs with no fire'.[80]

The sexual terms of that insult hardly seem coincidental. There was a feeling that Del Rey had somehow perpetrated a con and was withholding a kind of intimacy – realness – that audiences were owed. It was a charge she vehemently denied. As an artist, Del Rey recognised that 'realness' was still prized enough to be worth fighting for. 'Never had a persona,' she tweeted angrily in 2020 at a critic who had written a broadly positive review of her album *Norman Fucking Rockwell*. 'Never needed one. Never will.'[81] But there can be value in having a persona for some artists, if it keeps their flesh-and-blood person protected, and it's notable that Del Rey has rarely allowed her private life to become visible. *Spin* magazine, in an interview published the year after Amy died, called Del Rey 'Amy Winehouse, with the safety on'.[82] This sounds like an insult, but there was palpable relief in the phrase – this one, at least, wasn't going to kill herself in the pursuit of her art. And fake or otherwise, Del Rey is still here and still making music. Amy's ultimate reality was death.

7

Kim: Beauty

'Because I was horny and I felt like it'

It starts – of course it does – with the ass. Kim Kardashian walks through the kitchen of her family's house in Calabasas, California. 'I am starving,' she announces as she opens the fridge and leans inside to rummage for a snack, affording the camera a perfect rear view. Meanwhile, her mother, Kris Jenner, and younger sister Khloé Kardashian commentate.

'Don't you have a photoshoot tomorrow? Stop eating!' says Khloé.

'I think she has a little *junk* in the *trunk*,' stage-whispers Kris.

Then the credits roll, and we see most of the family

arranging themselves for a photo in front of an LA cityscape. Kim rushes in at the end and poses front and centre in a bright red skintight dress. Then her younger half-sister, Kylie Jenner, pulls a rope, and the glitzy backdrop falls away to reveal the family's plush but comparatively modest home. The point is made: this is a show about a family of wannabes whose Hollywood pretensions are nothing but a trompe l'oeil, and Kim is the biggest wannabe of them all.

When *Keeping Up with the Kardashians* began on the E! network in October 2007, the entertainment press treated it largely with contempt. Brian Lowry, writing for *Variety*, could see no merit – and no future – in it whatsoever. 'Once you get past Kim's prominently displayed assets, there's not much of a show here, and no discernible premise,' he tutted, going on to call Kim and her sisters 'talentless tarts', before concluding with the suggestion that viewers would soon dismiss reality TV's latest pretenders.[1] Instead, the series would last for twenty seasons and fourteen years with multiple spinoffs; its successor, called simply *The Kardashians*, began in 2022. Clearly, *Variety* had missed something. And yet, the review, while ostentatiously disgusted by the Kardashians, was not entirely wrong about the family. All that the public knew about the Kardashians at this point was that Kim had been in a sex tape, that she sometimes hung out with Paris Hilton, and that her father, Robert (who died in 2003), had been involved in the nineties' biggest celebrity criminal trial. The most famous cast member, by traditional standards, was Kim's stepfather, Bruce Jenner, who had been an Olympic hero in the seventies but was now eking out his former glories on the speaking circuit.* There were families like the Kardashians all over Los Angeles: fame-adjacent but not exactly famous, dwelling in the foothills

---

* In 2015, Jenner came out as a trans woman and now uses the name Caitlyn, but in her 2017 memoir, *The Secrets of My Life*, she refers to pretransition events using male pronouns and the name 'Bruce'. I do the same here.

of the entertainment industry. People who had been somebody once or who were related to someone who had been.

From *Variety*'s perspective, the Kardashians were of little
importance. Previous fly-on-the-wall domestic reality shows,
like *The Osbournes* and *Gene Simmons Family Jewels*, had
been built around people who'd earned their celebrity the
old way (respectively, Ozzy Osbourne and Gene Simmons,
both heavy metal singers with reputations for outrageous
behaviour). They gave a glimpse behind the curtain. With the
Kardashians, there was no curtain. Why would the American
public switch on their TVs to spend time with this collection
of nobodies, in preference to hanging out with their own
friends and families? But, for an audience inculcated into
noughties gossip culture, it was precisely the Kardashians'
nobody status that made them fascinating. Over the preceding
years, audiences had learned to treat fame cynically. It was a
property that seemed to be summoned from nothing more
than pure will. Anyone – however talentless, however stupid,
however lacking in class – could make it, so long as they were
desperate enough. What, then, could be more watchable than
a whole family putting this theory into practice as they tried to
scrabble their way to the top?

Kim had always wanted to be famous. As a teenager in the
nineties (she was born in 1980), she'd been obsessed with early
MTV reality show *The Real World* and even considered applying to be on it.[2] Instead, she had set herself up as a Hollywood
stylist, with clients including Paris Hilton and the singer
Brandy Norwood. Paris facilitated Kim's first appearance
on television, a blink-and-you'll-miss-it moment in the 2003
season one premiere of *The Simple Life*; the Brandy connection
would lead to an even more significant development in Kim's
assault on celebrity. But as the mid-noughties arrived and Kim
hit her mid-twenties, none of this had translated into stardom.

The emergence of social media, though, meant that there were other routes to attention, and the most important social network at this point was MySpace, which launched in 2003.

In 2006, *Vanity Fair* breathlessly profiled the MySpace scene. MySpace, wrote James Verini, 'has emerged as a new breed of communication medium for the Internet Age, a place where identity and performance mingle wantonly'. He rattled over the stats: 50 million registered profiles, 24.5 million unique monthly visitors, 170,000 new sign-ups daily, all eagerly adding the posts and pictures that came under the heading of 'user-generated content'. 'The average MySpace user spends over two hours a month on the site,' gasped Verini. Though this sounds unimpressive from the vantage point of the present – in 2022, the average TikTok user spent almost a full twenty-four hours using the app each month[3] – it represented a significant change in how people consumed media. User-generated content meant the emergence for the first time of what might be considered user-generated celebrities. MySpace, wrote Verini, 'is changing the nature of celebrity, ushering Andy Warhol's concept of baseless stardom into a bizarre new realm'. (Warhol probably didn't originate the dictum 'In the future, everyone will be world-famous for fifteen minutes', but it remains nonetheless bound to him.)[4]

Verini introduced readers to figures like Christine Dolce (screen name 'ForBiddeN'), 'an Orange County woman, allegedly 24, who, for reasons no one save herself seems able to discern, has racked up 706,000 friends ... with not much more than a housepainter's flair for eye shadow, a distaste for grammar, and cavernous cleavage'. Now Dolce had her own clothing line. Then there was Tila Tequila – 'a West Hollywood woman who looks like a sex-crazed Asian Kewpie doll' – who had 760,000 friends[5] and had converted that fan base into a record deal and a club tour.[6] An archived version of Kim's page from 2006 shows that she was a long way short of these heights. Under the name 'Princess Kimberly' (bio: 'I'm a princess, you're not, so there!'), Kim had accumulated a mere 856 friends. One of them was Brandy's brother, the rapper Ray J.[7] He and Kim had started dating in 2002, after the end of her first marriage, and they were together until 2006.[8]

In June 2006, TMZ included Kim in a post on 'The Curse of Paris Hilton', listing the terrible fates that had come to Paris's best friends so far. Paris had fallen out with Nicole Richie in 2004, and she was feuding with Lindsay. (Paris had been filmed laughing as her friend Brandon Davis called Lindsay 'Firecrotch', among other insults).[9] Now, wrote TMZ, Kim 'seems to be the Paris friend of the moment. She has also been linked in recent weeks to [former boy bander and Jessica Simpson's ex] Nick Lachey. But as the aforementioned list of Paris pals proves, watch your step, Kim!'[10] It would take another six months for the 'curse' to take hold, starting with a comment from Ray J on Kim's MySpace page. 'Let's show the world our sex tape,' he wrote (according to Kim).[11] And the world, it turned out, wanted to see.

When TMZ reported the rumours of a Kim and Ray J video in January 2007, Kim still wasn't famous enough for her name to make the headline. Nor, perhaps gallingly for him, was Ray J. Instead, the post was titled 'Paris' BFF's Sex Tape'.[12] It had been over three years since *1 Night in Paris*, but the conjunction of 'Paris' and 'sex tape' was still too exciting to resist. In other ways, though, public attitudes had moved on. Audiences had become more knowing, more weary. There had been a great many such tapes in the intervening period, and a set of standard practices had evolved around their acquisition and distribution. Some sex tapes were, clearly, stolen; some were leaked by one party without the consent of their partner; and some were made with the explicit intention of their being released. Inspired by the belief that Paris had gained both profit and profile from her tape, some of Hollywood's most desperate had set out to make their own mark on the celebrity porn canon.

One of these was Dustin Diamond, a former child actor who had played the nerdy character Screech in the sitcom *Saved by the Bell* and its spinoffs from 1989 to 2000. In 2006, TMZ reported that a tape of Diamond in a threesome had surfaced and was being shopped around by an agent with a track record for brokering celebrity porn deals.[13] Diamond denied that he was complicit, but TMZ didn't believe him,[14] and the scepticism was justified. In a 2013 interview for the Oprah Winfrey Network, Diamond confessed that he had orchestrated the whole thing after hearing the rumour that Paris had made $14 million from her tape: 'And my buddy said, "$14 million? Holy smokes, where's the Screech sex tape? You got to be worth at least a million." And I thought, "Yeah – yeah, maybe." And that's as simple as it was.'[15] Diamond's acting agent appeared hopeful that the tape would help his client break out of his child star image and get more bookings.[16] It didn't. Later, Diamond expressed regret over the whole thing and said that it hadn't even been him on the tape but, rather, a body double. 'I definitely got some money off of it, but it definitely wasn't worth what the fallout was,' he said. 'People to this day look down on me. There's a lot of people who are like, "how disgusting of you" – and I didn't really do it.'[17] He wasn't included in *Saved by the Bell*'s 2020 revival, and he died of lung cancer in 2021.[18]

The earliest mentions of Kim's tape suggested that, like the Screech tape, it was being released by a male star who was trying to kick his career out of the doldrums. On Christmas Day 2006, AOL (which two years earlier had been so outraged by Nipplegate that it demanded repayment of its Super Bowl sponsorship) ran the following rumour on its Black Voices site: 'Desperate times call for desperate measures! Sources say a certain R&B singer, who has never really caught a major

break, is peddling an X-rated home video to adult entertainment companies in hopes that it will do for his career what
it has done for Paris Hilton's. I'm also told that said singer
believes that releasing the video will serve as revenge to his ex-
girlfriend who recently dumped him for another entertainer.'[19]

Gossip blog IDon'tLikeYouInThatWay picked up on this
and put names to the story, along with its own scurrilous
elaboration:

> In a blind item over at The BV Buzz, Jawn Murray hints that
> Kim Kardashian might be in a soon to be released sex tape
> with Brandy's little brother, Ray-J ... Kim dumped Ray-J for
> Nick Cannon recently, so this sounds about right. Any girl
> with huge boobs and a big ass should always get the benefit
> of the doubt, but this girl hangs out with Paris Hilton, so I'm
> going to go ahead and believe this is true ... Wow, this girl
> has had more black guys inside her than a pair of handcuffs,
> so, if you're white, your only hope to get with this girl is to
> promise her oral sex. Chances are she'd jump on your face
> like that thing in *Alien*.[20]

From there, the story made its way to Fleshbot (part of
the *Gawker* network), albeit with the more egregious racism
stripped out.[21] In mid-January 2007, TMZ confirmed the
existence of the sex tape.[22] In February, the porn studio Vivid
acquired the tape from an 'undisclosed third party' and
released it as *Kim Kardashian, Superstar Featuring Hip-Hop
Star Ray J*. The title was a joke because ... who even was this
girl? The biggest joke, though, was on Ray J, who had been relegated to a supporting credit beneath a woman with zero claim
to fame. Fleshbot professed itself unexcited by the commercial
release of the tape. 'Since we doubt a company like Vivid would
risk selling something like this without having the necessary
2257 documentation [a statutory declaration of majority,

signed by the subjects] on hand, there's the sneaking suspicion that Kim might be in full cahoots with its distribution process, which kind of takes the edge off everything as far as we're concerned,' the blog said ruefully.[23] In fact, Kim had immediately sued Vivid for violation of the right to privacy, but in April she filed for dismissal; the settlement was rumoured to involve a payment of $5 million from Vivid to Kim,[24] a deal that Vivid CEO Steve Hirsch considered 'an amazing investment'. The legal disputes had only helped to raise the video's profile, he said.[25] Still, even if *Kim Kardashian, Superstar* seemed to some viewers to lack the erotic charge of an authentic privacy violation, Fleshbot continued to give the tape – and Kim – extensive coverage.[26]

Perez Hilton was one of those who felt that Kim's sex tape was suspiciously convenient. 'She created her own stardom by dating up – that and banging her boyfriend, Ray J, on a sex tape,' he wrote in his 2009 book, *Red Carpet Suicide*. 'Her fame took on new heights after that. Stardom finally came for her, just like Ray J did!'[27] (Ray J has claimed that the sex tape was released according to an agreement he, Kim and Kris had made, inspired by their observations of Paris's career.[28] Joe Francis, of *Girls Gone Wild* fame, has also boasted that he brokered the deal with Vivid on the Kardashians' behalf.[29] Kim and Kris have both denied any complicity in the leak.) By August 2007, Kim had 66,000 MySpace friends.[30] She wasn't Tila Tequila yet, but she was on her way. Her path to being the next Paris had begun. Unlike Paris, though – in fact, unlike any of the women in this book so far – Kim was able to approach her fame with a clear view of what it would entail. Britney, Lindsay, Aaliyah and Janet were children when their public lives began. Paris couldn't have foreseen the way the internet would shape her celebrity, and Amy was torn between her talent and her addictions. But by the time Kim began to appear on the gossip blogs, she was an adult and had been able to study everything that came before: the feeding frenzy over Britney and Lindsay, Nipplegate, *1 Night in Paris*.

Kim also had the benefit of her mother, now acting as her manager – Kris coined the word *momager* to cover her role – and all Kris's long service in the lower realms of the entertainment industry. 'When I first heard about Kim's tape, as her mother, I wanted to kill her. But as her manager, I knew that I had a job to do, and I really just wanted her to move past it,' says Kris in the first episode of *Keeping Up with the Kardashians*.[31] In her 2011 autobiography, Kris was more coy about the sex tape – she never overtly refers to it – but more explicit about that fact that it was a crisis she turned into an opportunity: 'There was so much media coverage swirling around Kim then, both positive and negative, that we knew that we had to act fast and take advantage of the moment,' she wrote.[32]

As Bruce's manager after their marriage in 1991, Kris oversaw his move into reality TV when, in 2003, he joined the US version of *I'm a Celebrity ... Get Me Out of Here!* and, in 2006, *Skating with Celebrities*. His children and stepchildren followed his example. Two of his sons from his first marriage starred in a short-lived show called *The Princes of Malibu* (2005), a kind of gender-swap *Simple Life*. And Kris's eldest daughter, Kourtney Kardashian, appeared in *Filthy Rich: Cattle Drive* from the same year, a show in which spoiled Hollywood spawn displayed their incompetence as ranchers. (It lasted one inglorious season.) Kim was in a position to observe all this up close and to draw her own conclusions about the operation of fame. But before any of that, she had a front-row seat for the most grotesque soap opera in nineties celebrity. Before Kim, there was O.J.

To Robert Kardashian, Orenthal James Simpson was his college best friend. To the public, he was O.J., or 'the Juice' – a transcendent talent in college football who had an even more glorious career in the National Football League between 1969 and 1979, after which he parlayed his charisma and good looks into acting and sportscasting. To Kris (who met O.J. through Robert in 1975), he was the entry point to a world of celebrity, glamour, success and wealth. 'I rushed out of the airport to meet Robert Kardashian for our first legitimate date. Sitting in a green Mercedes, waiting for me at the curb at the airport, were Robert and O.J. Simpson,' Kris recalled in her 2011 autobiography. '"This is O.J., my best friend," Robert told me, introducing me to the famous football player, while I'm thinking, Oh my God. Oh my GOD! We drove back to Robert's house in Beverly Hills: Robert Kardashian, O.J. Simpson, and me.'[33] But, by the nineties, O.J.'s light had dimmed. As Bruce Jenner also found, it was difficult to sustain sporting fame when your sporting days were behind you. O.J. had, wrote journalist Jeffrey Toobin, 'only a vaporous, peculiarly American kind of renown: he was famous for being O.J.'.[34] But O.J. remained close to Robert and Kris: to their four children, he was 'Uncle O.J.', and his wife, Nicole Brown, was 'Auntie Nicole'.[35]

To Nicole, O.J. was something else. During their marriage, she made multiple 911 calls reporting that he was beating her; in 1989, he pleaded no contest to domestic violence charges.[36] In 1992, the couple divorced.[37] On 12 June 1994, Nicole and Ron Goldman – a friend of hers who worked at the restaurant where she and her family had eaten that evening – were stabbed to death outside her Los Angeles home. O.J. was arrested, questioned and released. Later, on 17 June, when charges were announced, his legal team (which included Robert Kardashian in an advisory capacity) brokered an arrangement for O.J. to turn himself in. Instead, he fled, in a white Ford Bronco driven by his friend Al Cowlings. The subsequent police chase received blanket news coverage, with helicopters tracking the car's every move from the air. Crowds turned out on the streets to watch the action, as though this were one last run for the football ace, cheering him on with homemade signs: WE BELIEVE YOU O.J., SAVE THE JUICE, LET DA JUICE LOOSE.[38] When R. Kelly imagined himself persecuted by the media over his relationship with Aaliyah, he reached for the image of the white Bronco. It would, recalled Kris (mindful of the metrics as ever), 'turn out to be one of the biggest television events in history, with an estimated 95 million people watching'.[39]

And those who tuned in would have seen the first screen appearance of a Kardashian. It was Robert (divorced from Kris by now) who appeared in front of the media to read a message left by O.J. that sounded very much like a suicide note: 'I have nothing to do with Nicole's murder ... If we had a problem, it's because I loved her so much ... At times I have felt like a battered husband.'[40] The man delivering these words to the cameras and press was small and anxious-looking, with a distinctive shock of white at the temples of his thick black hair.[41] 'Who's the bloody mouthpiece?' a British tabloid journalist reportedly shouted out, and that was the Kardashian name's entry into public life.[42]

The case went to trial in 1995. O.J.'s position seemed hopeless. Besides his history of violence against Nicole and the attempted flight, there was extensive physical evidence tying him to the crime scene, and he had no alibi. His legal team, though, was not going to fight the case on its merits. The Los Angeles Police Department had been exposed as institutionally racist through multiple scandals, most significantly the beating of black motorist Rodney King by four LAPD officers, all of whom were acquitted at trial by a majority-white jury in 1992.[43] Under the leadership of activist lawyer Johnnie Cochran (who had represented Michael Jackson in his 1993 molestation trial),[44] the defence's main strategy was simply to point out that O.J. was a black man and that, as a black man, he could expect no fair treatment from the Los Angeles legal system. This was highly effective – O.J. was unanimously found not guilty by the majority-black jury – but also very strange, because O.J. had never previously associated himself with the cause of racial justice.

Part of the reason for O.J.'s popularity during his football career and after was that he offered a totally unthreatening version of blackness to white America. He recused himself from the civil rights struggle in the sixties. He socialised with wealthy white people and lived in a wealthy white neighbourhood. (On 17 June 1995, when he returned home after his attempted flight and saw the crowds of largely black supporters gathered to meet him, he reportedly wondered out loud, 'What are all these niggers doing in Brentwood?')[45] He had, if anything, been treated with undue softness by the LAPD, which, as well as being racist, was singularly in awe of celebrity. O.J. had become black only when it was convenient to him.

But, then, it was equally plausible that he had stopped being an honorary white only when he became an embarrassment. *Time* put a darkened version of his mug shot on the front cover the week after his arrest. The magazine denied any ill intent, but the president of the National Association of Black Journalists called it 'a conscious effort to make Simpson look evil and macabre, to sway the opinion of the reader to becoming fixated on his guilt'.[46] (In a 2004 *Chappelle's Show* sketch, the set-up is that a 'racial draft' is taking place, with different ethnic groups bartering for different celebrities: one joke has the white delegation insisting that O.J. be drafted as black.)[47] Actually, Simpson's popularity proved impressively resilient after his arrest. It was Nicole's reputation that suffered: the defence leaned into tabloid portrayals of her as a promiscuous party girl, which made it even harder for the prosecution to overcome both a general lack of sympathy for victims of domestic violence and the specific hostility from black women on the jury towards white women who dated black men. A key part of the defence strategy was to create 'an outlet for the resentment of black women toward the blond temptress who had snared this black hero,' wrote Toobin.[48] It was a cruel double bind for the dead woman: if Nicole was the bad one and O.J. was good, he couldn't have killed her, and even if he did, she must have deserved it.

The trial and the acquittal tore America open. It tore the Kardashians as well. While Robert stood resolutely by his friend, Kris believed absolutely in his guilt. (It says something about Kris's reverence for fame that, even after this, she could still sound uncomplicatedly starstruck when writing about O.J. in her autobiography; but it says something about her loyalty to Nicole that fame never swayed her perception of what was right.) The youngest of the Kardashian children, Rob, was seven when the trial began; Kourtney, the eldest, was fifteen. All four were caught in the middle, and often suffered the consequences of being associated with their father, who became a pariah as O.J.'s other white friends peeled away. In the 2011 book *Kardashian Konfidential*, written by Kourtney, Kim and Khloé, the sisters recalled that period like this:

And it was scary sometimes, too, even dangerous. People camped outside the house, not just media but people who were only there because they were angry. A lot of them got nasty, and our dad said the phone was tapped. We got bomb threats, and one former policeman told Dad he was going to hurt us kids, so Dad always told us to be very aware of who was around us or who might be following us. One time we were kicked out of a restaurant because they didn't want our dad there. Some of our friends' parents stopped letting them come over to our house.[49]

By the time Robert died of oesophageal cancer in 2003, he seemed at best tragic and at worst pathetic, a sorry casualty of the worship of fame. In 1997, O.J. lost a civil case brought against him by the families of Nicole Brown Simpson and Ron Goldman: the jury concluded that O.J. had 'willingly and wrongfully' caused the two deaths.[50] This left him in a strange position. He had been declared innocent in one court but condemned in another. He had no hope of recovering his former life – the assumed murderer of a white woman could never be white America's favourite black man. The taint of guilt also meant there was no way for him to pivot into the role of civil rights figurehead, even if he'd been capable of the necessary gravitas. After his legal expenses and the loss of the civil trial (which entailed extensive damages), he was also no longer wealthy. He may have escaped justice, but O.J. was left with very little apart from notoriety.

O.J. staggered through the noughties as a grotesque. In 2005, he made a straight-to-DVD prank show called *Juiced*, which included a skit of him trying to sell a damaged white Ford Bronco, telling would-be buyers that it had 'great escapability!'[51] The year after, he signed on to write a book called *If I Did It*, which offered a 'speculative' account of how he could have committed the murders, while still tenuously maintaining his innocence.[52] (Notably, the book does not detail any alibi for the time of the murders.) Still, there was lower for him to go. In 2008, he was convicted of robbing a sports memorabilia dealer and sentenced to nine years in prison: the verdict was handed down thirteen years to the day from his original acquittal for the 1995 murders.[53] In a curious detail, while O.J. was in a hotel room planning the heist in 2007, he happened to see Kim on TV doing a promo for *Keeping Up with the Kardashians*. When she mentioned her father Robert's legal career and his role in the 1995 trial, O.J. was scornful. (It perhaps wounded his ego to imagine that he owed anything to anyone but himself.) 'Baby, your dad was shit,' he yelled at the TV. He predicted that the Kardashians' show wouldn't last two weeks.[54]

*

Probably, Kim would have achieved celebrity with or without the sex tape: anyone who pursued it after what she'd experienced during the O.J. trial had to really want it. In 2013, Nick Lachey recalled to *Details* magazine how, on a date in 2006, he and Kim had been mysteriously met by thirty photographers when they left the cinema. 'There are certain ways to play this game, and some people play it well,' he said, laughing.[55] But the sex tape gave her an angle. It provided the media with a template for the kind of public figure she was, and it created a reason to write about her. It also helped to get the reality show commissioned. (*Keeping Up* launched the same week as Tila Tequila's MTV dating show, *A Shot at Love with Tila Tequila*.)[56] By 2011, Kim really was a superstar, and so *Kim Kardashian, Superstar* could be relegated to the fringes of her public myth. *Kardashian Konfidential* doesn't mention the tape at all, although it does have a section of tips for 'when you screw up big time and majorly embarrass yourself to the point where you want to move to a tiny country no one's ever heard of'. For that, the three sisters recommended the following:

1. Hold your head high.
2. Take responsibility.
3. Get through it by making the best of it.
4. Rely on your support system (in our case, our family).
5. Learn from it.
6. Move on.[57]

In 2011, Kim had moved on. But in 2007, she was still very much in stage three, and the sex tape both helped her to get coverage and gave a narrative spine to season one of *Keeping Up with the Kardashians*. In episode one, Kris comes to Kim with an invitation from *The Tyra Banks Show*. But there's a catch: 'You'd have to talk about the tape,' Kris tells Kim. 'I don't wanna talk about it,' says Kim poutily. (Although, of course, by having this conversation, she's already talking about it on camera.) They agree that it's too big an opportunity to pass up, though, and Kim moves on to practising her appearance, with Kourtney taking the Tyra role.

'Why did you make a sex tape?' asks Kourtney-as-Tyra.

'Because I was horny and I felt like it,' says Kim, laughing about it now that she's playing around with her sisters. When she comes back from taping *Tyra*, she tells the family it's been a success and she's ready to put the tape in her history.

But the show isn't done with the sex tape yet. After a first season in which the Kardashian sisters model a *Girls Gone Wild* bikini line and Kim does her first *Playboy* shoot, the final episode (called 'The Price of Fame') centres on the revelation that some nude pictures of a seventeen-year-old Kourtney are being shopped around by a photo agent. This time, we see the family immediately contact their lawyer, who takes it to the FBI, which puts a stop to the distribution of the photos. The Kardashians had consummately taken control of the narrative. Over the course of eight episodes, they had transformed themselves into a group of characters the audience could care about. The Kardashians' conversations in the first season are sometimes stagey, the storylines often contrived, but there is something compellingly honest about them all the same. The camera shows them reading the tabloids and the blogs, dissecting celebrities (including themselves) in the same way the audience of the show did. Their obsession with fame is the most relatable thing about them.

Plus, it was fun to see them succeed. Season two of *Keeping Up* shows how quickly the family had achieved its ambitions. It opens with Kim boasting to her family that her name has become the most-searched term on Google and AOL and then segues into a montage of the modern celebrity dream. 'I'm finally at a really happy place in my life right now,' she says in a to-camera 'confessional' segment. 'Everything from career to

family is going perfect. Every night it's a different red carpet
event, a different photoshoot. There's paparazzi everywhere.'
This triumph did not make Kim popular with everyone. In
2018, her BFF-ship with Paris came to end, after Paris sniped
in a radio interview that Kim's butt was 'gross! . . . like cottage
cheese inside a trash bag'.[58] But the barb was misplaced. Paris
might have been noticeably thinner than Kim – Perez Hilton
joked about Paris 'running around with a "motor in the back
of her Honda" nobody named Kim Kardashian to make herself look even skinnier'[59] – but not every audience agreed that
smaller was better.

Kim's body ruled her out of white-dominated high fashion
in the early noughties, which was still transfixed by the waif
shape.[60] But with her tits and ass, she looked like one of the
'video vixens' who populated rap videos. Her first cover was
for *Complex*, a hip-hop magazine.[61] *King*, a lifestyle magazine
marketed to black men, was clear about what its readers prized
in a model. Editor Datwon Thomas told the *New York Times* in
2004: 'They want to see the thick girls, the girls with . . . with,
you know, a big backside.'[62] Of course, *King* made Kim a cover
girl in 2007, with the line 'Breakin' the Color Barrier'.[63] Being
of Armenian descent, Kim strictly qualified as white (albeit
a tenuous sort of white within the paranoid racial sorting
system of America) – but, the magazine implied, she was still
hot enough for its black readers, and everyone knew she dated
black men. They'd seen the video. In the noughties, this was
still taboo. Polling showed that support for interracial marriage among Americans reached 70 per cent in 2003 – but this
still left a sizeable minority of objectors.[64] Among that rump,
according to Jerry Oppenheimer's muckraking biography of
the Kardashians, was Robert Kardashian, who reportedly
responded to Kim's 2000 marriage to the black music producer
Damon Thomas by railing, 'I know these black guys and I've
known them all my life, and I know they love white pussy.'[65]

While there are good reasons to take the words of an anonymous source under advisement, suspicion towards interracial relationships was not unusual. It showed in the attitudes towards Nicole Brown Simpson exposed by O.J.'s trial; it showed in the outrage over Janet Jackson's Super Bowl performance with Justin Timberlake; it showed in the decision to recut the 2000 movie *Romeo Must Die* to remove the kiss between Aaliyah and her Chinese co-star, Jet Li.[66] In pornography, the hostility was even more starkly exposed. Production companies were reluctant to film scenes between black men and white women because certain regional audiences in the US cable market wouldn't tolerate such 'intermixing', and some white female performers refused to work with black men because they believed it would damage their careers (or, more simply, because they were racist themselves). 'Interracial' was (and still is) considered a porn category in its own right – a niche sexual interest on par with gangbangs or BDSM.[67] Kim's sex tape might have been a private document of her and her boyfriend initially, but once it was public, it wasn't just celebrity pornography: it was celebrity *interracial* pornography. That gave it a frisson of the forbidden and confirmed Kim's desirability (and, theoretically, availability) to a black male audience.

Inevitably, people wondered whether plastic surgery had been involved in the creation of Kim's remarkable body. In the *King* interview, she waved the suggestion away. 'Everyone now says I have a fake butt or butt implant,' she said. 'I'm Armenian; you should see all the women in my family. The women have bigger breasts and bigger butts. That's how I was born. I can't help it. I'm not gonna fight it.'[68] In season six of *Keeping Up*, she even has an X-ray taken of her butt to prove she is implant-free. The Kardashians could be startlingly open about plastic surgery and aesthetics: Kim received Botox injections on the show, boob jobs were discussed at the dinner table on camera, and both Kris and Bruce were filmed undergoing facelifts in gory detail. In their world, there was no shame in such treatments – and yet, it was important to Kim to establish the authenticity of her ass.

But, as any plastic surgery-savvy viewer could have told you, the favoured procedure for creating a Kim-style figure wouldn't have shown up on an X-ray anyway. The route to ideal thickness was a procedure called the Brazilian butt lift, pioneered in the sixties by Dr Ivo Pitanguy. Rather than using silicone to alter the body, a BBL works on the principle of redistribution: fat is taken from where it's not wanted on the patient's body (for example, the stomach or back) and transplanted into the ass for a fuller, rounder shape. It's an operation that can create dramatic results. It's also startlingly dangerous. When the fat is injected into the buttock, there's a risk of it entering the muscle or the bloodstream, leading to an embolism. One in every three thousand BBLs results in the death of the patient. Even if the surgery proceeds without incident, recovery is painful – patients are advised not to sit down for two to four weeks – and there's the possibility of uneven results after the relocated fat has settled.[69] Nonetheless, women wanted it. Between 2002 and 2015, use of the procedure grew by 3,267 per cent, and that growth was credited largely to Kim's influence.[70]

It wasn't just the rise in surgery that made Kim's ass seem like a malevolent cultural force to some. Her ability to monetise her looks, and her high-profile relationships with black men, opened her up to a kind of resentment not unlike that once aimed at her Auntie Nicole. In 2011, Kim went on the (very short-lived) reality show *H8R* to confront one of her online critics, and the 'hater' she ambushed was a black woman called Deena. 'I don't like how you out here tanning, how you got the lip injections,' Deena complains in a confessional piece explaining her animosity for Kim. 'Frankly, the bitch is a thief. She's got the fake booty, she's all over the media with our men.'[71] (For the record, Kim denies ever having had her lips or cheeks enhanced.)[72] Kim's figure was not just a stereotypical object of desire in black male culture, it was also – stereotypically – a paler version of how black women were supposed to look.

Deena was making a raw version of an argument about Kim that would come to dominate Kardashian coverage from about 2014 on: that Kim's body and her image were a form of cultural appropriation, or 'blackfishing' – that is, altering one's appearance to look black. The discourse over Kim's ass was 'a conversation that is essentially about the black woman's body, minus the black woman', according to Kierna Mayo, vice-president of digital content for *Ebony*, speaking in 2014.[73] (The unacknowledged converse here is that Mayo was having a conversation about Kim's body minus Kim.) But if the bitch was a thief, what had she stolen, and from whom? Her ass, by definition, was her own, and Kim had always been curvy, regardless of any speculation over later interventions. And though the objectification of the big butt was mainstreamed in the noughties via hip-hop, the fact that big butts were associated with black culture is not the same thing as big butts being a distinctive characteristic exclusively of black women. Aaliyah's body was closer to Paris's than to Kim's.

Some naturally skinny black women undergo BBLs or other forms of augmentation because, paradoxically, they don't feel that their black bodies are black enough without the exaggerated hourglass shape.[74] In a 2022 podcast, rapper Nicki Minaj – someone who has regularly celebrated her own thick figure in her music – admitted on a podcast to having had 'ass shots' (presumably filler) performed by 'some random person' in the mid-noughties, because working alongside male artists who fetishised 'big booty women' had left her feeling that she wasn't 'complete or good enough'.[75] If many black women couldn't achieve the ideal butt without intervention, it's hard to argue that a white woman with a full figure is 'taking something' from black women, regardless of whether the booty in question is 'fake'.

But the cultural appropriation argument, in its strongest form, is not about whether Kim has a right to her own ass; it's about whether she has a right to be objectified for it. In the book *Butts: A Backstory*, cultural critic Janell Hobson tells author Heather Radke that 'the preference for big butts [is] coming from Black male desire. Straight up, point-blank. It's only through Black males and their gaze that white men are starting to take notice.'[76] White men had adopted a fetish that properly belonged only to black men – though any survey of Marilyn Monroe films or Rubens paintings would confirm that white men have historically been perfectly capable of objectifying round asses under their own cognisance – and Kim, according to Radke, 'would continue to use her butt to regularly, and unabashedly, appropriate elements of Black culture, and continue to make a huge amount of money while doing it'.[77]

To this way of thinking, everything about Kim and her family becomes suspect. The writer Allison P. Davis has even argued that the Kardashians' 'relationships with Black men, and the multiracial children they had with them, seemed to offer some sort of cultural cover for their appropriation'.[78] Notwithstanding the hedging work being done by the phrase 'seemed to', Davis is suggesting here that even Kim's most intimate ties of affection are part of an impulse to exploit blackness. And, yet, while the focus here is all on Kim, many of the criticisms aimed at her could more meaningfully be aimed at male targets. Deena's anger at Kim's being with 'our men' would have made more sense as anger directed at the black men who, influenced by a culture that values whiteness and lightness, saw a fair-skinned woman as a status symbol. Or, perhaps it was no more meaningful than IDon'tLikeYouInThatWay's degrading comment about Kim's having 'had more black guys inside her than a pair of handcuffs': simply an inverted form of America's angst over miscegenation.

If the definition of cultural appropriation is to simulate the appearance of blackness without paying the costs, it cannot apply to Kim's ass. Either it is a product of genetics, as she states, and so innocent of deceptive intent, or it is the result of the multiple surgeries some have attributed to her (including, according to the most sensationalist speculation, rib removal and repeated BBLs), in which case she has suffered the same bodily trauma that a black woman would have.[79] If it is unfair that Kim could profit from her butt in a way that no black woman has, the origins of that unfairness do not lie in her, but in the history of the society in which she lives. But it's also true that a significant portion of her power to compel attention derived from that history. Kim – because of her body, because of the kind of men who desired her, because of the kind of men she desired – existed on the fault line of race and sex in America.

Sometimes, as with her #BreakTheInternet cover for *Paper* magazine in 2014, Kim seemed to explicitly conjure those tensions: the image of her balancing a champagne glass on her butt was taken by photographer Jean-Paul Goude, who replicated a picture of the black model Carolina Beaumont he had taken in 1976 and was later published in a book titled *Jungle Fever*.[80] On the field of Kim's ass, the battle of the politics of attraction could be fought and fought again. It was an ass that (through Kim's sex tape and through the family association with the Simpson case, alluded to several times on *Keeping Up*) represented the taboo of interracial sex and an ass that (because no one outside the family knew whether it had grown to look 'black' or been crafted that way and because of Kim's white-ish status as an Armenian American) represented the fragility of racial categories altogether.

Kim embodied a new physical ideal, as Tina Fey wrote in her 2011 book *Bossypants*: 'Now every girl is expected to have Caucasian blue eyes, full Spanish lips, a classic button nose, hairless Asian skin with a California tan, a Jamaican dance hall ass, long Swedish legs, small Japanese feet, the abs of a lesbian gym owner, the hips of a nine-year-old boy, the arms of Michelle Obama, and doll tits. The person closest to actually achieving this look is Kim Kardashian, who, as we know, was made by Russian scientists to sabotage our athletes. Everyone else is struggling.'[81] (Fey herself lost thirty pounds before appearing on camera for *Saturday Night Live*.)[82] But if you watched *Keeping Up*, you would see that even Kim struggled, albeit in a discreetly telegenic way. However well her look was suited to the moment, there was always work that could be done to improve it. There were injectables, diets, exercise and shapewear, by her own account, and there were extreme surgical interventions, if you believed the rumours.

Perhaps the struggle was the point. The thick look was as unnatural for many women as the superskinny bodies exemplified by Paris had been, or the supersize breast augmentations seen in the nineties – as represented by Kim's predecessor in celebrity porn notoriety, Pamela Anderson. In 2004, sex advice columnist Dan Savage responded to a letter from a reader wondering where all the 'super tits' had gone by theorising about why 'super tits' had become popular in the first place:

> The sudden appearance of women with ridiculously huge boob implants was arousing in part because of its shock value. There was the shock of women with such exaggerated racks, of course, but there was also the more important and, sadly, the infinitely more arousing shock of women finding a novel new way to imperil their health in order to attract

the attention of men. Men have always found it arousing when women go to bizarre extremes – self-mutilation (bound feet) and self-torture (high heels) – to make themselves more attractive. That enormoboobs played into the deeply ingrained and thoroughly eroticized misogyny that plagues all human cultures to varying degrees was lost on most men.[83]

Once the novelty of gigantic breasts wore off, there was no value in having them, and it was time to move on to the next implausibly exaggerated version of the female body. Kim individually and the Kardashians as a whole, with their casual personal embrace of plastic surgery and injectables, and their explicit documentation of these procedures on their show, displayed the *work* involved in achieving beauty. This could be seen, as Savage suggested, as a bodily avowal of feminine subordination, but the display could also be seen as an assertion of status.

In his 1899 book *The Theory of the Leisure Class*, economist Thorstein Veblen had noted that some goods become perversely more desirable purely because they are costly, and so act as advertisements for the possessor's wealth. 'By further habituation to an appreciative perception of the marks of expensiveness in goods, and by habitually identifying beauty with reputability, it comes about that a beautiful article which is not expensive is accounted not beautiful,' he wrote.[84] However Kim had actually achieved her figure, the public interpreted her look as constructed, and this was to her advantage. She was hot because she looked like money. A Kardashian body was a purposeful work, and its purpose was not only – perhaps not even primarily – to be attractive, but also to announce that this was the body of a person with the resources to alter herself as she pleased.

*

October 2007 could have been an inauspicious moment to launch a reality show about unabashed materialism. ('There's a lot of baggage that comes with us,' says Kim in one of the first to-camera segments of the first episode. 'But it's like Louis Vuitton baggage. You always want it.') Just a month before, Northern Rock had collapsed – the first financial institution to fall victim to what was then called the credit crunch. In 2008, the global economy was acknowledged to be in full-blown financial crisis, leading to the United States' deepest downturn since the Great Depression. Up to this point, the noughties had been an economic miracle: between the beginning of 2000 and the end of 2006, global GDP rose from $36 trillion to $70 trillion.[85] The entire world got richer, and it seemed as though it would go on getting richer for ever. All this, though, was underwritten by an inflated market in high-risk (so-called subprime) mortgages in the United States. These were valuable not because of the profit that could be made on repayments, but because the financial markets had worked out a way for lenders to package and resell these loans to investors. This made credit, for a time, stunningly accessible. It also demolished the incentive for lenders to do due diligence on the people to whom they were lending. By a sort of economic alchemy, vast sums of money were being made out of people who had none. And then, as John Lanchester explained in his book *Whoops! Why Everyone Owes Everyone and No One Can Pay*, it all suddenly changed:

From 2005 onwards, across the industry, most of the lending was reckless and some of it was actively criminal. [Former subprime broker Richard] Bitner's estimate at the time he left the industry was that 70 percent of mortgage applications were erroneous or fraudulent ... A survey from 2007 found that by 2006 some 60 percent of subprime applicants were lying about their income by more than 50 percent – so more than half of applicants were lying by exaggerating their income by more than half … Gee, what could possibly go wrong?[86]

What went wrong was the housing market crashed, and a full-on global recession ensued.[87] The United States lost 2.6 million jobs in 2008.[88] As with most things in America, the impact did not fall equally: because black people had been targeted for predatory lending, they were also disproportionately victims of the subprime crisis.[89] (The financial crisis also helped Barack Obama become, in 2008, the United States' first black president: as a Democrat, he was able to run against the incumbent Republicans' record of Wall Street deregulation.)[90] The losses of 2008 weren't only material, though. Disturbingly, the crisis revealed the entire basis of economic life to have been conjured out of a fiction and to be no more substantial than, say, the Kardashians' fame. Scratch away at both, and you would very quickly discover a void.

And, yet, this newly poorer America did not turn away from primetime celebrations of the wealthy and vapid. Instead, audiences looked to reality shows like *Keeping Up with the Kardashians* for escapism – and, perhaps, for something crueller. In a column about the Bravo channel's reality offerings, *Variety*'s Brian Lowry wrote, 'If Bravo at times seems to exist mostly to rub our noses in the wealth of others, the channel's glitz-laden lineup simultaneously lets us look down on these shallow, materialistic boobs (and in the case of the *Real Housewives* franchise – which has spread from Orange County to New York and Atlanta – big fake ones as well).'[91] The Kardashians – and Kim more than any of them (apart, perhaps, from Kris) – understood that their appeal rested on their ability to be both idols and scapegoats. It was possible both to want to be them and to despise them for everything they were, often within the same episode. Take, for example, the immaculate moment from season six, when Kim is hysterical over the loss of a diamond earring, and Kourtney deadpans, 'Kim, there's people that are dying.' As a viewer, you could relish Kourtney judging Kim's materialism, or you could fantasise about sharing in Kim's lavishness – or, perhaps, a little of both.

For Kim, 2008 was probably most significant not for the collapse of the economy, but because it was the year she joined Twitter, which had launched in 2006. By the end of the year, she was one of the biggest deals on there, with almost 2.7 million followers. (Coincidentally, the final episode of *A Shot at Love with Tila Tequila* had been broadcast in June 2008, bringing to a close any possibility of the one-time Queen of MySpace's becoming a Queen of Reality.[92] Tequila's stint as a contestant on the 2015 season of *Celebrity Big Brother* ended after a few days when the programme's producers were made aware that she'd sent a number of tweets praising Hitler, including one with a photo of her dressed as a sexy concentration camp guard taken outside Auschwitz.[93] Attention seeking, it turned out, had its limits.) Kim's Twitter audience put her in the top tier of that newly minted aristocracy, the influencers, able to command a reported $10,000 per tweet for endorsing products such as a weight-loss supplement called QuickTrim.[94] She could also use the platform to promote her own branded projects, like the perfume she was developing.[95] 'I realized pretty quickly that social media was going to be used as my marketing tool and my free focus group,' she said in a 2019 interview.[96] Instagram (which launched in 2010) would prove to be an even more important platform for Kim after she joined in 2012: picture sharing was perfect for a celebrity whose appearance was everything, and by then, she'd hooked up with the man who was going to help refine the next iteration of her image.

The only other person who came close to Kim's level of

insight into the noughties' aspirational culture was the rapper Kanye West. 'All Falls Down', from his 2004 debut album, *The College Dropout*, sketches the story of a 'single black female addicted to retail', then expands it into a thesis on race and consumerism: 'Drug dealer buy Jordans, crackhead buy crack / And the white man get paid off of all of that.' On 2005's *Late Registration*, 'Diamonds from Sierra Leone' lays out the gem trade's complicity in violence against black Africans for the sake of the stones worn by rappers. But even in these early songs, Kanye positioned himself as a participant as well as a critic. He can see the ills in the system, but he cannot opt out. In 'All Falls Down', he admits that he's as invested in materialism as anybody, and in 'Diamonds', the idea that he might make the principled gesture of returning his own jewellery is brusquely dismissed. And, over time, his music became more and more about celebrity itself – and his own in particular. You could see this early on in the 2004 video for 'New Workout Plan', which featured Anna Nicole Smith prominently in the role of 'Ultimate Trophy Wife'.[97] You could see it too in his verse on the remix of N.E.R.D's track 'Everyone Nose (All the Girls Standing in Line for the Bathroom)', with its name drop of 'Paris, Lindsay, Britney'.* By his 2010 album, *My Beautiful Dark Twisted Fantasy*, it had become a full-on obsession. On the track 'Hell of a Life', he raps, 'I think I just fell in love with a porn star / Turn the camera on, she a born star.' Dating a woman with a sex tape was the ultimate status symbol, and by now, Kim was the highest-status woman to have a sex tape. Although Kanye was a respected artist, and she was still roundly regarded (in the words of *Variety*) as a 'talentless tart', they made sense together. In 2011 (after Kim's seventy-two-day marriage to basketball player Kris Humphries), Kanye and Kim started dating.

---

* See Chapter 3: Lindsay, for more on this song.

In their relationship, he was presented as the Svengali, reshaping her into an object worthy of him. On his first appearance on the show as her boyfriend, he cleared out her closet (the same job she'd once done for Paris in an episode of *The Simple Life*), rewriting her look to fit his own aesthetic. Pre-Kanye, *Vogue* editor Anna Wintour had banned the Kardashians from the Met Gala for the crime of having 'zero style'.[98] From 2013 on, Kim was welcomed to the Gala red carpet, and her looks were reliably sensational. In 2014, Wintour not only put Kim and Kanye on the cover of her magazine, but she also commissioned the custom designer dresses Kim wore for it.[99] The benefit cut both ways: while *Vogue* and the Met were blessed with Kim's relevance, their endorsement authenticated her as a celebrity. And with Kanye, too, there was symbiosis: Kim provided him with a trophy, but his validation allowed her to conquer echelons of society previously closed to her.

By the time their marriage was over – the couple divorced in 2022 – he was the one with the reputation for tabloid chaos. Kanye had always been provocative and unpredictable, but over time, those traits began to seem closer to madness than genius. He caused consternation by appearing to endorse Donald Trump during a concert shortly after Trump's victory in the 2016 presidential election. (He called Trump's communication style 'very futuristic'.)[100] Soon after, he cancelled the rest of the tour and was hospitalised for a 'psychiatric emergency'. He later revealed that he had been diagnosed with bipolar disorder.[101] One of his first acts after being discharged was to meet with Trump in New York City.[102] For a black man to support Trump was unusual, though not unheard of (Trump took 13 per cent of the black male vote in 2016 and 19 per cent in the next election);[103] but from Kanye, an artist who had always been so acutely political, it felt like a sign of disorder. By 2022, Kanye had escalated to open antisemitism and praise for Hitler, his paranoia appearing to take its shape from the same ready supply of anti-Jewish sentiment that had found a voice in Tila Tequila during the previous decade.[104]

Kim had her own dealings with Trump, with a very different outcome. In 2018, she met the president to lobby for the release of Alice Johnson, a black grandmother who had spent over two decades in prison for non-violent drug offences.[105] When Johnson was freed, it was the first in a series of victories for Kim in the distinctly unglitzy realm of justice reform: she would further this interest by going on to study law, like her father. But her campaigning relied as much on her social media savvy as it did on legal knowledge, and this was especially powerful with Trump, a social media president whose interest in policy was dwarfed by his interest in tweeting. No one was better placed to influence him than the woman who had turned influencing into an art form. Kanye's encounters with Trump had left him looking unstable, exploited and a traitor to the principles he had embodied at the start of his career. Kim came away from Trump not merely unscathed but enhanced.

It was the continuation of a pattern for Kim. Whenever it has seemed that someone else was in a position to make use of her, Kim has somehow extracted herself from the situation with the advantage. Ray J, Paris, Kanye, Trump, even *Vogue* – Kim prospered from all of them. Fame in the Upskirt Decade was rapacious. It left its subjects damaged, wounded and, in some cases, dead. But not Kim. Partly, that was an accident of timing. Because she began to seek fame later in the decade, she was able to harness the internet rather than merely be ambushed by it. She also had invaluable support in the form of Kris: whatever one may think about a mother leveraging the attention generated by her daughter's sex tape to win a reality show, there is no question that Kris is a model of care compared to many parents of celebrities, who can range from the catastrophically naïve to the outright abusive and exploitative.

But most important of all, Kim had knowledge. She grew up with the man on the Wheaties box sitting at her breakfast table, her Uncle O.J. had been America's most notorious fugitive and her Auntie Nicole had ended up a celebrity corpse. Long before Kim became famous, she learned how fame works and how to play the game to her own benefit. She absorbed the fundamental lesson of the noughties, which was that value could be conjured out of pure will. By accepting the commodification of her private life, her relationships, even her body, Kim was able to travel all the way from a sex tape to the White House. Kim was the one who made it, and in the process, she remade what beauty meant in the Upskirt Decade.

8

Chyna: Power

'I wanted to be wanted, I wanted to be cared for, I wanted respect'

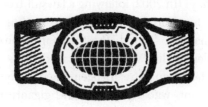

It's the World Wrestling Federation 2001 *Royal Rumble*. Chyna is sprawled on the canvas in front of an audience of 16,000 in the New Orleans Arena. Another 625,000 are watching the show on pay-per-view at home.[1] She's just taken a bad fall – not bad because it looks painful, but bad because it doesn't, and her efforts to appear stricken are more pathetic than the ruse itself. But even when she's flat on her back in a misfiring stunt, it's obvious why she's a star in the world of pro wrestling. Her tall frame is densely packed with solid muscle – she was billed on the commentary as 'standing six feet tall and close to the 200 pound mark,'[2] although she gave her own height as five feet, ten inches and was probably five foot nine.[3] She claimed she could bench-press an impressive 315 pounds.[4] Thick black Bettie Page-esque hair tangles around a striking face. A studded leather bikini strains across her extravagantly huge and obviously augmented breasts. (Because of her unusual stature, her implants had been custom designed: they were called the Chyna 2000s.)[5]

She was the first female wrestler to go up against the men. In 1999, she became the first, and remains the only, woman to win the WWF's Intercontinental Championship. Her ambition was to become 'the female Schwarzenegger'.[6] In the mythology of wrestling, Chyna is remembered as a trailblazer: 'Boldly treading into territories previously reserved for the Y chromosome contingent of the WWE locker room, Chyna broke as many gender barriers as she did bodies,' the WWE's site reads today.[7] (In 2002, following a lawsuit from the World Wide Fund for Nature, the World Wrestling Federation changed its name to 'World Wrestling Entertainment'.[8]) The Ninth Wonder of the World, they called her – the title of Eighth Wonder having already been taken in the eighties by André the Giant, who really did have gigantism and who, with his role in *The Princess Bride*, would become one of the first wrestlers to win mainstream popularity. Chyna was not actually a giant, though she was abnormally tall and unnaturally strong. She was given her ring name when she joined the WWF in 1997. It was ironic, she wrote in her 2001 autobiography, *If They Only Knew.* 'If you think of Chyna, you think of fine china, something fragile, something delicate, and ... here was this muscular, brutal woman who was beating the hell out of all these guys.'[9]

When Chyna took the fall in the *Royal Rumble*, though, she was not fighting a man. It was the end of a grudge match between her and a faction called Right to Censor – a stable of wrestlers dressed in white shirts and black ties, and characterised as moral majority conservatives. Right to Censor was introduced by WWF in 2000 as a mockery of the real-world moral majority conservatives in the Parents Television Council, which had accused the wrestling promotion of causing the deaths of four children. The PTC would go on to play a significant role in the fall of Janet Jackson; right now, though, its fictional counterpart was exercised over a different set of breasts.*

The year before, Chyna had been the cover star of the November issue of *Playboy*. Ever since, Right to Censor had been feuding with her, calling the pictorial 'nothing more than sugarcoated pornography!' This was received as a grave insult by Chyna and wildly cheered by wrestling audiences, who were robustly opposed to Right to Censor and the PTC, as well as being great fans of sugarcoated pornography.[10]

If reality TV was the signature art form of the noughties, pro wrestling lit the way. Before the nineties, wrestlers had by convention maintained the pretence that what happened in the ring was authentic. In the carny slang of the industry, the word for this is *kayfabe*. And wrestling is the truth, after a fashion. Wrestlers really do take blows from each other. They really hit the canvas. They get bruises, concussions and broken bones. They bleed – sometimes they cut themselves deliberately to ensure this. But this real violence happens in the course of choreographed and predetermined fights, which are performed in the service of planned storylines: there are heroes (*faces*) and villains (*heels*), rivalries and alliances, slapstick and tragedy, glorious title runs and gutting disappointments. Wrestling combines the physical rigour of ballet with the melodrama of soap opera and the thrill of genuine physical stakes. Its storylines have to absorb and accommodate life outside the fiction. Injuries, absences and animosities

---

* See Chapter 5: Janet for more on the story of the PTC and WWF.

must all sometimes be written into the narrative – or written around.

When Kim turned her sex tape into a narrative device, she was doing what wrestlers had been doing for decades: transforming life into entertainment. In 2008, she was a ring girl for *WrestleMania XXIV.* When she allowed herself to be cast in the role of antagonist to her family – as in, for example, the opening to season two of *Keeping Up with the Kardashians,* where her new-found celebrity status leads to her acting like a brat – she was performing what a wrestler would have recognised as a heel turn. Kim understood that, without conflict, there can be no drama, and that someone has to generate that conflict. More than that: Kim understood that audiences don't want merely to feel love for the characters on their screens; they also want to feel hate. As wrestlers had learned long ago, there is as much craft in winning the crowd's loathing as there is in earning their affection. And when Kim's marriage to Kris Humphries began to collapse almost before *Kim's Fairytale Wedding: A Kardashian Event* could make it to TV, she was experiencing the terrible moment when kayfabe breaks and the in-ring storytelling is undone by real life.

In wrestling, those moments had become ever more frequent since the arrival of the internet. Wrestling's scriptwriters had to contend with a new kind of media-literate fan: an audience that not only followed the action in the ring, but who also studied the industry behind it, eagerly trading locker room gossip on forums and through newsletters. By the late nineties, the rigid maintenance of kayfabe was dust, in the same way that the old securities of mainstream celebrity would soon collapse. Wrestling's most avid fans were traditionally called *marks*, their willingness to suspend disbelief making them tantamount to a con man's victims. Now, the fans started calling themselves *smart marks*, or '*smarks*' for short. For wrestling to work, it would have to embrace the

smudged line between reality and fakery and give those knowing viewers the compliment of acknowledging the artifice. A
wrestler's job is to *sell* this semi-fiction: to sell their character
(*gimmick*), to sell the storylines (*angles*), to sell the in-ring
combat by appearing to be really hurt even when they aren't.
(Although, as any wrestler knows, the best way to look hurt is
to get hurt.)[11]

Chyna did not sell her fall at the 2001 *Royal Rumble* very
well, but it's what comes next that really outraged fans. Her
opponent, Ivory, crawls over and extends an arm across
Chyna to pin her, which makes Ivory the winner of the
Women's Championship. Ivory's win, though, was not going
to be the main story here. 'Oh my God, she's not moving,' says
announcer Jim Ross, dropping from his habitual southern roar
into a low tone of concern. Sirens blare. Colour commentator
Jerry Lawler gets up from the desk and climbs into the ring to
check the apparently immobilised Chyna – something he had
last done in 1999, when wrestler Owen Hart died in the ring
in front of a live audience after a fall from a faulty harness. The
voice Ross uses was even referred to, informally, as 'the Owen
Hart voice', a signal to fans that events had slipped beyond
wrestling convention and should be taken very seriously.

The similarities were far too specific to be unplanned.
WWF had blatantly exploited a real death to sell a fake injury.
Even for a surpassingly crass medium, this was shocking.
'Really tasteless' was the *Wrestling Observer Newsletter*'s verdict, although it did concede that 'The work itself during the
match was a lot better than most WWF women's fare.' It then
awarded the match half a star, which shows the esteem in
which women's wrestling was generally held.[12]

At a time when female wrestlers in the WWF were branded
as 'divas' and when their main job was to titillate the audience with 'accidental' nudity, Chyna rejected being one of the
girls and insisted on going up against the men. She dedicated

herself to the creation of a body that was powerful enough to work with even more powerful opponents and then pushed that body harder still to meet the demands of feminine sexiness. But no matter how strong the body, most wrestlers are ultimately serfs within the kingdom of the promoter. Contracts routinely sign away the right for a wrestler or their estate to sue in the event of injury or death, even when it is caused by negligence on the part of the promoter. The wrestler is responsible for their travel and accommodation expenses. And, in what would prove to be a particularly ruinous clause for Chyna, the promoter holds copyright on a wrestler's 'ring name, likeness, personality, character, caricatures, costumes and gestures'. Even a wrestler's legal name will become property of the promoter. At the end of the contract, anything a wrestler brought with them reverts to the wrestler, but anything that was developed during the contract (for example, Chyna's name and gimmick) belongs to the promoter in perpetuity.[13] A performer who is naïve about intellectual property may well find themselves holding nothing at the end of their term – not even their identity.

In the World Wrestling Federation, Vince McMahon was king. McMahon had taken control of WWF from his father (also called Vince) in 1982, but he wasn't interested in simply keeping the family business going. Depending on how your interests aligned with his, McMahon was either a visionary or a shark. By buying up smaller regional promotions, he turned WWF into one of the most powerful brands in wrestling: only Ted Turner's World Championship Wrestling (WCW) could count as a rival. Between 1995 and 2001, WWF's flagship pre-recorded cable show, *Monday Night Raw*, would be aired at the same time as WCW's live broadcast, *Monday Nitro*, in a take-no-prisoners fight for ratings that became known as the Monday Night Wars.[14] It wasn't a coincidence that WCW chose a title that was phonetically identical to WWF's: this was a war of outstanding macho pettiness, which frequently spilled out on-screen.[15] *Nitro*'s live commentators would give away spoilers for the pre-taped *Raw* episode as it screened. *Raw* retaliated with a segment called 'Billionaire Ted's Wrasslin' Warroom', in which actors played unflattering parodies of WWF stars who'd defected to the opposition.[16]

Turner had deep pockets and a deep loyalty to the blue-collar pantomime of wrestling that many of his executives found perplexing. But McMahon had something that would prove even more valuable than Turner's capital. He had, simply, a ringmaster's genius for entertainment. Under his leadership, storylines began to incorporate romance, bizarre humour and crossover stars from sports and pop music: the fights were still centre stage, but what happened around them made them matter even more to the audience. McMahon recognised that he was dealing with a more sophisticated crowd, who didn't want to see one-dimensional goodies and baddies, but who hungered instead for anti-heroes and rebellion. In the time Chyna was with the company – known within the WWF as the Attitude Era – The Rock became a fan favourite by playing the part of a swaggering bully, while legit Olympic wrestling champion Kurt Angle's lectures about hard work and clean living (once classic face rhetoric) made him a heel. And McMahon made himself (and his wife and children) a part of the action, getting into the ring as a character called 'Mr. McMahon'. 'He turned his daughter into a villainous, conniving bitch, his wife into a meddlesome shrew, his son into the cowardly lion, himself into a blathering, pompous stuffed pigeon, all for fun,' wrote Chyna. But she thought of the real Vince McMahon, the one behind the kayfabe, as a father.[17]

Chyna would return from her phoney injury to win the title from Ivory, as narrative dictated – after all, at this point, Ivory was the heel, and Chyna was the face. There had never yet been a female crossover star from pro wrestling. Now Chyna looked ready to become the first: her 'female Schwarzenegger' dream must have seemed within reach. By playing a cartoon version of women's liberation to great effect, she had become one of the biggest names – and biggest earners – in the WWF. Soon after she won the Women's Championship, though, her WWF career would be over. A three-way collision between in-ring storylines, backstage politics and her personal life would see her cut loose from the WWF in the most crushing way. After that, she was set on a path towards self-destruction that took her through a sex tape, pornography and opioid addiction, and, eventually, to an early death. And as she fell, WWF was boosting the career of a man who represented in every way the backlash against women in America. The wrestling world that broke Chyna would also be the making of President Trump.

In Chyna's account, Vince McMahon had been unimpressed when she was first pitched to him. Not despite her remarkable size, but because of it. She was plainly too big – and, with her bulked-out frame and prominent jaw, too removed from conventional hotness – to be plausibly incorporated into storylines with the women wrestlers. But even an unusually large woman is smaller than most men, especially when the men in question are the enormous specimens who make up the majority of pro wrestlers. 'Forget it. Not gonna happen,' said an incredulous McMahon, according to Chyna's autobiography. 'Okay, so she hits a guy. What then? The guy's gonna hit her back? Unh-uh. No one's gonna work with her. No one's gonna sell her, it's taboo. And if they even did, who's gonna want to allow themselves to get beat up by a woman?'[18] Even for a heel, pummelling a woman would be a step too far (in the ring, at least). And for any male wrestler, being seen to lose to a woman would be a humiliation of his character. Whichever way the match turned out, fighting Chyna seemed to offer only downsides for a man.

But she had an influential sponsor in the form of Triple H, a rising star of WWF whose real name was Paul Levesque and whose real relationship to Chyna was boyfriend. McMahon may have had 'no interest in seeing a big woman ass-kicker',[19] but Triple H recognised how much value there was in his girlfriend's singular look, and he was in a position to talk McMahon round.

Chyna was introduced to WWF in 1997 as Triple H's bodyguard and became a member of D-Generation X, his stable. She specialised in interfering with his matches, often by delivering her trademark 'low blow' to his opponents – which was, exactly as you'd imagine, a crotch shot. Like Triple H, Chyna had trained at Walter 'Killer' Kowalski's wrestling school in Malden, Massachusetts, but she was never the greatest in terms of technique. She had discovered the discipline at the relatively late age of twenty-five after watching it on TV.[20] Within a year, she had made her first competitive appearance – fighting a man in drag, because there were no women big enough to give her a match.[21]

Her background was bodybuilding, which was notorious for cultivating an ungainly ring style. Male wrestlers who, like Chyna, came in under six feet often specialised in high-flying, risk-taking acrobatics, as was the case for Chris Benoit and Eddie Guerrero, deeply respected wrestlers who would go on to become two of McMahon's biggest stars. Chyna didn't have the agility for that. Other wrestlers compensated for limited skill by becoming experts at taking punishment. Mick Foley, who joined the WWF in 1996 and became most famous as the damaged weirdo Mankind, struggled to master the moves at the start of his career. 'I have several witnesses who can attest that I was the worst natural wrestler they ever saw,' he wrote. 'So when in the ring with me, the other students concentrated instead on what I was capable of – namely, taking an ass kicking.'[22] Foley's craft improved vastly, but his performances would always depend on his spectacular talent for taking bumps. By 1999, his catalogue of injuries ran to 'multiple concussions, a nose broken twice, a dislocated jaw, numerous knocked-out teeth, a broken wrist, a broken thumb, broken ribs, a broken toe, bone chips in his elbow, two herniated discs, more than 300 stitches, a torn abdominal muscle, a surgically repaired knee, and, oh yes, a partially amputated right ear!' All this was, declared the introduction to his autobiography, merely 'the retail price for success'.[23]

It seemed unlikely, though, that a wrestling audience would want to see a woman succeed in the same self-brutalising way – even if the male wrestlers had been willing to risk the hatred of the crowd by giving Chyna that kind of rough treatment. In fact, Chyna couldn't take heavy bumps: her breast implant had been ruptured by a simple 'clothesline' (a move in which a wrestler is struck across the neck or chest by running into an opponent's outstretched arm) in a 1998 bout, after which she had the custom set fitted.[24] Chyna couldn't meet the men as a physical equal. What she had, instead, was a gimmick, and her gimmick was 'being female'. She represented the nightmare fantasy of the empowered woman, the Amazon in the locker room. Carefully, the writers integrated her into the storylines, gradually building up her encounters with male wrestlers until the audience was ready to accept her as a force in her own right. Every time she landed a move on one of the men, she gained the appearance of power. Eventually, she looked powerful enough that viewers would tolerate her being on the receiving end of violence without its damaging her opponent's reputation. Winning the Intercontinental Championship over rival Jeff Jarrett in October 1999 was the pinnacle of that arc.

But she won it as a woman rather than purely as an athlete.

The match that gave her the title was the summation of a long-running 'battle of the sexes' angle. In the dramatic terms of wrestling, it was perfect because it gave something to both sides: Jarrett's boorishness shone a sympathetic light on Chyna's character, but the match also offered viewers the pleasure of seeing a troublesome woman being put down. Fans brought homemade signs to the match reading, CHYNA – MAKE THE SEXIST PIG SQUEAL! and MOP THE KITCHEN FLOOR WITH JARRETT'S ASS!, but also CHYNA SUCKS! GIVE HER A VACUUM CLEANER![25] – which is exactly what the WWF writers did. The Intercontinental Championship match was a 'Good Housekeeping' match, in which weapons were allowed. This had an obvious storytelling advantage: it was easier to believe Chyna could beat a man if she wasn't doing it with her bare hands. But it was the kind of weaponry involved that was really crucial: 'All the holy relics of house-wifery – pots, pans, vacuum cleaners, toilet seats, that kind of crap – would be laid out for us to use. The kitchen sink,' wrote Chyna.[26] For fans who loved Chyna – and there were a lot of these – the irony in this visual was all to her advantage. And for the fans who loved to hate her, the irony ran against her: she had the belt, but her winning only proved that, as a woman, she was naturally better with a mop. Even so, Jarrett held out for a rumoured $250,000 payday from WWF before he submitted to being beaten by a girl, and not everyone found it convincing.[27] Commentator Jim Ross, for one, said he always considered it a mistake.[28]

Chyna would win the Intercontinental Belt one more time, in August 2000, but not by beating a man: it would be in a mixed tag-team match, and she gained the victory by pinning her female opponent, Trish Stratus. Clearly, the WWF had reached the limits of what it felt it could achieve with Chyna as a ballbuster archetype. Part of the reasoning behind the 2001 *Royal Rumble* injury angle – as well as cementing Ivory's heel credentials – was to weaken Chyna in-story, preparing her for moving into the women's division. 'The idea seems to be that she's going to have a bad neck to show vulnerability and no longer wrestle against men, which is a good thing at this point because whatever novelty value that thing had is all played out,' concluded *Wrestling Observer* in its write-up of the pay-per-view.[29]

But there were other ways to use her, and one of these was in romance storylines – if *romance* is the right word for the WWF's unwholesome attitude towards sex. For example, Chyna was in an ongoing kayfabe relationship with Mark Henry, a black wrestler with a ladies' man gimmick and the nickname 'Sexual Chocolate'. This started when the couple was 'forced' to kiss by The Rock in order to humiliate Chyna, and it culminated in a deeply bad-taste reversal, when Chyna proposed a threesome with her friend 'Sammy'. 'Sammy', it was revealed on-screen, was a 'transvestite', and a disgusted Henry was shown throwing up.[30] Again, this angle worked both for and against Chyna, depending on where audience sympathies lay. ('Wouldn't play today, would it,' said Jim Ross in 2020, looking back at the storyline. '[If] you want to shit on transgender people, there's no way to do it.')[31] For her fans, this was an ingenious ruse by which she turned Henry's slea-ziness against him. For those who saw her as a comic figure, the punchline landed differently: Henry had been attracted to Chyna, the thinking went, only because he couldn't tell the difference between a man and a woman.

The barbs about Chyna looking manly were constant and cruel. When she went on *The Howard Stern Show* in 2001, Stern asked whether *Playboy* had airbrushed out her penis.[32] On the face of it, this was ridiculous. One of the things that Chyna's appearance in WWF made starkly obvious was the difference between male and female physicality. But it was true that there was something masculine about her. Partly, this came down to the fact that her disciplined mix of exercise and nutrition had produced a body composition with the usual female fat deposits stripped away: the only curves on Chyna's body were silicone. There was also the sexist assumption that a woman *shouldn't* be strong – something Chyna had encountered, to her cost, back when she was participating in fitness pageants, where she would lose to women whose less chiselled figures were more appealing to the judges.[33]

There was more to it, though. There was the prominent jaw (she had corrective surgery in 1998, after which her popularity soared).[34] And there was her fluting, raspy voice, which sounded almost like a man using falsetto. (She claimed this had been caused by her being repeatedly clotheslined in the throat.)[35] Taken together, this all points to one likely cause: anabolic steroid abuse. As well as promoting muscle growth far beyond what exercise alone can achieve and encouraging faster healing from injuries, steroids cause bone growth and thicken the vocal cords.[36] Long-term use leads to enlarged internal organs and a risk of heart attack – Eddie Guerrero died of heart failure in 2005, aged thirty-eight.[37] It also causes paranoia, aggression and delusions – when Chris Benoit murdered his wife, Nancy, and son, Daniel, in 2007 before killing himself, one of the posited factors was 'roid rage' from Benoit's long-term steroid abuse (although massive brain damage caused by repeated concussions was also likely to have contributed).[38]

Chyna adamantly denied ever taking steroids. She treated the allegations as another method of demeaning her by implying she hadn't really earned her muscles: 'Heaven forbid I did it on my own, with sweat and hard work,' she wrote.[39] Still, there's little room for doubt. Within the WWF, steroid use was an open secret – in 1991, Dr George Zahorian, a ringside physician for the WWF, was convicted of selling steroids to professional wrestlers.[40] Two years later, Vince McMahon was indicted on charges of steroid distribution. He maintained his innocence and was found not guilty, but explosive testimony from wrestlers during the trial made it clear that steroids were pervasive in the WWF locker room. Hulk Hogan – who for years had told 'all the little Hulkmaniacs' to 'say your prayers and eat your vitamins' before going on to family-friendly crossover success with films like *Mr. Nanny* – had testified that he regularly picked up steroids from company headquarters.[41] Chyna would certainly have encountered steroids before WWF, when she was on the bodybuilding circuit. When she joined WWF, the incentives to use only increased, as she transformed herself from the ripped woman of her fitness pageant era to the bulging superhuman in the wrestling ring. In a 2020 podcast, Jim Ross referred openly to Chyna's 'juicing'.[42]

The mood-altering effect of steroid abuse might also help explain why Chyna's exit from the WWF was so precipitous and so bitter. Or perhaps the basic facts of her situation in 2001 are sufficient explanation on their own. From the outside, she was well placed. She was popular with fans, her issue of *Playboy* had been a success, and in 2000 she'd even scored a guest role on the NBC sitcom *3rd Rock from the Sun*, playing a love interest to one of the main characters. Her character is Janice, a police officer whose strength puts her male colleagues to shame but who, deep down, wants to be seen as the soft and vulnerable woman she truly is. Perhaps this wasn't a huge stretch for Chyna, but she performed creditably enough for the role to be brought back in the two-part season finale. Her colleague The Rock had just made his movie debut, in *The Mummy Returns*, and was about to be rewarded with his own star vehicle in the form of follow-up *The Scorpion King*. Why shouldn't Chyna be the next wrestler to take Hollywood?[43]

Inside wrestling, though, things were more fraught for her. There was the matter of her relocation to the women's division, for one thing. Given Chyna's disparaging characterisation of women wrestlers 'who shake their asses, bat their eyelids, make out in the ring, do the whole Jezebel thing to entice men, then take them out with a shoe or something when they're not looking', she can't have been delighted by the future being laid out for her. With the intergender angle exhausted, what remained for her, according to Jim Ross, were storylines with 'sexual overtones, man-woman type deal. Or maybe she had a lesbian affair'. Her unhappiness showed in the ring, where she disrespected Ivory during their rematch by 'no-selling' (acting unhurt by) her attacks.[44] This was unprofessional, but it was also bad for Chyna personally, because it undid the work previously put into building her character up: if she could now beat Ivory without breaking a sweat, it made no sense that Ivory had been able to injure her in the first place.

Meanwhile, kayfabe had come crashing in on her private life. In 2000, Triple H was written into a romance storyline with Stephanie McMahon (Vince McMahon's daughter). This turned into a real-world relationship. Around the same time, Chyna and Triple H broke up.[45] Chyna took the split hard – in her autobiography, published after Triple H and Stephanie were married, she continued to refer to him as 'the man of my dreams'.[46] On its own, this would have been heartbreaking enough, but in the highly political landscape of WWF, it was a disaster. She lost not only the man she had expected to marry, but also the man she thought of as a surrogate father. Triple H was now her ex, and Vince McMahon was now his future father-in-law. She could hardly expect advantageous treatment from the writers in these circumstances, and her demotion to women's wrestling must have felt like a deliberate insult. Her distress began to show when she was at work, and management started to consider this emotional woman a liability.[47] (It is curious that no similar judgement was cast on Chris Benoit in 2007: right up until he murdered Nancy and Daniel, he was considered a star employee. After the deaths, but before the full details of Benoit's violence came out, he was even honoured with a televised tribute special.)[48]

Chyna's relationship with WWF was insecure because she had never developed a sure grasp of her place in wrestling's hierarchy. When her autobiography came out in 2001, it caused a minor scandal: she had written disrespectfully about her trainer, Killer Kowalski. In the macho, honour-based culture of wrestling, you paid your dues and genuflected to your elders: you certainly didn't mock your trainer's toupee and claim that he had done nothing for your career. 'She's the biggest liar I have ever come across,' an outraged Kowalski told the wrestling press.[49] Chyna had also offended by writing in critical terms of her treatment when she first arrived in the WWF: 'You come in new, everybody's checking you out. You come in new as a woman, they are checking you over. And if you come in as a woman who looks like she could break Xena [as in *Xena: Warrior Princess*, the fantasy action series starring Lucy Lawless] in half, it's over and out. You get everything from being called a dyke to getting propositioned for a threesome.'[50]

WWF management would deny that there was any truth to Chyna's allegations,[51] but those claims chimed with accounts from other female wrestlers. In 1999, Sable (real name Rena Mero) had brought a lawsuit against the WWF claiming (according to a report in the *New York Post*) that she had been stripped of her championship belt because she refused to do in-ring nudity, and further alleging 'unsafe conditions, sexual harassment – including a request to go to the mat in a lesbian storyline – and rampant steroid abuse'. (The parties settled, in a deal that required Mero to give up her stage name and barred her from wrestling for three years.)[52] Surprisingly, the case left no bad blood between Mero and her former employer, and she was brought back in 2003 for a storyline in which she played Vince McMahon's mistress.[53]

In 2001, Chyna had one more throw of the dice to save her

standing with the promotion. When her contract came up for renegotiation that year, she did what women have frequently been told they should do in hostile corporate situations: she leaned in and demanded what she considered to be her full value. When management offered her $400,000 a year, she countered by asking for $1 million. Her calculation may well have been that, as a burgeoning crossover star, she really was worth that much to the WWF, but she had badly misread her position. Even for a top-tier wrestler, $1 million was aiming high. For a wrestler with a played-out gimmick who had acquired a reputation for being unstable, and who showed no will to cooperate with the WWF's new plans for her, it was outrageous. Besides, who else was going to pay her that much? In the spring of 2001, WWF had bought out both WCW and smaller upstart company Extreme Championship Wrestling.[54] Vince McMahon was the only game in town, and as far as WWF management was concerned, asking for $1 million was tantamount to Chyna handing in her notice. Her time in the WWF was done.[55]

Some wrestlers are born to the trade. Owen Hart was the son of Stu Hart, the greatest wrestling trainer and promoter in Canada: of the twelve Hart children, all the boys became wrestlers, and all the girls married wrestlers.[56] The Rock's father and grandfather were wrestlers before him.[57] Eddie Guerrero belonged to a sprawling dynasty of *luchadores* (competitors in *lucha libre*, or 'freestyle', wrestling).[58] Other wrestlers, like Mick Foley and Chris Benoit, fall in love with the ring and will do anything to be a part of it after that.[59] Then there are those who seem to have nowhere else they belong – people like André the Giant, who simply do not fit into any other world; people like Chyna. The first time she saw wrestling, when she was in her mid-twenties, she shouted 'I can do that!' at the TV. She had no interest in women's wrestling, which she immediately pegged as 'all T&A', but the men's fascinated her, with 'its epic ambition, its winking boorishness, its harmless heroics'. Here was a realm where her size would be an asset rather than a mark of freakishness; where she would be celebrated, not rejected; a place she could call home.[60]

Any wrestler's account of their life has to be assessed as part of their gimmick. Chyna's character was the tough girl who overcame impossible odds – and so that was the story her autobiography told. It was not a narrative that served to flatter anyone else in it – the only person to come out well from her telling was Vince McMahon, whom she seemed able to separate from her criticisms of his business, but even that relationship was flimsier than she realised. Besides raising objections from Killer Kowalski and WWF management, her book was disputed by her parents, who were portrayed as neglectful, narcissistic and abusive – charges they denied. (However, the wrestling elements were happy to believe the worst about her family, and her family was happy to believe the worst about wrestling. Someone was to blame, after all.)[61] If Chyna was working an angle with her memoir, though, it didn't go over with the fans. One wrestling blog's review complained, 'Why is the result so goddamn ... well, *whiny*? ... little more than a "woe is me!" tale about what a horrible life she had.'[62]

If They Only Knew is an often angry, sometimes incoherent book. (The chronology of her pre-wrestling life is hard to put together.) At a minimum, it's misleading about her use of steroids. But even if the book is only partially reliable, it would still be fair to say Chyna had a horrible life.

She was born Joan Laurer in 1969 in Rochester, New York, to two people who – by Chyna's account – should probably never have been together. She described her father, Joe, as an adulterer, a conman and a drunk; her mother, Janet, 'routinely withheld affection, was suspicious of everyone, and had a wicked backhand'. Chyna claimed that during one parental fight, Janet dumped a bowl of spaghetti on Joe's head, and Joe responded by stabbing Janet in the thigh with a bread knife. The couple divorced when Chyna was three. She and her two older siblings lived with their mother and a procession of step-fathers, one of whom allegedly threatened to shoot himself in front of the children.[63] (Her sister Kathy recalled their father stabbing their mother, although in her telling, the weapon was a butcher's knife.)[64] Chyna's mother, though, told a podcast, 'I can't remember anything about her childhood that was negative.'[65] She would be estranged from both her parents at various times during her adult life, although she achieved a measure of reconciliation before her death. Her father died in 2014.[66] Her relationships with the adults she encountered outside the home were hardly more reliable. According to her autobiography, when she was in seventh grade – so twelve or thirteen years old – a male teacher kissed her and told her she was 'irresistible'.[67]

She connected this experience directly to her being 'always a big, different ... *visible* girl'.[68] And though she doesn't make the next link explicitly, there is a perfect, grim logic to the fact that, by the time she was thirteen, she had developed bulimia.[69] For a girl who felt she had no dependable caregivers in her life, her body may well have been the one thing in which she could have confidence. Now she was an adolescent, and that body was changing – changing in ways that attracted dangerous attention. By bingeing and purging, she could reclaim a fragile authority over her physical self, eliminating those betraying fat deposits that seemed to cause adult men to lose their compo-sure. Then her body found a new way to betray her: when she was sixteen, a routine gynaecology appointment revealed an 'ovarian tumor the size of a grapefruit'. (It was benign, and she made a full recovery after surgery.)

By now, Chyna had started working out seriously. 'All that

defined me as a woman in the physical sense just plain *hurt*,'
she wrote. 'I suffered becoming a woman. Maybe that's why
it was so important to be strong.'[70] This still wasn't enough to
make her safe in her own body. At a college party when she
was eighteen, she passed out drunk and woke up to find 'a
dick in my mouth while another guy was drilling for oil at the
other end'.[71] After she graduated, she spent her early twenties
drifting through abusive relationships and dead-end jobs –
beeper sales, topless bars, belly dancing. It wasn't enough for
her. 'I wanted to be wanted, I wanted to be cared for, I wanted
respect,' wrote Chyna in her autobiography.[72] When she
walked into Killer Kowalski's gym and learned that she had
not just the physique but also the presence to make it as a pro
wrestler, she must have felt as though everything lacking from
her life was finally about to be delivered. 'Chyna' wasn't just a
character she played on TV; she was the person Joan Laurer
had been born to become.

Now, losing her place in the WWF meant losing all that.
Even her name was taken from her – she began to go by 'Chyna
Doll' instead, but told Howard Stern during an interview that
this too was a potential infringement of the Chyna name and
gimmick owned by the WWF.[73]

She had one more fight on US television: in 2002, she com-
peted in Fox's *Celebrity Boxing*, against Joey Buttafuoco, a
man who was famous mainly because his seventeen-year-old
mistress, Amy Fisher (nicknamed 'the Long Island Lolita' by
the tabloids), had shot his wife, Mary Jo, in 1992. By itself, this
was degrading enough. More humiliatingly, Chyna lost to this
seedy, middle-aged amateur.[74]

With American wrestling effectively a McMahon monopoly, the only place left for her to go was Japan. New Japan Pro
Wrestling was a respected promotion, and many American
wrestlers had ultimately bettered their careers by spending time there. Chyna's tenure, though, would be brief and

ultimately unimpressive. NJPW booked her in the intergender
matches that were so important to her, and she won fans over
with her commitment in the ring. But her problems outside
it were once again impinging. Steroids are not the only substance routinely abused by wrestlers. 'A lot of wrestlers, if
they're prone to pills, they're gonna do downers,' Jim Ross has
said. 'Ambien, Xanax, OxyContin, and all that shit.'[75] Perhaps
Chyna's painful background meant she was always vulnerable
to addiction, but wrestling made it almost a certainty.

To stabilise the anxiety caused by steroids, users often
take tranquillisers like Valium.[76] And to manage the injuries
accumulated from years of taking bumps, wrestlers frequently
turn to opioids. In fact, one of the architects of the twentieth century's revolution in pain management was a wrestler
before he became an anaesthetist: John Bonica paid his way
through medical school by wrestling as the Masked Marvel,
an experience that left him with both chronic pain and an
abiding professional interest in diminishing that suffering.
He believed that doctors were too cautious about prescrib-
ing morphine to patients in pain, a belief that happened to
be shared by Richard Sackler of the Sackler pharmaceutical
dynasty. The two corresponded in the eighties, and Bonica's
ideas informed the development of the Sacklers' revolutionary
opioid products, MS Contin and, later, OxyContin – synthetic
forms of the naturally occurring narcotic in morphine.[77] These
are highly effective at managing pain, highly addictive and
perilously easy to overdose on, as users consume ever-bigger
amounts in pursuit of re-creating that first high. The Sacklers
became enormously wealthy, while people like Chyna became
desperately dependent. She was also drinking heavily.

In 2001, Chyna had been talking hopefully about a role in
the third *Terminator* movie.[78] In 2004, with wrestling closed
to her and Hollywood unreceptive, she made her debut in
a different kind of entertainment. That August, she started

touting a sex tape featuring her and her boyfriend, the wrestler Sean Waltman (ring name X-Pac).[79] In December, the film was picked up by Red Light District, the company that had distributed the Paris tape, and released it under the title *1 Night in China*, after the style of *1 Night in Paris*. (The copyright workaround was that, in the introductory sequences, Chyna and X-Pac are filmed in the *country* of China.)[80] Also in the style of Paris, the sex tape was followed by a move into reality TV: Chyna, using her real name, featured in the 2005 season of VH1's *The Surreal Life*, a kind of *Big Brother* for ex-celebs. Her stint there left many feeling disturbed. 'Joanie Laurer has been performing a one-woman show about self-annihilation,' wrote the *Globe and Mail*. It was 'the rough emotional equivalent of a snuff film'.[81] Waltman, now Chyna's ex, put a statement on his website calling the producers 'bottom feeders'.[82] In August, she was arrested for assaulting him.[83]

Chyna's issues didn't put her entirely beyond the pale for television. She retained a certain novelty value, which led to her appearance in the 2007 B-movie *Illegal Aliens* alongside her friend Anna Nicole Smith. By the time the film came out, Smith would be dead.[84] In 2008, Chyna was cast in *Celebrity Rehab with Dr. Drew*. (Exactly how effective that rehab was can be judged by her hospitalisation the following December: she had been found unconscious after her birthday party with cuts on her arms.)[85] But there was one industry that could definitely find a place for a woman disintegrating in full view. *1 Night in China* had been successful enough for Red Light District to release a follow-up in 2006. After that, Chyna made four studio porn films with Vivid, the company behind *Kim Kardashian, Superstar*.[86] (She'd legally changed her name to 'Chyna' in 2007,[87] so there were no longer any constraints on her using it.) The first of these was *Backdoor to Chyna*. Its cover included the inestimably bleak tagline 'From Kickin' ASS to Gettin' It Up the ASS.'[88] Chyna had once held herself superior to the 'T&A' element in women's wrestling. Now T&A was her profession. When she made her last Vivid film in 2013, she was forty-four – ancient in porn, where most women age out of being usable by their mid-twenties, but still young enough to have a future.[89] She had only three more years left to live.

Chyna still thought about wrestling. (In a chaotic 2005 appearance on *Howard Stern*, she referred to Vince McMahon as 'Vince McDick'.)[90] But in the kayfabe of World Wrestling Entertainment (as the World Wrestling Federation was now called), she didn't exist. The wrestling, and the storylines, had moved on without her.

Now that WWE was unchallenged in the realm of wrestling, McMahon set his sights on moving his promotion, and himself, into the centre of popular culture. As ever in wrestling, the way to build your profile is to pick the right fight. Chyna had been carefully introduced to the wrestling audience through a series of confrontations with opponents who served to showcase her strength and importance. Now McMahon would showcase himself for the public at large by setting up a confrontation with a man who represented the epitome of wealth, power and corporate success in America. It was time for Donald Trump to enter the ring.

Trump was generally referred to in the media as a real estate developer – like McMahon, Trump had taken on the family business – although an investigation by the *New York Times* cast doubt on the profitability of his enterprises.[91] More accurately, he was a reality star. Kayfabe Donald Trump was one of the world's greatest executives, and that image under-pinned the major source of his fortune. Because *Trump* was a byword for ruthless wealth and Manhattan glamour, any company that wanted to apply that image to their product simply needed to license his name: there were Trump steaks, Trump ties and Trump colognes.[92] (Describing her ideal man in a 2001 interview, Chyna had said, 'He doesn't have to be Donald Trump, but he has to have a good job.')[93] When NBC needed someone to front its business-based reality show *The Apprentice*, which started in 2004, Trump was the obvious choice. He knew how to sell the *appearance* of success. This was his gimmick. And if McMahon wanted to be seen by the public as a global impresario, Trump was the person he needed to fight – kayfabe, of course.

After some heated build-up, *WrestleMania 23*, in 2007, was where they met, in the so-called Battle of the Billionaires. Some had doubts about the billionaire status of both, but exaggeration is the nature of wrestling: add a little to your height, pump a bit of juice into your muscles and round up your wealth to the nearest nine zeroes.[94] The meet-up itself involved each man nominating a wrestler to fight on his behalf, with the loser submitting to have his head shaved – no trivial matter for Trump, who deducted $70,000 in hairstyling expenses during his time on *The Apprentice*.[95] To the crowd's delight, the match descended from farce into chaos, with Trump landing a clothesline on McMahon outside the ring before strapping his defeated rival into a barber's chair and gloatingly applying the razor. 'Trump understands the bullshit of wrestling better than, say, [wrestler] Michael Cole,' *Wrestling Observer* said admiringly, with the writer moved to add, 'I LOVE THE DONALD'.[96]

It's easy to see what McMahon gained from this arrangement: the day after *WrestleMania*, he and Trump shared a sofa on the *Today* show to be interviewed by Matt Lauer. For a $5 million payment to Trump's charity, McMahon had bought his way into the mainstream.[97] Perhaps less obvious is what Trump gained, besides the money. (In 2019, Trump was ordered to pay $2 million in damages to non-profit groups as part of a settlement after he admitted misusing money raised by the Donald J. Trump Foundation to promote his presidential bid, pay off business debts and purchase a portrait of himself. Trump described his infractions as 'small technical violations'.)[98] After all, Trump already had a primetime platform, in the shape of *The Apprentice*. But WWE allowed him to expand his persona to cartoonish heights, in front of an audience that was particularly important for him: white men without college degrees.[99] His appearance in WWE combined the grit of the outsider (he was challenging Vince McMahon, after all) with the glitz of success (on his first appearance in the ring, he was showered with banknotes and flanked by divas) and the contractual guarantee that he'd come out the winner.[100] Trump intrinsically understood the cynicism of wrestling. In wrestling, it is not that nothing serious ever happens. It is that the very form of wrestling mitigates against anything being taken seriously. This is a medium in which the workplace death of a beloved colleague like Owen Hart could be recycled into fiction before two years had passed.

If *The Apprentice* established Trump the businessman, WWE established Trump the president, and his presidency was entwined with wrestling. One of his first appointments placed McMahon's wife, Linda, in charge of the Small Business Administration.[101] Among his supporters, the GIF of Trump clotheslining McMahon became a way of celebrating every time Trump was perceived to have demolished an enemy. He understood the bullshit, in politics as in wrestling. During the 2016 presidential campaign, while Hillary Clinton prissily followed the rules, Trump delighted his supporters by breaking them, like the crowd-pleasing anti-hero he was. When Clinton called Trump's supporters 'a basket of deplorables', she had to apologise for her unbefitting language.[102] When footage emerged of Trump boasting about 'grabbing women by the pussy', no retraction was forthcoming: it cost him nothing, because he could both claim that he was being unserious – Trump called his words 'locker-room banter' in a statement, and he could have been thinking of the wrestling locker rooms Chyna had described – while enjoying the approbation of those who very seriously felt that a propensity to grab women by the pussy was an admirable trait.[103] As Chyna's run at the Intercontinental title had shown, there was a significant audience ready to take pleasure in the humbling of a powerful woman who chose to play with the boys. Trump v. Clinton put that storyline onto a global stage and gave the Trump fans the ending they wanted.

Chyna would not see Donald Trump become president. In April 2016, she died of what authorities considered to be an accidental overdose, although, with any addiction, it is difficult to trace the boundary between purposefully wishing to be dead and simply not caring if one's consumption is incompatible with living. Her autopsy revealed that she had taken the opioids oxycodone and oxymorphone as well as Valium, nordiazepam, temazepam and alcohol.[104] Her body was found on the twentieth, but she had probably died three days before, when she made her last social media post.[105] It took that long for anyone to check on her – a most lonely death for someone who had spent her life searching for belonging in all the wrong places. First wrestling, then reality TV and finally porn had taken her in and taken what they could from her. Once she was no longer usable, she was left to her demons.

During a podcast the year before, Triple H (her ex-boyfriend, now husband of Stephanie McMahon and vice-president of WWE) had underlined Chyna's exclusion from the WWE Hall of Fame and, by extension, from WWE itself: 'Does she deserve to go in the Hall of Fame? Absolutely ... It's a bit difficult, though, and this is the flip side of the coin that nobody looks at ... I've got an eight-year-old kid. My eight-year-old kid sees the Hall of Fame, and my eight-year-old kid goes on the internet to look ... and what comes up?'[106]

Chyna had won her popularity in wrestling by goading the moral majority with her 'sugarcoated pornography', but real porn was, apparently, too much for WWE to take. After all she'd been through, Right to Censor had won in the end. (Three years after her death, she was inducted in the Hall of Fame as part of D-Generation X, but she has never received individual recognition.)[107] The seeming hypocrisy of the WWE became even more apparent in 2022, when it was reported that the company had paid $12 million in 'hush money' to multiple women over allegations of sexual harassment and infidelity involving Vince McMahon.[108] McMahon, by then seventy-six, retired as CEO. Stephanie became co-CEO and chair, while Triple H took over creative direction.[109] If this was a reckoning, it was a short-lived one: in early 2023, he engineered a comeback and Stephanie resigned.[110]

Chyna's legacy is hard to pin down. She said she hoped to inspire girls with her strength, but in practice, she rarely supported other women – as with Ivory, she was more likely to denigrate her female colleagues than lift them up. It's true that she was one of the first women to unashamedly celebrate her own 'henchness', but she could hardly claim to have overturned objectification, given her move to, first, softcore and then hardcore pornography. The time of the female action hero would come, but it would be over a decade too late for Chyna. When that moment arrived, the pioneers were women like Ronda Rousey, a judo champion who moved to the mixed martial arts-based Ultimate Fighting Championship and then to WWE, dipping into Hollywood along the way. In 2019, Rousey fought Becky Lynch and Charlotte Flair in the headline match of *WrestleMania 35*. This contest marked the first time a women's bout had ever been the main event and, in all fairness, must be considered far more momentous than Chyna's brief novelty run in intergender contests. It showed that, finally, wrestling fans were both invested in the women's storylines and ready to accept female athleticism as spectacle. Chyna had pushed her body to its limits in the pursuit of power without ever seeming to understand that the institutions she attached to – wrestling, pornography, reality TV – all relied on exploiting her weaknesses.

9

Jen: Freedom

'I want to have it all'

When the Upskirt Decade began, Jennifer Aniston was not a hothoused hopeful or a needy wannabe. She wasn't a vulnerable neophyte at the mercy of her superiors; nor had she been around long enough to attain the veteran status that was so precarious for women in entertainment. At the start of 1999, she was twenty-nine years old and probably the most bankable star on definitely the biggest TV show in the world. NBC's Thursday night 'Must See TV' line-up (which included, at various times, *Seinfeld*, *ER* and *3rd Rock from the Sun*) had pushed the network back to primetime TV dominance, and

Friends was the jewel in that crown. The show launched in 1994, explicitly to reach the rising market of Gen Xers starting out on adult life in the big cities. And how better to find that audience than by putting it on-screen?[1] Jerry Seinfeld considered *Friends*'s basic elements – a sitcom about a group of singles in New York City – to constitute a do-over of his own show with a better-looking cast.[2] But *Friends* was more than *Seinfeld* with beautiful people. In contrast to *Seinfeld*'s self-imposed 'no hugging, no learning' rule, part of the point of *Friends* was that you got to see its characters grow and change over time, blurring the line between sitcom and soap opera.[3] The six main characters on the show seemed like people you would actually be friends with. 'I remember when I was a young person watching *Friends*, I thought, "This is how we talk,"' said Sean Hayes, who went on to play the character Jack in another Must See TV mainstay, *Will and Grace*.[4]

Jen's character, Rachel Greene, was the one who had the most growing and changing to do, so it made sense that audiences would become particularly attached to her. She's the last of the six to show up in the pilot episode, crashing into the coffee shop where the others are gathered, in a wedding dress, on the run from her own wedding. 'I just had to get out of there,' Rachel cries as she explains her situation. 'I started wondering, "Why am I doing this and who am I doing it for?"'[5] It's a smart upending of the typical rom-com plot: Rachel's story doesn't end when she gets to the altar but, rather, begins when she realises the man at the altar is entirely wrong for her. It was also a reflection of American lives in the nineties, albeit a melodramatic one. In common with people of all developed nations, Americans were getting married later, or not getting married at all, and the driving force of that trend was a generation of educated, ambitious young women for whom husbands and babies would come, if they came at all, after career and self-discovery.[6] By 1999, Rachel had been transformed from a princess reliant on her daddy's money into a capable young woman with a career in fashion – and a tantalising on-again, off-again relationship with Ross, played by David Schwimmer. She was the perfect example of the independent young woman making her way, and plenty of women chose to model themselves after her: the layered, face-framing hairstyle Jen wore on the show became a phenomenon in its own right, as millions of women went to their salons and requested 'the Rachel'.[7]

When she took the role of Rachel, Jen had begun to doubt that she would ever get her break. Shortly before *Friends*, she'd done the professional equivalent of jilting a fiancé when she turned down an invitation from producer Lorne Michaels to join the main cast of *Saturday Night Live*. 'I went into Lorne's office and I was like, "I hear women are not respected on this show,"' she told the *Hollywood Reporter* in 2021. 'I don't remember exactly what I said next, but it was something like, "I would prefer if it were like the days of Gilda Radner and Jane Curtin." I mean, it was such a boys' club back then, but who the fuck was I to be saying this to Lorne Michaels?!'[8] This was three years before the Tina Fey era opened up the possibilities for women to be funny on *SNL*; even so, it was a major opportunity to pass up. Jen's confidence was not misplaced, though. While she bounced around roles in underwhelming shows, television executives were paying attention.

NBC was so eager to get Jen that she was cast in *Friends* despite already being committed to the failing sitcom *Muddling Through*, on rival network CBS – and then, to ensure that CBS didn't tie her up purely for the sake of spoiling *Friends*, NBC killed *Muddling Through* by programming aggressively against it.[9] (CBS was led by Les Moonves. Given his fearsome reputation, NBC was probably justified in taking this approach.)* Jen was valuable, and along with the rest of

---

* For more on Moonves, see Chapter 5: Janet.

the *Friends* cast, she knew it. The six of them – three men, three women – formed what Schwimmer described as a 'mini-union' and negotiated a deal that not only placed them among the best-paid actors on TV, but also gave them syndication royalties.[10] Jen had kicked against the glass ceiling with regard to the *SNL* offer; now she had helped to create a micro-economy for herself and her co-stars with a perfect gender balance and no wage gap at all. Her professional life was more or less a self-made utopia. This success made her an object of admiration, but it also put her at the centre of an existential panic over women's choices in the noughties.

Friends made that panic part of its drama. Like the women who saw themselves in her, Rachel Greene was dealing with new dilemmas thrown up by the modern schedule for living. Deferring settling down brought choices and freedoms, but you still couldn't barter away the limits of the female body. Fertility remained finite. In the 2001 *Friends* episode 'The One Where They All Turn Thirty', Rachel goes through a landmark birthday – and becomes upset when she realises how far behind her 'plan' she actually is:

> See, I wanna have three kids ... I should probably have the first of the three kids by the time I'm thirty-five, which gives me five years. So if I wanna have a kid when I'm thirty five, I don't have to get pregnant until I'm thirty-four, which gives Prada four years to start making maternity clothes. Wait, but I do want to be married for a year before I get pregnant ... So I don't have to get married until I'm thirty-three. That's three years. That's three whole years. Oh, wait a minute though, I'll need a year and a half to plan the wedding. And I'd like to know the guy for like a year, year and a half before we get engaged, which means I need to meet the guy by the time I'm thirty ... According to my plan, I should already be with the guy that I'm gonna marry.[11]

For the young women watching, Rachel's distress was relatable: many would have their own plan, or at the least be aware that such choices would be forced on them at some point. But in the culture at large, one of the noughties' prevailing anxieties about women was that they were being altogether careless about their plan, complacently wasting their prime reproductive years in pursuit of education or professional advancement. Journalism of the period pushed an apocalyptic message about women's lives. A typical example appeared in *Time* in 2002, under the headline 'Making Time for a Baby', with a cover photo showing an adorable infant lying on top of an overflowing office in-box. In the article, fertility doctors bemoaned the naïveté of women who sought success within a workplace designed around men – men who had the advantage not only of more durable fertility, but also, traditionally, of a wife to pick up the childcare duties so their professional lives could continue unimpeded.

'Those women who are at the top of their game could have had it all, children and career, if they wanted it,' said one of the physicians quoted. 'The problem was, nobody told them the truth about their bodies.' According to the article, a woman's chances of conceiving declined rapidly after thirty – and after thirty-five, she had better prepare for a childless future. Sylvia Ann Hewlett, author of *Creating a Life: Professional Women and the Quest for Children*, said the issue was one of wishful thinking rather than straightforward ignorance. Childlessness had become a 'creeping non-choice' for middle-class women approaching midlife, she said, and yet, younger women were refusing to heed the warnings: 'The fact that the biological clock is real is unwelcome news to my 24-year-old daughter ... and she's pretty typical,'[12] Hewlett wrote.

Perhaps this was true of Hewlett's daughter. But *Friends* and other popular culture consumed by young women seemed to have little fear of alienating its audience with discussion of the so-called fertility cliff. In an episode of season seven of *Keeping Up with the Kardashians*, Kim and Khloé visit a reproductive clinic to discuss egg freezing and return with alarming news. 'At twenty-two your fertility is like here,' says Kim, holding her hand at eye level and lowering it as she speaks. 'At twenty-five, it goes down. Twenty-six. At thirty-two, it's like here' – she dramatically extends her thumb and forefinger to represent the narrow potential a woman in her thirties has of getting pregnant.[13] Actually, Kim may have been medically misinformed. In a 2012 article for *The Atlantic*, Jean Twenge explained that research on women's fertility was based largely on data that preceded modern medicine and that the chances of a woman in her late thirties conceiving were considerably better than Kim's hand gesture suggested.[14] Nonetheless, the average media-literate twenty-something woman in the noughties was unlikely to avoid the message that she was on a reproductive deadline.

In any case, Jen could hardly be accused of neglecting her personal life. In 1998, she had started dating Brad Pitt – a man so absurdly attractive that he could plausibly take the role of the demigod Achilles in the 2004 movie *Troy*. She was 'America's Sweetheart'; he was 'the sexiest man in the world'. In 2000, when she was thirty-one, they got married, putting her well ahead of the Rachel Greene plan. In a time when the intensity of celebrity coverage left few illusions about relationships, Brad and Jen offered a rare instance of purity. 'They seemed the most fortunate couple imaginable – two beautiful superstars who had hit the jackpot, earning not only fame and riches but also an enduring love,' wrote a *Vanity Fair* profiler who had met the two together.[15] People weren't just fans of Brad and Jen individually. They were fans of the *marriage*, which seemed to represent everything that could be hoped for in a twenty-first-century sexual union. The couple was even able to joke about their public selves. In a 2001 episode of *Friends*, Brad guest stars as Will Colbert, a formerly fat kid from Rachel's high school who reappears in her life, newly hot and enduringly bitter over her past treatment of him. It was funny to hear Brad Pitt snarl, 'I hate Rachel Greene,' because everyone knew that he loved Jennifer Aniston.[16]

When *Friends* ended in 2004, the obvious next step in the plan – a plan that both had discussed in interviews – would be for them to start a family. Instead, the still-childless couple fell apart. Inevitably, a public that had invested passionately in their relationship pored obsessively over the details of their break-up. What could have gone wrong with this golden union? Tabloids vied to supply the answer. Was Brad cheating on Jen with Angelina Jolie, his dangerously sexy co-star in the movie *Mr. & Mrs. Smith*? Had Jen pushed Brad away by refusing to compromise her career for the sake of a baby?[17] Interest reached such feverish heights that when Perez Hilton published the first photos of 'Brangelina' together – they were leaked to him by a magazine employee whose publication had been outbid for the pictures by a rival – he picked up enough traffic to crash his site. It was a defining moment in Hilton's career and in the shift of power from print to online outlets.[18]

When *Friends* brought its soap opera to its conclusion, it gave the audience everything they wanted. After multiple comings-together and fallings-apart (including getting drunkenly married, getting divorced, having a baby together and finally deciding they could never work as a romantic couple), Ross and Rachel end up together. In fact, in the final episode, she chooses Ross over her dream job in Paris, in a last-gasp realisation just before her plane takes off. Rachel Greene, the girl who ran away from her wedding to find out who she was supposed to be, has finally found the man worth sacrificing her hard-won career for. Rom-com logic ultimately won. The end of *Friends* was also the end of sitcoms' dominance on network TV: NBC's next hit in the Must See TV slot was a reality show called *The Apprentice*, starring Donald Trump.[19]

But with Rachel's fictional drama tied up, the public still wanted to see Jen in soap opera, still wanted to see her go through all the varieties of heartbreak and joy, still needed her to stand in for the noughties Everywoman and carry all the anxieties over professionalism, fertility and femininity that had attached to her. Jennifer Aniston was about to be cast, against her will this time, in the second great role of her career: as Sad Jen, the tragic third point in a love triangle with Brad Pitt and Angelina Jolie. For the rest of the decade, there was nothing she could say, and no example of her personal accomplishment or happiness she could show, that would convince the world it was mistaken.

While Jen entered the noughties as the consummate female success story, masculinity in the United States was having a crisis. 'As the nation wobbled toward the millennium, its pulse-takers seemed to agree that a domestic apocalypse was under way: American manhood was under siege,' wrote Susan Faludi in her 1999 book *Stiffed: The Betrayal of the Modern Man*.[20] This male malaise appeared to have its origins in a long-term restructuring of developed economies away from a reliance on blue-collar physical labour and towards service industries, in which conventionally feminine skills such as communication were prized over pure brawn. Masculinity – once an undoubted virtue, to be cultivated and celebrated – had started to appear in conjunction with the word *toxic* during the nineties.[21] And men also seemed to be losing their value on the domestic front. While, for women, the delay of marriage and maternity conferred the opportunity for them to flourish as independent adults, for men, the same period of freedom seemed only to connote prolonged immaturity.

You could see a gentle version of this masculine anxiety in the three male characters in *Friends*. Ross has a child as well as a job he loves and cares about, but he is divorced from his wife after her belated realisation that she's a lesbian. Joey (Matt LeBlanc) is an endearingly unreconstructed example of Italian American manhood, obsessed with sandwiches and girls. And Chandler (Matthew Perry) has a classic 'new economy' meaningless job, the uselessness of which becomes a running joke through the seasons. 'All right kids. I gotta get to work,' he announces in the first episode. 'If I don't input those numbers – it doesn't make much of a difference.'[22] When Monica has a long-running relationship with an older man, it makes sense because the men in her peer group seem so irredeemably childish.

One of Aniston's early films is a fantasy of men trying to escape from the Chandler nightmare. In the 1999 comedy *Office Space* (written and directed by Mike Judge), she has a small role – although, thanks to her success in *Friends*, second place in the credits – as the love interest of main character Peter, played by Ron Livingston. Peter works at a fictional computing firm called Initech. The pointlessness of his job drives him to despair. 'So, I was sitting in my cubicle today, and I realised, ever since I started working, every single day of my life has been worse than the day before it. So, that means that every single day that you see me, that's on the worst day of my life,' says Peter at one point. At home, he's henpecked and cuckolded by his type-A girlfriend, Anne (Alexandra Wentworth). After Initech brings in efficiency consultants with a view to outsourcing most jobs to Singapore, Peter and his two office friends Michael (David Herman) and Samir (Ajay Naidu) conspire to defraud the company using their programming skills. The plan fails because they're so white collar, they don't know how to launder the money, but they're saved when the Initech office building burns down, taking all evidence of their crime with it. Peter swaps the emasculating Anne for the far more desirable, and amenable, Joanna (played by Jen) and winds up taking a job in construction. At the end of the film, we see him covered in dirt, sifting through the wreckage of Initech, looking happier than he ever has. He's working fewer hours and getting paid more, and perhaps most important of all, he has gained the manly dignity of an honest day's sweat.[23]

While *Office Space* found comedy in the masculinity crisis, the Pitt-Aniston union's other contribution to cinema that year mined it for blackest satire. Like *Office Space*, *Fight Club* performed poorly in cinemas and became a success only upon home release. But when it found its audience, they embraced it wholeheartedly. *Fight Club* was taken up as an epoch-defining statement on the condition of man at the end of the millennium. Whether every viewer who saw himself in it truly understood the film is debatable, but the men who adopted *Fight Club* as a manifesto were not exactly wrong about the film's contents. David Fincher's movie, based on Chuck Palahniuk's savage novel, offered a powerful account of the problem with men and an equally powerful account of the lack of solutions. The nameless narrator, played by Edward Norton, is employed in soul-destroying data work, though, unlike Chandler in *Friends* and Peter in *Office Space*, *Fight Club*'s narrator knows what his work is for: he is employed by a car manufacturer to assess fatal malfunctions and calculate whether it's more cost-effective to recall the faulty vehicles or just pay out for the deaths some of them will likely cause. This makes him arguably less alienated from the product of his labour, but given that the product in question is intensely dehumanising, this hardly seems an improvement.

The narrator lives what he calls a 'single-serving life', one parcelled out between plane journeys and his condo, which has all the personality of an airport. 'Like everyone else,' says the narrator, 'I had become a slave to the Ikea nesting instinct ... I would flip through catalogues and wonder, "What kind of dining set defines me as a person?"'[24] (In the first

episode of *Friends*, Ross, Chandler and Joey are shown hap-
lessly trying to assemble some flatpack furniture. Clearly, Ikea
held a special place in the popular understanding of masculinity displaced.)[25] The *Fight Club* narrator has taken on the role
of consummate corporate citizen, and he is deeply unhappy
about it: he suffers from chronic insomnia, which he can only
alleviate by going to illness support groups and fraudulently
presenting himself as a sufferer of cancer, or brain parasites,
or tuberculosis. After these meetings, he can finally cry, and
sleep. And then he encounters Tyler Durden, played by Brad
Pitt – a man who not only presents the perfect image of masculinity, with his ripped torso and ruggedly handsome face,
but who is also uncannily skilled at articulating all the dissat-
isfaction the narrator feels with his place in the world.

'We're consumers,' Tyler tells the narrator. 'We are
by-products of a lifestyle obsession. Murder, crime, poverty –
these things don't concern me. What concerns me are celebrity
magazines, television with five hundred channels, some guy's
name on my underwear. Rogaine, Viagra, olestra.'[26] The men
of *Fight Club* cannot grow up because there is no version of
manhood for them to grow up into. 'I can't get married,' *Fight
Club*'s narrator complains to Tyler. 'I'm a thirty-year-old boy.'
For Faludi in *Stiffed*, the impossibility of maturity for men was
a consequence of the 'ornamental culture' that had begun to
dominate in the nineties and that no longer rewarded men for
fulfilling their traditional social roles: 'Constructed around
celebrity and image, glamour and entertainment, marketing
and consumerism, it is a ceremonial gateway to nowhere. Its
essence is not just the selling act but the act of selling the self,
and in this quest every man is essentially on his own, a lone
sales rep marketing his own image ... In an age of celebrity,
the father has no body of knowledge or authority to transmit
to the son. Each son must father his own image, create his
own Adam.'[27]

And 'creating his own Adam' is precisely what the narrator of *Fight Club* has done. Tyler, the film reveals, is not a separate person at all: he's the narrator's alter ego, a fantasy of everything ornamental culture believes a man should be, summoned unconsciously by the narrator so he can express his forbidden discontent. Faludi was a fan of *Fight Club* the novel, and Palahniuk admired *Stiffed* in turn.[28] The two authors shared an understanding of masculinity's failure, but they also recognised that a further question was implied: why did men as a whole seem incapable of acting to remedy their discontent? *Stiffed* had started as an enquiry into men's hostility towards women's liberation, wrote Faludi, but it became something else in the course of her research: 'Instead of wondering why men resist women's struggle for a freer and healthier life, I began to wonder why men refrain from engaging in their own struggle. Why, despite a crescendo of random tantrums, have they offered no methodical, reasoned response to their predicament? Given the untenable and insulting nature of the demands placed on men to prove themselves in our culture, why don't men revolt?' After all, this was what women had done. Faced with 'the problem that had no name', second-wave feminism had named it, and established a political movement.[29]

Fight Club, both the novel and the film, suggests an explanation for men's inertia: even when they did attempt to revolt, they could not rid themselves of the forms of the consumer culture they were ostensibly rebelling against. In one of the film's strangest moments, the narrator and Tyler talk about an underwear advertisement. 'Is that what a man looks like?' the narrator asks of some Adonis in briefs. But that, of course, is exactly what Brad looks like. The narrator can explain all the ways that late-stage capitalism is destroying men like him, but he still wants to look like Brad Pitt while he does it, and this is why he is doomed. The narrator complains to Tyler that he was deserted by his own father, who moved on to set up a new family every six years. 'The fucker's setting up franchises,' says Tyler: the breakdown of the nuclear family has commodified the paternal role. But the fight clubs the narrator frequents in the movie are also clearly established as franchises, and the narrator/Tyler is the father figure who leaves his symbolic 'sons' yearning for his attention and perpetrating deranged acts of loyalty to prove their love to him.

For some more highbrow critics, *Fight Club*'s ironies were a sign of intellectual hollowness and artistic failure rather than deliberate satire. Peter Rainer in *New York Magazine* called the film 'the squall of a whiny and essentially white-male generation that feels ruined by the privileges of women and a booming economy'.[30] Such attacks mistook *Fight Club* for one of frustrated masculinity's random tantrums, rather than seeing it as a film *about* the random tantrums. But the truth was that *Fight Club*'s ironies were easy to overlook when the visuals were so seductive, and many of the film's biggest admirers seemed equally to miss the point. Within a couple of years of the film's release, there were multiple reports of real-life fight clubs. 'Here City guys get to be like Muhammad Ali for the night and the next day who are the secretaries going to be talking about round the water cooler?' said a venture capitalist quoted in an *Evening Standard* article on white-collar boxing in London.[31] A student combatant at a Utah fight club said, 'I get headaches, my eye hurts, but it's fun ... just friends getting together to let off some steam. It's a rush.'[32] If the implicit argument of *Fight Club* was that men would rather get punched in the face than have therapy, the film's fans seemed happy to bear that out.

Fight Club set the tone for Brad's early noughties in that it showed him using his star power to support left-field projects. With Jen and business partner Brad Grey, he founded Plan B, a production company to support the kind of movies he wanted to be in. 'Some of his choices are not necessarily the most commercial choices,' Grey told *Vanity Fair*'s Leslie Bennetts in 2004. 'Brad will always gravitate toward what he has not done yet. It's about creativity.'[33] Meanwhile Jen seemed to have become a prisoner of her success on *Friends*. As Jim Burrows, who directed the *Friends* pilot, pointed out, 'Everybody was good-looking on that show, so the critics didn't realize how funny they were.'[34] During the time that *Friends* was running, the expansion of cable, and the competition for subscribers, had led to the rise of so-called prestige television. Shows like *The Sopranos* (HBO), *The Wire* (HBO) and *The Shield* (FX) established the idea of the serial drama as an American art form no less respectable than the best of cinema. But Jen was a network TV star, and that meant she was associated with entertainment rather than craft: when your full-time job is being America's sweetheart, it's difficult to play against type. Although she was a brilliant comedian and (as screenwriter Mike White's low-budget 2002 movie *The Good Girl* showed) a superb dramatic actress, her film roles rarely made use of her full range. She was playing largely either the lead in rom-coms or the love interest to the hero in comedies.

In *Rock Star* (2001), she's the loyal home town girlfriend who gives Mark Wahlberg's metal singer refuge from celebrity. In *Bruce Almighty* (2003), she acts opposite Jim Carrey, who plays a selfish, career-obsessed broadcast journalist, while she's the sweet-natured woman waiting for him to commit. In *Along Came Polly* (2004), she's the kooky dream girl who helps Ben Stiller's uptight character find himself. As the main character in *Rumor Has It* (2005), she was given more opportunities to be funny, but the film is still about her character ultimately coming to terms with her nerves over domesticity and settling down with her improbably loyal boyfriend, played by Mark Ruffalo. In other words, the point of Jen's character in almost all her films during this period was, if not to get married, then at the very least to be the kind of woman the male main character should *want* to marry. On-screen as well as off, she appeared to be a one-woman propaganda machine for heterosexual monogamy. Even when she was cast against type in the 2005 thriller *Derailed*, where she has a misfiring turn as a femme fatale, her character gets a moment of sympathy before dying by suggesting she really was in love with the man she tried to con.

Meanwhile, in 2004, Brad began work on a film that seemed designed to blow the whole concept of marriage to pieces. *Mr. & Mrs. Smith* is the story of a couple living a life of perfect suburban dullness. Their house is furnished with elegant blandness, the wife has dinner on the table at seven every evening, the two barely have sex and they hardly listen to each other when they talk about their days at work.

'There's this huge space between us, and it just keeps filling up with everything that we *don't* say to each other. What's that called?' Mrs. Smith wonders to a marriage counsellor in an early scene.

'Marriage,' the counsellor responds drily.[35]

The twist is that neither Smith is telling the other the truth, because both of them are assassins-for-hire, employed by rival agencies. When their cover is blown, each is assigned to kill the other, a dilemma that leads to the ultimate marital dispute. In the film's centrepiece confrontation, they hunt each other through their beautiful home until the entire place is torn apart. Finally stripped of all deceit, they realise they love each other after all, and have hot sex among the wreckage. Brad played Mr. Smith, Angelina Jolie played Mrs. Smith, and the rumour from the set was that there was very little acting involved in the couple's chemistry.

In January 2005, Brad and Jen issued a joint statement announcing their break-up. 'We would like to announce that after seven years together we have decided to formally separate,' it read. 'For those who follow these sorts of things, we would like to explain that our separation is not the result of any of the speculation reported by the tabloid media. This decision is the result of much thoughtful consideration. We happily remain committed and caring friends with great love and admiration for one another. We ask in advance for your kindness and sensitivity in the coming months.'[36] The end of any marriage is devastating, and that devastation is compounded when, in its dissolution, the private relationship is made public. Betrayals are revealed. Rumours spread. Plans once discussed openly in the casual expectation of a shared future become the humiliating evidence of your naïveté, the proof of your failure. This is even more true when the marriage is a celebrity one and its end is played out in print and on screens across the world. And when that marriage has been hailed as the century's ideal, and when you and your ex have been elevated to the status of avatars for your respective sexes, the pressure becomes extraordinary.

The collapse of Jen and Brad's marriage generated a global conversation about the nature of relations between men and women. Even more intrusively, it became a discussion about the condition of Jen's uterus and whether she was either willing or able to have the baby her husband apparently wanted. 'Perhaps the strongest clue to the cause of the end of this particular fairytale lies in Pitt's behaviour on an American television chat show last year,' explained a *Guardian* story on the couple's separation. 'Eyes welling up, the actor told the nation what he longed for. "I'm going to say it: kids, family, I am thinking family," he blurted out. But the only sign of issue from his marriage was a joint film project announced last year.'[37] In a tearful but defiant cover interview for *Vanity Fair* in September 2005, Jen pointed out the unfairness of this commentary. 'A man divorcing would never be accused of choosing career over children,' she said. 'That really pissed me off. I've never in my life said I didn't want to have children. I did and I do and I will! The women that inspire me are the ones who have careers and children; why would I want to limit myself? I've always wanted to have children, and I would never give up that experience for a career. I want to have it all.'[38] It was a robust answer to the prying, but it was also an answer that made her a public hostage to her reproductive prospects.

Jen's position was compounded by the fact that the woman who replaced her appeared to be everything she wasn't. Angelina Jolie had achieved fame around the same time as Jen, in the mid-nineties, breaking out in the 1995 cyber-thriller *Hackers* (she married her co-star, Jonny Lee Miller), then won the Best Supporting Actress Oscar for her role in *Girl, Interrupted* (1999) as the charismatic sociopath Lisa, which confirmed her as a major talent. Angelina rejected the conventional female rom-com track as taken by Jen. Instead, she pursued a mix of credible dramas and action films: genres either aimed at men or, at a minimum, not explicitly aimed at women. If Jen was Hollywood's vision of the woman other women could identify with, Angelina stood for everything the male id longed for, and her provocative self-presentation underlined that image. In interviews, she talked about her interest in knife play and S&M; her Oscar win was nearly overshadowed by her red carpet walk with her brother, James Haven, during which she kissed him on the lips for the cameras. 'Jolie's real-life over-the-top intensity and fuck-it-all attitude are nearly as unsettling as her screen performances,' said a breathlessly titillated 2000 profile in *Time*.[39]

When she signed on for *Mr. & Mrs. Smith*, though, she was in the midst of, if not an image reinvention, then at least a renewal of her persona. She had filed for divorce from Miller in 1999 and was married again, the next year, to Billy Bob Thornton, whom she had met on the set of the 1999 film

Pushing Tin. Thornton was nearly two decades her senior, and their marriage appeared to the public as one of hypersexed intensity, characterised by the vial of the other's blood each wore as a pendant. ('The necklaces were a very simple thing,' Thornton told a podcast in 2018. '"Hey, let's poke our fingers with a pen and smear a little blood on there, and when we're away from each other we'll wear the necklace." It was that easy. But by the time it came out in the press, it sounded like we were wearing a bucket of blood around our necks,' he said – as though the weirdness of the gesture were a function of the *volume* of bodily fluids.)[40] But Angelina pulled off one of her greatest shocks in 2002, by doing something that was almost normal: that year, when she was twenty-six, she and Thornton announced that they had adopted a Cambodian orphan named Maddox. 'Beneath the tattoos, black leather, and vial of her husband's blood beats, in Angelina Jolie, a maternal heart,' began a thoroughly bowled-over report in *People*,[41] and Angelina followed the adoption by taking on serious humanitarian work with the United Nations.[42]

Four months after announcing the adoption, Angelina filed for divorce from Thornton.[43] This phase of her public image showed her gaining in maturity without compromising either her sexiness or her male-approved status. In 2004, at the beginning of the *Mr. & Mrs. Smith* shoot, Jonathan Van Meter profiled her for *Vogue*. He had breathless praise for her 'masculine/feminine nature' and quoted Ethan Hawke (who had recently worked with Angelina) describing her as an exception to her sex: 'I don't know if I've worked with another woman who really knew how to be the lead of a movie.' Emphatically, Angelina was not like the other girls. Asked about playing Brad's wife in *Mr. & Mrs. Smith*, she told Van Meter, 'It's actually a very funny combination ... My opinion of marriage comes from a very cynical place, so the question "Do you want to kill your spouse?" is a serious thing. And he comes from a place of "What a funny idea, to kill the person you're married to," because he has a happy marriage.'[44] By the time the film wrapped, of course, that 'happy marriage' would be utterly shattered. While much of the gossip from the set was exceptionally salacious, one seemingly benign detail stood out in the coverage: it was rumoured that the paternally inclined Brad had spent long hours playing with Maddox.[45]

Before Brad and Angelina officially went public with their relationship, they appeared together in a lengthy pictorial in *W* magazine called 'Domestic Bliss', which showed the two as the epitome of the sixties suburban couple. Like *Mr. & Mrs. Smith*, the photo shoot drew on the lush, icy look of Douglas Sirk's mid-twentieth-century melodramas to represent the luxurious frustrations of a middle-class marriage. Brad and Angelina praying at the dinner table with five small boys who appear to be their sons; Brad scooping up an unconscious-looking Angelina from a shag-pile carpet, as though he came home to find her sloppy drunk on martinis and Valium; Brad and Angelina in bed, the picture blurred as though their passion were too intense for the camera.[46] For Jen, this was particularly cruel. In her own *Vanity Fair* profile, in 2005, she spoke sanguinely about it, but an unnamed 'friend' of hers offered the line that it was 'tremendously insensitive'.[47] Assuming the 'friend' was speaking with Jen's permission, this was a strategy that allowed Jen to place her injury on the record while avoiding the unattractive appearance of being an embittered ex.

There was no way to shield herself from the greater symbolism of her break-up, though. The disintegration of the Pitt-Aniston marriage became a morality play about two rival forms of femininity, with Jen's Everywoman pursuit of the plan pitched against Angelina's seductive chaos. You could even buy a T-shirt to show your allegiance: the Los Angeles boutique Kitson, which had found its market by allying tightly

with celebrity culture, offered TEAM JOLIE and TEAM ANIS-
TON designs. (The Hilton sisters were pictured wearing them,
Nicky plumping for Jen and Paris staying true to character by
taking Angelina's side.)[48] Coverage of Jen was sympathetic –
after all, she was the betrayed party here – but with an
unmistakable note of pity. She had bet everything on being
the good girl and had come up empty-handed. Meanwhile,
Angelina's unconventional family continued to grow. First,
she adopted a second baby, in 2005, and then, in January 2006,
she announced that she was expecting Pitt's child.[49] Jen's profile had been entwined from the start with the twenty-first
century's great question: how should a woman be? With the
formation of 'Brangelina', the answer appeared to have been
settled: probably not like Jen.

After her divorce, Jen briefly went out with the actor Vince
Vaughn and, subsequently, had a year-long relationship with
the singer John Mayer (which he later said ended because
he was an 'asshole').[50] In 2010, she began dating fellow actor
Justin Theroux, and the two were married from August 2015
to February 2018. There was little evidence of her being in a
state of permanent pining for her ex-husband. Her romantic
life was not, in itself, particularly interesting: TMZ, which
preferred its celebrities to come with DUIs and rehab stints,
called Jen the most boring star in Hollywood.[51] But TMZ
held itself to a high standard of veracity, only reporting what
it could confirm. Other gossip outlets took a more creative
approach, and for them, the Aniston-Pitt-Jolie love triangle
was too compelling to be allowed to die: bluntly, it sold magazines, and so it would have to be sustained in print even
if all evidence suggested that the principals had moved on.
Throughout the noughties and beyond, tabloid magazines ran
a steady stream of headlines informing their readers that Brad
and Angelina were breaking up, Jen was having a baby, Brad

and Jen were on the verge of reconciliation, or that Jen had told Brad to 'back off.' The fact that these stories were consistently contradictory and inevitably proved false did nothing to diminish their appeal. (Brad and Angelina eventually married in 2014. In 2016, Angelina filed for divorce, accusing Brad of abuse in subsequent legal actions; he denies the allegations.[52] Nonetheless, it hardly seems reasonable to credit the scattershot headlines of the previous decade with any powers of prediction.)

Some magazines were effectively writing fiction using paparazzi shots as prompts. Thanks in large part to the efforts of the photo agency Coleman-Rayner, which obsessively documented Jen, Brad and Angelina, there was no shortage of material to work with.[53] A fleeting expression, once captured on camera, could become the basis for any amount of speculation. An anonymous editor described this process to *Guardian* journalist Oliver Burkeman in 2009: 'You build the story around an emotion … What's happening with poor Jen this week? Well, John Mayer's seeing someone else, and for a woman of her age, that must be awful … So you construct a narrative of what a woman her age may be feeling.' The editor continued: 'The question is: how can we construct a story around a set of emotions that our readers are going to relate to? It can come from a genuine tip, or a photo. Or it can come out of our ass.'[54]

Regardless of what was actually happening in her life, Jen had been conscripted into being the face of the late-thirties female condition, and the assumption was that, without a man and a baby, that condition could only be an unhappy one. The one guiding rule of inventing stories about Jen, Burkeman added, was that, like any soap opera, they had to allow a note of hope: 'Despondency must be short-lived, because it's depressing – and, just as importantly, dull. (It would be just as dull were Aniston to find lasting peace with being single or childless ...)'[55] Ultimately, the purpose of the 'Sad Jen' journalism was not to reflect the truth of Jen's life. It was to reflect the worries that adhered to women of childbearing age in general. Alarmists had feared that women were naïve about their bodies. 'Sad Jen' was perhaps the era's greatest work of propaganda for the body clock.

Under the extensive fabrications, though, there was a fragment of truth: in her interviews during this period, Jen repeatedly stated her intention of becoming a mother, although the scrutiny around this part of her life was clearly uncomfortable for her. When Van Meter interviewed her for *Vogue* in 2008, he reported that Jen was 'visibly irritated' by the baby question. 'I've said it so many times,' she told him. 'I'm going to have children. I just know it.'[56] What she didn't say publicly was that, during this period, her private life was being consumed by the trying: 'It was really hard. I was going through IVF, drinking Chinese teas, you name it. I was throwing everything at it. I would've given anything if someone had said to me, "Freeze your eggs. Do yourself a favor." You just don't think it,' she told *Allure* in 2022.[57]

It didn't help that her post-divorce movies repeatedly returned to the themes of motherhood and marriage. Most awkwardly, there was *The Break-Up* (2006), in which she and Vaughn played a disintegrating couple. There was no way around the resonance with her private life. Sentimental drama *Marley & Me* (2008) cast her opposite Owen Wilson, as a wife balancing her career ambitions with her carefully planned drive for domesticity: in one of the standout scenes, she delivers a heartbreaking portrayal of a miscarriage. In *He's Just Not that Into You* (2009) she's the moany girlfriend trying to get an infantile boyfriend (Ben Affleck) to commit. And in *The Switch* (2010), which she executive-produced, her character is so eager to have a baby that she decides to become a single mother via donor sperm.

In 2009, in an acceptance speech at the Women in Film awards, Jen joked about the way her movie roles seemed to be dogging her personal life. 'It's funny,' she said, 'I kind of noticed something a couple years ago that there seemed to be this strange parallel to the movies I was doing and my life off screen. It started with, well, *The Good Girl*. Then that evolved into *Rumor Has It*, followed by *Derailed*, and then there was *The Break-Up* ...' She wrapped up with the punchline: 'So if any of you have a project titled *Everlasting Love with an Adult, Stable Male* ...'[58] But when she said this, she was single and forty. Jen would never have the baby the tabloids had so often promised. In 2021, the *Hollywood Reporter* asked her how her post-*Friends* life had differed from her expectations. 'The career was one thing,' Jen replied. 'I didn't know what was coming, and that's been nothing but blessed. It's a different caliber of work but I love it, no matter what, even if it's a terribly reviewed, dumb comedy, it doesn't matter if it brings me joy.' Then she continued: 'It was more personal stuff that I had expectations about that sort of shape-shifted, so to speak. That was what was jarring, that we all had an idea of what the future was going to be and we were going to go hunker down and focus on this or that and then it all just changed overnight, and that was it. But again, everything's a blessing if you're able to look at life's ups and downs in that way. And if it all hadn't happened, I would not be sitting here the woman that I am.'[59]

Perhaps some would classify Jen among those women for whom childlessness was a 'creeping non-choice', as Sylvia Ann Hewlett described it. It's worth noting, though, that a woman with Jen's resources has more options than most. Even without a partner, she could, like Angelina, have pursued adoption; or she could have had a baby via surrogacy, as Kim and Khloé Kardashian both did. She chose not to, which pokes some holes in the tabloid portrayal of her as a woman obsessed by baby hunger. And, despite all the ways Jen has been recruited to stand for the anguished tussle between career and motherhood, her ultimate contentment may be the most significant fact of all. Infertility is a source of deep grief – and yet, counter to the persistent message of the 'Sad Jen' confection, husbands and children do not bring automatic contentment for women. In fact, research by British academic Paul Dolan found that marriage and motherhood tend to make American women less happy. 'The healthiest and happiest population subgroup are women who never married or had children,' Dolan said in 2019. 'You see a single woman of 40, who has never had children – "Bless, that's a shame, isn't it? Maybe one day you'll meet the right guy and that'll change." No, maybe she'll meet the wrong guy and that'll change. Maybe she'll meet a guy who makes her less happy and healthy, and die sooner.'[60]

Beyond the noughties' concerted efforts to terrify women into reproduction lay an even greater fear: What if women didn't need a man and a baby to be happy? (Or, at any rate, what if they would be equally unhappy either way?) The insistence that women would inevitably find misery if they didn't follow the plan had been presented as well-intentioned advice, but perhaps it was closer to emotional blackmail: if women could be harrowed into shacking up and reproducing regardless of the immediate costs they bore, the workplace could be spared the bother of reforming itself to better fit female employees, who make up 47 per cent of the total US workforce.[61] (The United States remains the only developed economy with no nationally mandated paid parental leave – a policy deficiency that inevitably hits women hardest.)[62] More than that, men could be excused from reshaping themselves into desirable partners for educated, ambitious women: if women en masse could be convinced that settling down was their only option, then thirty-year-old boys could remain thirty-year-old boys.

The *Hollywood Reporter* interview was, in part, given to promote *The Morning Show*, the Apple TV+ drama that

marked Jen's first lead role in a television series since *Friends*.
The evolution of television that started with the cable wars of
the late nineties had continued through the following decades
and escalated again with the arrival of streaming services.
This had led to a resurgence of interest in *Friends*, and not
only among older viewers who wanted a nostalgic rewatch.
Millennials who would have been children at the time of
the first broadcast, and Gen Zs, who wouldn't even have
been born, were every bit as avid.[63] In 2018, Netflix signed a
deal worth $100 million to continue licensing the show – a
phenomenal price that was more than justified by *Friends'*
appeal.[64] But streaming needed new content as well as familiar
hits, and this meant another boom in original drama, as the
rival services all sought to commission their own must-see
TV. The fruits of this competition can be seen in shows like
Stranger Things (Netflix), *Rings of Power* (Amazon Prime),
multiple Marvel and *Star Wars* spinoffs (Disney Plus) and, on
Apple TV+, *The Morning Show*, which began in 2019.[65]

Friends had been a triumph for Jen, but it had also trapped
her in various less interesting iterations of the Rachel Greene
character. Now television had matured to the point where it
could again offer her a role to match her talents. After over a
decade of being largely disregarded for her cinematic work, Jen
won a Screen Actors Guild Award for her performance on *The
Morning Show*. In it, she plays Alex Levy, a TV news anchor
whose male co-host, Mitch Kessler (played by Steve Carrell),
is fired for sexual misconduct. It's a storyline that clearly maps
the real-life falls of men like Matt Lauer, Charlie Rose and Bill
O'Reilly, all of whom lost their jobs after allegations against
them emerged in the aftermath of the Harvey Weinstein
case.[66] (Lauer, Rose and O'Reilly all deny the accusations.) And
it's a drama with a sharp eye for institutional complicity and
the relationship of workplace politics to the delivery of justice.
Alex is appalled by Mitch's conduct and saddened by the loss

of him as a colleague, but his fall is also an opportunity for her. For Mitch, though, it's an inexplicable upheaval in the sexual order. 'I didn't rape anybody,' he screams at his assistants, as the extent of his public shaming becomes undeniable. 'I didn't jizz into a plant in front of anybody! If I fucked a couple of PAs and assistants, big fucking deal – they liked it! Since the dawn of time, men have used their power to attract women and now let's bust Mitch Kessler's head over it!'[67]

The crisis of masculinity, as mapped by Faludi and *Fight Club*, had not been resolved by the Upskirt Decade. In 2012, Hanna Rosin published *The End of Men: And the Rise of Women*, which repeated many of Faludi's conclusions about men's struggles but ended on a hopeful note. 'Maybe,' wrote Rosin, 'we are approaching the moment when men stop looking back, fretting that all the "real men" are dead, and allow themselves to go soft, a little.'[68] The scandals exposed by the MeToo movement showed that many men had little appetite for reinvention. Instead, they clung to dominance, using sex to assert their control over the women who had encroached on the workplace. And then, in 2016, disenfranchised masculinity found political expression in the election of Donald Trump. MeToo, which emerged as a mass movement in 2017, was essentially the backlash to the backlash: out of the betrayed promise of a female future came a moment of consciousness-raising in which many women not only acknowledged for the first time the harms done to them by men in positions of power, but also realised for the first time, through other women's testimony, how near universal such encounters with predators were. MeToo not only emboldened women to name their abusers, but also established the norm that women should be believed. After the grim years of the Upskirt Decade, this felt like restitution.

What was lacking, however, was a means of discriminating between substantive allegations and the less plausible ones.

Some targets deserved their destruction. The case for others – and one of the tensions of *The Morning Show*'s first season is whether this includes Mitch – was less clear-cut. The comedian turned US senator Al Franken, for example, was accused of sexual assault five weeks after the Harvey Weinstein allegations were published. In the moment, it seemed imperative that Franken submit to punishment. *Slate* published a column titled 'Al Franken Should Resign Immediately'. 'There is no rational reason to doubt the truth of [the] accusations, no legitimate defense of Franken's actions, and no ambiguity here at all,' it stated. The fact that Franken disputed the claims was held as further evidence of his turpitude: it was 'a case study in pseudo-apologetic denial, an effort to gaslight ... while purporting to express regret'.[69] Under pressure from his peers, Franken quit – and yet, two years later, the *New Yorker* raised possible discrepancies in his accuser's account that undermined her claims.[70] In lieu of due process, neither party could receive satisfaction.

But while MeToo offered a form of wild justice, women's formal rights in the United States were slipping away. In 2012, Rosin had regarded the professional, sexual and reproductive freedoms won by women in the previous decades as nonnegotiable. 'A society that has become utterly dependent on the unfettered ambition of women cannot possibly, with a straight face, reopen the debate about contraception,' she wrote confidently – and, it transpired, wrongly. Trump's appointment of conservative justices to the Supreme Court enabled the overturning of *Roe v. Wade* in 2022, ending American women's constitutional right to abortion. Speaking after the decision, Justice Clarence Thomas suggested that the same legal argument could also be deployed against (among other decisions) *Griswold v. Connecticut*, which had established the right to contraception.[71] The window of deferred maternity enjoyed by women had allowed both female liberty and male anxiety to flourish. Now, in the United States at least, there are determined efforts to close it.

This does not mean women will necessarily comply: one of the lessons of the demographic data is that, even with efforts to compel women towards childbearing, educated women will still have fewer babies and will do so later in their lives, if at all. But exercising this preference becomes dramatically more difficult without accessible legal abortion. In 2004, Rachel Greene and Jennifer Aniston had stood as twin visions of female liberty: the fictional one got to 'have it all', while the real one underwent a more complicated mixture of disappointments and accomplishments but, ultimately, built a life that must, by any standards, be considered a happy and successful one. Almost uniquely among women who experienced the most extreme form of noughties fame, Jen did not become a prisoner of her image, however relentless the efforts to impose that image on her. Her celebrity persona existed in parallel to a real life in which she found her own fulfillment. For the young women of the present-day United States, that freedom to make their own plan, with all the attendant risks and rewards, can no longer be taken for granted.

Conclusion

'Blurred Lines'

In March 2013, Pharrell Williams released a song. This was routine: Williams's music had soundtracked the noughties. As part of production and songwriting unit the Neptunes, he'd helped turn Britney from precocious schoolgirl into panting kitten, and Justin Timberlake into a bad-boy sex symbol. As part of the band N.E.R.D, he'd made 'Everyone Nose (All the Girls Standing in the Line for the Bathroom)', with its roll call of troubled party girls on the Kanye remix: 'Paris, Lindsay, Britney'. He'd worked with Gwen Stefani, Madonna, Kelis – and now he was working with Robin Thicke, a white soul singer who'd enjoyed minor commercial success since the late nineties without ever having a true breakout. (When Kim had her 'fairytale wedding' to Kris Humphries, inaugurating a marriage that would last all of seventy-two days, Thicke performed at the reception.) For Thicke, this song would be different. This song would be a global megahit, propelling him to the front of the public consciousness. It would also ruin him. The song was 'Blurred Lines', and it marked the end of the Upskirt Decade.

At first, 'Blurred Lines' didn't seem to strike anyone as being particularly controversial, with its lyrics addressed to a 'good girl' who, the narrator is convinced, 'must wanna get nasty'. 'I know you want it,' croons Thicke. *Spin* magazine called the song 'another fun slice of throwback soul from the perpetually underrated Thicke', and declared that the real reason to be excited about its release was the 'hilarious' video. In it, Williams, Thicke and rapper T.I. (all fully clothed) dance around a minimal set with three models: Emily Ratajkowski, Elle Evans and Jessi M'Bengue. The women are all dressed in white underwear – except in the unrated version of the video, where they wear nothing but flesh-coloured thongs while vamping with an oversize syringe, giant dice, a lamb and other absurd props. Near the end, foil balloons fill the screen spelling out the words ROBIN THICKE HAS A BIG DICK, and in a nod to the fact that the song was issuing into a social media world, #THICKE flashes on-screen intermittently.

'I wanted to deal with the misogynist, funny lyrics in a way where the girls were going to overpower the men,' said director Diane Martel. 'I directed the girls to look into the camera, this is very intentional and they do it most of the time; they are in the power position. I don't think the video is sexist.'[2] If she sounded defensive, it's because by the time she gave the interview, the song had become the focus of a firestorm over the objectification of women, and many people – women in particular – saw the 'Blurred Lines' video as very sexist indeed. That included, unhelpfully for Martel, Thicke himself. 'We tried to do everything that was taboo. Bestiality, drug injections, and everything that is completely derogatory towards women,' the singer told *GQ*. 'People say, "Hey, do you think this is degrading to women?" I'm like, "Of course it is. What a pleasure it is to degrade a woman. I've never gotten to do that before. I've always respected women."'[3]

The tenuous sense of irony that had sustained the Upskirt Decade was exposed here. What women understood to be a joke, the men took rather more seriously. In her 2021 book *My Body*, Ratajkowski alleges that Thicke groped her breasts during filming. (Martel has confirmed the account; Thicke did not respond to the claims.)[4] But while the video was outrageous, it was the lyrics that generated the sharpest reaction. The first inkling of offence came not from any of the feminist sites like Jezebel, but from the personal blog of a woman named Lisa Huynh. 'Has anyone heard Robin Thicke's new rape song?' she asked her readers. 'Basically, the majority of the song (creepily named "Blurred Lines") has the R&B singer murmurring [*sic*] "I know you want it" over and over into a girl's ear. Call me a cynic, but that phrase does not exactly encompass the notion of consent in sexual activity ... Seriously, this song is disgusting – though admittedly very catchy.'[5] This got picked up by the Daily Beast's Tricia Romano, who wrote a piece in June describing the song as 'kind of rapey'.[6] A few days later, BuzzFeed ran a post, titled 'Everyone Thinks Robin Thicke's "Blurred Lines" Is "Rapey"', rounding up social media denunciations of Thicke's song.[7] The engagement that the video had courted turned out to be its downfall.

It was a radicalising moment for young women. In November, University College London Students' Union banned the song. The 'fun slice of throwback soul' had become, according to Dorian Lynskey in the *Guardian*, 'the most controversial song of the decade'.[8] Jezebel – which had finally caught up to the fact that there were clicks in this outrage – described the unfortunate Thicke as 'a vengeful spirit who can be summoned by uttering "blundering male chauvinist" thrice into a dark mirror over a derivative R&B beat'.[9] Thicke's triumph had come, for him, at precisely the wrong moment. A burgeoning sense of injustice over the treatment of women needed a face, and he was perfectly placed to become it. In 2014, after the success of 'Blurred Lines' and its namesake album, he released a follow-up called *Paula*, after his then-estranged wife. It was, comprehensively, a flop: in the United Kingdom, it sold an appalling 540 copies in the first week. Things were slightly better in the United States, where the album sold 25,000 copies – until you realised this was a puny seventh of its predecessor's week-one sales. Outlets reported this with barely disguised pleasure. *Vanity Fair*'s 'Robin Thicke's New Album Sales Are So Bad You Might Think It's a Typo' was a typical gloating headline.[10]

Something had definitively shifted in the relationship between women and popular culture. The same month that 'Blurred Lines' came out, there was another watershed for Upskirt Decade mores. In a *Vanity Fair* cover interview with Nancy Jo Sales, Taylor Swift pointedly remarked that there was a 'special place in hell for women who don't help other women'. The comment was a response to an incident at the Golden Globes in January of that year, when hosts Tina Fey and Amy Poehler had made a joke about Taylor's much-publicised dating life.[11] For Taylor, this was the moment to take a stand over her press coverage: 'If you want some big revelation, since 2010 I have dated exactly two people,' she told Sales.[12] What was significant here was not merely that a celebrity should protest her media treatment – plenty of stars had done so before, and with much more cause than Taylor had here – but that Taylor was able to do so with an expectation of sympathy.

Born in 1989, Taylor was only three years younger than Lindsay, but those years represented a generational gulf. For Britney, Paris and Lindsay, the internet had been a brutal imposition, wrenching control of their images away from them. For Taylor, it was an accepted part of the order of life: she was on MySpace before she was famous, and later, Instagram would allow her to forge a direct relationship with her fans. She called herself an 'internet baby'.[13] If she was unhappy with her media treatment, she could simply appeal directly to her audience, which was more likely to applaud her for her integrity than penalise her for being a bad sport. And while the women who came before her were required to answer endlessly intrusive questions in order to justify their coverage – Britney and her hymen; Lindsay and her breasts; Jen and her uterus – by the time Taylor sat down with *Vanity Fair*, the order had shifted.

Celebrity coverage had always been a symbiotic business based on access. Outlets needed celebrities because the public was interested in celebrities, and celebrities needed the media to put them in front of the public. It was this very cosiness that created the space for bloggers like Perez Hilton, who covered celebrities as though fame itself were an affront to public morals and who gleefully broke stories that the old system might have kept quiet. But this situation could not survive the coming of social media. As a 2015 Awl essay by John Herrman noted, 'The sudden glut of Instagram photos of celebrities and by celebrities, often with newsworthy text attached, destroys a set of common arrangements ...' The media's dependence on celebrity was no longer reciprocated:

Let's say a celebrity couple is having a child (congratulations). A few years ago, they might have given this news to the tabloid willing to pay top dollar, or to the only celeb magazine that had refused to print a previous divorce rumor. The celebrity had power, but the magazine did as well ... With Instagram, the power shifts dramatically. A genuine Celeb Couple will have more combined followers on Instagram than virtually any publication, most of whom are actual fans. (There isn't a single celebrity publication in the top 100 Instagram accounts. *People*, as an example, the 10th largest magazine in the country with a 3.5 million issue circulation, has 1.1 million followers; Chrissy Teigen's Instagram pregnancy announcement went out to 4.1 million, and her partner John Legend's simultaneous post went to another 2.7 million.) If Celeb Couple posts a baby photo themselves ... publications would have to embed or print it *anyway*.[14]

So, if Taylor saw the attention paid to her love life as an injustice (despite repeatedly alluding to that love life in her songs), *Vanity Fair* was hardly going to compromise its relationship with her by strongly demurring. Celebrity journalism grew softer. Perhaps the ultimate example of this was a 2018 *Vogue* feature in which Beyoncé was presented 'in her own words' – effectively, allowed to interview herself.[15] The casual cruelty of the noughties no longer had a place. This was in large part because any celebrity with a large enough fan base to be worth covering also had the power to direct those fans against anyone perceived as an enemy. In 2018, writer Wanna Thompson was subjected to extensive harassment and abuse after tweeting that she thought it was time for rapper Nicki Minaj to find a new, 'mature' direction. Minaj responded directly, and her hostility was then magnified by her fans (called, collectively, 'Barbz'). In a sign of how cowed the media now was by celebrity, Thompson even lost her internship at an entertainment blog.[16]

There was still an appetite for dirt – TMZ remained, and remains, extraordinarily successful – but the default attitude towards the famous was a celebratory one. BuzzFeed, which for a period in the 2010s looked like it might be the future of journalism, had the motto 'No haters'. 'The site is one of the leading voices of the moment, thriving in the online sharing economy, in which agreeability is popularity, and popularity is value,' wrote Tom Scocca on *Gawker*, in a 2013 essay that bemoaned the rise of an aesthetic he defined as 'smarm'.[17] But Scocca was on the losing side of this culture war, and so was *Gawker*, although it would take three more years for it to fully acknowledge its defeat. In April 2013, *Gawker* published a post by John Cook with the self-explanatory title 'A Judge Told Us to Take Down Our Hulk Hogan Sex Tape Post. We Won't'.[18] The sex tape in question had appeared on *Gawker* the previous October and was very much business as usual for the *Gawker* family of sites, which had repeatedly hosted explicit personal material featuring both celebrities and civilians. Hogan – a former star of pro wrestling who had been disgraced in the steroid hearings – was exactly the kind of shopworn figure that suited *Gawker*'s self-ironising attitude towards fame.

Hogan's legal team initially attempted to use copyright law to suppress the tape, but as the video had been made without his knowledge – he had been secretly filmed by the woman he was having sex with and her husband – he could not claim to be the copyright holder.[19] His next legal approach was infringement of privacy, and here he had more success. Judge Pamela Campbell issued an order to remove both the tape and the post summarising its contents. *Gawker* deleted the video, begrudgingly, but saw no reason to comply when it came to the text. 'Campbell's order requiring us to take down not only a very brief, highly edited video excerpt from a 30-minute Hulk Hogan fucking session but also a lengthy written account from someone who had watched the entirety of that fucking session, is risible and contemptuous of centuries of First Amendment jurisprudence,' wrote Cook loftily. For good measure, he included a link to an externally hosted version of the tape. When the case was finally concluded in 2016, the jury found in Hogan's favour on all counts and awarded him damages of $140 million – more than enough to bankrupt *Gawker*.[20] No gossip site would be keen to replicate its hubris.

Gawker made many mistakes in its conduct with Hogan. One of its most serious was to assume that it was involved in a simple legal battle with a washed-up wrestler: in fact, Hogan's case was being secretly funded and directed by PayPal billionaire Peter Thiel. In 2007, when noughties cynicism was at its height, Valleywag (a *Gawker* blog) had outed Thiel in a post titled 'Peter Thiel Is Totally Gay, People'. Since then, Thiel had been looking to bring *Gawker* down, and the Hogan tape was his chance.[21] Thiel spared no resources in taking it. The comprehensiveness of *Gawker*'s defeat can be credited in large part to one particularly intelligent decision by Hogan's legal team, based on an insight gleaned from mock jury proceedings. 'It became very clear that the kind of jurors we wanted were overweight women,' said a member of Thiel's team, quoted by journalist Ryan Holiday in *Conspiracy*, his book about the case. 'Most people can't empathize with a sex tape, but overweight women are sensitive about their bodies and feel like they have been bullied on the internet. Men don't have that problem. Attractive women don't have that problem. They haven't been body shamed.'[22]

It's an irony, but a very routine one, that something that wounded primarily women ended up being addressed in a case in which a man was the victim. Sex discrimination case law has advanced more often than not through cases in which men were put at a disadvantage, even if the overall burden of unfairness tended to fall on women. What's more interesting here is that Hogan's lawyers had realised how pervasive online intrusion had become for women. When *1 Night in Paris* first leaked in 2003, Paris's high status was part of the reason she merited no sympathy. People were interested in the tape because Paris was rich, famous and hot; the fact that she was rich, famous and hot meant that she had sacrificed any expectation of privacy in advance. Ten years later, the experience of being publicly shamed was far more common. Any woman who had come into contact with the internet had either been on the receiving end of some humiliation or was able to sharply imagine the pain of being targeted.

The noughties had democratised celebrity. The epoch of the

famous-for-being-famous had stealthily evolved into a time when even the most obscure individual could have a public profile of some sort. The kind of parasocial relationships audiences had with the women of the Upskirt Decade – the angst over Britney's sexual propriety, the frenzied attention to Amy's body, the obsession with Jen's fertility – could now be developed towards anyone with a social media presence. Some took this as an opportunity, which led to the development of that new order of the quasi-famous known as influencers. Others experienced only the negative consequences: the judgement, the paranoia, the sense of having become a character in a drama being written by and for the benefit of other people. With the universal adoption of cameraphones, anybody could be unwittingly documented at any time. The idea that someone famous was 'asking for it' (the 'it' in question being intrusive coverage) simply by being famous grew less acceptable, as it became apparent that, should circumstances conspire, almost anyone of any standing could become subject to 'it'. Fame was once an elite trauma, and one that came at least with a certain promise of financial compensation. Now it's a baseline condition of modern life.

I lived through the noughties. I read the blogs. I listened to the music. I participated in the gossip. I laughed at the jokes. And yet, in writing this book, I haven't felt like I was revisiting familiar territory: I have felt as though I were entering an entirely alien landscape. Was there really a time when it was acceptable for television interviewers to press a twenty-one-year-old Britney to tears over a simple break-up? Did the whole news cycle truly spend a month focused on the terrible effects of Janet's exposed breast? Did the liberal New York City press actually run lurid daily updates on the existence of a private sex tape featuring Paris? Did porn blogs really openly mourn their disappointment over Kim's sex tape having been signed off on by its subject, rather than released without her consent? Did reality shows call women fat without compunction? Were life-threatening addictions treated as the stuff of primetime entertainment, rather than desperate afflictions? Was everyone okay with R. Kelly? The fact that the answer to all this is yes should not be shocking to me, because I was there, and in some cases, I was a participant. But I am shocked.

The underlying beliefs of the Upskirt Decade feel almost as foreign to me as those of the seventeenth-century witch trials, with the added confusion that instead of wondering, 'How could people have thought such things?' I am forced to ask, 'How could *I* have thought such things?' One of the most plaintive aspects of the *Gawker* trial was the moment when A. J. Daulerio, author of the original post, was cross-examined and forced to account not only for his reporting on Hogan, but for *Gawker*'s entire culture regarding privacy. 'Imagine what this must be like, there, in that witness box,' writes Holiday. 'Yes, you posted clips of a sex tape, but you're not the one who recorded it and you were at least half sincerely making an editorial point about the mundanity of celebrity and sex with the writing that went alongside. Now you are being depicted as some sort of rogue operator ... '[23] After all, many celebrities of similar stature to Hogan – most obviously Chyna – really had been complicit in the leak of their sex tapes. It would have been self-serving for *Gawker* to assume that Hogan fell into the same category, but it wasn't entirely improbable.

What Daulerio had done in posting the video was normal until, suddenly, it wasn't any more. There would be no more blurred lines. A hard-edged moral clarity began to form instead. For a post-noughties female celebrity, the biggest risk to her reputation isn't a sex tape or a cruelly scrutinised breakdown. (Mental illness can, in fact, be turned into highly sympathetic content, something ex-Disney stars Demi Lovato and Selena Gomez have both done in confessional documentaries.) What can maim a woman's career, however, is 'cancellation' for an actual or perceived moral offence. The same kind of mass outrage that had, for example, forced a public acknowledgement of R. Kelly's crimes could also be turned against figures guilty of far lesser infractions. And because women are in general punished harder for deviating from social norms, women proved particularly vulnerable. The ultimate example here is Chrissy Teigen – the model chosen by Herrman in his Awl essay as the personification of celebrity power in the social media age. Teigen had established her popularity with a punchily liberal Twitter presence and was often celebrated for her 'takedowns' of Donald Trump. But, in 2021, decade-old posts of hers resurfaced in which she seemed to tell reality wannabe Courtney Stodden (age sixteen in 2011) to kill herself. When Teigen sent those tweets, they were hardly notable. If women like Stodden had a purpose in the culture back then, it was surely to be hated. Ten years later, those same tweets looked abhorrent – and abhorrent by the standards that Teigen herself had embraced and enforced. In the immediate aftermath of the scandal, commercial partners distanced themselves from Teigen, and she was left socially isolated. (She has referred to herself as being in the 'cancel club'.)[24]

Taylor Swift also found herself on the sharp end of popular opinion after a clash with Kim and Kanye over whether she had approved the lyric 'I feel like me and Taylor might still have sex / Why? I made that bitch famous' in his 2016 track 'Famous'. After Kim released a video seeming to show Taylor as disingenuous, Taylor's social media comments were mobbed by Kim fans using the snake emoji to symbolise Taylor's supposed duplicity; an author at black culture blog The Root hyperbolically denounced Taylor as 'the most dangerous type of white woman'.[25] In 2019, Swift described the trauma of the experience to *Vogue*: 'A mass public shaming, with millions of people saying you are quote-unquote canceled, is a very isolating experience ... I don't think there are that many people who can actually understand what it's like to have millions of people hate you very loudly.'[26] In early 2023, singer Lizzo tweeted her own criticism of cancellation as a strategy. 'This may be a random time to say this but it's on my heart ... cancel culture is appropriation,' she wrote. 'There was real outrage from truly marginalized people and now it's become trendy, misused and misdirected.'[27] In the Upskirt Decade, a female celebrity's reputation was predicated on viciously policed sexual purity; in the 2020s, the purity test had become a moral one.

The resettlement of noughties norms was almost as arbitrary as the way they were applied in the first place. It was not strictly fair that a billionaire with a grudge was able to destroy *Gawker*, regardless of how indefensible much of *Gawker*'s content was. (Some of the *Gawker* sites were sold and continue today under new ownership, while *Gawker* itself was revived in 2021 under the banner of Bustle Digital Group. Without the no-prisoners tone of the original blog, though, it foundered and in February 2023 *Gawker* was shut down again.)[28] If Taylor was looking to make a point about sexism, a mild joke from two self-proclaimed feminist comedians was hardly the most egregious instance. And perhaps most pitiable of all, there's Robin Thicke – a man of middling success and little power in the music industry, catapulted into being the embodiment of rape culture thanks, in part, to a video directed by a woman. (Pharrell Williams, who held far more culpability for shaping noughties attitudes, was left unscathed: in 2014, *Stylist* ran a profile celebrating him for 'empowering women'.)[29] These moments did not signify justice, exactly, but they did represent a change: the snark, spite and violation that had been acceptable aspects of the treatment of celebrities (particularly women) were no longer to be tolerated.

Snark, spite and violation are hardly to be mourned. The Upskirt Decade was fantastically corrosive – primarily for the women who became its emblems and its targets, but also for every woman whose sense of self was formed within it. It is hard to understand why I accepted the things I accepted, because I no longer exist in a cultural miasma that insists that these things are indeed acceptable. Nonetheless, something was lost as well as gained. A world where celebrity coverage is directed by the twin forces of social media outrage and overweening star power is just as hollow, in its way, as the Upskirt Decade, and the shift from regarding famous women with contempt to regarding them with pity could sometimes be infantilising. For example, Janet was clearly treated indecently after the Super Bowl incident, but the shift to presenting her purely as a victim – both of the media and, more directly, of Justin Timberlake – that began around 2018 seemed to degrade her by another means.[30] Like all the women in this book, she was acting in the world as well as being acted upon. Janet did not choose the context in which she had to work, but more than anyone except Jen and, perhaps, Kim, she was in a position to exercise her judgement and make calls. It is disrespectful to pretend that she had no agency, however much that agency was constrained.

In many cases though, the women I've written about really were astonishingly young when they first had to contend with the predations of fame – Britney, Paris, Lindsay, Aaliyah. In others (Amy, Chyna), mental illness or addiction made them simply too fragile to survive the exploitation and exposure that came with an entertainment career. Nonetheless, every woman in this book is here because she has, or had, an extraordinary talent for fame. Somehow, despite the inhuman pressures on them, they made great work, too. One may note that they also made a lot of terrible work, as Lindsay and Jen both did. One may protest, in Paris's and Chyna's cases, that reality TV and wrestling are too lowbrow for greatness to come into it. One may be deeply sad for potential curtailed by death, as for Amy and Aaliyah. But successful creation in any medium is rare, and I would rather simply be glad for what we have.

I don't claim that the women here were role models or (God forbid) that the things they did were somehow 'feminist' or 'subversive'. I claim only that they were *interesting*, on their own terms, and not merely as sacrificial offerings to celebrity culture. Fame remains brutalising, and online life continues to hold particular danger for women. Sexism found new purchase in the public sphere during the noughties. The fall of some individual abusers after MeToo should not delude anyone into thinking that the entertainment industry has been turned into a safe space for women. There are always powerful men who will turn the institutions they run into machines for predation. Nonetheless, the way celebrity women were once treated feels unimaginable now. Sometimes, the register of progress is only in how utterly remote the past has become. The women in this book bore the full force of the Upskirt Decade – a period that set the terms for how we live now, a period that feels almost close enough to touch but that lies now beyond an impossibly vast gulf of technology and politics.

Acknowledgements

In one sense, I've been writing this book since I first saw the video for '... Baby One More Time'. In another, more convincing sense, the book started when Freya Sanders at UnHerd asked me to write about #FreeBritney. This led to a piece, which led to Ian Leslie's saying, 'I think this might be a book.' Congratulations, Ian! You were correct. The inestimable Caroline Hardman believed in the proposal and became my agent (which meant I also got the support of the redoubtable staff of Hardman and Swainson), her formidable colleague Sarah Levitt sold me to the United States, and queens of publishing Zoe Hood and Ursula Doyle at Fleet and Samantha Weiner and Sarah Robbins (with assistance from Juliet Dore) at Abrams carried me through the process of actually writing it. Holly Connolly did the beautiful illustrations. Thanks to all of you for helping make this happen. I sincerely hope you think the finished product is more *Mean Girls* and less *I Know Who Killed Me*.

Helen Lewis, Tracy King, Rebecca Reilly-Cooper, Gia Milinovich, Hadley Freeman, Janice Turner and Francis Wheen all gave crucial encouragement and comments that got me through the frankly vile business of producing a manuscript. Caroline Criado Perez gave hugely helpful suggestions on the issue of privacy. Thanks to Soph Wilkinson for reading the 'Lindsay' chapter and sharing her incredible Lindsay expertise with me. Thanks to Clare Ditum for reading 'Paris' and for all the dancing. Thanks to Jim DeRogatis for reading 'Aaliyah', which could never have been written without his exemplary journalistic pursuit of R. Kelly. Particular appreciation must go to Matt Elliott, who introduced me to the chaotic bad of sports entertainment by making me watch wrestling in his bedroom when we were teenagers. Rachel Hewitt and Francesca O'Neill both gave me boltholes in which to write, and to them I am truly grateful. Sorry about whatever I did to your cutlery drawers. To Dr T, who taught me history: you must be very sad that I know the dates of every sex tape and still not the Diet of Worms, but at least I tried this time.

My parents instilled in me a firm belief that nothing in culture is too trivial to be worth taking seriously, and they also showed bottomless confidence that I would find my feet eventually, despite my best efforts not to. Thank you, Mum and Dad. To my sister, Rachael, who I know would prefer that this book be about Soundgarden but who will read it anyway. To Maddy and Jay, who mean even more to me than *Blackout*. And last, thanks to my husband, Nathan, for his relentless and, honestly, sometimes quite annoying insistence that I write this book even when I really didn't want to. Love you all.

Notes

Introduction

1. Molly Haskell, *From Reverence to Rape* (New York: Penguin, 1973), p. 12.
2. State of Oklahoma v Riccardo Gina Ferrante, Motion to Quash, www.oklahomacriminallaw.com/Real%20Quash%20Peeping%20Tom.pdf.
3. 'Tulsa Peeping Tom Arrest', News on 6, 7 July 2006, www.newson6.com/story/5e368d022f69d76f620a471a/tulsa-peeping-tom-arrest.
4. State of Oklahoma v. Riccardo Gina Ferrante, Summary Opinion, www.oklahomacriminallaw.com/Ferrente%20Court%20of%20Criminal%20Appeals%20Ruling.pdf.
5. 'Court Drops Case of "Peeping Tom" in Target; Says Victim Was Not in Private Place', Fox News, 14 January 2015, www.foxnews.com/story/court-drops-case-of-peeping-tom-in-target-says-victim-was-not-in-private-place.
6. Catharine A. MacKinnon, *Toward a Feminist Theory of the State* (Cambridge, MA: Harvard University Press, 1991), p. 194.
7. John Estus, 'Voyeurism, Laws to Go High-tech: Peeping Statutes Don't Account for Public Sites', *Oklahoman*, 4 April 2008, eu.oklahoman.com/story/news/2008/05/04/voyeurism-laws-to-go-high-techbrspan-classhl2peeping-statutes-dont-account-for-public-sites-span/61597778007/.
8. 'Upskirt Photos Not Illegal, US Court Rules', Associated Press, 6 March 2014, www.cbc.ca/news/world/upskirt-photos-not-illegal-u-s-court-rules-1.2562395.
9. 'Without Your Vagina, There's No You!', Fleshbot, 30 March 2007, web.archive.org/web/20071221114437/http://fleshbot.com/sex/video/without-your-vagina-theres-no-you-248354.php.
10. Louise Gannon, '"I Find Being Sexy Embarrassing," Reveals Emma Watson', *Daily Mail*, 6 February 2009, www.dailymail.co.uk/home/moslive/article-1127838/I-sexy-embarrassing-reveals-Emma-Watson.html.
11. 'Vanessa Hudgens Is (Probably Not) Naked', Fleshbot, n.d. 2008, web.

archive.org/web/20081108073145/https://fleshbot.com/sex/wishful-thinking/vanessa-hudgens-is-probably-not-naked-297099.php.

12. '"HSM" Nude Pic: It's the Real Deal!', TMZ, 6 September 2007, web. archive.org/web/20081201021217/http://www.tmz.com/2007/09/06/hsm-nude-pic-its-the-real-deal/.

13. Simon Gage, 'Actress Vanessa Hudgens: I Want to Do This When I'm 60; I Want to Be Like Meryl Streep', Metro, 18 July 2013, metro.co.uk/2013/07/18/actress-vanessa-hudgens-i-want-to-do-this-when-im-60-i-want-to-be-like-meryl-streep-3887207/.

14. Ariel Levy, *Female Chauvinist Pigs: Women and the Rise of Raunch Culture* (London: Pocket Books, 2005), pp. 3–4.

15. Perez Hilton with Leif Eriksson and Martin Svensson, *TMI: My Life in Scandal* (Chicago: Chicago Review Press, 2020), p. 66.

16. Max Roser, Hannah Ritchie and Esteban Ortiz-Ospina, 'Internet', Our World in Data, n.d., ourworldindata.org/internet.

17. 'Time Spent Online Doubles in a Decade', Ofcom, 11 May 2015, www.ofcom.org.uk/about-ofcom/latest/media/media-releases/2015/time-spent-online-doubles-in-a-decade.

18. Roger Collis, 'Learning to Live Without Your BlackBerry', *New York Times*, 17 May 2007, www.nytimes.com/2007/05/17/travel/17iht-trfreq18.1.5752164.html.

19. A. E. Marwick and Danah Boyd, 'I Tweet Honestly, I Tweet Passionately: Twitter Users, Context Collapse, and the Imagined Audience', *New Media and Society* 13, No. 1 (2011): 114–33.

20. Penelope Trunk, 'Why I Tweeted About My Miscarriage', *Guardian*, 6 November 2009, www.theguardian.com/lifeandstyle/2009/nov/06/penelope-trunk-tweet-miscarriage.

21. Richard Pérez-Peña, '2 Celebrity Magazines Buck Circulation Trend', *New York Times*, 11 February 2008, www.nytimes.com/2008/02/11/business/media/11cnd-mag.html.

22. Perez Hilton with Jared Shapiro, *Red Carpet Suicide* (London: Celebra, 2009), p. 225.

23. Search Hollywood Tuna Archives at web.archive.org/web/20050425013826/http://hollywoodtuna.com/about.htm.

24. Emily Gould, 'How the *Gawker* Stalker Map Works: A Guide for Dummies, Outraged Famous People, and Old Folk', *Gawker*, 9 April 2007, www.gawker.com/250593/how-the-gawker-stalker-map-works-a-guide-for-dummies-outraged-famous-people-and-old-folk.

25. Emily Gould, 'Replaying My Shame', The Cut, 26 February 2020, https://www.thecut.com/2020/02/emily-gould-gawker-shame.html.

26. Nancy Jo Sales, 'The Suspects Wore Louboutins', *Vanity Fair*, March 2010, archive.vanityfair.com/article/share/e9cc0cc3-dbf1-4fab-8367-5fc7c05608e6.

27. Amélie Pedneault, Danielle A. Harris and Raymond A. Knight, 'Toward a Typology of Sexual Burglary: Latent Class Findings', *Journal of Criminal Justice* 40, No. 4 (July–August 2012): 278–84, www.sciencedirect.com/science/article/abs/pii/S004723521200075X.

28. Maureen O'Connor, '"Lindsay Was Crying" in Jail, Says Girl Who Tried to Rob Her', *Gawker*, 26 July 2010, www.gawker.com/5596844/

lindsay-was-crying-in-jail-says-girl-who-tried-to-rob-her.

29. Richard Lawson, '*Pretty Wild* Might Be the Worst Television Show Ever Made', *Gawker*, 29 March 2010, www.gawker.com/5504679/ pretty-wild-might-be-the-worst-television-show-ever-made.

30. Alex Pareene, 'Exclusive: Donald Trump's Brother Robert Has Billy Joel Tickets Tonight, Rented Party Bus, Pre-gamed in Murray Hill', *Gawker* Stalker, 15 March 2016, www.gawker.com/tag/gawker-stalker.

31. Barbara Penner, 'A World of Unmentionable Suffering: Women's Public Conveniences in Victorian London', *Journal of Design History* 14, No. 1 (2001): 35–51.

32. Hallie Rubenhold, *The Five: The Untold Lives of the Women Killed by Jack the Ripper* (London: Doubleday, 2019), p. 15.

33. Alwyn Collinson, 'How Black Friday Changed the Suffragette Struggle', Museum of London, 14 November 2018, https://www.museumoflondon.org.uk/discover/black-friday.

34. Jodi Kantor and Megan Twohey, 'Harvey Weinstein Paid Off Sexual Harassment Accusers for Decades', *New York Times*, 5 October 2017, www.nytimes.com/2017/10/05/us/harvey-weinstein-harassment-allegations.html.

35. Joanna Robinson, 'Rose McGowan Claims She Was Dropped by Her Agent for Speaking About Sexism in Hollywood', *Vanity Fair*, June 2015, www.vanityfair.com/hollywood/2015/06/ rose-mcgowan-fired-agent-sexism-hollywood.

36. Ronan Farrow, '"I Haven't Exhaled in So Long": Surviving Harvey Weinstein', *New Yorker*, 25 February 2020, www.newyorker.com/ news/q-and-a/i-havent-exhaled-in-so-long-surviving-harvey-weinstein.

1: Britney

1. 'Britney Wheeled Out on a Gurney', TMZ, 4 January 2008, www.tmz. com/2008/01/04/britney-wheeled-out-on-a-gurney/.

2. Michael Cragg, '"It Was a Bit of a Blur": Britney Spears on the Making of . . . Baby One More Time', *Guardian*, 11 August 2008, www.theguardian.com/music/2018/aug/11/ britney-spears-making-baby-one-more-time.

3. Rob Sheffield, 'How Britney Spears Changed Pop with "Baby One More Time"', *Rolling Stone*, 12 January 2019, https:// www.rollingstone.com/music/music-features/britney-spears-baby-one-more-time-anniversary-rob-sheffield-777564/ britney-spears-making-baby-one-more-time.

4. Polly Vernon, 'Like a Virgin?', *Guardian*, 6 June, 2000, www. theguardian.com/world/2000/jun/06/gender.uk1.

5. Vladimir Nabokov, *Lolita* (1955; repr. New York: Penguin, 1995), p. 135.

6. John Berger, *Ways of Seeing* (London: Penguin, 1972), p. 46.

7. Levy, *Female Chauvinist Pigs*, p. 30.

8. 'US Sales Database', RIAA, www.riaa.com/u-s-sales-database/.

9. 'Gold & Platinum', RIAA, www.riaa.com/gold-platinum/?tab_active=default-award&se=baby+one+more+time#search_section.

10. Eamon Forde, 'Oversharing: How Napster Nearly Killed the Music Industry', *Guardian*, 31 May 2019, www.theguardian.com/music/2019/may/31/napster-twenty-years-music-revolution.

11. 'US Sales Database'.

12. Concert Archives, 'Madonna Tours and Concerts', n.d. www.concertarchives.org/bands/madonna.

13. Concert Archives, 'Britney Spears Tours and Concerts', n.d. www.concertarchives.org/bands/britney-spears.

14. Mark Binelli, 'Britney Spears Finds It Hard to Be a Woman', *Rolling Stone*, 2 October 2003, www.rollingstone.com/music/music-news/britney-spears-finds-it-hard-to-be-a-woman-254714/.

15. Ann Hornaday, '"Crossroads": Britney's Fizzy Serving of Hot Pepsi', *Washington Post*, 15 February 2002, www.washingtonpost.com/archive/lifestyle/2002/02/15/crossroads-britneys-fizzy-serving-of-hot-pepsi/95e64090-0180-411e-a8af-6bf89004dd07/.

16. John Dingwall, 'Your Time Is Up, Jacko: Britney Wants Albums' Top Slot', *Daily Record* (Glasgow), 5 November 2001, www.thefreelibrary.com/otr..Off+the+record%3A+YOUR+TIME+IS+UP%2C+JACKO%3B+Britney+wants+albums+top...-a079729749.

17. Britney Fan, various tweets, twitter.com/BritneyHiatus/status/1360354816183132165.

18. Andy Swift, 'Loser', Details, 9 February 2021, tvline.com/list_item/details-magazine/.

19. Alex Denney, 'An Ode to Britney: The Making of the "Cry Me a River" Video', Dazed, 24 November 2017, www.dazeddigital.com/music/article/38186/1/cry-me-a-river-justin-timberlake-video-director-interview.

20. Binelli, 'Britney Spears Finds It Hard to Be a Woman'.

21. *Us Weekly* Staff, 'Britney Spears' Us Weekly Covers Through the Years', *Us Weekly*, 4 April 2019, www.usmagazine.com/celebrity-news/pictures/britney-spears-us-weekly-covers-through-the-years-20142111/42359-2/.

22. 'Britney Spears – Interview with Diane Sawyer @ ABC Primetime (2003)', YouTube, n.d., www.youtube.com/watch?v=FyI6PTuLYgw.

23. Lou Pearlman with Wes Smith, *Bands, Brands, and Billions: My Top 10 Rules for Making Any Business Go Platinum* (New York: McGraw-Hill, 2003), p. 20.

24. Ibid., p. 109.

25. Bryan Burrough, 'Mad About the Boys', *Vanity Fair*, 3 October 2007, www.vanityfair.com/news/2007/11/pearlman200711.

26. *The Boy Band Con: The Lou Pearlman Story*, directed by Aaron Kunkel (Pilgrim Media/Searchlight, 2019).

27. Liam Stack, 'Lou Pearlman, Svengali Behind Backstreet Boy and 'NSync, Dies at 62', *New York Times*, 22 August 2016, www.nytimes.com/2016/08/23/arts/music/lou-pearlman-dead.html.

28. John Seabrook, 'We Live in the Pop-Culture World that Lou

Pearlman Created', *New Yorker*, 27 August 2016, www.newyorker.com/
culture/culture-desk/
we-live-in-the-pop-culture-world-that-lou-pearlman-created.

29. Britney Spears and Lynne Spears, *Britney Spears' Heart to Heart*
(London: Hodder & Stoughton, 2000), back matter.

30. Britney Spears and Lynne Spears, *A Mother's Gift: A Novel* (New York:
Delacorte Press, 2001), flyleaf.

31. Pearlman with Smith, *Bands, Brands, and Billions*, p. 103.

32. Spears and Spears, *Britney Spears' Heart to Heart*, pp. 86–8.

33. Ibid., p. 118.

34. Binelli, 'Britney Spears Finds It Hard to Be a Woman'.

35. Jennifer Vineyard, 'Britney Talks Sex: Turns Out She Really Wasn't
that Innocent', MTV, 8 July 2003, www.mtv.com/news/9sefqc/
britney-talks-sex-turns-out-she-really-wasnt-that-innocent.

36. Bradley Stern, 'Annet Artani: From "Everytime" to "Alive"', MuuMuse,
February 2010, muumuse.com/2010/02/annet-artani-from-everytime-
to-alive.html/#more-5249

37. Heather Waugh and Heidi Parker, '"I Find It Very Suspect": Director
David LaChapelle Weights in on #FreeBritney After Old Music Video
Footage of Spears in a Cage Leaks Online', *Daily Mail*, 29 April 2019,
www.dailymail.co.uk/tvshowbiz/article-6973799/David-LaChapelle-
weighs-Britney-Spears-music-video-showing-cage-leaked.html.

38. Wenn, 'Britney: David LaChapelle Tricked Me
into Sexy Photos', ContactMusic, 2 October 2003,
www.contactmusic.com/britney-spears/news/
britney.-david-lachapelle-tricked-me-into-sexy-photos.

39. Esposito, Veronica, 'David LaChapelle: "I've never seen
what I do as objectification"', *Guardian*, 6 September
2022, www.theguardian.com/artanddesign/2022/sep/06/
david-lachapelle-photographer-fotografiska-new-york.

40. Waugh and Parker, '"I Find It Very Suspect"'.

41. John Berman and Edward Lovett, 'Britney Spears' Ex, Jason Alexander,
Reflects on 55-Hour Marriage: "I Was in Love"', ABC News, 3 February
2012, abcnews.go.com/Entertainment/britney-spears-jason-alexander-
reflects-55-hour-marriage/story?id=15506535.

42. *Britney & Kevin: Chaotic*, director Rob Klug (Fairy Zone, 2005).

43. Gil Kaufman, 'Britney Spears Sues over Bum Knee, Seeks $9.8
Million', MTV, 7 February 2005, www.mtv.com/news/1496626/
britney-spears-sues-over-bum-knee-seeks-98-million/.

44. Jennifer Vineyard, 'Britney Lashes Out Against Tabloid "Liars" on
Her Web Site', MTV, 30 March 2005, www.mtv.com/news/1499271/
britney-lashes-out-against-tabloid-liars-on-her-web-site/.

45. Lindsay Kimble, 'Emotional Bobby Brown Admits He Once Hit
Wife Whitney Houston and Details Using Drugs while Daughter
Bobbi Kristina Was Nearby', *People*, 2 December 2020, people.com/
celebrity/bobby-brown-admits-hitting-whitney-houston-details-
couples-drug-usage/.

46. Perez Hilton, 'Filthy Whore', Perez Hilton, n.d., perezhilton.com/
filthy-whore/.

47. Perez Hilton, 'Attention All Britney Fans', Perez Hilton, n.d., perezhilton.com/attention-all-britney-fans/.

48. Rosie Swash, 'Britney Spears's Former Manager Issued with Restraining Order', *Guardian*, 29 April 2009, www.theguardian.com/music/2009/apr/29/britney-spears-former-manager.

49. Spears and Spears, *Britney Spears' Heart to Heart*, p. 17.

50. Brandon Lowrey, 'Lutfi Testifies Britney Shaved her Head to Avoid Drug Testing', Reuters, 23 October 2012, www.reuters.com/article/entertainment-us-britneyspears-lutfi-idUSBRE89J01P20121023.

51. Sheila Marikar, 'Bald and Broken: Inside Britney's Shaved Head', ABC News, 19 February 2007, abcnews.go.com/Entertainment/Health/story?id=2885048&page=1.

52. Ryan Smith, 'Why Britney Spears Shaved Off Her Hair – Looking Back 15 Years Later', *Newsweek*, 15 February 2022, www.newsweek.com/why-britney-spears-shaved-off-her-hairlooking-back-15-years-later-1679388.

53. Donnell Alexander, 'The Paparazzi Who Stalked Britney Spears Have No Regrets', Insider, 18 February 2021, www.insider.com/the-paparazzi-who-stalked-britney-spears-have-no-regrets-2021-2.

54. Hilton with Shapiro, *Red Carpet Suicide*, p. 229.

55. Cowell's remarks in the *Sun* quoted in '"I Looked Like a Fat Pig," Says Britney After MTV Fiasco', *Daily Mail*, 13 September 2007, www.dailymail.co.uk/tvshowbiz/article-480947/I-looked-like-fat-pig-says-Britney-MTV-fiasco.html.

56. Sady Doyle, *Trainwreck: The Women We Love to Hate, Mock and Fear … and Why* (New York: Melville House, 2016), p. 175.

57. Binelli, 'Britney Spears Finds It Hard to Be a Woman'.

58. Claudia Rosenbaum, 'Breaking Down Britney Spears's Accusations Against Her Father', Vulture, 20 January 2022, www.vulture.com/2022/01/britney-spears-dad-allegations-finances.html.

59. *Us Magazine* Staff, 'Britney Spears Get a People's Choice Nod', *Us Magazine*, 10 November 2008, web.archive.org/web/20081113105106/https://britney-spears-nominated-for-peoples-choice-award.

60. Part 1 of *Britney: For the Record*, Daily Motion, www.dailymotion.com/video/x7lr2p.

61. 'Britney Spears: 28 Years in 28 Pictures', Page Six, 2 December 2009, pagesix.com/2009/12/02/britney-spears-28-years-in-28-pictures-2/.

62. Nicholas Hautman, 'Louis Walsh: "Britney Spears Was on So Much Medication on 'X Factor'"', Page Six, 14 June 2021, pagesix.com/2021/06/14/louis-walsh-britney-spears-was-on-medication-on-x-factor/.

63. Liz Day, Samantha Stark and Joe Coscarelli, 'Britney Spears Quietly Pushed for Years to End Her Conservatorship', *New York Times*, 22 June 2021, www.nytimes.com/2021/06/22/arts/music/britney-spears-conservatorship.html.

64. Emma Nolan, 'Jamie Spears' Lawyer Denies Britney's Birth Control Claims', *Newsweek*, 15 July 2021, www.newsweek.com/jamie-spears-lawyer-denies-britney-birth-control-claims-iud-1610027.

65. Jem Aswad, 'Read Britney Spears' Full Statement Against Her Conservatorship: "I Am Traumatized"', Variety, 23 June 2021, variety.

com/2021/music/news/britney-spears-full-statement-conservatorship-1235003940/.

66. Daphne Barak, '"Without My Help, Britney Might Be DEAD": His Words Will Infuriate the Legions of Britney Spears Fans Who Campaigned for Her Freedom – But, Speaking for the First Time, Her Father Jamie Insists the Controversial 13-Year Conservatorship SAVED Her', *Daily Mail*, 17 December 2022, www.dailymail.co.uk/news/article-11549597/Jamie-insists-Britney-Spears-controversial-13-year-conservatorship-saved-ruin.html.

67. 'Britney Spears Says She is Now Able to Use Cash, Have the Keys to Her Car After Being Freed from Conservatorship', CBS News Los Angeles, 17 November 2021, www.cbsnews.com/losangeles/news/britney-spears-use-cash-keys-to-car-freed-conservatorship/.

68. Quoted in Jacqueline Lindenberg, 'Britney Spears Lashes Out in Frustration over Documentaries Made About Her: "I Feel Like America Has Done a Wonderful Job at Humiliating Me"', *Daily Mail*, 9 July 2022, www.dailymail.co.uk/tvshowbiz/article-10998539/Britney-Spears-lashes-frustration-documentaries-her.html.

2: Paris

1. NYP Holdings v. Mario Lavenderia, Complaint, 2 May 2005.
2. Hilton with Eriksson and Svensson, TMI, p. 63.
3. Hilton with Shapiro, *Red Carpet Suicide*, p. 10.
4. 'Paris Hilton's Driving Could Lead to Jail', *Los Angeles Times*, 30 March 2007, latimes.com/archives/la-xpm-mar-30-me-paris30-story.html.
5. 'Paris Hilton Wins Big Outlaw of 2006—VH1's Big in 06 Awards', YouTube, n.d., www.youtube.com/watch?v=uf_P1iocuzc.
6. Bob Morris, 'Next Generation: The Hilton Sisters', *New Yorker*, 10 October 1999, www.newyorker.com/magazine/1999/10/18/next-generation-l-the-hilton-sisters.
7. Michelle Gotthelf, 'Debutantes They Ain't: Hot Young Heiresses Partying Up a Storm', *New York Post*, 15 October 2000, nypost.com/2000/10/15/debutantes-they-aint-hot-young-heiresses-partying-up-a-storm/.
8. Nancy Jo Sales, 'Hip-hop Debs', *Vanity Fair*, September 2000, archive.vanityfair.com/article/2000/9/hip-hop-debs.
9. Katherine E. Finkelstein, 'Jury Clears Combs and Bodyguard; Split Verdict for 3rd Defendant', *New York Times*, 16 March 2001, https://www.nytimes.com/2001/03/16/nyregion/jury-clears-combs-and-bodyguard-split-verdict-for-3rd-defendant.html.
10. Sales, 'Hip-hop Debs'.
11. Daniel R. Coleridge, 'Hilton's Sis Rejected Reality TV', *TVGuide*, n.d., web.archive.org/web/20030725004416/https://www.tvguide.com/newsgossip/insider/030722c.asp.
12. Leslie Ryan, '"Simple Life" New Reality at Fox Studio: 20th Tries on Genre for Size', *Television Week*, n.d., web.archive.org/web/20040215040316/http://www.tvweek.com/topstorys/112403simplelife.html.

13. Peter White, 'Paris Hilton Admits She Was "Playing a Character Before" as Heiress; Opens Up About YouTube Doc "This Is Paris" – TCA', Deadline, 18 January 2020, deadline.com/2020/01/paris-hilton-this-is-paris-character-youtube-1202834878/.

14. Josh Wolk, 'Are Paris and Nicole Rich Ditzes in the 1st Ep?', *Entertainment Weekly*, 2 December 2003, ew.com/article/2003/12/02/are-paris-and-nicole-rich-ditzes-1st-ep/.

15. Marc S. Malkin with Deborah Schoeneman, 'The Paris Hilton Sex Tape; Nicole Miller Gets Real; A Royal Pain', New York Metro.com, 8 August 2003, web.archive.org/web/20030815183515/http://www.newyorkmetro.com/nymetro/news/people/columns/intelligencer/n_9099/.

16. Elizabeth Spiers, 'Paris Hilton: Sex, Lies & Videotape, Cont'd', *The Kicker* (blog), New York Metro.com, 12 November 2003, web.archive.org/web/20031228135819/http://thekicker.nymetro.com/archives/000167.html.

17. 'Paris Hilton's PR Strategy: Avoidance,' CNN, 26 November 2003, edition.cnn.com/2003/SHOWBIZ/TV/11/26/television.paris.reut/.

18. *Never Mind the Buzzcocks*, episode 4, series 19, directed by John L. Spencer, aired November 16, 2006, on BBC Two.

19. Amanda Chicago Lewis, 'Pam and Tommy: The Untold Story of the World's Most Infamous Sex Tape', *Rolling Stone*, 22 December 2014, www.rollingstone.com/feature/pam-and-tommy-the-untold-story-of-the-worlds-most-infamous-sex-tape-194776/.

20. Richard Morgan, 'Revenge Porn: Jilted Lovers Are Posting Sex Tapes on the Web – And Their Exes Want Justice', Details, n.d., web.archive.org/web/20091113144122/http://www.details.com/sex-relationships/porn-and-perversions/200809/revenge-porn.

21. Mike Masnick, 'Since When Is It Illegal to Just Mention a Trademark Online?', TechDirt, 5 January 2005, www.techdirt.com/articles/20050105/0132239.shtml.

22. Paul Rogers, 'Streisand's Home Becomes Hit on Web: Star Had Sued Valley Mogul to Keep Photographs Off Site', *Mercury News*, 24 June 2003, www.californiacoastline.org/news/sjmerc5.html.

23. Mike Masnick, 'Fines and a Destroyed Phone for a Topless Cameraphone Snap Shot', TechDirt, 1 December 2004, www.techdirt.com/2004/12/01/fines-and-a-destroyed-phone-for-a-topless-cameraphone-snap-shot/.

24. Mike Rogers, 'The Fine Line of Celebrity Stupidity', MSNBC, 1 June 2003, www.californiacoastline.org/news/msnbc-stupidity.html.

25. Chris Clarke, 'The Price of Tides: Streisand Environmental Hypocrite', *CounterPunch*, 31 May 2003, www.californiacoastline.org/news/counterpunch.html.

26. Malkin with Schoeneman, 'The Paris Hilton Sex Tape'.

27. FTC, 'Sellers of Girls Gone Wild Videos to Pay $1.1 Million To Settle Charges of Unauthorized Shipping and Billing', 30 July 2004, www.ftc.gov/news-events/news/press-releases/2004/07/sellers-girls-gone-wild-videos-pay-11-million-settle-charges-unauthorized-shipping-billing.

28. Ryan Simkin, *FLASH! Bars, Boobs and Busted: Five Years on the*

Road with Girls Gone Wild (Santa Monica: 4 Park Publishing, 2010), p. 31.

29. Gloria Steinem, 'A Bunny's Tale: Show's First Exposé for Intelligent People', *Show*, May 1963, undercover.hosting.nyu.edu/files/original/5c9de8d1db51cede1395f6d6fa480ca24e872b76.pdf.

30. Mireya Navarro, 'The Very Long Legs of "Girls Gone Wild"', *New York Times*, 4 April 2004, www.nytimes.com/2004/04/04/style/the-very-long-legs-of-girls-gone-wild.html.

31. Simkin, *FLASH!*, p. 48; Aurora Snow, 'The Adult Industry Doesn't Pay! (As Much as You Think)', Daily Beast, 11 July 2017, www.thedailybeast.com/the-adult-industry-doesnt-pay-as-much-as-you-think.

32. Ariel Levy, 'Girls Get Naked for T-shirts and Trucker Hats', *Slate*, 18 March 2004, slate.com/news-and-politics/2004/03/girls-get-naked-for-t-shirts-and-trucker-hats.html.

33. Laura Miller, 'The Passion of Andrea Dworkin', Salon, 12 April 2005, www.salon.com/2005/04/12/dworkin_3/.

34. Reuters Staff, '"Girls Gone Wild" Founder Freed on Florida Charges', Reuters, 12 March 2008, www.reuters.com/article/us-francis-idUSN1221876020080312.

35. Simkin, *FLASH!*, p. 51.

36. Ibid., pp. 40–1.

37. Greta Christina, 'Girls Gone Wild', Greta Christina's Blog, n.d., web.archive.org/web/20070206020806/http://www.gretachristina.com/girlsgonewild.html.

38. Simkin, *FLASH!*, p. 75.

39. Ibid., p. 177.

40. See web.archive.org/web/20051104030454/http://www.exgfpics.com:80/blog/.

41. Tracy Clark-Flory, 'The Twisted World of "Ex-Girlfriend Porn"', Salon, 28 February 2011, https://www.salon.com/2011/02/28/exgirlfriend_porn/.

42. 'Misery Merchants: How Should the Online Publication of Explicit Images Without Their Subjects' Consent Be Punished?', *The Economist*, 4 July 2014, www.economist.com/international/2014/07/05/misery-merchants.

43. Kashmir Hill, 'Revenge Porn (Or: Another Reason Not to Take Nude Photos)', Forbes, 2 June 2009, web.archive.org/web/20110709024721/http://blogs.forbes.com/kashmirhill/2009/06/02/revenge-porn-or-another-reason-not-to-take-nude-photos/.

44. Richard Luscombe, 'Sex Video Gives Paris Hilton Publicity Money Can't Buy', *Guardian*, 7 December 2003, www.theguardian.com/world/2003/dec/07/arts.usa.

45. Hilton with Shapiro, *Red Carpet Suicide*, p. 56.

46. Reuters, 'Paris Hilton Sues Over Internet Sex Tape', CNN, 9 February 2004, www.edition.cnn.com/2004/tech/02/09/paris.lawsuit.reut/.

47. Marvad Corporation v. Donald Thrasher, 14 November 2003.

48. Salomon v. Hilton et al., First Amended Complaint, 2 January 2004.

49. Todd Peterson, 'Claim: Paris Hilton "Directed" Sex Tape', *People*,

24 February 2004, people.com/celebrity/claim-paris-hilton-directed-sex-tape/.

50. Stephen M. Silverman, 'Hilton, Salomon End Sex-Tape Legal Battle', *People*, 13 July 2004, people.com/celebrity/hilton-salomon-end-sex-tape-legal-battle/.

51. Paris Hilton with Merle Ginsberg, Confessions of an Heiress (New York: Fireside, 2004), p. 29.

52. Natalie Finn, 'Remembering How Moviegoers Got Psyched to "See Paris Die" in "House of Wax"', E! News, 6 May 2020, www.eonline.com/news/1148602/remembering-how-moviegoers-got-psyched-to-see-paris-die-in-house-of-wax.

53. Natalie Finn, 'Paris Hilton's Traumatic Trip to Jail Was 10 Years Ago: How She Revamped Her Life After the Celebutantes Gone Wild Era', E! News, 27 April 2017, www.eonline.com/news/846325/paris-hilton-s-traumatic-trip-to-jail-was-10-years-ago-how-she-revamped-her-life-after-the-celebutantes-gone-wild-era.

54. Ruth Kinane and Joey Nolfi, 'Sarah Silverman Says She "Immediately" Regretted Paris Hilton Jokes at 2007 MTV Movie Awards and Wrote Her to Apologize', *Entertainment Weekly*, 5 March 2021, ew.com/news/sarah-silverman-immediately-regretted-paris-hilton-jokes-wrote-to-apologize/.

55. 'Sarah Silverman Dragging Paris Hilton at the 2007 MTV Movie Awards', YouTube, n.d., www.youtube.com/watch?v=G_v3dN7TOk4&t=8s.

56. Lorena Mongelli, 'Paris Bawls in Jail: Shrink Pays Call', *New York Post*, 6 June 2007, web.archive.org/web/20070608150511/http://www.nypost.com/seven/06062007/news/nationalnews/paris_bawls_in_jail_nationalnews_lorena_mongelli.htm.

57. TMZ Staff, 'Paris DID Have to Spread 'Em!', In the Zone, TMZ, 6 June 2007, web.archive.org/web/20070609170039/http://www.tmz.com/2007/06/06/paris-did-have-to-spread-em/#c5295317.

58. Elizabeth Snead, 'Paris Is Set Free! Crying Works!', Styles and Scenes (blog), The Envelope, 7 June 2007, web.archive.org/web/20070609135618/http://stylescenes.latimes.com/fashion/2007/06/paris_gets_out_.html.

59. Mike Nizza, 'Paris Hilton Ordered Back to Jail', The Lede, *New York Times*, 8 June 2007, web.archive.org/web/20070611091018/https://thelede.blogs.nytimes.com/2007/06/08/paris-hilton-due-in-court/.

60. Jack Leonard and Doug Smith, 'Hilton Will Do More Time than Most, Analysis Finds', *Los Angeles Times*, 14 June 2007, web.archive.org/web/20070618015624/http://www.latimes.com/entertainment/news/la-me-paris14jun14,0,404958.story?coll=la-home-center.

61. Paul Harris, 'Why I Said "No" to Paris Hilton Mania', *Guardian*, 1 July 2007, www.theguardian.com/media/2007/jul/01/broadcasting.tvnews.

62. *Us Weekly* piece discussed on '"Countdown with Keith Olbermann" for July 2', Transcript, NBC News, 3 July 2007, www.nbcnews.com/id/wbna19581765.

63. Tracy Clark-Flory, 'Porn in a Flash', Salon, 25 November 2008, web.archive.org/web/20100523132107/http://www.salon.com/life/feature/2008/11/25/upskirting.

64. Greta Christina, 'Going Wild: A Feminist's Defense of the "Girls Gone Wild" Girls', Greta Christina's Blog, 15 August 2006, gretachristina. typepad.com/greta_christinas_weblog/2006/08/going_wild.html.

65. 'Paris Hilton: Feminist Icon to Be', *Gawker*, n.d., web.archive.org/ web/20031107032721/http://www.gawker.com/archives/009956.php.

66. Michaele L. Ferguson, 'Choice Feminism and the Fear of Politics', *Perspectives on Politics* 8, No. 1 (2010): 247–53.

67. Christopher Hitchens, 'Siege of Paris: The Creepy Populism Surrounding High-Profile Defendants', *Slate*, 11 June 2007, slate.com/ news-and-politics/2007/06/the-creepy-populism-surrounding-paris- hilton-and-scooter-libby.html.

68. Kaie O'Malley, 'Sorry Paris Hilton, We Should Have Had Your Back', *Elle*, 24 September 2020, www.elle.com/uk/life-and-culture/culture/ a34127722/paris-hilton-apology/.

69. Randi Bergman, 'All Hail the Unlikely Queen of Celebrity Fragrance', *Elle*, 21 January 2020, www.ellecanada.com/beauty/ paris-hilton-the-unlikely-queen-of-celebrity-fragrance.

70. Cait Munro, 'Can an Heiress Be Self-Made? Paris Hilton Thinks So', Refinery29, 30 July 2018, www.refinery29.com/en-us/2018/07/205006/ paris-hilton-interview-greed-self-made.

71. Sarah Ditum, 'Perez Hilton on Being the World's Most Notorious Gossip Blogger', *The Times*, 19 September 2021, www.thetimes.co.uk/ article/perez-hilton-on-being-the-worlds-most-notorious-gossip- blogger-l0fqvdvkr.

72. Provo Canyon School, Media Statement, 17 September 2020, provocanyon.com/wp-content/uploads/2020/10/ PCS_SaltLakeTribune_091720_pdf/.

3: Lindsay

1. Kenneth Turan, 'Happily Trapped', *Los Angeles Times*, 29 July 1998, www.latimes.com/archives/la-xpm-1998-jul-29-ca-7980-story.html.

2. Jett Otto, 'An Interview with Lindsay Lohan', IGN, 6 August 2003, updated 20 May 2012, www.ign.com/articles/2003/08/06/ an-interview-with-lindsay-lohan.

3. Greg Williams, 'Hell Hath No Fury Like a Showbiz Father Scorned', *New York Magazine*, 18 February 2005, www.nymag.com/nymetro/ news/people/features/11159/index1.html.

4. Associated Press, 'Lohan Parents' Divorce Heats Up on Long Island', *Today*, 7 August 2007, www.today.com/popculture/ lohan-parents-divorce-heats-long-island-1C9429793.

5. Stephen M. Silverman, 'Lindsay's Uncle Arrested for Alleged Scam', *People*, 22 June 2005, people.com/celebrity/ lindsays-uncle-arrested-for-alleged-scam/.

6. Umited States v. Paul Sullivan, Judgment in a Criminal Case.

7. Spencer Morgan, 'The Parent Trap', *Observer*, 15 August 2007, web. archive.org/web/20150825205613/http://observer.com/2007/08/ the-parent-trap-2/.

8. 'Lohan Seeks Press Muzzle', The Smoking Gun, 3 February 2005,

www.thesmokinggun.com/documents/crime/lohan-seeks-press-muzzle.

9. Williams, 'Hell Hath No Fury Like a Showbiz Father Scorned'.

10. Associated Press, 'Lohan Parents' Divorce Heats Up on Long Island'.

11. Robert Haskell, 'Lindsay Lohan', W, 1 April 2005, www.wmagazine.com/story/lindsay-lohan.

12. Morgan, 'The Parent Trap'.

13. Marcelle S. Fischler, 'For Lohan Matriarch, Like Daughter, Like Mother', New York Times, 21 October 2006, www.nytimes.com/2006/10/21/nyregion/nyregionspecial2/22limom.html.

14. Brian Lowry, 'Living Lohan', Variety, 26 May 2008, web.archive.org/web/20080607012539/https://variety.com/review/VE1117937255.html?categoryid=32&cs=1&nid=2609.

15. 'An Incomplete List of Attendees of the EW Pre-Emmy Party', Gawker, 21 September 2004, www.gawker.com/021968/an-incomplete-list-of-attendees-of-the-ew-pre-emmy-party/.

16. 'Harry Potter: Hermione Growth Spurt – SNL', YouTube, n.d., www.youtube.com/watch?v=uwfdFCP3KYM.

17. Gill Pringle, 'I'm Not a Girl, Not Yet a Woman', 13 June 2004, Guardian, www.theguardian.com/film/2004/jun/13/features.magazine.

18. Virginia Heffernan, 'Anchor Woman: Tina Fey Rewrites Late-Night Comedy', New Yorker, 26 October 2003, www.newyorker.com/magazine/2003/11/03/anchor-woman.

19. Vanessa Grigoriadis, 'Everybody Sucks', New York Magazine, 12 October 2007, nymag.com/news/features/39319/.

20. Defamer, n.d., web.archive.org/web/20041212003605/http://www.defamer.com/index.php?page=4.

21. 'Wilmer Valderrama Won't Be in Lindsay Lohan's "Rumors" Video', Popdirt.com, 25 September 2004, popdirt.com/wilmer-valderrama-wont-be-in-lindsay-lohans-rumors-video/33106/.

22. Stephen Hunter, '"Herbie: Fully Loaded": Old Engine in New Body', Washington Post, 22 June 2005, www.washingtonpost.com/wp-dyn/content/article/2005/06/21/AR2005062101765.html.

23. Robert K. Elder, 'Movie Review: "Herbie: Fully Loaded"', Metromix.com, n.d., web.archive.org/web/20051109100914/http://metromix.chicagotribune.com/movies/mmx-050621-movies-review-herbie,0,5936419.story?coll=mmx-movies_top_heds.

24. 'Defamer Preview: Lindsay Lohan's Too Big for Disney', Defamer, 18 February 2005, web.archive.org/web/20050221034141/http://www.defamer.com/hollywood/gossip/lindsay-lohan/defamer-preview-lindsay-lohans-too-big-for-disney-033598.php.

25. 'Lindsay Lohan Gets Booze Warnings on "Herbie" Set', Defamer, 15 September 2004, web.archive.org/web/20050221032729/http://www.defamer.com/hollywood/gossip/lindsay-lohan-gets-booze-warnings-on-herbie-set-021386.php.

26. Haskell, 'Lindsay Lohan'.

27. Todd Peterson, 'Lindsay Lohan Hospital Trip: "I Was Tired"', People, 22 November 2004, people.com/celebrity/lindsay-lohan-hospital-trip-i-was-tired/.

28. 'Lindsay Lohan's Breast a New Debate for 2005', Defamer, https://web.archive.org/web/20050217022544/http://www.defamer.com/hollywood/gossip/lindsay-lohan/lindsay-lohans-breasts-a-new-debate-for-2005-028964.php.

29. Haskell, 'Lindsay Lohan'.

30. Jennette McCurdy, *I'm Glad My Mom Died* (New York: Simon and Schuster, 2022), p. 88.

31. Leyla Mohammed, 'Demi Lovato Opened Up About Losing Her Virginity After Being Allegedly Raped by Someone Who Was Also on Disney', BuzzFeed, 25 August 2022, www.buzzfeednews.com/article/leylamohammed/demi-lovato-rape-disney-lost-virginity-teenager.

32. McCurdy, *I'm Glad My Mom Died*, pp. 190, 214; *Demi Lovato: Dancing With the Devil*, directed by Michael D. Ratner (YouTube Originals, 2020).

33. McCurdy, *I'm Glad My Mom Died*, p. 121.

34. Mickey Rapkin, 'Emilio Estevez Is No Bobby Kennedy', *GQ*, 4 October 2006, www.gq.com/story/rfk-assassinaton-bobby-kennedy-emilio-estevez.

35. Roger Ebert, 'A Hard Day's Plight', RogerEbert.com, 11 May 2006, www.rogerebert.com/reviews/just-my-luck-2006.

36. Geoffrey Macnab, 'I Used to Google My Name to See What Came Up – It Hurt', *Guardian*, 27 September 2006, www.theguardian.com/film/2006/sep/27/londonfilmfestival2006.londonfilmfestival.

37. Emily Nussbaum, '"Sex and the City": Tenth Anniversary', *New York Magazine*, 26 August 2011, nymag.com/news/9-11/10th-anniversary/sex-and-the-city/.

38. Heffernan, 'Anchor Woman'.

39. Terry Teachout, 'Tawdriness in Turnaround', *Wall Street Journal*, 4 January 2002, www.wsj.com/articles/SB1010103475159692400?mod=article_inline.

40. Grady Smith, 'Is Country Music Ready to Forgive the Dixie Chicks?', *Guardian*, 19 November 2015, www.theguardian.com/music/2015/nov/19/the-dixie-chicks-tour-is-country-music-ready-to-forgive.

41. 'A Shattered Nation Longs to Care About Stupid Bullshit Again', *The Onion*, 3 October 2001, www.theonion.com/a-shattered-nation-longs-to-care-about-stupid-bullshit-1819566188.

42. Amy Odell, *Anna: The Biography* (London: Allen and Unwin, 2022), p. 225.

43. Grigoriadis, 'Everybody Sucks'.

44. Emily Yahr, 'Harvey Weinstein's Behavior Was a Dark Inside Joke on Shows Like "Entourage" and "30 Rock"', *Washington Post*, 10 October 2017, www.washingtonpost.com/news/arts-and-entertainment/wp/2017/10/10/harvey-weinsteins-behavior-was-a-dark-inside-joke-on-shows-like-entourage-and-30-rock/.

45. Jodi Kantor and Megan Twohey, 'Harvey Weinstein Paid Off Sexual Harassment Accusers for Decades', *New York Times*, 5 October 2017, www.nytimes.com/2017/10/05/us/harvey-weinstein-harassment-allegations.html; Ronan Farrow, 'From Aggressive Overtures to Assault: Harvey Weinstein's Accusers Tell Their Stories', *New*

Yorker, 10 October 2017, www.newyorker.com/news/news-desk/
from-aggressive-overtures-to-sexual-assault-harvey-weinsteins-
accusers-tell-their-stories.

46. Jacob Stolworthy, 'Lindsay Lohan Defends Harvey Weinstein:
"I Feel Very Bad for Him"', *Independent*, 11 October 2017,
www.independent.co.uk/arts-entertainment/films/news/
harvey-weinstein-allegations-lindsay-lohan-defends-instagram-video-
georgina-chapman-wife-a7993966.html.

47. Marsha Kranes, 'Lindsay Bares Anguish', *New York Post*, 2 March
2005, nypost.com/2005/03/02/lindsay-bares-anguish/.

48. Evgenia Peretz, 'Confessions of a Teenage Movie Queen', *Vanity
Fair*, February 2006, archive.vanityfair.com/article/2006/2/
confessions-of-a-teenage-movie-queen.

49. Anita Gates, 'George Barris, Photographer Who Captured the
Last Images of Marilyn Monroe, Dies at 94', *New York Times*,
4 October 2016, www.nytimes.com/2016/10/05/arts/design/
george-barris-photographer-who-captured-the-last-images-of-
marilyn-monroe-dies-at-94.html.

50. Josh Grossberg, 'Lindsay Lohan: A Timeline of All Her Arrests (and
Boy, There Are a Lot of 'Em)', E! News, 29 November 2012, www.
eonline.com/news/367020/lindsay-lohan-a-timeline-of-all-her-
arrests-and-boy-there-are-a-lot-of-em.

51. 'Hollywood Big Blasts Lohan', The Smoking Gun, 28 July 2006, www.
thesmokinggun.com/documents/crime/hollywood-big-blasts-lohan.

52. Amy Bonawitz, '*Georgia Rule* Controversy Haunts Lohan',
CBS News, 9 May 2007, https://www.cbsnews.com/news/
georgia-rule-controversy-haunts-lohan/.

53. Todd Leopold, 'Lohan's "Killed Me" Sets Worst-Film Record', CNN,
23 February 2008, edition.cnn.com/2008/SHOWBIZ/Movies/02/23/
razzie.awards/index.html.

54. Ben Child, 'Lindsay Lohan Has Labour Pains as Film Goes Straight to
Cable', *Guardian*, 27 March 2009, www.theguardian.com/film/2009/
mar/27/lindsay-lohan-labour-pains-straight-to-cable.

55. 'Insurance Row Nearly Ends Lohan's Film Career', *Irish Examiner*, 7
June 2008, www.irishexaminer.com/lifestyle/arid-30365157.html.

56. Dave Itzkoff, 'A One-Way Ticket to Disaster', *New York Times*, 1
January 2008, https://www.nytimes.com/2008/01/01/arts/01iht-
30trainwreck.8972416.html.

57. Helen Pidd, 'I Don't Want to Sound Like a Piece of Poop, but . . .',
Guardian, 1 February 2008, www.theguardian.com/film/2008/feb/01/2.

58. Richard Lawson, 'Taradise Lost: Is Celebrity Hedonism Over?',
Gawker, 10 November 2008, www.gawker.com/5082289/
taradise-lost-is-celebrity-hedonism-over.

59. Zach Johnson, 'Lindsay Lohan on Samantha Ronson: "Two Toxic
People Cannot Be Together"', *People*, 26 November 2012, www.
usmagazine.com/celebrity-news/news/lindsay-lohan-on-samantha-
ronson-two-toxic-people-cannot-be-together-20122611/.

60. Perez Hilton, 'Lohan's Lesbian Love Triangle', Perez Hilton, n.d.,
perezhilton.com/lohans-lesbian-love-triangle/.

61. Sarah Nechamkin, 'The Last Photos of Marilyn Monroe', The Cut, 8 June 2017, www.thecut.com/2017/06/bert-stern-photos-of-marilyn-monroe-before-her-death.html.

62. Amanda Fortini, 'Lindsay Lohan as Marilyn Monroe in "The Last Sitting"', *New York Magazine*, 18 February 2008, web.archive.org/web/20130309011151/https://nymag.com/fashion/08/spring/44247/.

63. Gina Bellafante, 'Lohan Assumes the Pose: Monroe's Final Sitting', *New York Times*, 21 February 2008, www.nytimes.com/2008/02/21/arts/21iht-21loha.10266205.html.

64. Mike Collett-White, 'Lohan's "Macabre" Monroe Snaps an Internet Hit', Reuters, 23 February 2008, www.reuters.com/article/us-lohan/lohans-macabre-monroe-snaps-an-internet-hit-idUSN2262698320080222.

65. Abby Goodnough and Margalit Fox, 'Anna Nicole Smith Dies at 39', *New York Times*, 8 February 2007, www.nytimes.com/2007/02/08/arts/08cnd-smith.html.

66. Fortini, 'Lindsay Lohan as Marilyn Monroe in "The Last Sitting"'.

67. 'Lindsay is Sentenced to Jail Over Necklace Theft', BBC, 12 May 2011, bbc.co.uk/news/newsbeat-13371625.

68. Grossberg, 'Lindsay Lohan: A Timeline of All Her Arrests'.

69. Melissa Gira Grant, 'How Stoya Took on James Deen and Broke the Porn Industry's Silence', *Guardian*, 4 December 2015, www.theguardian.com/culture/2015/dec/04/how-stoya-took-on-james-deen-and-broke-the-porn-industrys-silence.

70. Bret Easton Ellis, 'Bret Easton Ellis: Notes on Charlie Sheen and the End of Empire', Daily Beast, 13 July 2017, www.thedailybeast.com/bret-easton-ellis-notes-on-charlie-sheen-and-the-end-of-empire.

71. Stephen Rodrick, 'Here Is What Happens When You Cast Lindsay Lohan in Your Movie', *New York Times Magazine*, 10 January 2013, www.nytimes.com/2013/01/13/magazine/here-is-what-happens-when-you-cast-lindsay-lohan-in-your-movie.html.

72. 'InAPPropriate Comedy', at web.archive.org/web/20130604181337/http://inappropriatecomedy.com/.

4: Aaliyah

1. 'A Vigil for Aaliyah', BBC News, 28 August 2001, news.bbc.co.uk/1/hi/entertainment/1512938.stm.

2. 'Vigil for Aaliyah', ABC News, 28 August 2001, abcnews.go.com/Entertainment/story?id=102746&page=1.

3. Thomas J. Lueck, 'New York Fans Grieve over Death of Aaliyah', *New York Times*, 29 August 2001, www.nytimes.com/2001/08/29/us/new-york-fans-grieve-over-death-of-aaliyah.html.

4. Air Accident Investigation Authority of the Bahamas, 'Aircraft Accident Report. F.S.I. File # A0619836', 30 August 2006, www.baaid.org/_files/ugd/fbeb16_0fa5141104984abf9a107bf1b6fd862f.pdf.

5. Kurt Eichenwald with Robin Pogrebin, 'Haste, Errors and a Fallen Star', *New York Times*, 8 September 2001, www.nytimes.com/2001/09/08/arts/haste-errors-and-a-fallen-star.html.

306   *Toxic*

6. Hyun Kim, 'Revisit Aaliyah's August 2001 Cover Story: "What Lies Beneath?"', Vibe, August 2001, https://www.vibe.com/features/editorial/aaliyah-august-2001-cover-story-what-lies-beneath-682260/.

7. Ernest Hardy, 'Aaliyah', *Rolling Stone*, 2 August 2001, web.archive.org/web/20011102125720/http://www.rollingstone.com/recordings/review.asp?aid=2042779&cf=1967.

8. Aaliyah, 'Aaliyah: MTV Diary in HD Full Episode', YouTube, n.d., www.youtube.com/watch?v=WlOYYd5T-CE.

9. Kathy Iandoli, *Baby Girl: Better Known as Aaliyah* (New York: Simon and Schuster, 2021), p. xvi.

10. Ibid., p. xii.

11. Ibid., p. 3.

12. Ibid., pp. 6–7.

13. 'She's Got That Vibe', Lyrics Genius, n.d., genius.com/R-kelly-and-public-announcement-shes-got-that-vibe-lyrics.

14. Camille Augustin, 'Aaliyah Week: "Age Ain't Nothing But a Number" & the Isley Brothers Cover that Placed Aaliyah on the Map', Vibe, 26 August 2016, www.vibe.com/features/editorial/age-aint-nothing-but-a-number-aaliyah-week-448053/.

15. Retha Powers, 'Brat Rap', *New York Times*, 5 March 1995, www.nytimes.com/1995/03/05/magazine/brat-rap.html.

16. Margo Jefferson, *On Michael Jackson* (London: Granta, 2018), p. 57.

17. Aaliyah, 'I'm So into You', Lyrics Genius, n.d., genius.com/Aaliyah-im-so-into-you-lyrics.

18. Aaliyah, 'No One Knows How to Love Me Quite Like You Do', Lyrics Genius, n.d., genius.com/Aaliyah-no-one-knows-how-to-love-me-quite-like-you-do-lyrics.

19. Touré, 'Aaliyah: 1979–2001', *Rolling Stone*, 11 October 2001, www.rollingstone.com/music/music-news/aaliyah-1979-2001-192667/.

20. Hip Hop News Uncensored, 'The Deleted R. Kelly and Aaliyah Interview that Will Make You Sick!!', YouTube, n.d., www.youtube.com/watch?v=wkguAwVeAPg.

21. Iandoli, *Baby Girl*, p. 30.

22. Augustin, 'Aaliyah Week'.

23. KlassicThrowbackTV, 'Throwback News: Aaliyah Marries R. Kelly (1994)', YouTube, www.youtube.com/watch?v=H7mZv2vHx58.

24. Jim DeRogatis, *Soulless: The Case Against R. Kelly* (New York: Abrams, 2019), p. 65.

25. Iandoli, *Baby Girl*, p. 81.

26. R. Kelly, *Soulacoaster: The Diary of Me* (New York: SmileyBooks, 2012), author's note.

27. Maria Bobila, 'Aaliyah's Stylist Derek Lee on Her Most Fashionable Music Video Moments', Nylon, 21 August 2020, www.nylon.com/fashion/derek-lee-on-styling-aaliyah-her-most-fashionable-music-videos.

28. Touré, 'Aaliyah: 1979–2001'.

29. Iandoli, *Baby Girl*, p. 81.

30. Kelefa Sanneh, 'A Pioneer, Briefly, of a New Sound', *New York Times*,

2 September 2001, www.nytimes.com/2001/09/02/arts/a-pioneer-briefly-of-a-new-sound.html.

31. Jim DeRogatis and Abdon Pallasch, 'R. Kelly Accused of Sex with Teenage Girls', *Chicago Sun-Times*, 21 December 2000, chicago.suntimes. com/2000/12/21/18423229/r-kelly-accused-of-sex-with-teenage-girls.

32. Kelly, *Soulacoaster*, dedication.

33. Kenneth Lanning, 'The Evolution of *Grooming*: Concept and Term', *Journal of Interpersonal Violence* 33, No. 1 (2018): 5–16, calio.org/wp-content/uploads/2019/03/the-evolution-of-grooming-concept-and-term.pdf.

34. DeRogatis and Pallasch, 'R. Kelly Accused of Sex with Teenage Girls'.

35. DeRogatis, *Soulless*, pp. 1–3.

36. Kimberlé Crenshaw, 'Mapping the Margins: Intersectionality, Identity Politics, and Violence Against Women of Color', *Stanford Law Review* 43, No. 6 (July 1991): 1241–99.

37. Eldridge Cleaver, *Soul on Ice* (New York: Delta, 1999), pp. 31–3.

38. John Kifner, 'Eldridge Cleaver, Black Panther Who Became GOP Conservative, Is Dead at 62', *New York Times*, 2 May 1998, www.nytimes.com/1998/05/02/us/eldridge-cleaver-black-panther-who-became-gop-conservative-is-dead-at-62.html.

39. Crenshaw, 'Mapping the Margins', p. 1242.

40. DeRogatis, *Soulless*, p. 77.

41. Kim, 'Revisit Aaliyah's August 2001 Cover Story: "What Lies Beneath?"'

42. Iandoli, *Baby Girl*, p. 48.

43. John Mulvey, 'Aaliyah', web.archive.org/web/20010718234116/https://www.nme.com/NME/External/Reviews/Reviews_Story/0,1069,8453,00.html.

44. Touré, 'Aaliyah: 1979–2001'.

45. Iandoli, *Baby Girl*, p. xviii.

46. Lueck, 'New York Fans Grieve over Death of Aaliyah'.

47. Touré, 'Aaliyah: 1979–2001'.

48. Joyce Wadler, 'Private Mass, Public Tribute for Singer', *New York Times*, 1 September 2001, www.nytimes.com/2001/09/01/nyregion/private-mass-public-tribute-for-singer.html.

49. Christopher John Farley, *Aaliyah: More Than a Woman* (New York: Pocket Books, 2001), pp. 2, 29, 40, 92, 93, 150, 183, 185.

50. See, for example, Caroline Sullivan, 'Obituary: Aaliyah: Singer Who Brought Style and Artistry to R&B', *Guardian*, 27 August 2001, www.theguardian.com/news/2001/aug/27/guardianobituaries.carolinesullivan; and Jon Pareles, 'Aaliyah, 22, Singer Who First Hit the Charts at 14', *New York Times*, 27 August 2001, www.nytimes.com/2001/08/27/arts/aaliyah-22-singer-who-first-hit-the-charts-at-14.html.

51. Sanneh, 'A Pioneer, Briefly, of a New Sound'.

52. Jim DeRogatis and Abdon M. Pallasch, 'City Police Investigate R&B Singer R. Kelly in Sex Tape', *Chicago Sun-Times*, 8 February 2002, web.archive.org/web/20020212051418/http://www.suntimes.com/output/news/cst-nws-kelly08.html.

53. Paul Flynn, 'Man in the Mirror: An Interview with R. Kelly', *Guardian*, 19 September 2004, www.google.com/amp/s/amp. theguardian.com/music/2004/sep/19/urban.

54. DeRogatis, *Soulless*, p. 117.

55. Ibid., p. 130.

56. See, for example, Normal1875, 'Have You Seen the Official R. Kelly Tape?', HBCU Sports Forums, 12 April 2002, www.hbcusports.com/ forums/threads/have-you-seen-the-official-r-kelly-tape.7585/.

57. Caroline Sullivan, 'Review: R. Kelly, Happy People/U Saved Me', *Guardian*, 20 August 2004,www.theguardian.com/music/2004/ aug/20/popandrock.

58. Kelefa Sanneh, 'R. Kelly at Radio City: Songs Served with a Side Order of Ham', *New York Times*, 20 April 2006, www.nytimes. com/2006/04/20/arts/music/r-kelly-at-radio-city-songs-served-with-a-side-order-of-ham.html.

59. Flynn, 'Man in the Mirror'.

60. DeRogatis, *Soulless*, pp. 203–4.

61. 'Rihanna Attack: The Official Blow-by-Blow', TMZ, 25 August 2009, www.tmz.com/2009/08/25/rihanna-attack-the-official-blow-by-blow/; https://completemusicupdate.com/article/ tmz-post-picture-of-beaten-rihanna/.

62. David Itzkoff, 'Chris Brown Sentenced', 26 August 2009, nytimes. com/2009/08/27/arts/music/27arts-chrisbrownse_brf.html.

63. John Seabrook, *The Song Machine: Inside the Hit Factory* (London: Vintage, 2015), p. 226.

64. 'Rihanna Breaks Silence over Chris Brown: "If It's a Mistake, It's My Mistake"', *Telegraph*, 30 January 2013, www.telegraph.co.uk/news/ celebritynews/9837484/Rihanna-breaks-silence-over-Chris-Brown-if-its-a-mistake-its-my-mistake.html.

65. 'Rihanna Exploits Beating in New Video', TMZ, 19 October 2011, www.tmz.com/2011/10/19/ rihanna-puts-chris-brown-lookalike-in-new-video/.

66. 'Wrigley Spits Out Chris Brown – For Good', TMZ, 6 August 2009, www.tmz.com/2009/08/06/wrigleys-spits-out-chris-brown-for-good/.

67. 'Chris Brown, "Graffiti"', *Billboard*, 19 January 2010, www.billboard. com/music/music-news/chris-brown-graffiti-1069883/.

68. Greg Kot, 'R. Kelly and the Music Industry's Complicity', Chicago Tribune, 18 January 2019, www.chicagotribune.com/entertainment/ music/ct-ent-r-kelly-sony-kot-0123-story.html.

69. Melissa Locker, 'Coming Soon to IFC: R. Kelly's "Trapped in the Closet: The Next Installment"', IFC, 20 March 2012, web.archive. org/web/20120322070647/https://www.ifc.com/fix/2012/03/ trapped-in-the-closet-announcement.

70. Alexis Petridis, 'How Did R. Kelly Create the World's Strangest Soap Opera?', *Guardian*, 20 August 2007, www.theguardian.com/music/ musicblog/2007/aug/20/howdidrkellycreatethewor.

71. Chuck Klosterman, 'Sex, Pies and Videotape', *Guardian*, 25 August 2007, www.theguardian.com/music/2007/aug/25/urban.dvdreviews.

72. Stephen Witt, 'Why Can't You Listen to Aaliyah? Ask Her Uncle',

Complex, 16 December 2016, www.complex.com/music/2016/12/
aaliyahs-music-isnt-online-and-her-uncle-barry-hankerson-is-the-
reason-why.

73. Richard Benson, 'How Terry Richardson Created Porn "Chic" and
Moulded the Look of an Era', *Guardian*, 29 October 2017, www.
theguardian.com/artanddesign/2017/oct/28/terry-richardson-porn-
chic-moulded-look-era-fashion-industry-photographer.

74. HB Team, 'Barack Obama x Terry Richardson Photograph',
Hypebeast, 16 September 2008, hypebeast.com/2008/9/
barack-obama-x-terry-richardson-photograph.

75. Niamh McIntyre, 'Terry Richardson: The Shocking List of Allegations
Facing the Fashion Photographer', *Independent*, 27 October 2017,
www.independent.co.uk/news/terry-richardson-sexual-allegations-
list-abuse-assault-fashion-photographer-models-a8022001.html.

76. Mark Di Stefano, 'Celebrity Photographer Terry Richardson Has
Been Banned From Top Magazines After Years Of Allegations From
Models', BuzzFeed, 24 October 2017, https://www.buzzfeed.com/
markdistefano/conde-nast-terry-richardson.

77. Stephanie Smith, 'Why Lady Gaga Scrapped R. Kelly Duet
Video', PageSix, 19 June 2014, pagesix.com/2014/06/19/
lady-gaga-scrapped-r-kelly-duet-video-after-controversies/.

78. Lady Gaga, 'I stand by anyone who has ever been the victim of sexual
assault', tweet, Twitter, 10 January 2019, twitter.com/ladygaga/
status/1083237788663697408.

79. Jim DeRogatis, 'Inside the Pied Piper of R&B's Cult', BuzzFeed,
17 July 2017, www.buzzfeednews.com/article/jimderogatis/
parents-told-police-r-kelly-is-keeping-women-in-a-cult.

80. Oronike Odeleye, as told to Mattie Kahn, 'The Cofounder
of #MuteRKelly on Where the Hashtag Goes Next',
Glamour, 3 May 2018, www.glamour.com/story/
oronike-odeleye-muterkelly-where-hashtag-goes-next.

81. Touré, 'Touré: R. Kelly Backlash Is Not a "Lynching"
but a Reckoning', *Rolling Stone*, 3 May 2018,
www.rollingstone.com/culture/culture-news/
toure-r-kelly-backlash-is-not-a-lynching-but-a-reckoning-628995/.

82. Kara Boomgarden-Smoke, 'More Publishers Cut Ties
With Terry Richardson', *Women's Wear Daily*, 26
October 2017, https://wwd.com/business-news/media/
more-publishers-cut-ties-with-terry-richardson-11037284/.

83. Jem Aswad and Shirley Halperin, 'R. Kelly Dropped by Sony
Music', *Variety*, 18 January 2019, variety.com/2019/biz/
news/r-kelly-dropped-sony-music-1203106180/.

84. Troy Closson, 'R. Kelly Is Convicted of All Counts After Decades of
Accusations of Abuse', *New York Times*, 27 September 2021, nytimes.
com/2021/09/27/nyregion/r-kelly-racheteering-sex-trafficking.html.

85. Troy Closson and Emily Palmer, 'R. Kelly Sexually Abused Aaliyah
When She Was 13 or 14, Witness Says', *New York Times*, 13
September 2021, www.nytimes.com/2021/09/13/nyregion/r-kelly-
trial-aaliyah.html.

86. Tony Closson and Emily Palmer, 'Ex-Manager Says R. Kelly Thought Aaliyah, 15, Was Pregnant with His Baby', *New York Times*, 20 August 2021, updated 28 September 2021, www.nytimes.com/2021/08/20/nyregion/r-kelly-trial-racketeering.html.

87. Robert Chiarito and Julia Jacobs, 'R. Kelly Sentenced to 20 Years for Child Sex Crimes', 23 February 2023, nytimes.com/2023/02/23/arts/music/r-kelly-sentenced-federal-child-sex-crimes.

88. Iandoli, *Baby Girl*, pp. 166–7.

89. *Queen of the Damned*, directed by Michael Rymer (Warner Bros., 2002).

5: Janet

1. Samuel Spencer, 'Yes, the Halftime Performers at the Super Bowl Do Get Paid – But Not Much', *Newsweek*, 12 February 2022, www.newsweek.com/super-bowl-2022-halftime-show-performers-paid-1678068.

2. Allen St John, '6-Minute Shuffle: How the NFL Sets Up a Super Bowl Halftime Stage', *Popular Mechanics*, 11 February 2022, www.popularmechanics.com/adventure/sports/a5307/4344900/.

3. Noam Scheiber, 'The Way We Live Now: 9-21-03: Questions for Michael Powell; King of All Media', *New York Times Magazine*, 21 September 2003, www.nytimes.com/2003/09/21/magazine/the-way-we-live-now-9-21-03-questions-for-michael-powell-king-of-all-media.html.

4. Shaheem Reid, 'Janet Jackson's Super Bowl Show Promises "Shocking Moments"', MTV, 28 January 2004, www.mtv.com/news/1484644/janet-jacksons-super-bowl-show-promises-shocking-moments/.

5. Stephen Labaton, 'Federal Regulators Give Approval to Viacom's Buyout of CBS', *New York Times*, 4 May 2000, www.nytimes.com/2000/05/04/business/federal-regulators-give-approval-to-viacom-s-buyout-of-cbs.html.

6. Andrea DenHoed, '"Wardrobe Malfunction": The Anatomy of a Phrase', *New Yorker*, 31 January 2014, www.newyorker.com/culture/culture-desk/wardrobe-malfunction-the-anatomy-of-a-phrase.

7. ecraviotto2003, 'U2 at XXXVI Superbowl [sic] 2002 Full Halftime Show', YouTube, n.d., www.youtube.com/watch?v=jiE8v29h6zI.

8. See Ben Ratliff, 'Justified', *Rolling Stone*, 28 November 2002, www.rollingstone.com/music/music-album-reviews/justified-184824/; Caroline Sullivan, 'Review: Justin Timberlake: Justified', *Guardian*, 1 November 2002, www.theguardian.com/music/2002/nov/01/popandrock.artsfeatures6; and Denise Boyd, 'Justin Timberlake Justified Review', BBC, 2002, https://www.bbc.co.uk/music/reviews/vdmq/.

9. Michael Jackson, *Moonwalk* (London: William Heinemann, 2009), p. 33.

10. Janet Jackson, *True You: A Journey to Finding and Loving Yourself* (New York: Gallery Books, 2011), p. 33.

11. Ibid., p. 1.

12. Jackson, *Moonwalk*, p. 26.
13. Jackson, *True You*, p. 10.
14. Jackson, *Moonwalk*, p. 28.
15. Laura Italiano, 'A Look Back at Joe Jackson's Tormented Relationship with the Kids He Made Stars', PageSix, 28 June 2018, pagesix.com/2018/06/28/a-look-back-at-joe-jacksons-tormented-relationship-with-the-kids-he-made-stars/.
16. Jackson, *True You*, p. 41.
17. Ibid., p. 40.
18. Jackson, *Moonwalk*, p. 152.
19. Jackson, *True You*, p. 87.
20. *Janet Jackson*, directed by Benjamin Hirsch (Lifetime, 2002).
21. 'Jukebox Tabs for Fats Domino Songs, 1957', The Charts, University Libraries, exhibitions.lib.umd.edu/fatsdomino/legacy/charts.
22. Joseph Vogel, 'The Nation that Janet Jackson Built', *The Atlantic*, 15 September 2014, www.theatlantic.com/entertainment/archive/2014/09/the-world-changing-aspirations-of-rhythm-nation-1814/380144/.
23. David Ritz, 'Janet Jackson: The Joy of Sex', *Rolling Stone*, 17 September 1993, www.rollingstone.com/music/music-news/janet-jackson-the-joy-of-sex-56099/.
24. Jackson, *True You*, p. 125.
25. Chris Willman, 'Unfair Warning: Are Hip-hop Artists Being Held to a Different Standard?', *Entertainment Weekly*, 14 August 2001, web.archive.org/web/20090421120002/http://www.ew.com/ew/article/0,,171027,00.html.
26. 'Singapore Upholds Janet Jackson Ban', BBC News, 5 June 2001, news.bbc.co.uk/1/hi/entertainment/1370650.stm.
27. *Malfunction: The Dressing Down of Janet Jackson*, directed by Jodi Gomes (Left/Right, 2022).
28. 'Apologetic Jackson Says "Costume Reveal" Went Awry', CNN, 3 February 2004, http://edition.cnn.com/2004/US/02/02/superbowl.jackson/.
29. Ibid.
30. Mike, 'Janet Jackson Super Bowl XXXVIII Halftime Show (2004)', YouTube, n.d., www.youtube.com/watch?v=JzipWoXgVm0.
31. 'Janet's Breasts Make Net History', BBC News, 5 February 2004, news.bbc.co.uk/1/hi/technology/3461459.stm.
32. Lisa de Moraes, 'CBS Gave 90 Million an Eyeful', *Washington Post*, 3 February 2004, www.washingtonpost.com/archive/lifestyle/2004/02/03/cbs-gave-90-million-an-eyeful/2be7d6d3-b059-46b8-a899-b3d6d4fb967b/.
33. 'Alexander McQueen A/W 1995: "Highland Rape"', Long Live McQueen (blog), Tumblr, the-widows-of-culloden.tumblr.com/post/57900804593/alexander-mcqueen-a-w-1995-highland-rape.
34. *Hustler*, October 2004, hustlermagazine.com/magazines/october-2004/.
35. Steven Williams 'Lil' Kim Set to Unintentionally Appear in "Hustler" Magazine for Wardrobe Malfunction', ContactMusic, 21 July 2004,

www.contactmusic.com/lil-kim/news/lil.-kim.s-shocking-genital-pictures.

36. de Moraes, 'CBS Gave 90 Million an Eyeful'.

37. *Malfunction: The Dressing Down of Janet Jackson.*

38. 'Apologetic Jackson Says "Costume Reveal" Went Awry'.

39. 'Jackson, Timberlake Apologize for Flash', *USA Today*, 3 February 2004, usatoday30.usatoday.com/life/television/news/2004-02-03-jackson-timberlake-apologize_x.htm.

40. 'Janet's Bared Breast a PR Stunt?', CBS News, 2 February 2004, www.cbsnews.com/news/janets-bared-breast-a-pr-stunt/.

41. 'Jackson, Timberlake Apologize for Flash'.

42. Nic Hopkins, 'AOL Demands $10M Refund After Jackson Mishap', *Sunday Times*, 6 February 2004, www.thetimes.co.uk/article/aol-demands-dollar10m-refund-after-jackson-mishap-bc2mdmd7lkj.

43. 'Janet Jackson: Supreme Court Approves Super Bowl Ruling', BBC News, 29 June 2012, www.bbc.co.uk/news/entertainment-arts-18651908.

44. Frank Ahrens and Lisa de Moraes, 'FCC Is Investigating Super Bowl Show', *Washington Post*, 3 February 2004, www.washingtonpost.com/archive/politics/2004/02/03/fcc-is-investigating-super-bowl-show/3d523644-ed7a-41ad-a2f1-dcee9b07b9cf/.

45. 'Notice of Apparent Liability for Forfeiture', File No. EB-04-IH-0011, NAL/Accct. No. 200432080212, law2.umkc.edu/faculty/projects/ftrials/conlaw/FCCjackson.html.

46. Rob Brown, 'The Powell and the Glory', *Guardian*, 29 October 2001, www.theguardian.com/media/2001/oct/29/mondaymediasection.afghanistan.

47. Jeannine Aversa, 'Auto Wreck Led Colin Powell's Son to Establish His Own Identity', Seattle Times, 16 August 1998, archive.seattletimes.com/archive/?date=19980816&slug=2766859.

48. Brown, 'The Powell and the Glory'.

49. Ibid.

50. Stephen Labaton, 'Federal Regulators Give Approval to Viacom's Buyout of CBS', *New York Times*, 4 May 2000, www.nytimes.com/2000/05/04/business/federal-regulators-give-approval-to-viacom-s-buyout-of-cbs.html/.

51. 'Powell Leaving FCC: Chairman Announces Resignation to Pursue Unnamed Opportunities; Led Fights on Obscenity, Ownership', CNN Money, 21 January 2005, money.cnn.com/2005/01/21/news/newsmakers/powell_resigning/.

52. Tom Shales, 'Michael Powell and the FCC: Giving Away the Marketplace of Ideas', *Washington Post*, 2 June 2003, www.washingtonpost.com/archive/lifestyle/2003/06/02/michael-powell-and-the-fcc-giving-away-the-marketplace-of-ideas/ed8c1f3a-be25-4214-92f6-25353f487e38/.

53. Stephen M. Silverman, 'No, Janet Won't Be at Grammys, After All', *People*, 4 February 2004, people.com/awards/no-janet-wont-be-at-grammys-after-all/.

54. David Segal, 'The Grammys' Hip-Hop Parade', *Washington Post*, 9

February 2004, www.washingtonpost.com/archive/lifestyle/2004/02/ 09/the-grammys-hip-hop-parade/cd0ace41-b367-49a8-a281-5775594 d50fc/.

55. Tony Kornheiser, 'Newscycled Items that Are Left to Be Trashed', *Washington Post*, 13 March 2004, www.washingtonpost.com/archive/ sports/2004/03/13/newscycled-items-that-are-left-to-be-trashed/ cde1f646-bc04-42ff-81d8-71054bb26578/.

56. Cady Lang, 'A Comprehensive Guide to Justin Timberlake's Rocky History with the Super Bowl Halftime Show', Time, 2 February 2018, time.com/5129559/janet-jackson-justin-timberlake-super-bowl-2018/.

57. PublicApologyCentral, 'Janet Jackson Discusses Wardrobe Malfunction at Super Bowl Halftime Show', YouTube, n.d., youtu.be/ aavUakg4S74.

58. Gary Susman, 'Justin Apologizes in Order to Appear at Grammys', *Entertainment Weekly*, 7 February 2004, ew.com/article/2004/02/07/ justin-apologizes-order-appear-grammys/.

59. Gary Susman, 'Disney World Removes Janet Jackson-Inspired Statue', *Entertainment Weekly*, 3 March 2004, ew.com/article/2004/03/03/ disney-world-removes-janet-jackson-inspired-statue/.

60. Sam Francis, 'Morality Not the Only Target on Monday Night Football', VDARE, 26 November 2004, web.archive. org/web/20120204040022/https://vdare.com/articles/ morality-not-the-only-target-on-monday-night-football.

61. Justin McCarthy, 'US Approval of Interracial Marriage at New High of 94%', Gallup, 10 September 2021, news.gallup.com/poll/354638/ approval-interracial-marriage-new-high.aspx.

62. Beatrice Loayza, 'The Imperfect Legacy of Aaliyah's Romeo Must Die', Vulture, *New York Magazine*, 27 August 2021, www.vulture. com/2021/08/the-imperfect-legacy-of-aaliyahs-romeo-must-die.html.

63. Lola Ogunnaike, 'Seriously Kidding About Race', *New York Times*, 23 February 2005, www.nytimes.com/2005/02/23/arts/seriously-kidding-about-race.html.

64. Neal Travis, 'FCC Turns Eminem Song into "Fine Art"', *New York Post*, 6 June 2001, nypost.com/2001/06/06/ fcc-turns-eminem-song-into-fine-art/.

65. Lynda Richardson, 'Public Lives; She Wants Her MTV. Actually, She's Got Her MTV', *New York Times*, 11 June 2003, www.nytimes. com/2003/06/11/nyregion/public-lives-she-wants-her-mtv-actually-she-s-got-her-mtv.html.

66. John T. McWhorter, 'Oh, R-o-b, the Bad Words Won't Go Away', *Washington Post*, 28 December 2003, www.washingtonpost.com/ archive/opinions/2003/12/28/oh-r-o-ob-the-bad-words-wont-go-away/0e20aa72-d71f-495d-b1f8-489ba9a9960f/.

67. *Parents Television Council 2005 Annual Report*, 2005, https://web. archive.org/web/20060428212424/http://www.parentstv.org/PTC/ joinus/AR2005.pdf.

68. Brian Fitzpatrick, 'Does Watching TV Damage Character?' Human Events, 12 June 2007, web.archive.org/web/20070613015557/http:// www.humanevents.com/article.php?id=21069.

69. Julia A. Seymour, 'Media Myth: Networks Stick to Warming Theme Despite Avalanche of Chilling News', MRCBusiness, 4 March 2009, web.archive.org/web/20160119204107/http://www.mrc.org/media-myths/media-myth-networks-stick-warming-theme-despite-avalanche-chilling-news-0.

70. *Exxon Mobil Corporation 2004 Worldwide Contributions and Community Investments*, 2004, www.documentcloud.org/documents/1019878-2004-exxon-giving-report.

71. Bob Thompson, 'Fighting Indecency, One Bleep at a Time', *Washington Post*, 9 December 2004, www.washingtonpost.com/archive/lifestyle/2004/12/09/fighting-indecency-one-bleep-at-a-time/2be1a76e-bc1b-4e1d-898f-9f09d4f40ad8//

72. Paul Farhi, 'TV Watchdog Apologizes for False Claims on Wrestling', *Washington Post*, 9 July 2002, www.washingtonpost.com/archive/lifestyle/2002/07/09/tv-watchdog-apologizes-for-false-claims-on-wrestling/dacca2ea-5431-4bfe-bc90-e759739e7b9f/.

73. Brian Fritz and Christopher Murray, *Between the Ropes: Wrestling's Greatest Triumphs and Failures* (ECW Press, 2006), ebook.

74. Parents Television Council, 'Take Action Against CBS' Outrageous Super Bowl Stunt', PTC, PTC E-Alert, 2 February 2004, web.archive.org/web/20040423085937/http://www.parentstv.org/ptc/publications/ealerts/2004/0202.asp.

75. Parents Television Council, 'File Your Formal FCC Indecency Complaint Against the February 1 CBS Broadcast of "NFL Super Bowl XXXVIII Half-Time Show" Now!', PTC Action Alert, PTC, 21 February 2004, web.archive.org/web/20070930201025/https://www.parentstv.org/ptc/action/superbowl/main.asp.

76. Testimony of Michael K. Powell, Chairman, Federal Communications Commission, Before the House Energy and Commerce Committee, Subcommittee on Telecommunications and the Internet, 11 February 2004, Rayburn House Office Building, Washington, DC, docs.fcc.gov/public/attachments/DOC-243802A3.pdf.

77. Jennifer 8. Lee, 'Musicians Protesting Monopoly in Media', *New York Times*, 18 December 2003, www.nytimes.com/2003/12/18/arts/musicians-protesting-monopoly-in-media.html.

78. Shales, 'Michael Powell and the FCC'.

79. Edmund Sanders, 'Senators Scold Radio Chain for Tuning Out Dixie Chicks', *Los Angeles Times*, 9 July 2003, www.latimes.com/archives/la-xpm-2003-jul-09-fi-cumulus9-story.html.

80. Jonah Goldberg, 'Very Different Visions', Townhall, 12 September 2008, townhall.com/columnists/jonahgoldberg/2008/09/12/very-different-visions-n852447.

81. Devin Gordon, 'What Happened to Jon Stewart?' *The Atlantic*, 21 April 2011, www.theatlantic.com/culture/archive/2022/04/the-problem-with-jon-stewart-tucker-carlson/629608/.

82. Parents Television Council, 'Take Action Against CBS' Outrageous Super Bowl Stunt'.

83. Shales, 'Michael Powell and the FCC'.

84. Brian Hiatt, 'Janet's Super Bowl Stunt Could Cost $550K', *Entertainment Weekly*, 19 July 2004, ew.com/article/2004/07/19/janets-super-bowl-stunt-could-cost-550k/.

85. Ronan Farrow, 'Les Moonves and CBS Face Allegations of Sexual Misconduct', *New Yorker*, 27 July 2018, www.newyorker.com/magazine/2018/08/06/les-moonves-and-cbs-face-allegations-of-sexual-misconduct.

86. Lawrie Mifflin, 'Viacom Set to Acquire CBS in Biggest Media Merger Ever', *New York Times*, 8 September 1999, archive.nytimes.com/www.nytimes.com/library/financial/090899cbs-viacom-deal.html.

87. Yashar Ali, 'Exclusive: Les Moonves Was Obsessed with Ruining Janet Jackson's Career, Sources Say', *Huffington Post*, 9 July 2018, www.huffingtonpost.co.uk/entry/les-moonves-janet-jackson-career_n_5b919b8ce4b0511db3e0a269.

88. Daniel Kreps, 'Nipple Ripples: 10 Years of Fallout from Janet Jackson's Halftime Show', *Rolling Stone*, 30 January 2014, www.rollingstone.com/culture/culture-news/nipple-ripples-10-years-of-fallout-from-janet-jacksons-halftime-show-122792/.

89. soapluvr, 'Janet on Letterman', YouTube, n.d., www.youtube.com/watch?v=p2zyp7uACbg.

90. Chuck Philips, 'Janet Jackson Spins a New Record: $80-Million Deal', *Los Angeles Times*, 12 January 1996, www.latimes.com/archives/la-xpm-1996-01-12-mn-23892-story.html.

91. Neil Strauss, 'Damita Jo', *Rolling Stone*, 24 March 2004, www.rollingstone.com/music/music-album-reviews/damita-jo-248247/.

92. Alexis Petridis, 'Review: Janet Jackson, Damita Jo', *Guardian*, 26 March 2004, www.theguardian.com/music/2004/mar/26/popandrock.shopping.

93. Ibid.

94. Strauss, 'Damita Jo'.

95. Ian Wade, 'Janet Jackson: Damita Jo Review', BBC, 2004, www.bbc.co.uk/music/reviews/gmcz/.

96. Lola Ogunnaike, 'Capitalizing on Jackson Tempest', *New York Times*, 4 February 2004, www.nytimes.com/2004/02/04/arts/capitalizing-on-jackson-tempest.html.

97. Andrew Court, 'Janet Jackson Felt "Guilty by Association" Amid Michael Jackson's Abuse Trial', *New York Post*, 3 January 2022, nypost.com/2022/01/03/janet-jackson-speaks-out-about-michael-jackson-abuse-trial/.

98. 'Janet Jackson signs new deal', NME, 16 July 2007, web.archive.org/web/20071216073525/https://www.nme.com/news/janet-jackson/29708.

99. Susan Faludi, *Backlash: The Undeclared War Against Women* (New York: Vintage, 1993), p. 182.

100. Jackson, *True You*, p. 1.

101. 'Celebs Who Balloon Between Projects', TMZ, 12 January 2006, www.tmz.com/2006/01/12/celebs-who-balloon-between-projects/.

102. Jackson, *True You*, p. 3.

103. Ibid., p. 186.

104. 'Gaming the Rules: Politicians Should Be Kept Out of Regulation', *The Economist*, 24 July 2003, www.economist.com/leaders/2003/07/24/gaming-the-rules.

105. Michael K. Powell, 'Don't Expect the Government to Be a V-Chip', *New York Times*, 3 December 2004, www.nytimes.com/2004/12/03/opinion/dont-expect-the-government-to-be-a-vchip.html.

106. Farrow, 'Les Moonves and CBS Face Allegations of Sexual Misconduct'.

107. John Koblin, 'Leslie Moonves Receives Nothing from CBS Exit Package', *New York Times*, 14 May 2021, nytimes.com/2021/05/14/business/media/leslie-moonves-cbs-severance.html.

108. Brittany Spanos, 'Janet Jackson's Rock and Roll Hall of Fame Acceptance Speech: "Induct More Women"', *Rolling Stone*, 29 March 2019, www.rollingstone.com/music/music-news/janet-jackson-rock-and-roll-hall-of-fame-2019-814263/.

109. Maria Sherman, 'How Justin Timberlake Came Undone', *Slate*, 18 November 2021, slate.com/culture/2021/11/justin-timberlake-reckoning-britney-spears-janet-jackson.html.

110. Nina Braca, 'Everything Justin Timberlake Has Said About the 2004 Super Bowl Controversy', Billboard, 18 January 2018, www.billboard.com/music/music-news/justin-timberlake-2004-super-bowl-controversy-statements-8094956/.

111. Sherman, 'How Justin Timberlake Came Undone'.

112. Gary Susman, 'Academy Blasts ABC over Oscar Tape Delay', *Entertainment Weekly*, 11 February 2004, ew.com/article/2004/02/11/academy-blasts-abc-over-oscar-tape-delay/.

113. Rob Tannenbaum, 'How Hip-Hop Inched Its Way to the Super Bowl Halftime Stage', *New York Times*, 10 February 2022, www.nytimes.com/2022/02/10/arts/music/super-bowl-halftime-hip-hop.html.

114. 'Anna Nicole Flashes Crowd at MTV Event', Fox News, 13 January 2015, www.foxnews.com/story/anna-nicole-flashes-crowd-at-mtv-event.

115. Jim Hopkins, 'Surprise! There's a Third YouTube Co-founder', *USA Today*, 11 October 2006, http://web.archive.org/web/20121004011143/usatoday30.usatoday.com/tech/news/2006-10-11-youtube-karim_x.htm.

116. Jan Hoffman, 'Justin Bieber Is Living the Dream', *New York Times*, 31 December 2009, www.nytimes.com/2010/01/03/fashion/03bieber.html.

6: Amy

1. Janis Winehouse, *Loving Amy: A Mother's Story* (London: Bantam Press, 2014), p. 273.

2. Alexandra Topping, 'Amy Winehouse died of alcohol poisoning, second inquest confirms', *Guardian*, 8 January 2013, www.theguardian.com/music/2013/jan/08/amy-winehouse-alcohol-poisoning-inquest.

3. Winehouse, *Loving Amy*, p. 273.

4. Sarah Bull, 'Amy Winehouse, 27, Found Dead at Her London Flat After Suspected "Drug Overdose"', *Daily Mail*, 26 July 2011, www. dailymail.co.uk/tvshowbiz/article-2018020/Amy-Winehouse-dead-London-flat-drug-overdose.html.

5. Hadley Freeman, '"God, I never thought we'd be this old!": Miquita Oliver and Simon Amstell on Popworld turning 20', *Guardian*, 1 May 2021, www.theguardian.com/tv-and-radio/2021/may/01/miquita-oliver-and-simon-amstell-on-popworld-turning-20.

6. Eternal Amy Winehouse, 'Amy Winehouse BRIT Awards Campaign Popworld 2004', n.d., www.youtube.com/watch?v=H1kuCS9uX9s.

7. Winehouse, *Loving Amy*, p. 71.

8. Ibid., p. 73.

9. Henrietta Roussoulis, 'Amy Winehouse: The Q Interview', *Independent*, 18 January 2004, www.independent.co.uk/arts-entertainment/music/features/amy-winehouse-the-q-interview-74363. html; Winehouse, *Loving Amy*, p. 53.

10. Tyler James with Sylvia Patterson, *My Amy: The Life We Shared* (London: Macmillan, 2021), ebook.

11. *Amy*, directed by Asif Kapadia (Film4 Productions, 2015); Winehouse, *Loving Amy*, p. 131.

12. Winehouse, *Loving Amy*, p. 84.

13. James with Patterson, *My Amy*, ebook.

14. Winehouse, *Loving Amy*, p. 90.

15. 'Amy Winehouse – Frank', BBC, n.d., web.archive.org/web/20121110175202/http://www.bbc.co.uk/dna/collective/A1364744.

16. Beccy Lindon, 'Amy Winehouse, Frank', *Guardian*, 17 October 2003, www.theguardian.com/music/2003/oct/17/jazz.shopping1.

17. Winehouse, *Loving Amy*, p. 90.

18. Amy Winehouse, 'Stronger Than Me', Lyrics Genius, n.d., genius.com/Amy-winehouse-intro-stronger-than-me-lyrics.

19. Roussoulis, 'Amy Winehouse: The Q Interview'.

20. Gary Mulholland, 'Charmed and dangerous', *Guardian*, 1 February 2004, www.theguardian.com/music/2004/feb/01/popandrock. amywinehouse.

21. Richard Rushfield, *American Idol: The Untold Story* (New York: Hachette, 2011), p. 3.

22. Roussoulis, 'Amy Winehouse: The Q Interview'.

23. Mulholland, 'Charmed and dangerous'.

24. Rushfield, *American Idol*, pp. 11–12.

25. Michael Hogan '"Nasty" Nigel Lythgoe on the legacy of Pop Idol: "Did I create a monster? In no way, shape or form"', *Telegraph*, 13 January 2021, www.telegraph.co.uk/tv/0/nasty-nigel-lythgoe-legacy-pop-idol-did-create-monster-no-way/.

26. Rushfield, *American Idol*, p. 17.

27. *The Talent Show Story*, directed by Kerry Allison and Yvette Lyons (Shiver/Talkback Thames, 2012).

28. Kym Marsh, *From the Heart* (London: Hodder & Stoughton, 2011), p. 65.

29. Ibid., p. 168.

30. 'Hear'Say announce split', *Guardian*, 1 October 2002, www.theguardian.com/culture/2002/oct/01/artsfeatures1.
31. Rushfield, *American Idol*, p. 91.
32. Nancy Jo Sales, 'Sirens for Scandal', *Vanity Fair*, May 2002, nancyjosales.com/wp-content/uploads/2015/05/3AMgirls.pdf.
33. Miranda Sawyer, 'Hot Gossip', *Observer*, 27 January 2002, www.theguardian.com/theobserver/2002/jan/27/features.magazine17.
34. Ibid.
35. Jessica Callan, *Wicked Whispers: Confessions of a Gossip Queen* (London: Michael Joseph, 2007), ebook.
36. Sawyer, 'Hot Gossip'.
37. Sarah Hall, 'What the Editor Said to the Supermodel: "You Are a Celebrity Who Has Voraciously Invaded Your Own Privacy"', *Guardian*, 13 February 2002, www.theguardian.com/media/2002/feb/13/pressandpublishing.privacy.
38. Emma Brockes, 'Sienna Miller on taking on the tabloids: "It was so toxic – what women were subjected to"', *Guardian*, 23 April 2022, www.theguardian.com/film/2022/apr/23/sienna-miller-on-taking-on-tabloids-so-toxic-what-women-subjected-to.
39. 'Why the phone-hacking story won't go away', *The Economist*, 12 November 2020, www.economist.com/britain/2020/11/12/why-the-phone-hacking-story-wont-go-away.
40. Judgments – Campbell (Appellant) v. MGN Limited (Respondents), www.bailii.org/uk/cases/UKHL/2004/22.html.
41. John Plunkett, 'Stirring Up the Froth', *Guardian*, 16 February 2004, www.theguardian.com/media/2004/feb/16/pressandpublishing.mondaymediasection.
42. Sawyer, 'Hot Gossip'.
43. Winehouse, *Loving Amy*, p. 143.
44. Darren and Elliott Bloom with Matt Trollope, *Amy: A Life Through the Lens* (London: Omnibus Press, 2016), p. 7.
45. James with Patterson, *My Amy*, ebook.
46. 'New CDs', *New York Times*, 12 March 2007, www.nytimes.com/2007/03/12/arts/music/12choi.html.
47. Will Hermes, 'Amy Winehouse's "Back To Black": *EW* Review', *Entertainment Weekly*, 9 March 2007, ew.com/article/2007/03/09/back-black/.
48. Joshua Klein, 'Amy Winehouse: Back to Black', Pitchfork, 28 March 2007, web.archive.org/web/20080605042226/http://www.pitchforkmedia.com/article/record_review/41866-back-to-black.
49. MTV News Staff, 'Grammy 2008 Winners List', MTV, 10 February 2008, www.mtv.com/news/y2utwa/grammy-2008-winners-list.
50. Jenny Eliscu, 'The Diva and Her Demons: *Rolling Stone*'s 2007 Amy Winehouse Cover Story', *Rolling Stone*, 23 July 2011, web.archive.org/web/20110725013229/https://www.rollingstone.com/music/news/the-diva-and-her-demons-rolling-stones-2007-amy-winehouse-cover-story-20110723.
51. James with Patterson, *My Amy*, ebook.

52. Ibid.
53. Ibid.
54. Winehouse, *Loving Amy*, p. 115.
55. Mitch Winehouse, *Amy, My Daughter* (London: HarperCollins, 2012), p. 69.
56. Harriet Gibsone, 'Ronnie Spector: Kanye West is "a Dick"', *Guardian*, 13 November 2013, www.theguardian.com/music/2013/nov/13/kanye-west-ronnie-spector.
57. *Keeping Up with the Kardashians*, episode 9, season 2, directed by David Bresenham, aired 11 May 2008, on E!.
58. Sarah Harding with Terry Ronald, *Hear Me Out* (London: Penguin, 2021), p. 4.
59. 'Girls Aloud's Sarah Harding Enters Rehab for Depression', BBC, 12 October 2011, https://www.bbc.co.uk/news/newsbeat-15274546.
60. James with Patterson, *My Amy*, ebook.
61. Winehouse, *Amy, My Daughter*, p. 57.
62. Eliscu, 'The Diva and her Demons'.
63. James with Patterson, *My Amy*, ebook.
64. Louise Carpenter, 'Blake Fielder: Guilt, Loss and Amy', *The Times*, 20 June 2015, thetimes.co.uk/article/blake-fielder-civil-guilt-loss-and-amy-jrbsr-9w6m0h.
65. Rushfield, *American Idol*, p. 60.
66. Mike Nizza, 'Britain's Boldly Anti-Rehab Star', *New York Times*, 21 February 2007, thelede.blogs.nytimes.com/2007/02/21/britains-boldly-anti-rehab-pop-star/.
67. Perez Hilton, 'Warning: This is Too Real', Perez Hilton, n.d., perezhilton.com/warning-this-is-too-real/.
68. Perez Hilton, 'We Just Spoke With Amy Winehouse', Perez Hilton, n.d., perezhilton.com/we-just-spoke-with-amy-winehouse/.
69. Winehouse, *Loving Amy*, p. 171.
70. Winehouse, *Amy, My Daughter*, p. 215.
71. James with Patterson, *My Amy*, ebook.
72. Winehouse, *Amy, My Daughter*, p. 216.
73. 'In Court Today: Blake Fielder Civil Due to Be Sentenced', *The Times*, 21 July 2008, thetimes.co.uk/article/in-court-today-blake-fielder-civil-due-to-be-sentenced-rlxbmd07ws2.
74. Adrian Shaw, '"Amy Winehouse's Money Used to Bankroll Bribe Plot", Court Heard', Mirror, 11 June 2008, mirror.co.uk/3am/celebrity-news/amy=winehouses-money-used-to-bankroll-312742.
75. Winehouse, *Amy, My Daughter*, p. 230.
76. Perez Hilton, '$2 Million Mess', Perez Hilton, n.d., perezhilton.com/2-million-mess/.
77. Douglas Wolk, 'Frank – Amy Winehouse', Pitchfork, 14 November 2007, pitchfork.com/reviews/albums/10900-frank/.
78. Alexandra Topping, 'Amy Winehouse Died of Alcohol Poisoning, Second Inquest Confirms', *Guardian*, 8 January 2013, www.theguardian.com/music/2013/jan/08/amy-winehouse-alcohol-poisoning-inquest.
79. Duncan Cooper, 'Lana Del Rey is Anyone She Wants to Be', Fader, 4

June 2014, www.thefader.com/2014/06/04/cover-story-lana-del-rey-is-anyone-she-wants-to-be.

80. Lindsay Zoladz, 'Born to Die – Lana Del Rey', Pitchfork, 30 January 2012, pitchfork.com/reviews/albums/16223-lana-del-rey/.

81. Spencer Kornhaber, 'The Plot Against Lana Del Rey', *The Atlantic*, 15 September 2019, www.theatlantic.com/entertainment/archive/2019/09/lana-del-rey-says-she-never-had-persona-really/597883/.

82. Jessica Hopper, 'Deconstructing Lana Del Rey', Spin, 30 January 2012, www.spin.com/2012/01/deconstructing-lana-del-rey/2/.

7: Kim

1. Brian Lowry, 'Keeping Up With the Kardashians', *Variety*, 10 October 2007, variety.com/2007/scene/markets-festivals/keeping-up-with-the-kardashians-1117935063/.

2. Lynsey Eidell, 'The Reality-TV Show Kim Kardashian Originally Wanted to Audition For', *Glamour*, 28 August 2015, www.glamour.com/story/kim-kardashian-the-real-world.

3. Simon Kemp, 'Digital 2022: July Data Statshot Report', Datareportal, 21 July 2022, datareportal.com/reports/digital-2022-july-global-statshot.

4. Rachel Nuwer, 'Andy Warhol Probably Never Said His Celebrated "Fifteen Minutes of Fame" Line', *Smithsonian Magazine*, 8 April 2014, www.smithsonianmag.com/smart-news/andy-warhol-probably-never-said-his-celebrated-fame-line-180950456/.

5. James Verini, 'Will Success Spoil MySpace?', *Vanity Fair*, March 2006, archive.vanityfair.com/article/2006/3/will-success-spoil-myspace.

6. 'MySpace Phenom Tila Tequila to Tour', TMZ, 16 July 2007, www.tmz.com/2006/07/26/myspace-phenom-tila-tequila-to-tour/.

7. Sophie Kleeman, 'Here's Kim Kardashian's 9-Year-Old Myspace Page – It's Even Funnier Than You Think', Mic, 12 June 2015, www.mic.com/articles/120575/here-s-kim-kardashian-s-9-year-old-myspace-page-it-s-even-funnier-than-you-think.

8. Kat Pettibone, 'Kim Kardashian and Ray J's Relationship Timeline: Their Sex Tape, Cheating Confessions and More', *Us Magazine*, 5 May 2022, www.usmagazine.com/celebrity-news/pictures/kim-kardashian-ray-js-relationship-sex-tape-timeline/.

9. 'Brandon Davis – "Firecrotch" Originator Burned by Massive Casino Debt', TMZ, 7 May 2015, www.tmz.com/2015/05/07/brandon-davis-debt-lost-money-las-vegas-casinos/.

10. 'The Curse of Paris Hilton', TMZ, 26 June 2006, www.tmz.com/2006/06/26/the-curse-of-paris-hilton/.

11. 'Kim Kardashian: I'm Not Shopping the Sex Tape', TMZ, 17 January 2007, www.tmz.com/2007/01/17/kim-kardashian-im-not-shopping-the-sex-tape/.

12. 'Paris' BFF's Sex Tape – It's a Pisser', TMZ, 17 January 2007, www.tmz.com/2007/01/17/paris-bff-kim-ks-sex-tape-its-a-pisser/.

13. 'Screech Sex Tape?!', TMZ, 17 September 2006, www.tmz.com/2006/09/27/screech-sex-tape/.

14. 'Did Screech Know the Sex Tape Was Coming?', TMZ, 28 September 2006, www.tmz.com/2006/09/28/did-screech-know-the-sex-tape-was-coming/.

15. Lynn Okura, 'Dustin "Screech" Diamond Talks About His Sex Tape Debacle (VIDEO)', Huffpost, 2 December 2013, www.huffpost.com/entry/dustin-diamond-sex-tape-screech_n_4351031.

16. 'Screech Sex Tape?!'.

17. 'The One Thing Dustin Diamond Is Most Embarrassed About', Where Are They Now, Oprah Winfrey Network, n.d., www.youtube.com/watch?v=GWtctcYcDeo.

18. Chancellor Agard, 'How the Saved by the Bell Revival Honored Dustin Diamond in the Season 2 Premiere', *Entertainment Weekly*, 24 November 2021, ew.com/tv/how-saved-by-the-bell-season-2-honored-dustin-diamond/.

19. Jawn Murray, 'BV Buzz', AOL Black Voices, 25 December 2006, web.archive.org/web/20070113234355/http://blackvoices.aol.com:80/black_entertainment/bvbuzzcanvas/_a/dec-25-2006/20061221143709990001.

20. Todd, 'Kim Kardashian Might Be a Porn Star', IDon'tLikeYouInThatWay, 26 December 2006, web.archive.org/web/20070227062748/http://www.idontlikeyouinthatway.com/2006/12/kim-kardashian-might-be-porn-star.html.

21. 'Morning Wood: Ghosts of Sex Tapes, Past and Future', Fleshbot, 18 December 2006, web.archive.org/web/20070305003411/http://www.fleshbot.com/sex/morning-wood/morning-wood-ghosts-of-sex-tapes-past-and-future-224769.php.

22. 'Paris' BFF's Sex Tape – It's a Pisser'.

23. 'Kim Kardashian, Superstar', Fleshbot, n.d., https://web.archive.org/web/20070708143210/http://www.fleshbot.com/sex/celebrity/kim-kardashian-superstar-234663.php.

24. David Sullivan, 'Kim Kardashian Drops Vivid Lawsuit', Adult Video Network, 29 April 2007, web.archive.org/web/20071022133949/http://www.avn.com/index.cfm?objectId=98649D44-C294-9975-F33A043901001070.

25. djvlad, 'Vivid CEO Steven Hirsch on How the Kim K & Ray J Deal Came Together (Flashback)', 11 September 2022, www.youtube.com/watch?v=5mkGdBLSKMI.

26. 'DVD Review: Everything You Wanted To Know About "Kim Kardashian, Superstar" But Were Afraid To Watch', Fleshbot, 22 March 2007, web.archive.org/web/20070418095720/https://fleshbot.com/sex/hype/dvd-review-everything-you-wanted-to-know-about-kim-kardashian-superstar-but-were-afraid-to-watch-246457.php.

27. Hilton with Shapiro, *Red Carpet Suicide*, p. 71.

28. Caroline Blair, 'Ray J claims Kim Kardashian, Kris Jenner were in on sex tape leak', Page Six, 4 May 2022, pagesix.com/2022/05/04/ray-j-claims-kim-kardashian-kris-jenner-were-in-on-sex-tape-leak/.

29. Scaachi Koul, 'Inside the Stunning Rise and Fall of Girls Gone Wild', HuffPost, 26 May 2023, www.huffpost.com/entry/girls-gone-wild-joe-francis_n_645ee736e4b005be8ff3951e.

30. Kleeman, 'Here's Kim Kardashian's 9-Year-Old Myspace Page'.
31. *Keeping Up with the Kardashians*, episode 1, season 1 (2007).
32. Kris Jenner, *Kris Jenner ... and All Things Kardashian* (New York: Simon and Schuster, 2011), p. 257.
33. Ibid., p. 28.
34. Jeffrey Toobin, *The Run of His Life: The People v. OJ Simpson* (New York: Arrow Books, 2016), p. 44.
35. Kourtney Kardashian, Kim Kardashian and Khloé Kardashian, *Kardashian Konfidential* (New York: St Martin's Press, 2010), p. 29.
36. Toobin, *The Run of His Life*, p. 2.
37. Ibid., p. 14.
38. Sara Boboltz, 'Here's What You Might Not Remember About O.J. Simpson's Police Chase', HuffPost, 9 February 2016, www.huffingtonpost.co.uk/entry/american-crime-story-oj-simpson-bronco-chase_n_56b8f737e4b01d80b2475fc7.
39. Jenner, *Kris Jenner*, p. 162.
40. O.J. Simpson, *If I Did It* (London: Gibson Square, 2016), pp. 231–2.
41. Michael Ness, 'O.J. Kardashian Reads Letter', 28 January 2014, www.youtube.com/watch?v=7nPQeSCjQNw.
42. Jerry Oppenheimer, *The Kardashians: An American Drama* (New York: St Martin's Press, 2017), p. xvi.
43. 'After The Riots; A Juror Describes the Ordeal of Deliberation', *New York Times*, 6 May 1992, web.archive.org/web/20090425194252/ https://www.nytimes.com/1992/05/06/us/after-the-riots-a-juror-describes-the-ordeal-of-deliberations.html.
44. Adam Bernstein, 'Lawyer Johnnie Cochran Played Key Role in Famous Cases', Seattle Times, 30 March 2005, www.seattletimes.com/nation-world/ lawyer-johnnie-cochran-jr-played-key-role-in-famous-cases/.
45. *O.J.: Made in America*, produced and directed by Ezra Edelman (ESPN Films, 2016).
46. Toobin, *The Run of His Life*, pp. 70–1.
47. Comedy Central, 'Chappelle's Show – The Racial Draft', 31 December 2017, www.youtube.com/watch?v=2z3wUD3AZg4.
48. Toobin, *The Run of His Life*, p. 254.
49. Kardashian, Kardashian and Kardashian, *Kardashian Konfidential*, p. 29.
50. B. Drummond Ayres Jr, 'Civil Jury Finds Simpson Liable in Pair of Killings', *New York Times*, 5 February 1997, www.nytimes.com/1997/02/05/us/civil-jury-finds-simpson-liable-in-pair-of-killings.html.
51. Harmon Leon, 'I Was O.J. Simpson's Accomplice (On His Hidden-Camera Prank Show)', Vice, 12 June 2014, https://www.vice.com/en/article/5gkaba/i-was-oj-simpsons-accomplice-on-his-hidden-camera-prank-show-juiced.
52. Edward Watt, 'Publisher Calls Book a Confession by O.J. Simpson', *New York Times*, 17 November 2006, www.nytimes.com/2006/11/17/books/17ojbook.html.
53. Steve Friess, 'O.J. Simpson Convicted of Robbery and Kidnapping',

New York Times, 4 October 2008, www.nytimes.com/2008/10/04/world/americas/04iht-simpson.1.16687098.html.

54. *OJ: Made in America*, episode 5.

55. Matt Belloni, 'Nick Lachey', Details, May 2013, web.archive.org/web/20130420055811/http://www.details.com/celebrities-entertainment/music-and-books/201305/nick-lachey-98-degrees-tour.

56. Gina Bellafante, 'The All-Too-Easy Route to Stardom', *New York Times*, 13 October 2007, www.nytimes.com/2007/10/13/arts/television/13bell.html.

57. Kardashian, Kardashian and Kardashian, *Kardashian Konfidential*, pp. 110–11.

58. Molly Friedman, 'Paris Hilton Is Not A Fan Of Kim Kardashian's "Cottage Cheese In A Trash Bag" Butt', *Gawker*, 17 April 2008, web.archive.org/web/20120829233132/https://gawker.com/381060/paris-hilton-is-not-a-fan-of-kim-kardashians-cottage-cheese-in-a-trash-bag-butt.

59. Hilton with Shapiro, *Red Carpet Suicide*, p. 129.

60. 'The Power of Kim Kardashian', episode of *Honestly with Bari Weiss*, Apple Podcasts, 2021.

61. 'KIM KARDASHIAN Cover: Feb/March 2007', Complex, 5 February 2007, web.archive.org/web/20070304010355/http://www.complex.com/blogs/?p=1991.

62. Lola Ogunnaike, 'New Magazines for Black Men Proudly Redefine the Pinup', *New York Times*, 31 August 2004, www.nytimes.com/2004/08/31/arts/new-magazines-for-black-men-proudly-redefine-the-pinup.html.

63. 'Kim Kardashian', *King*, 17 May 2010, https://web.archive.org/web/20150913074819/https://king-mag.com/kim-kardashian-3/.

64. Justin McCarthy, 'US Approval of Interracial Marriage at New High of 94%', Gallup, 10 September 2021, https://news.gallup.com/poll/354638/approval-interracial-marriage-new-high.aspx.

65. Oppenheimer, *The Kardashians*, p. 67.

66. Beatrice Loayza, 'The Imperfect Legacy of Romeo Must Die', Vulture, 27 August 2021, www.vulture.com/2021/08/the-imperfect-legacy-of-aaliyahs-romeo-must-die.html.

67. 'Lexington Steele Interview', Rog Reviews, December 2001, www.rogreviews.com/interviews/lexington_steele2.asp; 'Sophie Dee', Xcitement, 2010, web.archive.org/web/20100630012304/http://www.xcitement.com/interview/?page_id=907.

68. Page Six Staff, 'Family Way', Page Six, 15 August 2007, pagesix.com/2007/08/15/family-way/.

69. Sophie Elmhirst, 'Brazilian Butt Lift: Behind the World's Most Dangerous Cosmetic Surgery', *Guardian*, 9 February 2021, www.theguardian.com/news/2021/feb/09/brazilian-butt-lift-worlds-most-dangerous-cosmetic-surgery.

70. Amin Kalaaji, MD, PhD, Stine Dreyer, MS, Line Vadseth, MD, Ivana Maric, MD, Vanja Jönsson and Trond H Haukebøe, MD, 'Gluteal Augmentation with Fat: Retrospective Safety Study and Literature Review', *Aesthetic Surgery Journal* 39:3, March 2019, pp. 292–305, academic.oup.com/asj/article/39/3/292/5040466.

71. PulverSilva101, 'Kim Kardashian AMBUSHES Hater!!', 23 July 2012, www.youtube.com/watch?v=H8ph3cTj0pE.

72. Danielle Pergament, 'Kim Kardashian and I Analyzed Each Other's Faces', *Allure*, August 2022, www.allure.com/story/kim-kardashian-cover-interview-august-2022.

73. Bethonie Butler, 'Yes, Those Kim Kardashian Photos Are About Race', *Washington Post*, 21 November 2014, www.washingtonpost.com/blogs/she-the-people/wp/2014/11/21/yes-those-kim-kardashian-photos-are-about-race/.

74. Habiba Katsha, 'Body Trends Come And Go, But Black Women Can Never Win', HuffPost, 13 November 2022, www.huffingtonpost.co.uk/entry/body-trends-black-women-can-never-win_uk_636bb75ee4b06d3e42567051.

75. 'A Conversation with Nicki Minaj & Joe Budden', directed by Drew Morris (Joe Budden TV, 2022), YouTube, https://www.youtube.com/watch?v=LSmMQEsBzmE.

76. Heather Radke, *Butts: A Backstory* (New York: Simon and Schuster, 2022), p. 199.

77. Ibid., p. 214.

78. Allison P. Davis, 'The End of Kim and Kanye's Wild Ride', *Vulture*, 26 April 2021, www.vulture.com/article/kim-kardashian-kanye-west-divorce.html.

79. Lorry Hill, 'Kim Kardashian: Plastic Surgery (2000–2020)', BODY Edition, 28 September 2020, www.youtube.com/watch?v=6gObY8qEchQ.

80. Barbara Herman, 'The Man Behind Naked Kim Kardashian Photos, Jean-Paul Goude, Has A Race Problem', *International Business Times*, 13 November 2014, www.ibtimes.com/man-behind-naked-kim-kardashian-photos-jean-paul-goude-has-race-problem-1723182.

81. Tina Fey, *Bossypants* (New York: Little, Brown, 2011), p. 22.

82. Virginia Heffernan, 'Anchor Woman', *New Yorker*, 26 October 2003, www.newyorker.com/magazine/2003/11/03/anchor-woman.

83. Dan Savage, 'Savage Love: On the Racks', The Stranger, 15 July 2004, web.archive.org/web/20060625020725/https://www.thestranger.com/seattle/SavageLove?oid=18774.

84. Thorstein Veblen, *The Theory of the Leisure Class: An Economic Study of Institutions* (1899; repr. Oxford: Oxford University Press, 2007), p. 89.

85. John Lanchester, *Whoops! Why Everyone Owes Everyone and No One Can Pay* (London: Penguin, 2010), p. xii.

86. Ibid., pp. 111–12.

87. 'Great Recession', Britannica, n.d., www.britannica.com/topic/great-recession.

88. Louis Uchitelle, 'US Lost 2.6 Million Jobs in 2008', *New York Times*, 9 January 2009, www.nytimes.com/2009/01/09/business/worldbusiness/09iht-jobs.4.19232394.html.

89. Ta-Nehisi Coates, 'The Case for Reparations', *The Atlantic*, June 2014, www.theatlantic.com/magazine/archive/2014/06/the-case-for-reparations/361631/.

90. Don Gonyea, 'Financial Crisis Gave Candidate Obama a Boost',

NPR, 8 September 2009, www.npr.org/templates/story/story.
php?storyId=112651600

91. Brian Lowry, 'Tying Pop Culture to Economy is a Leap',
Variety, 11 February 2009, variety.com/2009/tv/news/
tying-pop-culture-to-economy-is-a-leap-1117999987/.

92. 'A Shot at Love with Tila Tequila', IMDb, n.d., www.imdb.com/title/
tt1263572/.

93. THR Staff, 'Tila Tequila "Removed" From "Celebrity Big Brother"
Reportedly Due to Past Nazi Remarks', *Hollywood Reporter*,
28 August 2015, www.hollywoodreporter.com/tv/tv-news/
tila-tequila-removed-celebrity-big-818664/.

94. Michael Learmonth, 'Here's Who Gets the Highest Ad Rates
Online', Business Insider, 21 December 2009, www.businessinsider.
com/heres-who-gets-the-highest-ad-rates-online-2009-12;
Katie J. M. Baker, 'Stop Lying To Your Young, Impressionable
Fanbase, Kim Kardashian!', Jezebel, 2 March 2012, jezebel.com/
stop-lying-to-your-young-impressionable-fanbase-kim-k-5890088.

95. Julie Naughton, 'Kim Kardashian Discusses First Scent', *Women's
Wear Daily*, 2 October 2009, wwd.com/beauty-industry-news/
beauty-features/kim-kardashian-discusses-first-scent-2324791/.

96. Jonathan Van Meter, 'In the 2010s, Fame Went Multi-Platform Kim
Kardashian West on life as a brand and her political awakening', The
Cut, 25 November 2009, www.thecut.com/2019/11/kim-kardashian-
west-on-her-decade-of-multi-platform-fame.html.

97. Khal, 'Remember That Time Anna Nicole Smith Was in Kanye West's
"The New Workout Plan" Video?', Complex, 8 February 2007, www.
complex.com/pop-culture/2017/02/anna-nicole-smith-kanye-west-
the-new-workout-plan-video.

98. Amy Odell, *Anna: The Biography* (London: Allen and Unwin,
2022), p. 220.

99. Ibid., pp. 288–9.

100. Joe Coscarelli, 'Kanye West Calls Out Beyoncé and Praises Trump in
Onstage Tirade', *New York Times*, 20 November 2016, www.nytimes.
com/2016/11/21/arts/music/kanye-west-beyonce-donald-trump-
speech.html.

101. Joe Coscarelli, 'Kanye West is Hospitalized for "Psychiatric
Emergency" Hours After Canceling Tour', *New York Times*, 21
November 2016, www.nytimes.com/2016/11/21/arts/music/kanye-
west-hospitalized-exhaustion.html; Jon Caramanica, 'Into the Wild
with Kanye West', *New York Times*, 25 June 2018, www.nytimes.
com/2018/06/25/arts/music/kanye-west-ye-interview.html.

102. Katie Rogers, 'Kanye West Visits Donald Trump', *New York Times*, 13
December 2016, www.nytimes.com/2016/12/13/us/politics/kanye-
trump-tower-visit.html.

103. Ashitha Nagesh, 'US election 2020: Why Trump gained support
among minorities', BBC News, 22 November 2020, www.bbc.co.uk/
news/world-us-canada-54972389.

104. Hadley Freeman, 'Don't Punish Kanye West', UnHerd, 11 October
2022, unherd.com/2022/10/dont-punish-kanye-west/.

105. 'Alice Johnson freed after Trump grants clemency plea', BBC News, 7 June 2018, www.bbc.co.uk/news/world-us-canada-44390737.

8: Chyna

1. 'WWF PPV Statistics 2001', OSW Review, n.d., oswreview.com/history/wwf-ppv-statistics-2001/.
2. 'Chyna vs. Ivory', Daily Motion, n.d., https://www.dailymotion.com/video/x98voa.
3. Joanie Laurer [Chyna] with Michael Angeli, *If They Only Knew* (New York: ReganBooks/HarperCollins, 2001), p. 80.
4. Ibid., p. 132.
5. Ibid., p. 84.
6. 'GEICO Presents: Chyna' episode in podcast *Grilling JR* (2020), www.stitcher.com/show/the-jim-ross-report/episode/geico-presents-chyna-80346998.
7. 'Chyna', WWE, www.wwe.com/superstars/chyna.
8. Richard Sandomir, 'Sports Business: Wildlife Fund Takes Down Wrestlers in Name Game', *New York Times*, 7 May 2002, nytimes.com/2002/05/07/sports/sports-business-wildlife-fund-takes-down-wrestlers-in-name-game.html.
9. Laurer with Angeli, *If They Only Knew*, p. 246.
10. Swatzify, 'Chyna's PlayBoy Cover RAW: Sep 25, 2000', 8 August 2021, www.youtube.com/watch?v=6aR-ry6aqyw.
11. Mick Foley, *Have a Nice Day: A Tale of Blood and Sweatsocks* (New York: HarperCollins, 1999), p. 43.
12. *Observer* Staff, 'January 29, 2001 Wrestling Observer Newsletter: Royal Rumble Review, Shawn Michaels to Return, More', *Wrestling Observer Newsletter*, 29 January 2001, members.f4wonline.com/wrestling-observer-newsletter/january-29-2001-wrestling-observer-newsletter-royal-rumble-review.
13. Chris Smith, 'Breaking Down How WWE Contracts Work', Forbes, 28 March 2015, www.forbes.com/sites/chrissmith/2015/03/28/breaking-down-how-wwe-contracts-work/; see also 'Exhibit A: Titan Sports Inc. Booking Contract', Martha Hart v World Wrestling Entertainment Inc.
14. 'Vince McMahon', Britannica, n.d., www.britannica.com/biography/Vince-McMahon.
15. Jim Smallman, *I'm Sorry, I Love You: A History of Professional Wrestling* (London: Headline, 2018), p. 176.
16. Ibid., p. 182.
17. Laurer with Angeli, *If They Only Knew*, p. 22.
18. Ibid., p. 186.
19. Ibid., p. 184.
20. Ibid., pp. 123–4.
21. Ibid., p. 157.
22. Foley, *Have a Nice Day*, p. 97.
23. Ibid., pp. vii–viii.
24. Laurer with Angeli, *If They Only Knew*, pp. 80–4.

25. Ibid., p. 264.
26. Ibid., p. 265.
27. Ibid., p. 274; Bob Holly and Ross Williams, *The Hardcore Truth: The Bob Holly Story* (Toronto: ECW Press, 2013), p. 140.
28. 'GEICO Presents: Chyna'.
29. *Observer* Staff, 'January 29, 2001 Wrestling Observer Newsletter'.
30. Jesse Holland, 'On this date in WWF history: Mark Henry gets humiliated by Chyna in front of his mama', Ringside Seats, 18 January 2012, www.cagesideseats.com/2012/1/18/2713632/ wwf-wwe-mark-henry-humiliated-chyna-raw-dx-video-sammy.
31. 'GEICO Presents: Chyna'.
32. *Observer* Staff, 'F$W~!#336 – WWF Profits Down 71 Percent – December 3, 2001', *Wrestling Observer*, 3 December 2001, members.f4wonline.com/figure-four-weekly/ f4w336-wwf-profits-down-71-percent-december-3-2001-89091.
33. Laurer with Angeli, *If They Only Knew*, p. 206.
34. Rex Jones, '10 Ways Wrestlers Changed Their Appearance Through Surgery', WhatCulture, 8 February 2021, whatculture.com/wwe/10-ways-wrestlers-changed-their-appearance-through-surgery-2?page=4.
35. Laurer with Angeli, *If They Only Knew*, p. 14.
36. 'Anabolic Steroid Misuse', NHS, n.d., www.nhs.uk/conditions/ anabolic-steroid-misuse/.
37. Ryan Clark, 'Eddie Guerrero Autopsy Results – Massive Heart Failure', Wrestling Inc, 17 November 2005, https://www.wrestlinginc. com/news/2005/11/eddie-guerrero-autopsy-results-489609/.
38. See Matthew Randazzo, *Ring of Hell* (Beverly Hills: Phoenix Books, 2008).
39. Laurer with Angeli, *If They Only Knew*, p. 176.
40. 'Sports People: Pro Wrestling; Prison for Doctor', *New York Times*, 29 December 1991, www.nytimes.com/1991/12/29/sports/sports-people-pro-wrestling-prison-for-doctor.html.
41. 'A Promoter of Wrestling is Acquitted', *New York Times*, 23 July 1994, www.nytimes.com/1994/07/23/nyregion/a-promoter-of-wrestling-is-acquitted.html.
42. 'GEICO Presents: Chyna'.
43. Benjamin Svetkey, 'The Rock is the secret weapon in "The Mummy Returns"', *Entertainment Weekly*, 11 May 2001, https://ew.com/ article/2001/05/11/rock-secret-weapon-mummy-returns/.
44. 'GEICO Presents: Chyna'.
45. Julia Emmanuele, 'A Championship Couple! Stephanie McMahon and Paul "Triple H" Levesque's Relationship Timeline', *Us Magazine*, 11 January 2023, www.usmagazine.com/celebrity-news/pictures/wwes-stephanie-mcmahon-and-wrestler-triple-hs-relationship-timeline/.
46. Laurer with Angeli, *If They Only Knew*, p. 235.
47. 'GEICO Presents: Chyna'.
48. Randazzo, *Ring of Hell*, p. 340.
49. John Powell, 'Killer Kowalski Slams Chyna's Book', Slam Wrestling, 6 February 2001, slamwrestling.net/index.php/2001/02/06/ killer-kowalski-slams-chynas-book/.

50. Laurer with Angeli, *If They Only Knew*, p. 229.
51. 'GEICO Presents: Chyna'.
52. Adam Miller, 'Lady Wrestler Settles Legal Fight Out of Ring', *New York Post*, 29 July 1999, mypost.com/1999/07/29/lady-wrestler-settles-legal-fight-out-of-ring.
53. *Observer* Staff, 'December 22, 2003 Wrestling Observer Newsletter: Build to Cactus Jack Vs. Randy Orton, Armageddon Review', *Wrestling Observer Newsletter*, 22 December 2003, members.f4wonline.com/wrestling-observer-newsletter/december-22-2003-observer-newsletter-build-cactus-jack-vs-randy-orton.
54. Smallman, *I'm Sorry, I Love You*, p. 238.
55. 'GEICO Presents: Chyna'.
56. Tim Ott, 'Inside the Hart Family Wrestling Dynasty', Biography, 18 May 2021, www.biography.com/news/bret-hart-family-wrestling.
57. Ron Dicker, 'The Rock Shares Awesome Throwback Of Grandfather And Andre The Giant', HuffPost, 7 December 2019, www.huffingtonpost.co.uk/entry/dwayne-johnson-grandfather-andre-the-giant-photo_n_5d289108e4b02a5a5d599470.
58. Russ Good, 'The Tragic Life Of Eddie Guerrero', Wrestling Inc., 12 September 2022, www.wrestlinginc.com/1005497/the-tragic-life-of-eddie-guerrero/.
59. Foley, *Have a Nice Day*, p. 13; Randazzo, *Ring of Hell*, p. 23.
60. Laurer with Angeli, *If They Only Knew*, pp. 123–4.
61. 'GEICO Presents: Chyna'; *Vice Versa: Chyna*, written and directed by Marah Strauch (Vice TV, 2021).
62. Jim McLenna, '*If They Only Knew*, by Chyna', Girls With Guns, 1 January 2003, girlswithguns.org/if-they-only-knew/.
63. Laurer with Angeli, *If They Only Knew*, pp. 27–30.
64. Jason King, 'The Great Fall of Chyna: How WWE's Greatest Female Wrestler Disappeared', Bleacher Report, 15 September 2016, thelab.bleacherreport.com/the-great-fall-of-chyna/.
65. WrestlingINC, 'Documenting Chyna Part 1 feat. Chyna's Mom Jan LaQue & Anthony Anzaldo' (2020), youtu.be/E_-pPS1YW_8.
66. Vince Russo, 'Joanie Laurer aka Chyna Talks Triple H, WWE Hall of Fame, and More' (2015), www.youtube.com/watch?v=rmIjyMiR2Ys&t=5803s.
67. Laurer with Angeli, *If They Only Knew*, p. 33.
68. Ibid., p. 12.
69. Ibid., p. 54.
70. Ibid., pp. 34–5.
71. Ibid., pp. 111–12.
72. Ibid., p. 112.
73. *Observer* Staff, 'August 2, 2004 *Observer* Newsletter: Summerslam Card Finalized, Raw Iron Man Match, More', *Wrestling Observer Newsletter*, 2 August 2004, members.f4wonline.com/wrestling-observer-newsletter/august-2-2004-observer-newsletter-summerslam-card-finalized-raw-iron.
74. NostalgiaMania – Wrestling, 'Celebrity Boxing – Joanie "Chyna" Laurer vs Joey Buttafuoco (2002-05-22)', 18 June 2021, www.

youtube.com/watch?v=VOhjG-UOy9E; Eric Killelea, 'Flashback: Amy Fisher Becomes "Long Island Lolita"', *Rolling Stone*, 19 May 2017, www.rollingstone.com/culture/culture-news/ flashback-amy-fisher-becomes-long-island-lolita-193012/.

75. 'GEICO Presents: Chyna'.
76. Randazzo, *Ring of Hell*, p. 37.
77. Patrick Radden Keefe, *Empire of Pain: The Secret History of the Sackler Dynasty* (London: Picador, 2021), pp. 175–6.
78. Lonnie Tepper, 'Profile: Great Wall of Chyna', *Iron Man*, 1 July 2001, www.ironmanmagazine.com/profile-great-wall-of-chyna/.
79. *Observer* Staff, 'August 2 2004 *Observer* Newsletter'.
80. 'F4W~!#493 – Vince Hoarding Lifejackets As the Ship Sinks – 12/6/04', *Wrestling Observer*, 6 December 2004, members.f4wonline.com/figure-four-weekly/ f4w493-vince-hoarding-lifejackets-ship-sinks-12604-88251.
81. Lynn Crosbie, 'When Chyna cracked, Surreal became too real', *Globe and Mail*, 13 August 2005, www.theglobeandmail.com/arts/ when-chyna-cracked-surreal-became-too-real/article984600/.
82. Sean Waltman, 'Statement', Sean Waltman, 9 March 2009, web. archive.org/web/20050407191611/http://www.seanwaltman.com/ statement.html.
83. Crosbie, 'When Chyna Cracked'.
84. 'Anna Nicole Smith mocks herself in final role', CNN, 23 April 2007, web.archive.org/web/20070427025657/http:/edition.cnn.com/2007/ SHOWBIZ/Movies/04/23/film.annanicole.lastrole.ap/index.html.
85. 'Chyna Hospitalized – Too Wasted For Shrinks', TMZ, 28 December 2008, www.tmz.com/2008/12/28/chyna-taken-to-the-hospital/.
86. 'Joanie Laurer Filmography', Adult Film Database, n.d., www. adultfilmdatabase.com/actor/joanie-laurer-36148/.
87. 'Decree Changing Name', 2 November 2007, web.archive. org/web/20160303211419/http://www.aolcdn.com/ tmz_documents/1107_chyna_wm.pdf.
88. *Backdoor to Chyna*, directed by B. Skrow (Vivid, 2011).
89. Anthony Volastro, 'How Do Porn Stars Plan for Retirement?', CNBC, 21 March 2014, www.cnbc.com/2014/03/21/-porn-stars.html.
90. *Observer* Staff, 'January 24, 2005 Wrestling Observer Newsletter: 2004 *Wrestling Observer Newsletter* Awards Issue', *Wrestling Observer*, 24 January 2005, members.f4wonline.com/ wrestling-observer-newsletter/january-24-2005-observer-newsletter-2004-wrestling-observer-newsletter.
91. Russ Buettner, Susanne Craig and Mike McIntire, 'The President's Taxes: Long-Concealed Records Show Trump's Chronic Losses and Years of Tax Avoidance', *New York Times*, 27 September 2020, nytimes.com/interactive/2020/09/27/us/Donald-trump-taxes.html.
92. Zane Anthony, Kathryn Sanders and David A. Fahrenthold, 'Whatever Happened to Trump Neckties? They're Over. So Is Most of Trump's Merchandising Empire', *Washington Post*, 13 April 2018, www.washingtonpost.com/politics/ whatever-happened-to-trump-ties-theyre-over-so-is-most-of-trumps-

merchandising-empire/2018/04/13/2c32378a-369c-11e8-acd5-35eac230e514_story.html.

93. Teper, 'Great Wall of Chyna'.

94. Timothy L. O'Brien, 'What's He Really Worth?', *New York Times*, 23 October 2005, https://www.nytimes.com/2005/10/23/business/yourmoney/whats-he-really-worth.html; Tim Keeney, 'Vince McMahon Recognized as Billionaire by Forbes', Bleacher Report, 4 March 2014, https://bleacherreport.com/articles/1980066-vince-mcmahon-recognized-as-billionaire-by-forbes.

95. James Poniewozik, 'Donald Trump Was the Real Winner of "The Apprentice"', *New York Times*, 28 September 2020, https://www.nytimes.com/2020/09/28/arts/television/trump-taxes-apprentice.html

96. *Observer* Staff, 'F4W~!615 – Wrestlemania XXIII – April 9, 2007', *Wrestling Observer*, 9 April 2007, members.f4wonline.com/figure-four-weekly/f4w615-wrestlemania-xxiii-april-9-2007-89536.

97. Joe Palazzolo, 'WWE's Board Finds Vince McMahon Paid $5 Million to Donald Trump's Charity', *Wall Street Journal* , 17 August 2022, https://www.wsj.com/articles/wwes-board-finds-vince-mcmahon-paid-5-million-to-donald-trumps-charity-11660774043.

98. Alan Feuer, 'Trump Ordered to Pay $2 Million to Charities for Misuse of Foundation', *New York Times*, 7 November 2019, nytimes.com/2019/11/07/nyregion/trump-charities-new-york.html.

99. 'An examination of the 2016 electorate, based on validated voters', Pew Research Center, 9 August 2018, www.pewresearch.org/politics/2018/08/09/an-examination-of-the-2016-electorate-based-on-validated-voters/.

100. *Observer* Staff, 'F4W~!#615 – WrestleMania XXIII – April 9, 2007'.

101. Jonathan Martin, Chris Buckley, Amy Chozick and Maggie Haberman, 'Trump Taps Linda McMahon to Head Small Business Administration', *New York Times*, 7 December 2016, www.nytimes.com/2016/12/07/us/politics/donald-trump-transition.html.

102. Roxanne Roberts, 'Hillary Clinton's "Deplorables" Speech Shocked Voters Five Years Ago – But Some Feel It Was Prescient', *Washington Post*, 31 August 2021, www.washingtonpost.com/lifestyle/2021/08/31/deplorables-basket-hillary-clinton/.

103. David A. Fahrenthold, 'Trump Recorded Having Extremely Lewd Conversation About Women in 2005', *Washington Post*, 8 October 2016, www.washingtonpost.com/politics/trump-recorded-having-extremely-lewd-conversation-about-women-in-2005/2016/10/07/3b9ce776-8cb4-11e6-bf8a-3d26847eeed4_story.html.

104. Corinne Heller, 'Chyna's Autopsy Report Reveals Cause of Death: Prescription Drugs And Alcohol', E! Online, 22 December 2016, www.eonline.com/news/817759/chyna-s-autopsy-report-reveals-cause-of-death-prescription-drugs-and-alcohol.

105. Hailey Branson-Potts and Brittny Mejia, 'Days Before Her Death, Wrestling Star and Actress Chyna Posted a Rambling YouTube Video', *Los Angeles Times*, 21 April 2016, www.latimes.com/local/lanow/la-me-ln-chyna-video-20160421-story.html.

106. Sean Rueter, 'Triple H's Reasons for Excluding Chyna from the Hall of Fame Don't Hold Water, and Are an Example of WWE's Sexism', Cageside Seats, 3 February 2015, www.cagesideseats.com/wwe/2015/2/3/7969849/triple-h-reasons-for-excluding-chyna-from-the-wwe-hall-of-fame-example-wwe-sexism.

107. Tristan Jung, 'D-Generation X to be Inducted into the WWE Hall of Fame', Sports Illustrated, 18 February 2019, www.si.com/wrestling/2019/02/18/dx-wwe-hall-of-fame-induction-2019-tripleh-chyna.

108. Joe Palazzo, Ted Mann and Joe Flint, 'WWE's Vince McMahon Agreed to Pay $12 Million in Hush Money to Four Women', *Wall Street Journal*, 8 July 2022, www.wsj.com/articles/wwes-vince-mcmahon-agreed-to-pay-12-million-in-hush-money-to-four-women-11657289742.

109. Dan Mangan, 'Vince McMahon retires as WWE chief amid probes into alleged misconduct of pro wrestling boss', CNBC, 22 July 2022, www.cnbc.com/2022/07/22/vince-mcmahon-retires-as-chief-of-wwe-amid-probes-into-alleged-misconduct.html.

110. Manish Pandey, 'WWE: Stephanie McMahon resigns as father Vince becomes chair again', BBC, 11 January 2023, www.bbc.co.uk/news/newsbeat-64237701.

9: Jen

1. Warren Littlefield with T. R. Pearson, *Top of the Rock: The Rise and Fall of Must See TV* (New York: Doubleday, 2012), p. 133.

2. Scott Feinberg, '"Awards Chatter" Podcast – Jerry Seinfeld ("Comedians in Cars Getting Coffee")', *Hollywood Reporter*, 27 August 2016, www.hollywoodreporter.com/news/general-news/awards-chatter-podcast-jerry-seinfeld-923565/.

3. Littlefield with Pearson, *Top of the Rock*, p. 153.

4. Ibid., p. 169.

5. 'The One Where Monica Gets a Roommate', episode 1, season 1, *Friends*, directed by James Burrows, aired 22 September 1994, on NBC.

6. Arthur J. Norton and Louisa F. Miller, 'Marriage, Divorce, and Remarriage in the 1990s', US Department of Commerce, Economics and Statistics Administration, Bureau of the Census, October 1992, www2.census.gov/library/publications/1992/demographics/p23-180.pdf.

7. Natalie Stone, 'Jennifer Aniston's "Rachel" Haircut: The Story Behind the Iconic Photo of Her Wildly Popular "Friends" Hairdo', *People*, 25 October 2017, people.com/tv/jennifer-aniston-story-behind-friends-rachel-haircut-photo/.

8. Lacey Rose, 'Jennifer Aniston Has No Regrets', *Hollywood Reporter*, 8 December 2021, www.hollywoodreporter.com/feature/jennifer-aniston-interview-morning-show-friends-murder-mystery-sequel-1235058142/.

9. Littlefield with Pearson, *Top of the Rock*, p. 141.

10. Ibid., p. 159; Lynette Rice, *Entertainment Weekly*, n.d., web. archive.org/web/20090719103906/http://www.ew.com/ew/article/0%2C%2C275935%2C00.html.

11. 'The One Where They All Turn Thirty', episode 14, season 7, Friends, directed by Ben Weiss, aired 8 February 2001, on NBC.

12. Nancy Gibbs, 'Making Time for a Baby', *Time*, 15 April 2002, content. time.com/time/subscriber/article/0,33009,1002217,00.html.

13. 'Baby, Baby, Baby', episode 18, season 7, *Keeping Up with the Kardashians*, aired 6 September 2012, on E!

14. Jean M. Twenge, 'How Long Can You Wait to Have a Baby?', *The Atlantic*, July/August 2013, www.theatlantic.com/magazine/archive/2013/07/how-long-can-you-wait-to-have-a-baby/309374/.

15. Leslie Bennetts, 'The Unsinkable Jennifer Aniston', *Vanity Fair*, September 2005, archive.vanityfair.com/article/2005/9/the-unsinkable-jennifer-aniston.

16. 'The One with the Rumor', episode 14, season 7, *Friends*, directed by Gary Halvorson, aired 22 November 2001, on NBC.

17. Bennetts, 'The Unsinkable Jennifer Aniston'.

18. Sarah Ditum, 'Perez Hilton on Being the World's Most Notorious Gossip Blogger', *Sunday Times*, 19 September 2021, www.thetimes. co.uk/article/perez-hilton-on-being-the-worlds-most-notorious-gossip-blogger-l0fqvdvkr.

19. Bill Carter, *Desperate Networks* (New York: Doubleday, 2006), p. 265.

20. Susan Faludi, *Stiffed: The Betrayal of the Modern Man* (London: Chatto & Windus, 1999), ebook.

21. Ibid.

22. 'The One Where Monica Gets a Roommate'.

23. *Office Space*, directed by Mike Judge (20th Century Studios, 1999).

24. *Fight Club*, directed by David Fincher (Fox 2000 Pictures, 1999).

25. 'The One Where Monica Gets a Roommate'.

26. *Fight Club*.

27. Faludi, *Stiffed*, ebook.

28. Diana Abu-Jaber, 'Susan Faludi Coaches *Fight Club* Author', *Slate*, 24 November 1999, www.salon.com/1999/11/24/faludi_4/.

29. Faludi, *Stiffed*, ebook.

30. Peter Rainer, 'Pulling Punches', *New York Magazine*, 25 October 1999, nymag.com/nymetro/movies/reviews/1248/.

31. Patrick Sawer, '*Fight Club* for City Boys', *Evening Standard*, 16 October 2003, www.standard.co.uk/hp/front/fight-club-for-city-boys-7285297.html.

32. Audrey Perry, 'Students put up their dukes at Provo fight club', Daily Universe, 9 April 2000, universe.byu.edu/2000/04/09/students-put-up-their-dukes-at-provo-fight-club/.

33. Leslie Bennetts, 'Aspects of Brad', *Vanity Fair*, June 2004, archive. vanityfair.com/article/2004/6/aspects-of-brad.

34. Littlefield with Pearson, *Top of the Rock*, p. 154.

35. *Mr. & Mrs. Smith*, directed by Doug Liman (Regency Enterprise, 2005).

36. Gary Susman, 'Brad Pitt and Jennifer Aniston Separate',

Entertainment Weekly, 10 January 2005, ew.com/article/2005/01/10/brad-pitt-and-jennifer-aniston-separate/.

37. Vanessa Thorpe, 'The One Where Brad and Jen Vow to Stay Friends for Ever', *Guardian*, 9 January 2005, www.theguardian.com/world/2005/jan/09/arts.artsnews.

38. Bennetts, 'The Unsinkable Jennifer Aniston'.

39. Jeffrey Ressner, 'Rebel Without a Pause', *Time*, 24 January 2000, content.time.com/time/subscriber/article/0,33009,995905-1,00.html.

40. Jessica Bailey, 'Billy Bob Thornton Opens Up About What It Was Really Like To Be Married To Angelina Jolie', *Grazia*, n.d., graziamagazine.com/articles/billy-bob-thornton-opens-up-about-what-it-was-really-like-to-be-married-to-angelina-jolie/.

41. *People* Staff, 'Jolie News', *People*, 25 March 2002, people.com/archive/jolie-news-vol-57-no-11/.

42. *People* Staff, 'Jolie Talks About "Borders" and Babies', *People*, 23 October 2003, people.com/celebrity/jolie-talks-about-borders-and-babies/.

43. Jonathan Van Meter, 'Learning to Fly', *Vogue*, March 2004, web.archive.org/web/20040504212442/http://www.style.com/vogue/feature/022304/page2.htm.

44. Ibid.

45. Russell Scott Smith, 'Killer Sex – Hot Tales of Brad And Angelina From the Set of "Mr. and Mrs. Smith"', *New York Post*, 5 June 2005, nypost.com/2005/06/05/killer-sex-hot-tales-of-brad-and-angelina-from-the-set-of-mr-and-mrs-smith/.

46. *W* Staff, 'Domestic Bliss: Angelina Jolie and Brad Pitt at Home', *W Magazine*, 1 July 2005, www.wmagazine.com/gallery/brad-pitt-angelina-jolie.

47. Bennetts, 'The Unsinkable Jennifer Aniston'.

48. Priya Elan, 'Celebrity Shirts: Getting the Message Off Their Chest', *Guardian*, 9 July 2016, www.theguardian.com/lifeandstyle/2016/jul/09/hiddleston-swift-t-shirt-slogans-make-feelings-loud-and-clear.

49. *People* Staff, 'Angelina Jolie Pregnant', *People*, 11 January 2006, people.com/celebrity/angelina-jolie-pregnant/.

50. Alexandra D'Aluisio, 'Jennifer Aniston's Dating History: A Complete Timeline of Her Exes and Flings', *Us Magazine*, 11 February 2022, www.usmagazine.com/celebrity-news/pictures/jennifer-anistons-dating-history-timeline-of-her-famous-exes/paul-sculfor/.

51. 'Paparazzi Chaos ... Over Jen Aniston?', TMZ, n.d., www.tmz.com/watch/0-82kpldfo/.

52. Julia Jacobs, 'Angelina Jolie Details Abuse Allegations Against Brad Pitt in Countersuit', *New York Times*, 4 October 2022, https://www.nytimes.com/2022/10/04/movies/angelina-jolie-brad-pitt-lawsuit.html.

53. 'Ducking Hell', Popbitch, n.d., popbitch.com/emails/ducking-hell/.

54. Oliver Burkeman, 'The Brangelina Industry', *Guardian*, 24 June 2009, www.theguardian.com/lifeandstyle/2009/jun/24/magazines-media-aniston-jolie-pitt.

55. Burkeman, 'The Brangelina Industry'.
56. Jonathan Van Meter, 'Jennifer Aniston: Prime Time', Vogue, 1 December 2008, www.vogue.com/article/jennifer-aniston-prime-time.
57. Danielle Pergament, 'Jennifer Aniston Has Nothing to Hide', Allure, December 2022, www.allure.com/story/jennifer-aniston-december-2022-cover-interview.
58. Scott Huver, 'Jennifer Aniston Pokes Fun at Her Life and Movies', *People*, 13 June 2009, people.com/movies/jennifer-aniston-pokes-fun-at-her-life-and-movies/.
59. Rose, 'Jennifer Aniston Has No Regrets'.
60. Sian Cain, 'Women Are Happier Without Children Or a Spouse, Says Happiness Expert', *Guardian*, 25 May 2019, www.theguardian.com/lifeandstyle/2019/may/25/women-happier-without-children-or-a-spouse-happiness-expert.
61. 'Women in the labor force: a databook', US Bureau of Labor Statistics, April 2021, www.bls.gov/opub/reports/womens-databook/2020/home.htm.
62. Ellen Francis, Helier Cheung and Miriam Berger, 'How Does the US Compare to Other Countries On Paid Parental Leave? Americans Get 0 Weeks. Estonians Get More Than 80', *Washington Post*, 11 November 2021, www.washingtonpost.com/world/2021/11/11/global-paid-parental-leave-us/.
63. *Guardian* readers and Rachel Obordo, '"Spoiler alert: Ross and Rachel date!" – teens on why they love Friends', *Guardian*, 6 February 2019, www.theguardian.com/tv-and-radio/2019/feb/06/spoiler-alert-ross-and-rachel-date-teens-on-why-they-love-friends.
64. Edmund Lee, 'Netflix Will Keep "Friends" Through Next Year in a $100 Million Agreement', 4 December 2018, www.nytimes.com/2018/12/04/business/media/netflix-friends.html.
65. Ian Leslie, 'Watch it while it lasts: our golden age of television', *Financial Times*, 13 April 2017, www.ft.com/content/68309b3a-1f02-11e7-a454-ab04428977f9.
66. Maria Elena Fernandez, 'The Morning Show Was a Challenge Kerry Ehrin Couldn't Resist', Vulture, 1 November 2019, www.vulture.com/2019/11/the-morning-show-kerry-ehrin-interview-me-too.html.
67. *The Morning Show*, episode 1, season 1, directed by Mimi Leder, aired 1 November 2019, on Apple TV+.
68. Hanna Rosin, *The End of Men: And the Rise of Women* (New York: Viking, 2012), p. 267.
69. Mark Joseph Stern, 'Al Franken Should Resign Immediately', *Slate*, 16 November 2017, slate.com/news-and-politics/2017/11/al-franken-should-resign-immediately.html.
70. Jane Mayer, 'The Case of Al Franken', *New Yorker*, 22 July 2019, www.newyorker.com/magazine/2019/07/29/the-case-of-al-franken.
71. Sheryl Gay Stolberg, 'Thomas's Concurring Opinion Raises Questions About What Rights Might Be Next', *New York Times*, 24 June 2022, www.nytimes.com/2022/06/24/us/clarence-thomas-roe-griswold-lawrence-obergefell.html.

Conclusion

1. Jordan Sargent, 'The 15 Most Hilarious Parts of Robin Thicke's "Blurred Lines" Video', *Spin*, 22 March 2013, www.spin.com/2013/03/robin-thicke-blurred-lines-video-gif-ti/.

2. Eric Ducker, 'Q&A: Veteran Music Video Director Diane Martel on Her Controversial Videos for Robin Thicke and Miley Cyrus', *Grantland*, 26 June 2013, grantland.com/hollywood-prospectus/qa-veteran-music-video-director-diane-martel-on-her-controversial-videos-for-robin-thicke-and-miley-cyrus/.

3. Stelios Phili, 'Robin Thicke on That Banned Video, Collaborating with 2 Chainz and Kendrick Lamar, and His New Film', *GQ*, 6 May 2013, www.gq.com/story/robin-thicke-interview-blurred-lines-music-video-collaborating-with-2-chainz-and-kendrick-lamar-mercy.

4. Emily Duggan and Laura Hackett, 'Blurred Lines Singer Robin Thicke Assaulted Me On Set, Says Emily Ratajkowski', *Sunday Times*, 3 October 2021, www.thetimes.co.uk/article/blurred-lines-singer-robin-thicke-assaulted-me-on-set-says-emily-ratajkowski-dkgq83cpf.

5. Lisa Huynh, 'In the News: Robin Thicke's Rape Song, Tennessee Legislation, and My Continued Obsession with Sheryl Sandberg', Feminist in L.A., 2 April 2013, web.archive.org/web/20130624072912/http://feministla.blogspot.com/2013/04/in-news-robin-thickes-rape-song.html.

6. Tricia Romano, '"Blurred Lines," Robin Thicke's Summer Anthem, Is Kind of Rapey', Daily Beast, 17 June 2013, www.thedailybeast.com/blurred-lines-robin-thickes-summer-anthem-is-kind-of-rapey.

7. Ryan Broderick, 'Everyone Thinks Robin Thicke's "Blurred Lines" Is "Rapey"', BuzzFeed, 20 June 2013, www.buzzfeed.com/ryanhatesthis/everyone-thinks-robin-thickes-blurred-lines-is-rapey.

8. Dorian Lynskey, 'Blurred Lines: The Most Controversial Song of the Decade', *Guardian*, 13 November 2013, www.theguardian.com/music/2013/nov/13/blurred-lines-most-controversial-song-decade.

9. Callie Beusman, 'Robin Thicke Has Truly Out-Sleazed Himself This Time', Jezebel, 24 October 2013, jezebel.com/robin-thicke-has-truly-out-sleazed-himself-this-time-1451553568.

10. Katey Rich, 'Robin Thicke's New Album Sales Are So Bad You Might Think It's a Typo', *Vanity Fair*, 8 July 2014, www.vanityfair.com/hollywood/2014/07/robin-thicke-paula-album-sales.

11. Allison Stubblebine, '"There's a Special Place In Hell ...": A Timeline of Tina Fey and Taylor Swift', Billboard, 4 October 2017, www.billboard.com/music/pop/tina-fey-taylor-swift-feud-timeline-7988945/.

12. Nancy Jo Sales, 'Taylor Swift's Telltale Heart', *Vanity Fair*, April 2013, archive.vanityfair.com/article/2013/4/taylor-swifts-telltale-heart.

13. Ibid.

14. John Herrman, 'Access Denied', The Awl, 3 December 2015, www.theawl.com/2015/12/access-denied/.

15. 'Beyoncé In Her Own Words', *Vogue*, September 2018, www.vogue.com/article/beyonce-september-issue-2018.

16. Joe Coscarelli, 'How One Tweet About Nicki Minaj Spiraled Into Internet Chaos', *New York Times*, 10 July 2010, www.nytimes.com/2018/07/10/arts/music/nicki-minaj-wanna-thompson-twitter-stans.html.

17. Tom Scocca, 'On Smarm', *Gawker*, 5 December 2013, www.gawker.com/on-smarm-1476594977.

18. John Cook, 'A Judge Told Us to Take Down Our Hulk Hogan Sex Tape Post. We Won't', *Gawker*, 25 April 2013, www.gawker.com/a-judge-told-us-to-take-down-our-hulk-hogan-sex-tape-po-481328088.

19. Ryan Holiday, *Conspiracy: A True Story of Power, Sex, and a Billionaire's Secret Plot to Destroy a Media Empire* (London: Profile, 2018), p. 112.

20. Ibid., p. 7.

21. Ibid., p. 35.

22. Ibid., p. 220.

23. Ibid., p. 235.

24. Rasha Ali, '"There Is No Winning": Chrissy Teigen Opens Up About Being in the "Cancel Club"', *USA Today*, 15 July 2021, eu.usatoday.com/story/entertainment/celebrities/2021/07/15/chrissy-teigen-cancel-club-status-canceled-bullying-mean-tweets/7976685002/.

25. Damon Young, 'How Taylor Swift Is the Most Dangerous Type of White Woman, Explained', The Root, 18 July 2016, www.theroot.com/how-taylor-swift-is-the-most-dangerous-type-of-white-wo-1822521310.

26. Abby Aguirre, 'Taylor Swift on Sexism, Scrutiny, and Standing Up for Herself', Vogue, 8 August 2019, www.vogue.com/article/taylor-swift-cover-september-2019.

27. Ashley Lasimone, 'Lizzo Says That "Cancel Culture Is Appropriation"', *Hollywood Reporter*, 8 January 2023, www.hollywoodreporter.com/news/general-news/lizzo-cancel-culture-appropriation-social-media-1235293274/.

28. Wolfgang Ruth, 'Gawker Is Gawn, Awgain', Vulture, 1 February 2023, www.vulture.com/2023/02/gawker-shut-down-bustle-digital-media-group.html.

29. Stylist Team, 'Pharrell Williams on empowering women, spirituality and the "Happy" song', *Stylist*, 2014, www.stylist.co.uk/people/pharrell-williams-on-empowering-women-spirituality-and-the-happy-song/21235.

30. Chris Richards, 'This is How Justin Timberlake Lost the Super Bowl', *Washington Post*, 4 February 2018, www.washingtonpost.com/news/arts-and-entertainment/wp/2018/02/04/this-is-how-justin-timberlake-lost-the-super-bowl/.